American Fiction Since 1940

KT-547-134

Longman Literature in English Series

General Editors: David Carroll and Michael Wheeler
Lancaster University

For a complete list of titles see pages ix and x

THE LIBRARY
GUILDFORD COLLEGE
of Further and Higher Education

American Fiction Since 1940

WITHDRAWN

Tony Hilfer

Longman

London and New York

813. 5 MIL
78630

Longman Group UK Limited,
Longman House, Burnt Mill,
Harlow, Essex CM20 2JE, England
and Associated Companies throughout the world.

Published in the United States of America
by Longman Publishing, New York

© Longman Group UK Limited 1992

All rights reserved; no part of this publication may be
reproduced, stored in a retrieval system, or transmitted in
any form or by any means, electronic, mechanical,
photocopying, recording, or otherwise without either the
prior written permission of the Publishers or a licence
permitting restricted copying in the United Kingdom
issued by the Copyright Licensing Agency Ltd.,
90 Tottenham Court Road, London W1P 9HE.

First published 1992
Second impression 1993

British Library Cataloguing-in-Publication Data
A catalogue record for this book is
available from the British Library

ISBN 0 582 49351 X CSD
ISBN 0 582 49350 1 PPR

Library of Congress Cataloging-in-Publication Data
Hilfer, Anthony Channell.
  American fiction since 1940 / Tony Hilfer.
  p.   cm. – (Longman literature in English Series)
  Includes bibliographical references and index.
  ISBN 0-582-49351-X. – ISBN 0-582-49350-1 (pbk.)
  1. America fiction – 20th century – History and criticism.
I. Title.   II. Series.
PS379.H55   1992
813'.5409–dc20   91–43421 CIP

Set 7L in Bembo
Produced by Longman Singapore Publishers (Pte) Ltd
Printed in Singapore

Contents

Editors' Preface

The multi-volume Longman Literature in English Series provides students of literature with a critical introduction to the major genres in their historical and cultural context. Each volume gives a coherent account of a clearly defined area, and the series, when complete, will offer a practical and comprehensive guide to literature written in English from Anglo-Saxon times to the present. The aim of the series as a whole is to show that the most valuable and stimulating approach to the study of literature is that based upon an awareness of the relations between literary forms and their historical contexts. Thus the areas covered by most of the separate volumes are defined by period and genre. Each volume offers new and informed ways of reading literary works, and provides guidance for further reading in an extensive reference section.

In recent years, the nature of English studies has been questioned in a number of increasingly radical ways. The very terms employed to define a series of this kind – period, genre, history, context, canon – have become the focus of extensive critical debate, which has necessarily influenced in varying degrees the successive volumes published since 1985. But however fierce the debate, it rages around the traditional terms and concepts.

As well as studies on all periods of English and American literature, the series includes books on criticism and literary theory, and on the intellectual and cultural context. A comprehensive series of this kind must of course include other literatures written in English, and therefore a group of volumes deals with Irish and Scottish literature, and the literatures of India, Africa, the Caribbean, Australia and Canada. The forty-seven volumes of the series cover the following areas: Pre-Renaissance English Literature, English Poetry, English Drama, English Fiction, English Prose, Criticism and Literary Theory, Intellectual and Cultural Context, American Literature, Other Literatures in English.

David Carroll
Michael Wheeler

Longman Literature in English Series
General Editors: David Carroll and Michael Wheeler
Lancaster University

Pre-Renaissance English Literature

* ⋆ English Literature before Chaucer *Michael Swanton*
* English Literature in the Age of Chaucer
* ⋆ English Medieval Romance *W. R. J. Barron*

English Poetry

* ⋆ English Poetry of the Sixteenth Century (Second Edition) *Gary Waller*
* ⋆ English Poetry of the Seventeenth Century (Second Edition)
  George Parfitt
* English Poetry of the Eighteenth Century, 1700–1789
* ⋆ English Poetry of the Romantic Period, 1789–1830 (Second Edition)
  J. R. Watson
* ⋆ English Poetry of the Victorian Period, 1830–1890 *Bernard Richards*
* English Poetry of the Early Modern Period, 1890–1940
* ⋆ English Poetry since 1940 *Neil Corcoran*

English Drama

* English Drama before Shakespeare
* ⋆ English Drama: Shakespeare to the Restoration, 1590–1660
  Alexander Leggatt
* ⋆ English Drama: Restoration and Eighteenth Century, 1660–1789
  Richard W. Bevis
* English Drama: Romantic and Victorian, 1789–1890
* English Drama of the Early Modern Period, 1890–1940
* English Drama since 1940

English Fiction

* ⋆ English Fiction of the Eighteenth Century, 1700–1789
  Clive T. Probyn
* ⋆ English Fiction of the Romantic Period, 1789–1830 *Gary Kelly*
* ⋆ English Fiction of the Victorian Period, 1830–1890 (Second Edition)
  Michael Wheeler
* ⋆ English Fiction of the Early Modern Period, 1890–1940 *Douglas Hewitt*
* English Fiction since 1940

English Prose

* English Prose of the Seventeenth Century, 1590–1700 *Roger Pooley*
English Prose of the Eighteenth Century
English Prose of the Nineteenth Century

Criticism and Literary Theory

Criticism and Literary Theory from Sidney to Johnson
Criticism and Literary Theory from Wordsworth to Arnold
Criticism and Literary Theory from 1890 to the Present

The Intellectual and Cultural Context

The Sixteenth Century
* The Seventeenth Century, 1603–1700 *Graham Parry*
* The Eighteenth Century, 1700–1789 (Second Edition) *James Sambrook*
The Romantic Period, 1789–1830
* The Victorian Period, 1830–1890 *Robin Gilmour*
The Twentieth Century: 1890 to the Present

American Literature

American Literature before 1880
* American Poetry of the Twentieth Century *Richard Gray*
* American Drama of the Twentieth Century *Gerald M. Berkowitz*
* American Fiction 1865–1940 *Brian Lee*
* American Fiction since 1940 *Tony Hilfer*
* Twentieth-Century America *Douglas Tallack*

Other Literatures

Irish Literature since 1800
Scottish Literature since 1700

Australian Literature
* Indian Literature in English *William Walsh*
African Literature in English: East and West
Southern African Literature in English
Caribbean Literature in English
* Canadian Literature in English *W. J. Keith*

* *Already published*

Author's Preface

The greatest problems this book presents are of selection and assessment, especially of authors of the 1970s to the 1990s, a question taken up in Chapter 9. I feel no doubt that in a study dealing with contemporary writers, I have neglected some important authors and included a few soon to be forgotten. Choices had to be made and those in this book represent my considered judgement.

One whole area of writing left out is popular fiction, not because I regard popular genres as unimportant and unworthy but because I believe them to be critically unintelligible except in terms of their own historically evolved conventions which this study does not give me the scope to elaborate. John Cawelti's *Adventure, Mystery, and Romance* does this for the detective novel and my *The Crime Novel* does it for that form. I know little of science fiction although it is clear that Isaac Asimov, Robert Heinlein, Philip K. Dick and Ray Bradbury have written important and influential novels in this genre while Ursula LeGuin's anthropologically inflected feminism has given a new dimension to it.

Finally, the reader needs to know that the parenthetical citations following quotations are to chapter numbers since these usually are the same in various hardback and paperback editions. In the case of novels divided into books as well as chapters, the citation gives book followed by chapter as in (1:5), that is, Book 1, Chapter 5.

Introduction

A striking feature of American fiction since 1940 is the movement on all fronts from the margins to the centre. African American, Southern and Jewish writers emerge as major talents, as signalized by the belated critical recognition of Faulkner and the immediate impact of Bellow, crowned by their respective Nobel Prizes. And in a poll of professors of American literature, *Invisible Man* by the African American writer Ralph Ellison was most often named as the most important American novel since 1945.[1]

Stylistically we see an initial continuity of the dominant modes of the 1920s and 1930s, traditional realism, naturalistic social protest, and a symbolically inflected modernist poetic realism. Increasingly, however, the symbolism begins to displace the realism as traditional images of self and society diminish in the face of imperializing discourses of mass media and the social sciences (as Americans term such disciplines as sociology, psychology and anthropology) that reduce the contemporary self to a package, explanatory labels attached. In the 1960s postmodernist writers turn this discourse back on itself although their parodies of sociological and bureaucratic language very nearly concede the loss of substantial human values which such language reflects.

Thus, literary developments responded to major historical changes and, more directly, to the philosophical, psychological and sociological discourses used to moralize or rationalize such changes. These discourses, frequently employed to interpret contemporary fiction, are also its subject matter, the floating debris of ideas, clichés, fears and presentiments that novelists draw on as ideas of order or targets of satire. The Second World War, for instance, appears in fiction already thoroughly ideologized, presented usually as accelerating the American version of the authoritarian society. *The Naked and the Dead* and *Catch-22* tell less about men in battle than the *Iliad*, their real subject being the dehumanizing effects of the emerging corporate capitalist garrison state. John Horne Burns's *The Gallery* contrasts American occupation troops unfavourably with the more 'natural' Italians of Milan.

Literature and politics

The immediate effect of the war was a discrediting of overt ideology generally, whether of the left or right. Indeed, the left, defined as a politics aimed at restructuring the socioeconomic order so as to equalize wealth and power, all but disappeared in the 1950s, due to its 1930s identification with Marxism. The right continued to exert political pressure by its overt appeal to anti-communist hysteria and later, responding to the civil rights revolution, in a more covert appeal to race and class antagonism. Pervasive anti-communism greased the skids into the Vietnam War, an outcome so distressing that it very nearly revived the moribund left. However, the new left of the 1960s, though changing consciousness to some degree, failed greatly to alter existing institutions or found new ones.

For that matter, American writers generally tend towards liberalism or nihilism rather than radicalism, with a scattering of self-conscious reactionaries. The typical American literary ideology is individualism and the typical attitude towards politics as group action is ambivalent, even evasive. Even in the 1930s it was literary and cultural critics rather than novelists who became most involved in Communist Party politics, the high water mark of such involvement coming in 1932 with a declaration of support for the party by Sherwood Anderson, Erskine Caldwell, John Dos Passos, Theodore Dreiser, Granville Hicks and Sidney Hook, among others. Then came waves of disinvolvement, notably after Stalin's purges of 1935–7 and the Hitler–Stalin pact of 1939, a chronology that differed somewhat for the few but significant African Americans initially attracted by the Communist Party's stand for racial equality and a form of black nationalism. The party lost this constituency when, as a result of Hitler's attack on Russia, it called on African Americans to suspend their quest for racial justice and serve unprotestingly in a segregated army, a stand that disgusted Ralph Ellison, previously a fellow traveller, and further alienated Richard Wright, a party member already disillusioned with its attempts to tell him what to write (though Wright's open break did not come until 1944).

By 1950 the disillusion with radical politics had become an anti-ideological ideology, the development of which was influenced by seminal works of political philosophy and social psychology. Sir Karl Popper indicted Marx along with Plato and Hegel in *The Open Society and its Enemies* (1943). In 1950 Richard Wright and five other writers formerly influenced by communism officially repudiated it in their essays in *The God that Failed*. In 1951 Hannah Arendt's *The Origins of Totalitarianism* argued for the structural identity of Nazi and communist totalitarianism, and Eric Hoffer, a self-educated longshoreman, attacked ideological thinking generally in *The True Believer*. Perhaps most revealing of the new outlook was the 1950 book, *The Authoritarian Personality*, the outcome of a research project directed by the refugee German intellectual T.W. Adorno. This book, clearly intended to forewarn Americans against their own authoritarian tendencies, interpreted such tendencies not in historical and economic terms but as manifestations of a malignant psychological type, prone to rigidity of thought, repression of impulse and intuition, and intolerance of differences. The nonconformist rather than the radical was cast as the antithesis to the authoritarian personality.

If malevolent politics were a reflex not of class but of personality type what seemed needed was not a radical restructuring of society but a wary introspection into the the spiritual limitations as well as possibilities of the self. In a prototype book of 1950s culture criticism, *The Liberal Imagination*, Lionel Trilling attacked what he saw as the oversimplifications of the liberal social critique. Trilling favoured the work of art that is 'complex, personal and not literal', implying 'the awareness of complexity and difficulty'. Literature, as opposed to sociology or political philosophy, is uniquely relevant to a viable politics because it is 'the human activity that takes the fullest and most precise account of variousness, possibility, complexity, and difficulty'. Trilling, however, fails to ground his alternative values, coming nearest in a vague gesture towards Freud, who 'is clearly in the line of . . . classic tragic realism'.[2] This seems to mean that self and society are grounded in neurosis, a condition from which we are supposed to derive a grim satisfaction due to the complexity and difficulty with which it rewards us.

Liberal idealists became the straw men of 1950s culture criticism. Reinhold Niebuhr complained that they lacked a sense of sin: 'In the liberal world the evils in human nature and history were ascribed to social institutions or to ignorance or to some other manageable defect in human nature or environment'.[3] Original sin was a much better explanation even for critics who were not quite theists. A dissenting critic commented, 'Religion now has its fellow travellers'.[4]

So indeed had capitalism which now seemed, with all its flaws, a mode more conducive to personal liberty than communism, much less fascism. In a *Partisan Review* symposium on whether alienation had become obsolete for American writers, Philip Rahv attributed the changed attitudes of the intellectuals to 'the exposure of the Soviet myth and the consequent resolve to be done with Utopian illusions and heady expectations. In their chastened mood American democracy looks like the real thing to American intellectuals. Its incontestable virtue is that, for all its distortions and contradictions, it actually exists'.[5] Intellectuals shifted their discontent from the social and political to the existential and psychological. As Norman Mailer sourly noted, 'It has become as fashionable to sneer at economics and emphasize "the human dilemma" as it was fashionable to do the reverse in the thirties'.[6] Economics seemed less of an issue as the war economy finally delivered America from depression. The relative prosperity of the 1950s precluded the necessity of a major redistribution of income as a rising tide of prosperity floated most boats, based though this affluence was on Cold War defence spending.[7]

Although no longer envisioning a viable alternative to the capitalist system, American intellectuals were distressed by the trend toward conformity and depersonalization signified by giant corporations run by managerial bureaucrats. The significant opposition was between conformity and autonomy, an opposition guaranteeing the moral complexity recommended by Trilling *et al.*, since the choice of autonomy was open to endless self-questioning. In the 1930s one could oppose the boss by joining a union, thus asserting a clear moral and political identity. By the 1950s, however, the existentialist ethos of personal authenticity seemed to permit one to become autonomous without having to tell anyone or do anything, thus allowing a rather wide margin for what the existentialists themselves had begun to call 'false consciousness'. In the more ambiguous post-war America even the would-be conformist's situation was problematic since in a society of rapid technological transformation dependent on shifts in fashion demanded by the economics of consumerism, it was difficult to be certain what one was to conform *to*. Thus, the 'other-directed person' of David Riesman's 1950 sociological study *The Lonely Crowd* suffers from 'diffuse anxiety',[8] while William H. Whyte notes in *The Organization Man* (1956) that the 'quest for normalcy is one of the great breeders of neurosis'.[9] The then radical Norman Mailer, finding it difficult to target his opposition, took this difficulty as the dirtiest trick his society could play: 'I would propose that the artist feels more alienated when he loses the sharp sense of what he is alienated from. In this context, I wonder if there has been a time in the last fifty years when the American artist has felt more alienated.'[10] It is no wonder that Freudianism became the all but official psychology of post-war American intellectuals, and existentialism the philosophy. Both answered anxieties all the more pressing in ratio to their indefiniteness. Fiction, in turn, becomes characterized by diffuse anxiety and normal neurosis.

Literature and technology

Many Americans felt pride and awe at the innovations of technology. Released from wartime restrictions, American technology and commerce exploded into a profusion of exciting products. Even the atom bomb was initially perceived as a scientific marvel, a form of white magic – until the Russians made one too. But technology had a bizarre side effect, some forms of it seeming to undermine the authority even of perceptual reality. Romantic poets had protested against science for its materialism but the new science and technology began to seem positively ghostly, a kind of white noise. The scientific concepts of entropy and indeterminacy became rhetorical figures in American fiction, indicating that civilization was spinning out its energy into terminal idiocy and that perception was foredoomed never to see beyond its own reflection. Despite their provocation of metaphysical gloom, these concepts could be played out in quite enjoyable vertigo games, leaving the reader delightedly dizzy.

Technology impacted perception most directly in the 'graphic revolution' described by Daniel Boorstin as inundating Americans with a 'current of hot and cold running images' so striking that images threatened to displace 'real experience'. By the late twentieth century the man on the spot, the viewer of the experience where it actually happened, began to feel confused and limited. The full flavour of the experience seemed to come only to the "viewer", 'the man in the television audience. . . . The man there in person was spacebound, crowd-confined; while the TV viewer was free to see from all points of view, above the heads of others and behind the scenes. Was it he who was *really* there?'[11] In such instances as the instant replays of Jack Ruby shooting and re-shooting Lee Harvey Oswald, televisual experience became uncanny. Simultaneously television encouraged the reduction of politics to the art of packaging, a branch of advertising specializing in a product that is the advertisement itself, an image not of but substituting for reality, in Boorstin's term a 'pseudo-event'.[12] The pseudo-event is contrived solely for the purpose of reproduction – the astronaut moon landing was the product not of scientific needs but of those of public relations, essentially a massive pseudo-event. Pseudo-debates, proving a candidate's dexterity at instant cliché, became important to the electorate's choice of a president. Television news finally gave up reality altogether as a ground for political choice, frankly rating political candidates on their competence at projecting an image.[13] While the degree to which Americans believed in this pseudo-world was debatable (it is significant that they offset their presidential symbols by the pragmatism of their choice of congresspersons to represent their direct material interests), its sheer pervasiveness poisoned public discourse.

Literature and criticism

Previously, the centre of power in making and unmaking literary reputations had been journalists like H. L. Mencken or freelance men of letters like Edmund Wilson who wrote for a broad general public, not easily definable as either elite or mass. By the 1950s a new group of academic critics, empowered by a boom in higher education resulting from the extension of educational benefits to Second World War veterans in the 'GI Bill of Rights', and writing for an audience they educated to their specialized critical vocabulary, increasingly displaced the journalists. Two diverse sets of critics, the Southern-derived and academically affiliated 'New Critics' and the New York intellectuals of The Partisan Review, arrived at relatively common ground on a recently formed American literary canon consisting of novelists properly mythic, symbolic, ironic, tragic and at least proto-modernist who wrote aesthetically organic symbolic romances about , as William Faulkner put it, 'the problems of the human heart in conflict with itself which can alone make good writing'.[14] This critical tendency was epitomized in Mark Schorer's celebrated essay arguing that a proper literary technique 'discovers the complexity of the modern spirit, the difficulty of personal morality, and the fact of evil – all the untractable elements under the surface which a technique of the surface alone cannot approach'.[15] Interesting if vague notions about technique, evil, and a somewhat reified version of the human heart became the vogue in the newly influential circles of academic criticism.

The institutionalization and growing influence of American literature as an academic field allowed academic critics to become arbiters of what was 'serious' in contemporary as well as past literature, and the extraordinary growth of the paperback industry allowed even difficult writers access to a growing reading audience newly trained to apprehend irony and complexity. Soon a dual track of literary reputation developed. On the one track were writers, usually realists not overly complex in technique, who sold well to a large audience after being seriously reviewed in the New York Times or the Saturday Review of Literature. On the other track were writers taught while still living, sometimes even rather early in their careers, as classics in university courses and who owed their reputation primarily to articles in academic quarterlies.

Another effect of the boom in college enrolment was that writers themselves came to have a closer association with the universities. Before the Second World War relatively few writers had college educations. After it, college education became more the rule than the exception. Indeed, a growing number of novelists became college teachers, sometimes in the new 'creative writing' programmes, sometimes in areas they could draw on for material, as with Saul Bellow's teaching of western intellectual history. The post-1950 generations of writers then were directly influenced by the reigning academic ideas and the fashions of literary criticism – they learned them in class. Only the less interesting novelists wrote to rule, turning out novels stuffed with readily explicable symbols and archetypes. The innovative novelists ran unique variations on academic themes, sometimes extending and/or deepening them, as frequently questioning and/or undermining them.

Certainly one effect of this was to make writers more self-conscious about literary tradition and literary craft, probably a contributing factor to the rise of metafiction. Another important effect of academic institutionalization was that some of the most interesting critical commentary on contemporary writers tended increasingly to come from the writers themselves in the form of essays and interviews. The literary interview has become a major critical genre, with collections of interviews with various writers coming out as books, as in the (to date) seven volumes of *Writers at Work*, drawing from the *Paris Review* interviews. Although writers are capable of misrepresenting or even misreading their own work, it is true that some of the most acute comments on current writers can be found in their self-reflections.

Unfortunately, the most brilliant literary criticism of the post Second World War period also became effectually prescriptive, marginalizing, even stifling, certain forms of literary expression. The critics managed to construe naturalistic social protest fiction as simplistic by the simple device of reading it simplistically. Naturalistic fiction soon became as unfashionable as radical politics. A reading of American literature as being primarily in what Richard Chase defined as the romance tradition became a ruling critical paradigm. This view of American literature as symbolic exploration of the isolated self trying to evade social definition was anticipated in D. H. Lawrence's *Studies in Classic American Literature* (1923) but the books that promoted it to academic orthodoxy were F. O. Matthiessen's *American Renaissance* (1941), Henry Nash Smith's *Virgin Land* (1950), R. W. B. Lewis's *The American Adam* (1955), Richard Chase's *The American Novel and its Tradition* (1957) and Leslie Fiedler's *Love and Death in the American Novel* (1960). American Studies, a relatively new academic field, was dominated by this myth and symbol approach which saw American fiction in terms of its archetypes of the self rather than its engagements with society. The typical American heroes were Cooper's Deerslayer, Twain's Huck Finn, Melville's Ishmael and Fitzgerald's Gatsby. Tony Tanner in his brilliant *City of Words* adds Updike's Rabbit and Ellison's Invisible Man, among others, as he carries the romance reading, perhaps rather too uncritically, through contemporary fiction. The realistic novel with its more complex social texture was marginalized by this critical view and the naturalistic novel dismissed as hardly worth considering. Moreover, as Nina Baym observed in her sardonic critique of the critical paradigm, 'Melodramas of Beset Manhood: How Theories of American Fiction Exclude Women Authors,' women writers are conspicuous by their absence from the romance tradition.[16] For that matter, Robert Penn Warren had perceived the existence of the archetype and the problems with it before the fact. Warren constructs Jack Burden's drive to California in *All the King's Men* as an ironic reprise of Huckleberry Finn's lighting out for the territories. Thus even before Smith and R.W.B. Lewis in *The American Adam* theorized on the American fantasy of recovering innocence by fleeing from a stratified social world, Warren had subjected the myth to a conservative deconstruction. In sum, the myth-symbol school developed brilliant new insights on American literature while also contributing to the turn away from social concerns by writers and critics and to a narrowing of the American literary canon.

Other important intellectual influences on American fiction from the 1940s on are what Philip Rieff called *The Triumph of the Therapeutic*, that is, the displacement of traditional moral and theological explanations for human behaviour by psychiatric ones, with illness replacing badness as the prime cause of vicious behaviour and spiritual despair redefined as emotional depression. In the opinion of some contemporary culture critics, the therapeutic revolution contributed to the marginalization of political protest, indeed of political thinking generally, encouraging Americans to consider their authentic self as the inner self, known through self-awareness, aided by a psychological descriptive vocabulary, as opposed to the social self, manifested by public word and act. In *The Culture of Narcissism* Christopher Lasch declares 'Economic man . . . has given way to the psychological man of our times – the final product of bourgeois individualism.'[17] Lasch argues that this is an individualism compounded out of psychological clichés, 'psychobabble' as it has been called. Supplementing, though to some degree counteracting the triumph of the therapeutic was the post-Second World War importation of existentialist philosophy which in the late 1940s and through the 1950s became very nearly the official American philosophy. Kierkegaard, Camus and Sartre were the most salient figures in the early stage of existentialist influence, with a somewhat later recognition of the key importance of Heidegger. But it should be noted that in the case of existentialism, as with psychology and literary criticism, writers were as apt to react away from as to adopt the new perspectives. Existentialism is the ideological subtext of some novels and a target for parody in others. The postmodernist novel was anti-existentialist, though, to a degree, harking back to the proto-existentialist radical relativism of Nietzsche.

Literature, race and gender

The focus, then, shifted from the class consciousness of the 1930s to the existential anxiety and therapeutic hopes and fears of the 1950s. But race, and then gender, moved into the political vacuum as vital issues.

Some cracks in the massive American institutionalization of racial discrimination appeared as early as the 1940s: Eleanor Roosevelt, the wife
of the President, espoused racial justice in her influential newspaper col-
umn, and Gunnar Myrdal's *An American Dilemma* (1944) exposed the
basic contradiction between American democratic theory and racist practice. The American Cold War posture of defender of the 'free world'
seemed hypocritical in the face of the political disenfranchisement of
African Americans. But though Truman ended some federal discrimina-
tory practices by presidential decree, the routine segregation upheld by
state laws did not come under major challenge until the Supreme Court
decision of 1954 that declared segregation in the public schools to be
unconstitutional. Only in 1964 did the massive Civil Rights Bill pushed
through by President Johnson ban most other forms of legalized and
customary segregation. Since 1940 five decades of struggle have elimi-
nated legally institutionalized forms of racial discrimination and enabled
major political gains for African Americans, but the economic consequences of past and present racism were felt no less in 1990 than in
1940, the condition of the urban black underclass having become, if
anything, more desperate. Some African American writers, however,
came into the mainstream before the political breakthrough; seminal
works by Wright, Petry, Ellison and Baldwin were published before the
1954 Supreme Court decision. It is illustrative of the force of the 1950s
critical paradigm that in Ellison and Baldwin, writers whose lives were
clearly circumscribed by political oppression, 1950s concerns for identity
and – in Ellison – even the romance theme of unfettered individuality
take precedence over political protest. Finally, as late as 1990 the political as well as economic possibilities for African Americans were limited
by the Republican Party's clear, if not overt, 'Southern strategy' of appealing
to hostility towards African American attempts to improve their condition.

Jewish Americans made less qualified gains during this period, in the
economic as well as the political realm. While residual anti-Semitism
existed in 1990, it no longer had the force and fashionableness of pre-
Second World War racism. The discovery of the death camps at the end
of the war led to a certain philo-Semitic reaction, as will be explored in
Chapter 4. By the 1950s, then, Jewish American literature, Southern
literature and, if not African American literature, at least two African
American novelists had moved to the centre of the American literary
scene. If anything, it was non-Southern white male writers who began
to feel marginal, due less to this competition than to the general decline
of a traditional Protestant middle-class value system. This odd self-as-
cribed marginalism, which will be the subject of Chapter 7, has been noted
by Jewish American writers, ever alert to the possibilities for self-hatred:

> I think everybody in this country has a minority complex. Even
> the majority. They're guilty about being the majority. (Heller)[18]

'Self-hating *Jews*? Henry, America is full of self-hating *Gentiles*, as far as I can see – it's a country full of Chicanos who want to look like Texans, and Texans who want to look like New Yorkers, and any number of Middle Western Wasps who, believe it or not, want to talk and act and think like Jews.' (Roth, *The Counterlife* (3))

This applies, however, only to the *realists*. Postmodernist Anglo male novelists turned an aggressive, even confident alienation to literary advantage, as will be seen in the writings of William Gass and others.

Women, for their part, suffered more from irrational male hostility than self hatred. The re-emergence of women as a political force was foreshadowed by Betty Friedan's *The Feminine Mystique* in 1963 which attacked the pattern of socializing women into solely homebound maternal roles. In 1966 Friedan founded the National Organization of Women. From this base, feminism took off in the 1970s with Kate Millett's *Sexual Politics* in 1970 and the founding of *Ms*, a mass media feminist magazine, in 1972. Feminist thought anticipated the 1980s vogue of academic Marxism in repoliticizing literary discourse and has had a major effect in leading to not only new discoveries but new perspectives, alterations of the field of consciousness. By 1990 there were many competing modes of feminist thought, some drawing on the psychoanalytic theories of Jacques Lacan, who revised Freud in a poststructuralist fashion, some going in a traditionalist Marxist direction, some deriving from the alliance of academic Marxism with poststructuralism, a curiously dematerialized form of Marxism. Feminist literary criticism is now well institutionalized and has become one of the most politically powerful critical modes as measured by key positions in the leadership of the Modern Language Association and on the editorial boards of various academic quarterlies. Yet the influential Marxist poststructuralist 'theory' wing of feminism has a highly problematic relation to modern American women's fiction, as will be argued in Chapter 8.

Conclusion

The various emergences in American fiction from 1940 to 1990 tend to take literary form in one of four modes, going from the soon superseded mode of naturalistic social protest to the currently critically favoured mode of postmodernism.

The first of these, naturalistic social protest, usually centres on characters destroyed by psychological, social and economic forces beyond their control. As shown by C. C. Walcutt, naturalistic fiction tends towards determinism but somewhat contradictorily also protests social injustice and is reformist or revolutionary in its political implications.[19] (Though, it should be noted, the naturalistic novel can go in the direction of nihilism as well.) In the 1930s John Dos Passos, John Steinbeck and James T. Farrell wrote major naturalistic novels and there is a naturalistic inflection in Faulkner's work of the period. Despite naturalism having been pronounced dead in the early 1950s, a few writers stubbornly persisted in writing strong naturalistic novels while others subsumed naturalistic ideas into a predominantly realist mode.

The second mode, poetic or modernist realism, is fiction in which though character and plot follow predominantly realist conventions much of the meaning inheres in subtextual webs of symbolism that intimate interior states of the character and/or metaphysical concepts about the world. This dominant mode of the 1940s and 1950s tended to give up the social and political world in despair, turning to the subjective self seeking meaning in personal relationship. But that these quests frequently eventuated in solipsistic loneliness or perversely dysfunctional relationship hints at a social or metaphysical structure disallowing personal autonomy and thwarting love.

The third mode, traditional realism, is fiction about characters who seem recognizably like those of the reader's experience and whose moral choices and their consequences are the focus of the novel. This mode never disappeared during the period of this study though it tended towards the poetic at some points and the postmodern at others. Some recent novelists, believing that postmodernism ends up by dissolving the self in order to save it from conditioning, have turned back to realism, reasserting the possibilities of identity and community.

The fourth mode, postmodernism, is stylistically recognizable by a studied affectlessness of tone sometimes coupled with horrific content, by disorienting games with narrative conventions, and by baroque, allegorically suggestive elaborations of plot. The postmodernist self is not a moral agent but merely the sum of its roles. As such, however, it can be judged aesthetically, as a dull or scintillating performer. This self inheres less in characters than in an imperial, sometimes solipsistic narrative voice moving characters and readers about as pawns in a literary game. The affective relation of reader to protagonist that centres the reader's moral response in traditional realism is absent or even, as in Nabokov's use of perverse first-person narrator–protagonists, mocked. The postmodernist novel has a certain American logic, relating as it does to a persistent American denial of the essential self, consistent in interior subjectivity and fixed social role. There are consistencies between the postmodernist and the nineteenth-century American romance tradition earler described. The myth of an American society that allows for relatively unimpeded social mobility gives Americans a sense of identity as fluid and performative, a question of choice, rather than historical and determinate, a matter of destiny, though Southern fiction reacts against this mythology. A critique of American social ideas is entitled *The Hidden Injuries of Class*, an unlikely title for a European critique where the injuries of class seem transparent.[20]

Crosscutting these modes is the emergence of new literary voices, African American, Southern and Jewish, ready to use any or all modes through which they can represent their special experience. Thus, of the African American novels in Chapter 3, Wright's and Petry's are naturalistic, Baldwin's poetic realist, and Ellison's anticipates postmodernism. Yet all of these are at the same time novels expressive of an African American experience of denial and oppression by and invisibility to the strange, pathological white world that defines their boundaries. Likewise, although Saul Bellow, Bernard Malamud and Cynthia Ozick have major differences, they have each a somehow recognizable Jewish voice. That there is such a thing as the Jewish American novel is proven by the fact that the most Protestant of American novelists, John Updike, has written two of them, *Bech* and *Bech is Back*. In turn, *Something Happened* by the Jewish writer Joseph Heller is a demonic version of another subtype to be later considered, the white male Protestant realist novel of anxiety and resentment. Such are the happy uses of distinction.

The organization of this book is intended to show these various emergences in their complex relation to contemporary historical circumstances. The first chapter sets the stage by describing the increasing privatization of literary imagination in the 1940s. I then examine the emergence of African American, Southern and Jewish American fiction and their different modes of response to cultural and political trends. The next two sections delineate the postmodernist turn, a turn away from the relative humanism characteristic of the previous emergences. Though traditional realist fiction continued throughout the period this book covers, I treat it after postmodernism in order to show how realist fiction begins to respond to the postmodernist challenge. A second chapter on realism focuses on women's fiction which has been predominantly in the realist mode. The study concludes with the two most effective writers working from the 1960s through to the 1980s, the late postmodernist stylist Donald Barthelme and the extraordinary, virtually unclassifiable Toni Morrison. All these groupings are intended to make accurate and useful distinctions but my greater concern is to point to individual talents never completely containable within any critical categories.

Notes

1. 'Professors' Choice', *The Wilson Quarterly* (Winter, 1978), 136-37.

2. *The Liberal Imagination* (Garden City, New York, 1957), pp. 2, xii–xiii, 54.

3. *The Irony of American History* (New York, 1952), p. 4.

4. Meyer Schapiro in 'Religion and the Intellectuals', *The Partisan Review Anthology*, ed. William Phillips and Philip Rahv (New York, 1962), p. 418.

5. 'Our Country and Our Culture', *Partisan Review* **19** (1952), 304.

6. 'Our Country and Our Culture', 300.

7. Gabriel Kolko, *Main Currents in Modern American History* (New York, 1984), pp. 317–18.

8. David Riesman, Nathan Glazer, Reuel Denney, *The Lonely Crowd* (1950; repr. Garden City, New York, 1953), p. 42.

9. William H. Whyte, *The Organization Man* (1956; repr. Garden City, New York, 1957), pp. 440-41.

10. 'Our Country and Our Culture', 299.

11. Daniel Boorstin, *The Democratic Experience* (New York, 1973), pp. 393, 390.

12. Boorstin, *The Image: A Guide to Pseudo-Events in America* (1962; repr. New York, 1964).

13. The concept of the image displacing reality now associated with Jean Baudrillard was common knowledge among such culture critics of the 1950s and 1960s as Irving Howe, Philip Roth, Marshall McLuhan and Daniel Boorstin. For Baudrillard's version see *Simulations* (New York, 1983) and 'The Ecstacy of Communication' in Hal Foster (ed.), *The Anti-Aesthetic* (New York, 1983), pp. 126-34.

14. 'Upon Receiving the Nobel Prize for Literature' in *Essays, Speeches and Public Letters*, ed. James B. Meriwether (London, 1967), p. 119.

15. Mark Schorer, 'Technique as Discovery' in *Forms of Modern Fiction*, ed. William Van O'Connor (1948; repr. Bloomington, Indiana, 1959), p. 28.

16. *American Quarterly* **33** (1981), 123-39.

17. *The Culture of Narcissism* (New York, 1979), p. 22.

18. 'An Impolite Interview with Joseph Heller' in *Catch-22: A Critical Edition*, ed. Robert M. Scotto (New York, 1973), p. 469.

19. C. C. Walcutt, *American Literary Naturalism: A Divided Stream* (Minneapolis, 1956).

20. Richard Sennett and Jonathon Cobb, *The Hidden Injuries of Class* (New York, 1972).

Chapter 1
From Social Protest to Solipsism

The 1940s: endings and beginnings

1940 was a watershed year in American fiction. It was the year of Richard Wright's *Native Son* and Carson McCullers's *The Heart is a Lonely Hunter*, their first and best novels, and of Faulkner's last great novel, *The Hamlet*. In retrospect, with the death of Scott Fitzgerald, it seems a year more of endings than beginnings. Nathanael West, whose talent was so innovative that it was not assimilated until the mid 1950s, died in a car crash. And though the careers of some of the major American writers of the 1930s carried over into the new decade and beyond, their best work was mostly behind them. Hemingway's Spanish Civil War novel *For Whom the Bell Tolls* (1941) was his last major novel. *Across the River and into the Trees* (1950) has a protagonist, Colonel Cantwell, who mimics the tough stoicism of previous Hemingway protagonists but in contrast to their evocations of ironic control and endurance of loss Cantwell seems merely irritable while Hemingway's prose has become mannered, even exhibitionistic. Hemingway's final popular success, *The Old Man and the Sea* (1952), is self-consciously universal and noble, replete with the pseudo-profundities American writers are apt to produce when the Nobel Prize is hovering about (Hemingway received it in 1954). The worst feature of the novel, an insufferably arch imitation of Spanish vocabulary and syntax intended to sound wise and elemental, was a carry-over from *For Whom the Bell Tolls* where it had a purpose. While *For Whom the Bell Tolls* is uneven, the protagonist not quite focused and the heroine sentimentalized, other characters are splendidly realized and the horror and waste of the war are powerfully presented.

Dos Passos failed to follow the completion of his naturalistic trilogy *USA* with fiction of a comparable quality, though *Midcentury* (1961) has some interest in its re-use of the trilogy's rhetorical techniques of pocket biography and camera eye from a now conservative perspective. Most of

Steinbeck's novels after *The Grapes of Wrath* (1939) are surprisingly slight. Indeed, the power of *The Grapes of Wrath* was not in its thin and sentimentalized characters but its descriptions of natural and social processes, notably its initial depiction of the dust storm. His attempts at psychological depth in *East of Eden* (1952) and *The Winter of Our Discontent* (1961) are unconvincing. There is a certain brooding intensity in the former but Steinbeck's heavy-handed play on the biblical story of Cain and Abel portends more than the novel delivers.

In addition to some of the major writers of the 1930s, an important genre of the period was also in eclipse. Steinbeck, Dos Passos and James T. Farrell had written primarily in the naturalistic genre and even Faulkner and Hemingway – especially in *To Have and Have Not* (1937) – had incorporated naturalistic elements into their 1930s fiction. Farrell's finest work, the Studs Lonigan trilogy, was completed in 1935 but the Danny O'Neill series, less structurally satisfactory, has scenes of considerable power and carries on from *A World I Never Made* in 1936 to *The Face of Time* in 1953. But as formalist 'New Criticism' proceeded to marginalize social protest naturalist fiction as a supposedly innately inartistic form, writers like Farrell began to disappear critically. As I shall show in Chapter 2, Richard Wright's *Native Son* had a major impact but by 1945, the year of Ann Petry's *The Street*, naturalism was well on its way to critical marginalization. Thus, Harriette Arnow's *The Dollmaker* (1954), a minor classic of naturalistic social protest, received little critical respectability although it has attracted enough readers to stay continuously in print. And social protest becomes ever more subordinated to a bleak vision of unredeemed brutality, as in Nelson Algren's rewriting of his 1935 social protest novel, *Somebody in Boots*, into *A Walk on the Wild Side* (1956) which drops the protest and most of what is social as well. In the 1940s fiction of McCullers, Warren and Mailer we see the naturalistic impulse being gradually modified by various social and literary pressures.

Carson McCullers and Jane Bowles: perspectives become freaky

The turn from the social emphasis of the 1930s to interior experience is evident in Carson McCullers's *The Heart is a Lonely Hunter* (1940). Indeed, we see the turn as well as some of its causes within this extraordinarily original novel by a twenty-three-year old author. *The Heart is a Lonely Hunter* is a prototype of poetic realism, developing themes that became characteristic of 1940s and 1950s fiction. This fiction does not show an end of alienation as some critics assert, but rather a shift in the source of it from the political and economic to the personal and psychological. There is a sort of class conflict with something like the bourgeoisie as antagonist but the protagonists are defined as outcasts not by economic but by psychosexual traits and it is difficult to conceive of any sociopolitical solution to their dilemma. What political hopes they have eventuate, as if inevitably, in frustration and fresh distress. This pervasive doubt of political transformation itself reflects a historically specific political situation but to the protagonists, even the novelists, their dilemma appears as immutable as fate, in sharp contrast to the social protest fiction of the 1930s.

The five main characters of *The Heart is a Lonely Hunter* are thematically linked by their inability to accept or effectively function in their world. Two of these characters are politically radical, Jake Blount, a working-class radical concerned with economic injustice, and Doctor Benedict Mady Copeland, an African American who protests the blatant racial injustice of 1939 Georgia. Neither finds an audience able to comprehend their convictions. Copeland meets with incomprehension when he tries to explain Marx's labour theory of value. He is asked, 'Were he the Mark in the Bible?' His attempt to shape his family into a radical cadre leads only to his loss of close relations with them. The son he named Karl Marx now goes by the name of Buddy. His attempt to control, consciously a political motivation, is presented by McCullers as psychologically symptomatic, a compulsion obsession. Though McCullers certainly believes protest is justified, the world of the novel is so constituted that it can lead only to personal illness rather than to social change. The first encounter of the town's sole radicals results in a disastrous misunderstanding and later they argue at cross purposes about political tactics. In response Copeland feels a 'murderous darkness. Yet now he could not clearly recall those issues which were the cause of their dispute'. Though Blount's ideal is to make man 'a social creature', neither he nor Copeland can sustain an individual much less a social relationship.

The problem is that in McCullers's world no one understands anyone, so not only radical politics but *any* politics is precluded. Of course, this precludes community as well. Not only Blount and Copeland but Mick Kelly, a twelve year old girl struggling to find identity and vocation, and Biff Brannon, owner of the New York Café, seek communion with the deaf mute Singer. Each supposes that he/she alone has a true relation to Singer when in fact none does. A non-community of the lost and lonely, they separately visit Singer. The one occasion where their visits coincide results in a strained silence. This is because another structural attribute of McCullers's world is that love can never be symmetrical: A will always love B who loves C who loves A, a structure even more apparent in McCullers's novella *The Ballad of the Sad Café*. So Biff Brannon moons over Mick who moons over Singer.

Singer writes in a letter to the man *he* loves, Antonapoulos, that Blount 'thinks that he and I have a secret together but I do not know what it is'. But he does not send the letter because Antonapoulos cannot read. Near the end of the novel Blount is caught up in an outbreak of violence that begins as a race riot but soon loses even so irrational a vestige of articulation: 'He did not see who he hit and he did not see who hit him. But he knew that the line-up of the fight had changed and now each man was for himself'. This last section of the novel carries the characters through the day of 21 August 1939. On 1 September 1939 Nazi Germany invaded Poland, surely an intended parallel.

It is not clear that McCullers has earned a parallel that makes so evident a claim for significance. The schematic structure of her world seems arbitrary and the novel stands in a paradoxical relation to its own theme, showing us the links between the characters that they are unable to discern, communicating what they are unable to articulate. Thus in a sense the readers constitute the interpretive community (to appropriate Stanley Fish's term for institutionalized critical interpreters) missing in the world of the novel. But this community is itself paradoxical, a lite- rary elite with democratic sympathies, perceiving but quite unable to intervene in McCullers's world of obsessed solipsists blindly colliding. In a world such as she constructs politics could be only the vainest of en- deavours, as seen in the futile encounter of Blount and Copeland, two factions of one.

The novel's historical resonance lies precisely in its turn from history and politics to psychopathology as the privileged explanation for things as they are. Richard Gray points out that history is the 'absent presence' of the novel.[1] Clearly this was the intended significance of '21 August 1939'. The inability of the characters to relate themselves effectively to a a place in history or to political possibility *is* their place in history, a representative failure. Yet McCullers's insistence on the universality of muteness and deafness reflects a personal more than a national dilemma. This is apparent in the character closest to the writer's identity, Mick Kelly, a girl on the verge of adolescence. That she is too young to have political ideas makes her the better mirror of what McCullers shows as the condition underlying the political futility of Blount and Copeland. This condition, one that torments all the characters of this and other McCullers novels, is the unnameability and impossibility of desire. Early in the book Mick, accused of being unloving, reflects on how in fact she has fixated desire upon 'one person after another' and that 'every time it was like some part of her would bust in a hundred pieces'. Desire is elusive and disintegrative: 'Her face felt like it was scattered in pieces and she couldn't keep it straight. The feeling was a whole lot worse than being hungry for any dinner, yet it was like that. I want – I want – I want – was all that she could think about – but just what this real want was she did not know' (1:3). A post-Second World War American intellectual, cognizant of existential philosophy, would label this feeling as 'angst' but such labelling begs the question of the causes and the meaning of the prevalence of the theme of anxiety in 1940s and 1950s fiction, a prevalence that seems too historically special for the universalist metaphysics of existentialism to explain.

At least one explanation for McCullers's version of it involves the sexual cross purposes of the characters. McCullers was a bisexual who, to Katherine Anne Porter's horror, followed her about as Mick does Singer and Biff Mick; like her characters, she seemed to find insuperable barriers to reciprocal love.[2] In its hints and whispers *The Heart is a Lonely Hunter* marks a shift in the area of conflict from class to sex as the crux of oppressiveness, marginality, difference. Indeed, along with work by Jane Bowles, Truman Capote and others, McCullers's novel marks something of a homosexual emergence in the literature of the 1940s. But reciprocal love does in fact exist between homosexuals whereas McCullers's characters share an underlying disability for relationships generally.

The encoding of McCullers's psychological dysfunction into the structure of her plot renders dubious any critical claims for the universality of *The Heart is a Lonely Hunter* yet in some ways its trail of disconnections characterizes 1940s and 1950s fiction. Moreover, her novel has a peculiar force not only in its despair of politics but in its religious nihilism and stylistic texture. Singer has a dream that encapsulates the novel's pyramid of desire.

> There were dull yellow lanterns lighting up a dark flight of stone steps. Antonapoulos kneeled at the top of these steps. He was naked and he fumbled with something that he held above his head and gazed at as though in prayer. He himself knelt halfway down the steps. He was naked and cold and he could not take his eyes from Antonapoulos and the thing he held above him. Behind him on the ground he felt the one with the mustache and the girl and the black man and the last one. They knelt naked and he felt their eyes on him. And behind them were the uncounted crowds of kneeling people in the darkness. (2:7)

The iron laws of McCullers's world forbid the revelation of the object of desire probably because the only object is desire. And the god at the apex is an idiot.

McCullers is hardly more reliable about faith than about love yet the passage has a certain eerie power due to the inventiveness of the image and the authority of the language. The prose affects through its scrupulous flatness, its avoidance of decorative adjectives or rhetorical flourishes. McCullers derived this style from the Russian realists with whom Southern writers had sociological and aesthetic affinities: 'The technique briefly is this: a bold and outwardly callous juxtaposition of the tragic with the humorous, the immense with the trivial, the sacred with the bawdy, the whole soul of man with a materialistic detail'. Southern writers were misconceived as cruel because they not only describe horrific events without telling the reader how to feel about them but go on 'with no shift of tone to some trivial detail'. Thus farce and tragedy 'are superimposed one upon the other so that their effects are experienced simultaneously'.[3] Despite her lack of overtly figurative language McCullers's fiction is poetic rather than traditional realism, both characters and the overall design of the novel having primary meaning not as mimesis but as symbol. This is not to deny that McCullers presents an accurate picture of her economically as well as emotionally depressed mill town. And her characters are not unbelievable so much as superseded by the symbolic design. Alfred Kazin catches this: 'The consistency of her theme absorbed the town into itself, made the immediate landscape hot with silent emotion.'[4] McCullers overdetermined her theme of the muteness and deafness of the self, a theme that never quite escapes from a peculiar privacy of vision. McCullers's judgement of Dostoievsky's relation to the problems of his novels seems more applicable to herself: 'Sociologically these problems could never be solved, and besides Dostoevsky was indifferent to economic theories. And it is in his role as a Messiah that Dostoevsky fails to meet the responsibilities he has assumed. The questions he poses are too immense. They are like angry demands to God.'[5] Except that McCullers's work evokes not anger but a strangely luminous depressiveness.

McCullers was acquainted with a writer who resembled her in theme if not style, Jane Bowles. Both wrote about freaks although Bowles complained about McCullers that 'Her freaks aren't real'. Certainly Bowles's were different because seen through the 'curious, slanted and witty style' that as McCullers wrote to Bowles, gave her 'boundless delight'.[6] *Two Serious Ladies* (1943) is indeed a stylistic delight built around an unpredictably freakish perspective. As in McCullers radical political ideology is self-consciously considered, given its due, and dismissed from centre stage. Bowles counterposes a satirical undercutting of the 1920s idea of a community of the aesthetically sensitive with a *reductio ad absurdum* of the ideology of business enterprise.

> 'I'll tell you about it,' said Arnold. 'There were many people there, the majority of whom were creative artists, some successful and rich, others rich simply because they had inherited money from some member of the family, and others with just barely enough to eat. None of these people, however, were interested in money as an objective but would have been content, all of them, with just enough to eat'.
>
> 'Like wild animals,' said his father, rising to his feet. 'Like wolves! What separates a man from a wolf if it is not that a man wants to make a profit?' (1)

Bowles's world is consistently askew, continually outflanking expectation. The weird essence of it is built on turns and counterturns of phrase and demands quotation. As Miss Gamelon says to Miss Goering, 'you can never sit down for more than five minutes without introducing something weird into the conversation. I certainly think you have made a study of it' (3). The everyday takes on a bizarre aspect in Miss Goering's surprise that social organization exists even on Staten Island.

> She was delighted to see the flag in this far-off place, for she hadn't imagined that there would be any organization at all on the tip of the island.
> 'Why, people have lived here for years,' she said to herself. 'It is strange that I hadn't thought of this before. They're here naturally, with their family ties, their neighborhood stores, their sense of decency and morality, and they have certainly their organizations for fighting the criminals of the community'. She felt almost happy now that she had remembered all this. (3)

The ring of the prose anticipates Donald Barthelme by some twenty years. Characters are articulately uncertain: ' "How amusing," said Mrs Copperfield, "or perhaps it was depressing" ' (1). Odd attitudes are asserted as if self-evident: 'She was suffering as much as she had ever suffered before, because she was going to do what she wanted to do . . . . . She knew it would not make her happy, because only the dreams of crazy people come true' (2). Original distinctions are made: 'You look like a prostitute and that's what you are. I don't mean a small-time prostitute. I mean a medium one' (3). Responses seem inappropriate.

> 'What kind of men come in here?' he asked her.
> 'Oh,' said Miss Goering, 'all sorts of men, I guess. Rich and poor, workers and bankers, criminals and dwarfs'.
> 'Dwarfs,' Arnold's father repeated uneasily. (3)

These are camp mannerisms, to a degree, used by writers since Oscar Wilde as a way of inverting or at least eliding culturally normative perspectives. Yet though style is foregrounded, the two protagonists Miss Goering and Mrs Copperfield are engaging, even elegant in their tactless candour and unpredictable quirks. Mrs Copperfield, the character who most resembles the author, travels somewhat unwillingly with her husband to Panama, where she falls in love with the good-natured prostitute Pacifica, refuses to travel further with her husband and begins to go to pieces. At this point she receives a letter from her husband which logically and dispassionately dissects her. Out of the absurdist ambience of her novel Bowles conveys here a convincing sense of panic: 'Mrs Copperfield rose to her feet. "Pacifica," she shouted, "Pacifica!" ' (2).

Robert Penn Warren and Norman Mailer: naturalism becomes problematic

Politics as subject and naturalism as philosophy are both central and problematic in two important 1940s novels, Robert Penn Warren's *All the King's Men* (1946) and Norman Mailer's *The Naked and the Dead* (1948). In Warren's novel naturalism is foregrounded from procedure to problem, put simultaneously into use and into question. In a 1953 retrospect Warren declared that he intended 'to compose a highly documented picture of the modern world' centred on a dictatorial politician. The parallels to Theodore Dreiser's Cowperwood trilogy and Frank Norris's *The Pit* with their documentary procedure and ruthless businessman protagonists is evident; by the 1940s power had shifted from the economic to the political arena. But Warren also felt 'the necessity for a character of a higher degree of self-consciousness than my politician, a character to serve as a kind of commentator and *raissonneur* and chorus'. Warren wished 'to avoid writing a straight naturalistic novel, the kind of novel the material so readily invited'.[7] The novel's main theme is the conversion of its narrator, Jack Burden, from a nihilistic version of naturalism to a belief in the possibility of love and redemption. Warren's invention of this narrator is the foundation of the novel, the source of its brilliance and greatest flaw, a flaw representative of the moral dilemma of the 1940s.

Warren's difficulty was in finding a credible language for moral responsibility, a language neither too ideal to fit the dread realities of his time nor too complicitous with those realities in a self-defeating cynicism. This is the burden of the symbolically named narrator. In the novel's allegorical scheme his role is to find a new thesis at a higher level to resolve the antithesis of idealism and naturalism, innocence and will, as represented in the characters of Adam Stanton, 'the man of idea', and Willie Stark, 'the man of fact', each 'incomplete with the terrible division of their age' (10). Stark will and fact opposed to Adamic innocence – the allegory is overt. But there is a question as to how possible the idealist side of the opposition seems in the toxic narrative environment of Jack Burden's and Willie Stark's cynical rhetoric. Warren tries not very successfully to convince us that Jack is philosophically reborn towards the end of the novel but Adam, Stark's allegorical antagonist and eventual assassin, is never alive enough on the page to live up to his ideological or plot function.

Willie Stark does come alive – a remarkable portrayal of a character obviously based on Huey Long, the populist Governor then Senator and virtual dictator of the state of Louisiana until his assassination in 1935 by a young doctor.[8] Ruthless in his use of power, tolerant of corruption as a means of greasing the wheels, Stark has yet democratized political and economic power, providing access to roads, health care and education to previously deprived farmers and workers. Jack, who works for Stark as a kind of historical researcher of his opponents' indiscretions, responds to hearing someone has called Stark corrupt: 'Graft is what he calls it when the fellows do it who don't know which fork to use' (3). Or as Stark puts it, 'It is just a question of who has got his front feet in the trough when slopping time comes' (9). Stark is a cynical philosopher of sorts, a character who could be a Brecht hero. Yet the fount and origin of his philosophy is not Marx's *Capital* but the Westminister Confession; Stark learned about human nature in Presbyterian Sunday School. When Jack argues that there may be no dirt to find on a particularly upright person, Stark's reply is Calvinistically axiomatic: 'Man is conceived in sin and born in corruption and he passeth from the stink of the didie to the stench of the shroud. There is always something' (1). He is, of course, right.

Stark speaks for Warren in his scorn of the sort of innocent idealism that is blind to what the Westminister Confession calls an 'original corruption, whereby we are utterly disposed, disabled, and made opposite to all good, and are wholly inclined to evil. . . '. Influenced by Niebuhr, Warren shares his distrust of optimistic naivety. However, even Jack Burden sometimes feels his automatically cynical ripostes are overdone: '*Christ, Jack, you talk like a snot, Christ, you are a smart guy*'. He is given to nasty similes: 'the .38 Special which rode under his left armpit like a tumor'; 'a look on her face as though her garter belt had busted in church. . . ' (1). It is an enjoyably mean point of view but as Roger Sale points out, Raymond Chandler, whose tough detective novels were a probable source, did it better. Sale sees Jack's cynicism as forced, inauthentic, an attempt by Warren to have it both ways as Jack later slides into metaphysical moralization, without having altogether dropped his intonations of snide superiority.[9] It is true that Warren intends that we should be ultimately unconvinced by Jack's cynical voice and the world view that goes with it. Jack even intimates that he is telling the story in a style he now repudiates: 'And the good old family reunion, with picnic dinner under the maples, is very much like diving into the octopus bank at the aquarium. Anyway, that is what I would have said back then, that evening' (1). But not only does the cynical voice continue, if somewhat diminuendo, beyond Jack's rebirth of faith but the illuminated voice in which he attempts to enunciate moral truth is far *less* convincing than his nasty one. And most of Warren's best hits at idealism, which he has no intention of taking back, are in the nasty voice. Earlier Jack is faulted for overidealizing Adam's sister, failing to make love to her. What is most inventive in the novel is its vision of the human condition as so pervaded by sin that the best politics is that which frankly recognizes and builds on this condition, graft and good roads going together in a sort of Calvinist pragmatism. When Warren tries to transcend morally this engagingly scandalous position his prose goes fuzzy, replete with orotund abstractions about Time and Truth that are asserted about events in the novel without convincingly connecting with them. Jack Burden's mother, a minor character who has not been made very real to us, is trotted on stage near the end to give a silvery scream that restores Jack to the possibility of love and moral responsibility. Writers of popular melodrama motivate such plot devices more skilfully. The root of the problem, however, is not in the characterization or plotting but in the moral vision.

The problem is that Original Sin interpenetrates the texture of the novel whereas Love and Redemption float above its surface as factitiously beautified platitudes. Warren approves of love and goodness but his fictional imagination is captured by cynicism and nihilism. Thus Warren replicates in his style and structure what he terms 'the terrible division of our age'. He gives speeches on redemption and dramatizes sin. In this and other novels of the 1940s the language of impasse and negation is alive and urgent, that of solution and engagement hollow and evasive. This is not to say that Warren implicitly concedes to nihilistic naturalism. Indeed, some of the most impressive passages in the novel undercut Jack's tendency to relax into meaninglessness. In a symbolic flight west Jack embraces the philosophy of the Great Twitch, a view of the world in terms of scientific determinism. The twitch is that of 'the nerve, like a dead frog's leg in the experiment when the electric current goes through'. It is also that of an old man to whom Jack gives a ride on his way back from California.

> The only thing remarkable about him was the fact that while you looked into the sun-brittled leather of the face, which seemed as stiff and devitalized as the hide on a mummy's jaw, you would suddenly see a twitch in the left cheek, up toward the pale-blue eye. You would think he was going to wink, but he wasn't going to wink. The twitch was simply an independent phenomenon, unrelated to the face or to what was behind the face or to anything in the whole tissue of phenomena which is the world we are lost in. (8)

Jack went to California trying to escape from his enmeshment in a world of moral complications. Warren is mocking the American Adam fantasy that one can escape historical evil by moving west and beginning life anew. But what now lies west is not territories to light out for but Long Beach, California, presented as the dead end of the American dream of 'innocence and a new start' (7). The secular humanist dream is incarnated in a technology of stimulus and response signified by the neon sign 'flickered on and off to the time of my heart, systole and diastole' (7) and by the Great Twitch: 'That is what you have to go to

California to have a mystic vision to find out. That the twitch can know that the twitch is all. Then, having found that out, in the mystic vision, you can feel clean and free. You are at one with the Great Twitch' (8). The American romanticist retrieves innocence through an Adamic figure who moves west to find new possibilities of self in divorce from society. The American naturalist removes guilt by reducing action to behaviour, moral choice to conditioned response. Both, as Warren sees it, are equivalent to the prefrontal lobectomy Jack witnesses Adam perform. Adam's description of the pre-operative patient is clearly intended by Warren to remind us of Pascal's analysis of the misery into which we fall when we lack sufficient distraction from the truth of the human condition.

> The way he is now he simply sits on a chair or lies on his back on a bed and stares into space. His brow is creased and furrowed. Occasionally he utters a low moan or an exclamation. In some such cases we discover the presence of delusions of persecution. But always the patient seems to experience a numbing, grinding misery. But after we are through with him he will be different. He will be relaxed and cheerful and friendly. He will smooth his brow. He will sleep well and eat well and will love to hang over the back fence and compliment the neighbors on their nasturtiums and cabbages. He will be perfectly happy. (8)

Warren anticipates the 1950s suburban idyll.

The problem is that after having convincingly questioned naturalism, Warren cannot effectively move beyond it. He makes a fine case against the tendency, clearly apparent in Steinbeck and Dos Passos, to privilege the collective over the personal and reduce choice to reflex. That he implicates suburban secularism in the same figure is a *tour de force*. But Warren's belief in freedom and redemption seems curiously unattached to his characters even when he rhetorically insists on their freedom (as when Jack interprets the complicity in the assassination of one of Stark's humiliated flunkies as a confirmation of free will when it appears in the face of Warren's own presentation of it as a mere reflex of hatred). One of the book's finest prose moments is the opening passage which puts the reader, using second person address, in a scene that while it allegorically illustrates the fatality of technological mesmerization, works primarily through the intensity of its evocation of its Southern highway.

> To get there you follow Highway 58, going northeast out of the city, and it is a good highway and new. Or was new, that day we went up it. You look up the highway and it is straight for miles, coming at you, with the black line down the center coming at you and at you, black and slick and tarry-shining against the white of the slab, and the heat dazzles up from the white slab so

that only the black line is clear, coming at you with the whine of
the tires, and if you don't quit staring at that line and don't take a
few deep breaths and slap yourself hard on the back of the neck
you'll hypnotize yourself and you'll come to just at the moment
when the right front wheel hooks over into the black dirt
shoulder off the slab, and you'll try to reach to turn off the igni-
tion just as she starts the dive. (1)

In *The Naked and the Dead* (1948) Norman Mailer, working from politically radical premises, constructed a world structurally similar to that
Warren created, working from conservative premises. In both, the true
commitments are those signified not by rhetorical argument but by prose
vitality. In a 1948 interview Mailer described the book he thought he
had just written, a social protest naturalistic novel in the vein of Farrell,
Dos Passos and Steinbeck: 'The book finds man corrupted, confused to
the point of helplessness, but it also finds that there are limits beyond
which he cannot be pushed, and it finds that even in his corruption and
sickness there are yearnings for a better world'.[10] Mailer's technique of
interpolating pocket biographies of his characters in segments called 'The
Time Machine' and his use of a chorus to show group response reminds
us of Dos Passos. The naturalistic theme of time eroding possibilities
already limited by culturally stunted consciousness is especially evident in
Mailer's portrayal of Gallagher, the Boston Irishman, a character angrier
than Farrell's Studs Lonigan and whose political naivety takes a more
violent form but who resembles Studs in his inability to articulate his
vague intuitions of a better world. Farrell's Danny O'Neill is a politicized rebel (see p. 15), as are characters in Steinbeck and Dos Passos.
But the most radical characters in *The Naked and the Dead*, Valsen and
Hearn, finally despair of finding limits beyond which they cannot be
pushed. Both are in fact pushed into the margin of the book's action as
if Tom Joad and Jim Casey had been reduced to ineffectual minor characters in *The Grapes of Wrath*. Diane Trilling noted that what differen-
tiated Mailer from the previous generation of naturalists was 'the loss of
faith in both the orderly and the revolutionary processes of social development, our always increasing social fragmentation and our always diminishing trust in social possibility'.[11] Norman Podhoretz slightly
oversimplifies in saying that in the course of writing his novel Mailer
discovered 'that American liberalism is bankrupt' but is exact in declaring
that Mailer was looking for 'not so much a more equitable world as a
more exciting one, a world that produces men of size, and a life of huge
possibility, and this was nowhere to be found in the kind of liberalism to
which he committed himself in the earliest phase of his literary career'.[12]
Trilling, Podhoretz and other critics saw that Mailer's imagination was
more excited by his politically reactionary characters, General Cummings
and Captain Croft.

Cummings, however, is still a primarily negative and rather conventionalized character. Mailer uses him to develop his theory that the Second World War, in the scale of industrial and military organization it necessitated, moved America closer to fascism in the guise of fighting against it. The true enemy, as in many war novels, is the officer class rather than the opposing army. General Cummings proclaims 'This is going to be the reactionary's century, perhaps their thousand year reign' (3). Cummings anticipates Riesman and Whyte in theorizing that the 'natural role of twentieth-century man is anxiety', seeing the creation of a 'fear ladder' (6) as a valid strategy for imposing control. But Cummings's power philosophy is undercut by a certain spinsterish quality, a sexual hysteria apparent in his covert courtship of Lieutenant Hearn and in his fear and loathing of his wife, who seeks *her* power in extra-marital relationships after recognizing his basic coldness to her. Cummings's philosophy seems especially refuted by a final victory accidentally won by a subordinate distracted with diarrhoea and more concerned with bowel than troop movements. Cummings himself has speculated on the 'tragic curve', an analogy to the wind resistance that deflects the symmetry of a projectile. The mass inertia of his troops is the resistance for which he is unable to find a formula: 'It had all been too pat, too simple. There was order but he could not reduce it to the form of a single curve. Things eluded him' (6). Mailer sees Cummings's defeat as a victory for human possibility, an instance of a saving disorder in the nature of things.

Hearn is 'partially convinced the General was a great man' (3). Yet the equivalent to the troubling charisma of Willie Stark is not Cummings but Croft, the cold and dangerous Texan. In the novel Mailer thought he was writing, Croft is one of the two ideological villains, a rigid misogynist, as obsessed with power as Cummings but with a more personal and thus more directly violent relation to the troops he tries to control. He is crazier than Cummings, acting more on impulse than plan. If anything, Mailer was closer in temperament in the 1940s to Cummings; he went to war planning to write a major novel about it, read *Infantry Journal* and carried Spengler's *Decline of the West* in his knapsack. Yet Croft is the character who foreshadows Mailer's later fascination with the hipster, the 'white negro', the existential killer.

Mailer briefly served as a rifleman in the Philippines in the Second World War, during the Luzon campaign in an Intelligence and Reconnaissance unit that derived from a division of the Texas National Guard. He adopted a Texas accent for protective coloration that he fell back on in later years when acting out the tough guy role. The appeal of this role was its antithesis to the identity Mailer found 'absolutely insupportable – the nice Jewish boy from Brooklyn'.[13] Croft, then, is Mailer's antithetical self, the kind of American archetype that Clint Eastwood embodies in films.

His narrow triangular face was utterly without expression. There seemed nothing wasted in his hard small jaw, gaunt firm cheeks and straight short nose. His gelid eyes were very blue . . . he was efficient and strong and usually empty and his main cast of mind was a superior contempt toward nearly all other men. He hated weakness and he loved practically nothing. There was a crude unformed vision in his soul but he was rarely conscious of it. (5)

Mailer acknowledges the affinity: 'Beneath the ideology in *The Naked and the Dead* was an obsession with violence. The characters for whom I had the most secret admiration, like Croft, were violent people.'[14] For Mailer it is the irrationality of Croft's violence that is its saving grace. Early on we see Croft seriously disturbed when his 'sudden and powerful conviction that he was going to win the pot' in a game of poker turns out wrong. However, the confirmation of his intuition that Hennessy, a raw replacement, will die on the first day of battle opens 'such vistas of such omnipotence that he was afraid to consider it directly. All day the fact hovered about his head, tantalizing him with odd dreams and portents of power' (1:2). Like later Mailer heroes he is exhilarated by danger and violence. Sex is just another battle ground, as with Sergius O'Shaughnessy of Mailer's notorious 'The Time of Her Time' who calls his penis 'The Avenger'. Croft spurs himself to superior sexual performance with the inner incantation, 'Crack . . . that . . . WHIP!' (2:6). Croft's odd blend of superstition, sadism and aspiration becomes focused on Mount Anaka.

> Croft was moved as deeply, as fundamentally as caissons resettling in the river mud. The mountain attracted him, taunted and inflamed him with its size. . . . He stared at it now, examined its ridges, feeling an instinctive desire to climb the mountain and to stand on its peak, to know that all its mighty weight was beneath his feet. His emotions were intense; he knew awe and hunger and the peculiar unique ecstasy he had felt after Hennessy was dead, or when he had killed the Japanese prisoner. He gazed at it, almost hating the mountain, unconscious at first of the men about him. 'That mountain's mighty old,' he said at last. (3:1)

Mailer noted that the greatest literary influence on his novel was *Moby-Dick*; Croft's fascination with the mountain parallels Ahab's with the whale. The title, 'Plant and Phantom', of Part 3 of the novel, in which Croft attempts his ascent of the mountain, derives from Nietzsche's metaphor for the merely biological as opposed to spiritual dimension of mankind. Mailer wanted to use this as the title for the whole novel but decided that *The Naked and the Dead* was 'another way of saying it – the naked being the fanatics, the men obsessed with vision'.[15] Both Cummings and Croft are so obsessed but Cummings is too rationalistic, too much the organization man, too plastic really to qualify for Mailer's curious version of spiritual heroism. By the 1960s Mailer had decided that Americans were losing touch with the world of nature and instinct: 'such things as television and plastics are probably doing us much more harm, and getting us much closer to totalitarianism than the FBI or CIA ever would'. Cummings's violence has an abstract quality, mediated through the bureaucracy he controls; he is essentially in accord with the plastic world Mailer loathes. Croft's violence, in contrast, is hands on, as was that of the Utah murderer Gary Gilmore, about whom Mailer wrote a fascinated and ambivalent book. In 1986 Mailer declared that a Croft would be unacceptable to the contemporary, evidently plasticized army; he would be profiled as 'psychologically unstable', 'too intense'.[16] Croft encodes Mailer's concept of manhood: 'being a man is the continuing battle of one's life, and one loses a bit of manhood with every stale compromise to the authority of any power in which one does not believe'.[17] For Croft, that is any power outside the self.

Mailer's novel, like Warren's, has unresolved moral ambivalences but Mailer's ends more successfully. In Warren the substitution of moral platitudes for the grit of Willie Stark's cynical wisdom is a let-down, but Mailer carefully calibrated the dual anti-climaxes of his conclusion – the battle won not by Cummings's grand strategy but by accident, Croft's brutal and heroic trail drive of his men up Mount Anaka defeated by a swarm of hornets. Mailer's veneration of violence is morally dubious but he is canny enough to recognize that for characters like Croft victory only feeds a megalomania bound to eventuate in defeat or even ignominy. Besides being overly dependent upon luck such a drive for predominance is innately self-destructive. And the strength of a single will is ultimately undermined by the mute but collective recalcitrance of those over whom it attempts domination.

Diana Trilling points to the internal contradiction recurrent in Mailer's writing 'between his overriding fear, in politics, of an authority which makes its law in defiance of the decent social values and his powerful attraction to the same authority in the personal or spiritual realm'.[18] The Naked and the Dead powerfully projects this contradiction. Mailer's later novels are more self-consciously aware of the contradiction but less successful in finding forms proper to its dramatization. Mailer, it now seems clear, benefited from the naturalistic tradition. The prose in The Naked and the Dead is serviceable rather than stirring but in the manner of Dreiser, Dos Passos and Farrell the cumulative effect can be strong, as in the episode of the two soldiers ordered to carry a critically wounded comrade through miles of dense jungle and over rapids back to the base, an action that begins as an externally defined duty and ends as an existential errand. There is also the naturalistic device of taking the reader on a descent deeper into contingencies of the material world than allowed for under previous literary protocols. No 1948 reader of *The Naked and the Dead* will forget the scene in which Hennessy in his first and last exposure to combat learns what the veterans' advice to keep 'a tight ass-hole' means and dies after hysterically leaving the shelter of his foxhole to empty his pants (1:2). The prose in Mailer's later fiction is likely to mount higher when it works and fall flatter when it does not. *An American Dream* (1965) has fine flights of performative prose on the topics of Mailer's typical obsessions – macho power games, the metaphysics of anal intercourse, etc. – but within a narrative that never for a moment presents a credible character or persuades us that its world means anything on any level of reality, symbolism or allegory. The later novels are more interesting to read about than to read because Mailer conceives wonderful literary ideas but is unable, lacking such prefabricated devices as those offered by the naturalistic tradition, to find a form for their development in convincing *scenes*. His characters seem like parodies without a real model whose dialogue is so unmotivated, so obviously the writer speaking through the character, that their lines would look more natural enclosed in cartoon balloons. It is in his best non-fiction that Mailer's voice comes alive. This is because the characters are already there for him, allowing him to concentrate on what he has come to do best, contrive his unique rhetorical compound of dottiness and perception.

Paul Bowles, Truman Capote, J. D. Salinger, Jack Kerouac: the impasse of solipsism

In a *Partisan Review* essay on 'Psychoanalysis and Literary Culture Today' Alfred Kazin observed that the social significance of Norman Mailer's *The Deer Park* (1955) was its lack of any: 'Mailer is not interested in the political significance of his material, though he feels he *should* be; he is concerned with sex as an ultimate expression of man's aloneness'. This turn towards solipsism was the defining characteristic of recent fiction by McCullers, Nelson Algren, Jack Kerouac and Paul Bowles as well as Mailer, a fiction that seems 'like a nightmare from which the dreamer may never escape into the unpatterned relief of the real world'.[19] The presentation of what another critic called 'the landscape of nightmare'[20] is the explicit theme of Paul Bowles's *The Sheltering Sky* (1948). Published the same year as *The Naked and the Dead*, the alienation in this novel is personal and metaphysical rather than political. Its protagonists, Port and Kit Moresby, remind us of Mr and Mrs Copperfield as both couples do of Paul and Jane Bowles but *The Sheltering Sky* presents them without the quirky charm of *Two Serious Ladies*. Less interesting stylistically than the earlier novel, it has a certain bleak force as the most programmatically nihilistic novel of the 1940s, its protagonists proving successful in their quest through the Sahara for the 'perfect zero' (19). The feel of this idiosyncratic novel is best conveyed in an image and a story from it. The image is the titular one of the sheltering sky. Port says of the Sahara sky that 'I often have the sensation when I look at it that it's a solid thing up there, protecting us from what's behind'. Which is, of course, 'Nothing. . . . Just darkness. Absolute night.' (13). The story, told to Port at the instigation of an Arab woman, is of three prostitutes whose dream is to have tea in the Sahara. They join a caravan and go off at night 'to look for the highest dune so they can see all the Sahara' but by the time they find it they are so tired that they take a nap. Some days later another caravan discovers them: 'they were still there, lying the same way as when they had gone to sleep. And all three of the glasses . . . were full of sand. That was how they had tea in the Sahara.' When Port comments inadequately 'It's very sad' the woman responds '*Ei oua!*', roughly translatable as *Yes sir!* (5). That Port then wants to sleep with the Arab woman shows that despite (or because of) his self-involved nihilism, he has missed the point.

Bowles's nihilism gives his novel an arid quality, rather like that attributed to Port: 'Although it was the basis of his unhappiness, this glacial deadness, he would cling to it always, because it was also the core of his being; he had built the being around it' (17). Yet *The Sheltering Sky* is rather appealing in comparison with the mixture of solipsism and sentiment found in the works of Truman Capote, J. D. Salinger and Jack Kerouac. It is true that the twenty-four-year-old author of *Other Voices, Other Rooms* (1948) was in complete control over his highly textured prose and complex symbolic pattern, with its extended allusion to Hans Christian Anderson's 'The Snow Queen'. Moreover in 1948 it took a certain courage to write a novel on the theme of not just sexual but homosexual initiation. (In the same year Norman Mailer's publisher required the substitution of the word 'fug' for an everyday army usage.) Capote's dramatization of his protagonist's sexual ambivalence as he is caught between the tomboy Idabel (based on Capote's childhood friend Harper Lee, later author of the children's classic *To Kill a Mockingbird*) and Cousin Randolph, the transvestite Snow Queen, has a certain poignancy. But there is something dishonest about the moral perspective of the novel. It begins with an epigraph from Jeremiah 17:19: 'The heart is deceitful above all things, and desperately wicked. Who can know it?' If this frames anything it is Cousin Randolph's seduction of the protagonist, Joel Knox. Yet the presentation of this within the novel is as Joel's discovery of an inevitable rather than wicked identity. The purpose of the biblical quotation seems to be to give the novel a factitious portentousness. In the 1940s and 1950s a number of novelists, lacking a social vision, fell back on original sin to give their narratives an unearned moral density. In the age of Auschwitz sin should be taken more seriously.

The year 1948, it should be noted, was not only that of Capote's novel but that of Gore Vidal's *The City and the Pillar* and Tennessee Williams's *One Arm and Other Stories* (1954), all of which developed homosexual themes. Homosexual experience, as earlier noted, seemed to be emerging from the shadows. Yet though the careers of these writers continued apace, no general homosexual emergence ensued. James Purdy's novels of the 1960s and John Rechy's *City of Night* (1962) ran original variations on homosexual themes but their work was not supplemented by enough other writers to form the critical mass of a subgenre, a movement. It is possible that such a subgenre will emerge in the 1990s, consonant with the activism of gay politics and the increasing visibility of the gay cultural presence. If so, some forerunners will have been David Leavitt's *The Language of Cranes* (1986) and David Feinberg's AIDS novel, *Eighty-Sixed* (1989). Rita Mae Brown's *Rubyfruit Jungle* (1973) and Cecil Dawkins's understated and witty *Charleyhorse* (1985) may be harbingers of an emerging fiction expressing lesbian experience though the former seems designed for lesbian readers only.

Two extraordinarily influential but now dated novels of the 1950s, J. D. Salinger's *The Catcher in the Rye* (1951) and Jack Kerouac's *On the Road* (1957), confirm the impasse of solipsism in their very attempts to break out of it. In a 1959 essay Gore Vidal commented that in recent American writing Love had 'replaced the third act marines of a simpler time as *deus ex machina*'.[21] This easy answer vitiates both novels. Salinger had a perfect ear for the rhythms of adolescent language and this may be enough to help his work survive but his reduction of the problem of existentialist authenticity to the difficulties of a wise child in a world of phonies seems a massive projection of self-pity. Moreover, the protagonist's profession of love for everyone in general is rather inconsistent with his nicely specified disgust for almost all those people he actually knows. The critical reaction against Salinger in the late 1950s is exemplified by Mary McCarthy's malicious comment about the group hero of his later fiction, the Glass family (who appear on a television show called 'It's a Wise Child').

> And who are these wonder kids but Salinger himself, splitting and multiplying like the original amoeba?
> In Hemingway's work there was hardly anyone but Hemingway in a series of disguises, but at least there was only one Papa per book. To be confronted with the seven faces of Salinger, all wise and lovable and simple, is to gaze into a terrifying narcissus pool.[22]

Raise High the Roofbeams, Carpenter is the Glass family story that most nearly transcends such defects especially in its opening scene, an absurd comedy of manners at an abortive wedding.

On the Road (1957) won celebrity as the prototype novel of the so-called 'beat generation', though this was not actually a generation but a small group of individuals who embraced an alternative lifestyle heavy on drugs, cool jazz and mysticism from which, somewhat mysteriously, two genuine talents, Allen Ginsberg and William Burroughs, actually emerged. Kerouac's novel is similar to Salinger's except substituting all-purpose ecstasy for all-purpose love. The prose has some fine impressionistic snapshots of America as it looked from a car window or at a far West bus stop but the quality of experience is out of accord with the pumped-up rhetoric and on the novel's own showing it is difficult to see what the prose is getting so excited about. In both Salinger and Kerouac sentiment is curiously unrelated to its nominal objects, interior rather than relational.

Notes

1. Richard Gray, *The Literature of the South: Modern Writers of the American South* (Baltimore, 1987), p. 273.

2. Virginia Spencer Carr, *The Lonely Hunter* (Garden City, NY, 1974), p. 156.

3. 'The Russian Realists and Southern Literature', *Decision* 2:1 (1941), 15–16.

4. Alfred Kazin, *Bright Book of Life: American Novelists and Storytellers from Hemingway to Mailer* (Boston, 1973), p. 53.

5. 'The Russian Realists and Southern Literature', 18.

6. Millicent Dillon, *A Little Original Sin: The Life and Works of Jane Bowles* (NY, 1981), pp. 209, 382. Bowles wrote in a letter that 'there is nothing original about me/But a little original SIN'. Dillon, p. 99.

7. 'Introduction to the Modern Library Edition of *All the King's Men*' in *Twentieth Century Interpretations of All the King's Men*, ed. Robert H. Chambers (Englewood Cliffs, NJ, 1977), p. 95.

8. See Ladell Payne, 'Willie Stark and Huey Long: Atmosphere, Myth or Suggestion?', *American Quarterly* 20 (Fall, 1968), 580–95.

9. Roger Sale, 'Having It Both Ways' in *All the King's Men: A Critical Handbook*, ed. Maurice Beebe and Leslie A. Field (Belmont, California, 1966), pp. 168–75.

10. *Conversations with Norman Mailer*, ed. J. Michael Lennon (Jackson, Mississippi, 1988), p. 14.

11. Diana Trilling, 'The Moral Radicalism of Norman Mailer' in Robert F. Lucid (ed.), *Norman Mailer: The Man and his Work* (Boston, 1971), pp. 115–16.

12. Norman Podhoretz, 'Norman Mailer: The Embattled Vision' in Lucid, pp. 67–68.

13. Hilary Mills, *Mailer: A Biography* (NY, 1982), p. 29.

14. *The Presidential Papers* (NY, 1963), p. 136.

15. *Conversations with Norman Mailer*, p. 7.

16. *Conversations with Norman Mailer*, pp. 321, 340.

17. *Advertisements for Myself* (NY, 1959), p. 222.

18. Diana Trilling, p. 127.

19. Alfred Kazin, 'Psychoanalysis and Literary Culture Today' in *The Partisan Review Anthology*, ed. William Phillips and Philip Rahv (NY, 1962), pp. 238, 240.

20. Jonathan Baumbach, *The Landscape of Nightmare: Studies in the Contemporary American Novel* (NY, 1965).

21. 'Love, Love, Love', *The Partisan Review Anthology*, p. 231.

22. *The Writing on the Wall and Other Literary Essays* (NY, 1970), p. 39.

Chapter 2
The Emergence of African American Fiction

The literary context for Richard Wright's *Native Son*

The publication of Richard Wright's *Native Son* in 1940 changed the face of African American literature. This literature had a brief vogue in the 'Harlem Renaissance' of the 1920s with novels by Langston Hughes and Claude McKay among others, though the most significant novel by an African American man was Jean Toomer's non-Renaissance classic *Cane* (1923), an intense, lyrical work built around the prototype 1920s theme of the opposition of materialism and sexual repressiveness to passionate self-expression. Some of the novel is set in rural Georgia where racial tension mixes with sexual rivalry to produce an undertone of simmering frustration and rage that finally explodes into violence. But Toomer then turned to the Gurdjieff movement, losing interest in fiction, so the achievement of *Cane* was not followed up. By the 1930s the literature of the Harlem Renaissance was no longer in vogue.[1]

Ralph Ellison, writing on 'Recent Negro Fiction' for *New Masses* in 1941, showed no regret for the virtual disappearance of some types of African American fiction. From his then radical perspective, Ellison condemned the 'exoticism' of novels that exploited a supposed 'primitivism' to entertain a predominantly white reading audience. Ellison equally repudiated a type of fiction he described as 'apologetic in tone and narrowly confined to the expression of Negro middle-class ideals'. In contrast, he found recent work 'marked by a slow but steady movement toward a grasp of American reality', with *Native Son* now in 'the front rank of American fiction'.[2] Wright had quickly become a reference point, writers being attacked for lacking his political commitment or praised for transcending his alleged limitations. Ellison himself later qualified his praise of Wright so as to defend his own very different novel, *Invisible Man,* and James Baldwin launched a pre-emptive strike against Wright in 'Everybody's Protest Novel' in order to free up his own literary space. It all came full circle when Irving Howe criticized *Invisible Man* for not being political enough, as Ellison had done with earlier African American novels.

In fact, some of the novels Ellison had dismissed in his *New Masses* essay were of real distinction; Nella Larsen's *Quicksand* (1928) and *Passing* (1929) are 'middle-class novels' that especially repay close reading. Deborah E. McDowell shows that the real subject of *Passing* is not the titular one of 'passing' for white but the self-delusions of the compulsively proper and unreliable narrator of the novel, an African American lady who sublimates sexual desire into the compulsion to control not only the behaviour but the thoughts and feelings of her husband and child. She too passes for white in having internalized a 'white' code of repression and respectability as the only way in which African Americans can attain self-esteem. Her inadmissible attraction to the beautiful woman who is more literally 'passing' leads to a complex series of evasions culminating in murder.[3] A later novel in this mode is Gwendolyn Brooks's subtle, brilliant *Maud Martha* misperceived in 1953 as a gentle and lyrical depiction of middle-class black life but really, as Mary Helen Washington shows, 'a novel about bitterness, rage, self-hatred and the silence that results from suppressed anger'.[4] Moreover, Zora Neale Hurston's *Their Eyes Were Watching God* (1937), an 'exotic' novel attacked by both Ellison and Wright, is now on the verge of canonization. For Wright the novel had no theme and the wrong audience: 'The sensory sweep of her novel carries no theme, no message, no thought. In the main her novel is not addressed to the Negro, but to a white audience whose chauvinistic tastes she knows how to satisfy.'[5] The novel does in fact have a theme, Janie Starks's search for emotional and sexual fulfilment, her implicit protest against not so much racial but gender oppression. It seems significant that a man about to write a novel about a man that kills two women should misunderstand a novel by a woman about a woman who leaves one man and kills two. But Ellison's and Wright's main objection was that Hurston's novel seemed to present African Americans as passionate primitives, a stereotype often used by white writers on slumming expeditions, as in Sherwood Anderson's *Dark Laughter* (1925), DuBose Heyward's *Porgy and Bess* (1925), Carl Van Vechten's *Nigger Heaven* (1926) and Julia Peterkin's *Scarlet Sister Mary* (1928) – this last a novel of some merit despite its suspect origin as the work of a white woman married to a South Carolina plantation manager. Hurston's novel, however, is centred not in primitivism but in Hurston's experiences growing up in an all African American Florida town and in her extensive and sympathetic study of African American folklore. Besides the feminist theme invisible to Wright and Ellison her work has the 'sensory sweep' Wright acknowledged, especially in Hurston's extraordinary descriptions of her characters' work in the rice fields of the Florida 'muck' and their survival of a hurricane.

Essentially the objections of Wright and Ellison were prescriptive, as was later the case when some critics attacked Wright and Ann Petry for being too political and naturalistic while others attacked Ellison and Baldwin for not being political and naturalistic enough. As June Jordan suggests, these 'choose between' games blaming one African American writer for not being sufficiently like or unlike another have become a waste of time better put to understanding the various writers in their historical context.[6] To see Wright's value does not necessitate trashing Hurston or vice versa.

Yet the attacks are understandable as the reflex of shifts in political ideology and literary convention. In the early 1940s Wright and his young ally Ellison defined their residual 1930s ethos by attacking what seemed to them modes of African American writing that were insufficiently radical. By the 1950s a less radical Ellison and the young James Baldwin were attacking Wright for a mode of writing that was overly radical and insufficiently ironic, existentialist and formalist, both missing how subjectively intense and formalistically complex a work Native Son actually is. Indeed in Wright, Ellison, Baldwin, Petry, just as in Carson McCullers, we can see how politics becomes solipsized and solipsism becomes politicized. An underlying theme in the four African American writers is how, in the absence of community, communication breaks down into the collision of mutually solipsistic sensibilities, divided not only by class, race and gender but by the lack of a basis for discourse. No one in these novels can talk to anyone, an impasse unbridgeable except through the writer's desperate attempt to break through to the reader. We shall see, however, from the 1970s to the 1990s, a renewed quest after the possibilities, never easily attainable, of community, a development that comes with the reassertion of traditional realism, with its emphasis on the interrelation of characters rather than their mutual isolation.

Richard Wright: the smothering world of Bigger Thomas

Wright's Native Son (1940) is written against what was thought to be the reassurances of respectability intrinsic to the middle-class novel, the ingratiating cuteness intrinsic to the primitivist novel and the sentimental pathos intrinsic to the proletarian novel, the terms of success of Wright's own stories of black victimization and pathos, Uncle Tom's Children (1938). The very success of these tales of victimization and pathos disgusted him: 'I found that I had written a book which even bankers' daughters could read and weep and feel good about. I swore to myself that if I ever wrote another book, no one would weep over it; that it would be so hard and deep that they would have to face it without the consolation of tears.'[7] Wright wished readers to feel threatened and implicated. The novel became the first African American novel selected for the Book of the Month Club and a best seller not despite but because of the powerful anxieties provoked by its portrayal of a terminally alienated character, Bigger Thomas, who resorts to horrifying violence in response to the cultural violence deployed against him. As a contemporary reviewer declared, Wright 'neither sentimentalizes nor excuses Bigger, though he explains him. The result is something new in American fiction and something terrifying.'[8]

The first section of the novel, 'Fear', opens unforgettably with the image of the rat that terrorizes Bigger's mother until backed against the wall by Bigger where 'it reared once more and bared long ugly fangs' (1), enabling Bigger to pound it to death with a saucepan. This scene epitomizes the novel on several levels. It works technically as documentary naturalism, paralleling Wright's later non-fiction account in *Twelve Million Black Voices* of the dreadful overpriced one-room 'kitchenettes' African American families were forced into due to their exclusion from the city-wide housing market. Politically, the novel draws on Marxist ideas as when it reveals that Bigger's employer, Mr Dalton, a philanthropic contributor to charitable causes for African Americans, is the absentee landlord of Bigger's slum kitchenette building and is ideologically blind to the obvious contradiction. In the economy of the novel the price of his blindness is precisely the life of his daughter, Mary, accidentally killed by Bigger, in part because of the oppressive effect of the kitchenette. Bigger is structurally in the position of the rat he had killed, walled into a dangerously hostile world with little margin for survival. Psychologically it is significant that Bigger symbolically kills the rat twice more: the descriptions of his killings of Mary and Bessie clearly echo the rat scene. Finally and inevitably Bigger becomes the cornered rat, in a structural rhyme, as he is backed against the wall by hateful white newspaper reporters, 'his teeth bared in a snarl' (3). By this point documentary details have been subsumed into images of the claustrophobic, smothering white world that impinges on Bigger from the beginning and from all directions – laterally from the building wall with the campaign poster of the District Attorney who will later prosecute him, vertically in the white writing an aeroplane leaves, reminding Bigger that African Americans are excluded from the occupation of pilot. Bigger internalizes this world as a white block in his solar plexus, a constricting, choking sensation, the outcome of the unremitting frustration and fear of subsisting in a prison world.

Bigger kills Mary Dalton out of fear rather than rage in another scene that Wright overdetermines as brilliantly as the rat scene. Bigger has become the Dalton chauffeur and is ordered to take Mary to a college event. But she instructs him to pick up her communist lover, Jan. Jan takes over the wheel and as what he supposes to be a clear demonstration of interracial solidarity Mary and Jan insist on sitting next to Bigger on the front seat for ideological reasons perfectly unintelligible to him. The actual effect of their presence is to increase his intolerable sense of constriction: 'There were white people to either side of him: he was sitting between two white vast looming walls' (1). Mary becomes too drunk to walk unaided so Jan tells Bigger to sneak her back to her bedroom. When she passes out as Bigger lowers her to her bed he feels a mixture of fear and desire. But what precipitates the killing is the appearance of Mary's blind mother. Terrified by 'the awesome white blur floating towards him', Bigger presses a pillow over Mary's face to keep her quiet, only later realizing the significance of having heard 'a long slow sigh go up from the bed into the darkened room, a sigh which afterwards, when he remembered it, seemed final, irrevocable' (1). He has smothered her.

Bigger's smothering world is in part linguistically constituted. The language, like the imagery of the novel, forms a transumptive chain while also a fertile source of confusion and error. If Bigger is dumbfounded at Mary and Jan's inept gesture at racial brotherhood they are at least as ignorant of his world. They try to show their sympathy by breaking into a chorus of 'Swing Low, Sweet Chariot'. The Daltons in Bigger's job interview speak in a vocabulary – words like 'procedure', 'environment', 'analysis', 'evoke' – mystifying to Bigger.

> The long strange words they used made no sense to him; it was another language. He felt from the tone of their voices that they were having a difference of opinion about him, but he could not determine what it was about. It made him uneasy, tense, as though there were influences and pressures about him which he could feel but not see. He felt strangely blind. (1)

Whites reveal their blindness to his language when they fail to recognize the African American syntax of the fake ransom note Bigger sends so as to mislead the investigation of Mary's disappearance: '*Do what this letter say*' (2). Critics complain that Wright's own language is too abstract and propagandistic, especially in the lengthy defence argument by Bigger's lawyer, Boris Max, which constructs Bigger as exemplary of racial victimization. However, as Laura Tanner argues, not only is Max's speech another linguistic appropriation of Bigger by a language alien to him but so also is the narrator's relatively abstract and sociologically knowing language.[9] There is no public language to express Bigger's turmoil.

Bigger's acts speak for desires hardly to be named, present in the depths of consciousness. Bigger kills his girlfriend Bessie as he did the rat with repeated blows to the head; she mirrors for him his powerless entrapment. The white newspaper reporters and the District Attorney are more fascinated by the rape they are certain he committed, that they clearly *want* him to have committed, than by his killing of Mary, much less of Bessie, who is very nearly forgotten about. Bigger himself desires Mary after the fact and tries, retroactively, to convert an unintended act of fear into a willed act of racial and sexual assertion. The novel calculatedly avoids the privileging of a linguistic–moral perspective that would provide aesthetic distance and ideological closure. The reader cannot get *out* of the novel.

In the graphic details of the novel, collated from sensational newspaper crime stories, Wright combines the documentary with the oneiric, pulling the reader into a nightmare vision of the process of Bigger's disposition of Mary's body in the furnace, the necessity of cutting off her head to make her fit. Wright learned from Henry James how to centre most perceptions in the novel in his protagonist's point of view but whereas in James this serves primarily to expand our sense of possibility, in *Native Son* it has the effect of locking us into Bigger's nightmare. As a Marxist Wright constructed Bigger as a primitive rebel from the lumpenproletariat who reacts with spasmodic personal violence to social oppression because the communal vision of revolutionary politics is not accessible to him. But by *Native Son* the communist version of this vision had become less accessible for Wright himself, though the public denunciation of the American Communist Party in his contribution to *The God that Failed* was some years off. Moreover, within the novel Bigger has little more relation to a black community than to an interracial one. His mother, sister and girlfriend impinge on him primarily as shaming or irritating presences, his kitchenette world being too constrictive to allow the free space for relationship. The nearest he comes to a viable community is with his street gang, but even here he is too busy competing with his peers in macho posturing to hear or be heard by them. Bigger's solipsism, then, is politically inflected by Wright, shown as the logical result of a suppression so total as to preclude the possibility of relationship. But though Wright well understood the futility of mere personal rebellion he was by *Native Son* thinking in terms more existentialist than communist. Three currents come together here: an American tendency, often noted by the French, towards a home-made variety of existentialism – an instinctive, unrationalized version; the obvious relation of the existentialist sense of entrapment and alienation to the historical situation of African Americans; and the influence of such proto-existentialist precursors as Dostoevsky, Unamuno and Malraux, all of whom Wright had read and assimilated. *The Outsider* (1953), written after Wright had read and met Jean-Paul Sartre and become self-consciously existentialistic, reads more like an existentialist primer than a novel but 'The Man Who Lived Underground' (1944) in *Eight Men* is a superbly eerie fable of arbitrariness and absurdity. Its plot of a man who discovers the unspeakable truths of the 'normal' world by literally going underground into the sewers parallels Sartre's *Nausea* and anticipates Camus's *The Stranger* as a fable of alienation. It is also a major source for Ralph Ellison's *Invisible Man*, not only in the plot device of the descent to the underground but in the thematic shift from political rebellion to existential alienation.

Ralph Ellison: the joke of African American identity

In *Native Son* Wright quite deliberately breaks all the rules – no African American writer had created a protagonist so close to the white racist stereotype of the 'bad nigger' – and all but defies the reader to come to terms with the book. Ellison, in contrast, calculatedly set out to write a canonical American classic, all but advertising its relation to the great tradition of nineteenth-century American fiction, even anticipating by some years Lewis's *American Adam* and Chase's American romance thesis, building as they did on F. O. Matthiessen's construction of the American canon and its privileged themes in *American Renaissance*. In effect, Ellison shelves himself somewhere between Melville and Twain. It is thus no accident that *Invisible Man* became a consensus critical choice as the most important American novel since the Second World War.[10] The novel dazzlingly decentres and puts into play political concepts of revolt versus acquiescence and black nationalism versus communist conspiracy; psychological concepts of the self seen as essence versus the self seen as a series of roles; and finally even its own status as a narrative that is by turns realistic, surrealistic, symbolic and allegorical. Existentialism, Marxism, Freudianism, even Emersonianism become counters in a game Ellison plays. As a spectacular performative speech act *Invisible Man* is reminiscent of Twain's *Huckleberry Finn*, Faulkner's *The Sound and the Fury* and, most of all, Melville's *The Confidence Man* but is far from the overt social protest novel Ellison had earlier called for. By the time he wrote *Invisible Man*, Ellison had considerably distanced himself from the radicalism of his *New Masses* essays and from his association with Richard Wright. Though (or because) clearly influenced by Wright, Ellison now self-consciously opposed him, attacking Wright for being 'overcommited to ideology' and reductive in his characterization of Bigger: 'he was designed to shock whites out of their apathy and end the circumstances out of which Wright insisted Bigger

emerged. Here environment is all – and interestingly enough environment conceived solely in terms of the physical, the non-conscious. Well,
cut off my legs and call me Shorty.'[11] Ellison misses how Wright elaborates complications despite Bigger's inarticulateness through a demonstration of the inadequacy of various modes of discourse that attempt to
contain and rationalize Bigger, Ellison's own comment participating in
such containment. Ellison may have misapprehended Wright because his
own technique is so different though ending in a similar solipsistic bind.
In *Native Son* the reader vividly feels Bigger's presence without being
able securely to account for him; whereas in *Invisible Man* the protagonist
lacks physical and emotional presence as he dissolves almost entirely into
a hypnotic voice that accounts for so much, in such pyrotechnical feats
of discourse, that the reader becomes intellectually dizzy. Wright induces
dread; Ellison induces vertigo.

The novel's allegory is structured around episodes, each of which
show historical and political facets of a counterfeit society run by confidence men. The epitome of Ellison's demystification of these leaders is
the description of the statue of the founder of the African American
college the protagonist briefly attends.

> Then in my mind's eye I see the bronze statue of the college
> Founder, the cold Father symbol, his hands outstretched in the
> heartbreaking gesture of lifting a veil that flutters in hard, metallic
> folds above the face of a kneeling slave; and I am standing puz-
> zled, unable to decide whether the veil is really being lifted, or lo-
> wered more firmly in place; whether I am witnessing a revelation
> or a more efficient blinding. (2)

The statue exactly matches that of Booker T. Washington on the campus
of Tuskegee Institute, where Ellison had studied music. Ellison is making
a point about Washington's policy of accommodation to Southern white
political power in return for supposed economic advancement. When
the protagonist is expelled from college for letting a white trustee see
too much reality, he is duped with letters of, in effect, disrecommenda-
tion. This fulfils his dream of opening a briefcase only to find a Russian
doll series of envelopes stating 'To Whom It May Concern. . . Keep
This Nigger-Boy Running' (1).

Every episode in the novel is structured around some incident that
does just this. All American institutions are in on the joke. In New York
the protagonist works for Liberty Paints, a factory that produces Optic
White, the right white, used to whitewash various national monuments.
The protagonist discovers that its dazzling purity can be achieved only
by a mixture with a 10 per cent black solution. That is, the African
American 10 per cent of the American population is by the logic of
binary opposition what makes the American majority 'white'. In the

next episode the protagonist joins The Brotherhood, an obvious caricature of the Communist Party, USA. The Brotherhood turns out to be
counterfeit in a fashion structurally similar to the society it intends to
subvert, and its leader, Brother Jack, a trickster not unlike the college
president with his recommendation letters, the founder who is pulling
the veil of ignorance down rather than up, etc. Later episodes show the
same pattern.

Since every character in *Invisible Man* allegorically represents a view-
point either aligned with or alternative to the status quo, differences
between characters are differences in positions. Ellison's own ambivalen-
ces are especially evident in Ras the Destroyer and B. P. Rinehart, characters memorable beyond their space in the narrative because of the
intensity of Ellison's investment in the attitudes they dance out. Ras
represents the temptation of the kind of black nationalism Marcus Gar-
vey had preached (a movement analogous to that of the later Black
Muslims) and though Ellison rejects this as a viable political possibility he
feels an emotional appeal in the totality of Ras's rejection of the white
world. He remembers writing this section 'at a vacation spot where we
met some white liberals who thought the best way to be friendly was to
tell us what it was like to be Negro'.[12] Ellison uses Ras simultaneously
to exorcize his rage at such fatuousness while satirizing the lack of political realism in the Black Nationalist agenda. 'Ras' is the Ethiopian word
for prince and in the riot which comes near the end of the novel Ras
acts out his African fantasy by riding on a great black horse in African
garb carrying a spear. But one of the streetwise rioters casually assimilates
him into white American folklore: 'Ole Ras didn't have time to git his
gun so he let fly with that spear and you could hear him grunt and say
something 'bout that cop's kinfolks and then him and that hoss shot up
the street leaping like Heigho, the goddam Silver!' (25). Ellison mocks
the notion that Black Nationalism can escape American cultural (especially pop cultural) enmeshment by fiat.

Rinehart represents a position less easily dismissed, harder to distinguish from Ellison's own attitude and even from the narrative strategy of
the book. The novel relativizes and mocks all fixed positions, all social
roles, but Rinehart seems the very principle of such decentring as the
protagonist discovers that Rinehart's identity varies with the setting in
which he appears (the operative word).

> Still, could he be all of them: Rine the runner and Rine the
> gambler and Rine the briber and Rine the lover and Rinehart
> the Reverend? Could he himself be both Rind and heart? What
> is real anyway? But how could I doubt it? He was a broad man, a
> man of parts who got around. Rinehart the rounder. It was true
> and I was true. His world was possibility and he knew it. He was
> years ahead of me and I was a fool. I must have been crazy and

blind. The world in which we lived was without boundaries. A vast seething, hot world of fluidity, and Rine the rascal was at home in it. It was unbelievable, but perhaps only the unbelievable could be believed. Perhaps the truth was always a lie. (23)

Ellison returns to Rinehart almost compulsively in essays and interviews and though his protagonist is influenced by many false prophets, Rinehart is the only one he tries to *become*, donning the Rinehart mask of snapbrim hat and dark sunglasses. The trickster's initials, B. P. , stand for Bliss Proteus, establishing Rinehart as a model protean self, ' man of parts'.[13] At the conclusion of the novel Rinehart is identified with possibility, surely the keyword in Ellison's political and philosophical vocabulary.

I believed in hard work and progress and action, but now, after first being 'for' society and then 'against' it, I assign myself no rank or any limit, and such an attitude is very much against the trend of the times. But my world has become one of infinite possibilities. What a phrase – still it's a good phrase and a good view of life, and a man shouldn't accept any other; that much I've learned underground. Until some gang succeeds in putting the world in a strait jacket, its definition is possibility. Step outside the narrow borders of what men call reality and you step into chaos – ask Rinehart, he's a master of it – or imagination. (Epilogue)

The hero himself, however he keeps attempting true belief, is a protean man, though less insouciant than Rinehart. In fact, we never learn his name. He is, then, a hero in the tradition of the American romance, a self-created one like Cooper's Natty Bumppo who gets a new name in every novel, Fitzgerald's Jay Gatsby who used to be James Gatz, Twain's Huckleberry Finn who assumes so many pseudonyms he has trouble keeping them straight, and Melville's confidence man who is like Rinehart a man of parts, that is, dramatic roles, but who has not only a name but many of them, though his real name might as well be Proteus. Yet the protagonist's attempt to play Rinehart (that is, to play a player) is disastrous with as many people trying to keep him running or stop him dead as in his previous avatar of Brotherhood apostate. And he differs from Rinehart in questioning even the protean identity, thus becoming in his final avatar the consistent ironist who must finally turn upon irony itself.

Invisible Man has the strong and weak points of a voice novel, a novel of consciousness rather than character. In an 'Introduction' for a later edition of *Invisible Man* Ellison tells how he was trying to write a more conventional kind of novel which the voice of Invisible Man possessed and dislocated: 'For while I had structured my short stories out of familiar experiences and possessed concrete images of my characters and their backgrounds, now I was confronted by nothing more substantial than a taunting, disembodied voice.'[14] But this gives him a major problem at the end of the novel with his attempt to reassert the possibility of a democratic interracial community: how can the protagonist get from 'the invisible music of my isolation' (Prologue) to 'a socially responsible role to play' (Epilogue) only by means of a 'tauntingly disembodied voice'? For one thing, as an Adamic American romance hero, Ellison's protagonist is defined and valued for his evasion of social identity. Moreover, the other characters are primarily alternative thoughts in the narrator's head, figures of his speech. This makes for a richness of solipsistic identity but can hardly establish the grounds for community. For that, one needs other people. What the protagonist does move towards – and it is difficult enough – is personal integration. Perhaps this prepares him for reintegration with a community except that he has but one character, the reader, with whom to negotiate his new identity. Throughout the narrative voice, like that of *Moby-Dick* and *The Adventures of Huckleberry Finn*, gets past readers' defences by cajoling, conning and joking them into acquiescence, finally coopting them into the text to the point that it speaks for as well as to them.

> 'Ah,' I can hear you say, 'so it was really all a build-up to bore us with his buggy jiving. He only wanted us to listen to him rave!' But only partially true: Being invisible and without substance, a disembodied voice, as it were, what else could I do? What else but try to tell you what was really happening when your eyes were looking through? And it is this which frightens me:
> Who knows but that on the lower frequencies, I speak for you?
>   (Epilogue)

The one rabbit this voice is unable to pull out of its hat is community. But otherwise his performance is astonishing. Scarcely a page, scarcely even a line goes by without a pun, a joke or an allusion as this voice plays out its bag of tricks. For instance, after an industrial accident at Liberty Paints the protagonist is reborn from a machine, even cut free from an electric umbilical cord, emerging as a lobotomized or electroshocked (Ellison leaves this vague) 'new man', as a doctor assures him. Yet within pages, he finds himself on a subway train as 'a young platinum blonde nibbled at a red Delicious apple . . . . The train plunged' (11). In Ellison's world even a reborn Adam is due for a quick fall. Later his protagonist supposes he has solved his identity problem when he is able unashamedly to relish characteristically rural African American food, a hot Carolina yam being sold by a street vendor: 'They're my birthmark,' he exclaims, and mixing Popeye with Yahweh, 'I yam what I yam!' (13). But when he bites into a second yam it is sour, frostbitten. Rural Southern folk experience, though resonant in the novel, does not always perfectly translate to northern cities. The book is built around such combinations of comic riff with allegorical suggestion. Ellison once interrupted an earnest interviewer to ask, 'Look, didn't you find the book at all *funny*?' and is on record as finding America 'a land of masking jokers'; for Ellison, at his most serious, American identity *is* a joke.[15]

James Baldwin and identity crisis

It is not a joke for James Baldwin, who agonizes over the questions of identity that Ellison ironizes over. Baldwin's fine first novel, *Go Tell it on the Mountain* (1953), is the autobiographically based story of young John Grimes's attempt to cope with the intense pressure of his family and his world on his own as yet inchoate sense of self. Certainly one of the major pressures is that of race but the white world, in contrast to the crucial encounters of Bigger Thomas and Invisible Man, impinges on him only indirectly, primarily through its effects on the family members with whom he is struggling to come to terms, his mother, aunt and father, though all these problems are enclosed within the pressure cooker atmosphere of Harlem. His ensuing identity crisis is psychological and religious rather than political. Indeed, Baldwin's essay 'Everybody's Protest Novel' (1949) seems designed to clear the ground for his fictional focus on psychological identity by attacking what he supposed to be Wright's political reductionism: 'The failure of the protest novel lies in its rejection of life, the human being, the denial of his beauty, dread, power, in its insistence that it is his categorization alone which is real and cannot be transcended.'[16] In fact, this description applies better to the alienated and self-pitying characters in some of Baldwin's later and lesser novels than to the undismissable Bigger Thomas. Baldwin's defensiveness about Wright as a literary father figure, one who helped him get a major grant, may account for this odd denial of the dread and power so evident in *Native Son*.

In its psychological focus, its lyrical style, and its theme of a a universal quest for love always already perversely deflected, Baldwin's novel less resembles *Native Son* or even *Invisible Man* (published only a year earlier) than *The Heart is a Lonely Hunter*. In fact, if McCullers's novel enacts the turn from politics, in Baldwin it is a *fait accompli*. This may account for Baldwin's attack in 'Notes for a Hypothetical Novel' where he sketches

> one of those long, warm, toasty novels. You know, those novels
> in which the novelist is looking back on himself, absolutely infatu-
> ated with himself as a child and everything is in sentimentality.

But I think we ought to bring ourselves up short because we don't need another version of *A Tree Grows in Brooklyn* and we can do without another version of *The Heart is a Lonely Hunter*.[17]

McCullers's novel is no more 'warm and toasty' than *Go Tell it on the Mountain* and Baldwin's comment probably projects retroactive guilt about his own concentration on the personal as opposed to the political. The centre of the novel is the psychological conflict between John Grimes and his tormented, ingrown, fanatical father Gabriel, who has twisted religion into an expressive form of his hatred of his family and his world. Baldwin varies lyrically evocative imagery with psychologically exact analysis to reveal Gabriel's vindictiveness as a massive projection of self-hatred, a form of denial of his own failures as a man, a husband and a father. John is the target of Gabriel's most intense anger because, though John does not know it, Gabriel is not his biological father. Gabriel had married John's mother knowing that she was pregnant from a lover who had committed suicide. Gabriel has gone from considering the marriage as an act of charity and of penance for his own sexual misdeeds to reconstructing it in convenient Old Testament terms as a drama of a noble martyr wronged by a harlot and her bastard. He resents John for not being his own unacknowledged illegitimate son Royal, who died, never knowing his father's identity, in a bar fight. Gabriel casts himself as an Old Testament patriarch, divinely promised a royal line but thwarted by the interposition of the illegitimate claimant, John. Echoes of the biblical stories of Ishmael, Isaac, Jacob (Israel) and Esau abound. Gabriel's sister perceives his bad faith: 'I know you thinking at the bottom of your heart that if you just make *her*, her and her bastard boy, pay enough for her sin, *your* son won't have to pay for yours' (3).

The keywords of Baldwin's novel, as in other 1940s and 1950s works of psychological lyricism, are *love* and *heart* and there is the same pervasive but undefined sense of some primal curse, a version of original sin. Some passages could be seamlessly interpolated into novels by McCullers and Capote: 'Time was indifferent, like snow and ice; but the heart, crazed wanderer in the driving waste, carried the curse forever' (3). Some critics see the novel's ambiguously imagistic ending as a weakness but such endings are a convention of the psychological–lyrical novel. The terms of resolution are religious as John's conflict is momentarily resolved in an overpowering conversion experience on what his church calls the 'threshing floor' where spiritual wheat is separated from chaff. *The Fire Next Time* retells this story as biography, Baldwin interpreting the psychology of his conversion as a momentary escape from the destructive temptations of Harlem street life besides jumping him ahead of his father in religious prestige. But the ending makes as much sense from a traditional religious perspective: Gabriel is a hypocrite, a whited sepulchre, lacking in charity and incapable of a genuine conversion because too adept at seeing the mote in his neighbour's eye rather than the beam in his own. In contrast John's undeserved suffering prepares him for the reception of Grace.

Baldwin got into difficulties in his later political essays and politicized novels due to an insufficient analysis of how the personal is the political, though the two powerfully fuse in the classic autobiographical essay 'Notes of a *Native Son*' which reads as a coda to *Go Tell it on the Mountain*. Baldwin here recodes his father's rage as a paranoia induced by the white world, a rage his son now shares as a result of his encounter with malevolent racism. The insult of being refused service at a restaurant leads Baldwin to a nearly suicidal counter-attack as a white mob chases him through the streets, all of which becomes correlative to the public violence of the Harlem riot of 1943, a riot that erupts on the day of his father's funeral, thus uniting private and public intensities. But in subsequent works such as *Giovanni's Room* (1956), in which the main characters are white homosexuals, and *Another Country* (1962), which descends into pure bathos, Baldwin's attempts to rationalize politics in terms of the love–heart–terror ethos of the psychological–lyrical novel are thoroughly unconvincing.

Ann Petry and the vagaries of canonization

Baldwin's novel is important to the African American literary canon though peripheral to the American, Wright's central to the former and problematic for the latter, Ellison's central to both. In contrast, Ann Petry's *The Street*, written in 1945 and only recently reprinted, remains somewhat peripheral to the African American canon and invisible to the American. Yet it is one of the finest novels of the 1940s, an instance of the vagaries of literary canonization. The reprinting of the novel is, of course, the result of literary politics: the emergence of African American women as cultural players. But why did Petry's novel, initially fairly well received, gradually disappear from literary consciousness? This would seem to be because of a triple marginalization based on race, gender and, not least, genre.

Despite the breakthrough of Richard Wright there was no African American literary renaissance of the 1940s. African American writing did not become re-visible until 1952–3 with Ellison and Baldwin. The lack of a continuous critical tradition led to Petry's book being nodded towards and then quickly forgotten. Moreover, even after Ellison and Baldwin the focus was on male African American writers, Leroi Jones

(Imamu Baraka) and Eldridge Cleaver having their brief moment in the game of choose-between. But the most marginalizing factor may well have been genre rather than gender. Petry published a novel of naturalistic social protest just as critics were busy declaring this form of fiction officially obsolete. This had become so much an article of faith that by 1958 a critic of African American literature could contend that the 'war boom had siphoned off the discontent of the 1930s, but the Wright school persisted as an anachronism'.[18]

Evidently another such anachronism was the Harlem riot of 1943. Although a positive revaluation of naturalistic fiction is now under way, as late as 1985 a critic can be found praising Petry for how in a later work she 'moves beyond the naturalistic vision' of *The Street* and, better yet, 'moves even further beyond economic determinism'.[19] Would that we all could!

Petry commented on this critical trend in 1950: 'After I had written a novel of social criticism . . . I slowly became aware that such novels were regarded as a special and quite deplorable creation of American writers of the twentieth century. It took me quite a while to realize that there were fashions in literary criticism and that they shifted and changed much like the fashions in women's hats.'[20] Naturalistic social protest may have gone out of fashion but the social wrongs such fiction depicted had not and Petry's novel shows her characters suffocating much as Bigger Thomas had within the walls of a socioeconomically created ghetto. As in *Native Son* the documentary fuses into the phenomenological, the symbolic and even the solipsistic. Petry's Harlem has a darkness with 'a heavy syrupy quality – soft and thick like molasses, only black' (9), as oppressive as whatever lies behind Paul Bowles's sheltering sky. Petry's characters, trapped in mutual incomprehension of each other's fears and desires, are figures in a round robin of victimization, each feeling thwarted by some other. But contrary to Wright's novel, the protagonist Lutie Johnson is a woman, the prey of African American as well as white predatoriness. This protagonist's world is hell and Petry draws on Dante in her presentation of it, the superintendent of Lutie's building even possessing a Cerberus-like hound.

Lutie must live with her young son on a dangerous street in a constrictingly small apartment space, the Harlem equivalent of Wright's Chicago 'kitchenette', paying more than she can afford or could be charged in a competitive, unsegregated housing market. She has a brief hope of escaping her trap through her singing but finds that the only path to a career goes through Junto, a white man more interested in her body than her talent. Junto is also the absentee owner of her apartment building and even when Lutie strikes out in murderous rage at his thwarting power she kills a mere surrogate, his African American tool. Petry's plot convincingly specifies the socioeconomic forces that entrap her characters while its phenomenological imagery encloses the reader in a pathological world. In one sequence Lutie feels pursued by a felt silence, a silence that has presence. Finally, it assumes a recognizable form.

> Inside her apartment she stood motionless, assailed by the deep, uncanny silence that filled it. It was a too-sharp contrast with the noise in the street. She turned off the radio and then turned it on again, because she kept listening, straining to hear something under the sound of the music.
>
> The creeping, silent thing that she had sensed in the theatre, in the beauty parlor, was here in her living room. It was sitting on the lumpy studio couch.
>
> Before it had been formless, shapeless, a fluid moving mass – something disembodied that she couldn't see, only sense. Now, as she stared at the couch, the thing took on form, substance. She could see what it was.
>
> It was Junto. (18)

Junto in fact is present only in Lutie's consciousness, yet her perception of his pervasive presence is both imaginatively and politically accurate in that he and what he represents structurally determine Lutie's 'choice' of the apartment and her life there. The passage forces the reader to *feel* the encroachment of evil while *seeing* its political source. Such a vision may become obsolete about the time that social evil does.

Community and gender in African American fiction of the 1980s

The protagonists of the novels above by Wright, Ellison, Baldwin and Petry are locked into desperate worlds of thought and feeling in which the outside world, other minds, appear primarily in the mode of threat and limit rather than resource and possibility. In contrast, a major concern of African American fiction of the 1980s has been the relationships of the protagonist, whether to lover, wife, brother, family generally or community or the interlocking of all these. The new emphasis appears in titles reflective of place: David Bradley's *The Chaneysville Incident* (1981); John Edgar Wideman's *Hiding Place* (1981) and *Philadelphia Fire* (1990); Gloria Naylor's *The Women of Brewster Place* (1983) and *Linden Hills* (1985). John A. Williams's *!Click Song* (1982) plays on an African language fricative that becomes a symbol for the possibilities of authentic communication. Relationship is excruciatingly problematic in these novels with a high potential for breakdown and catastrophe yet it is presented as a *possibility* and given a social and historical density.

An instance is Wideman's Homewood trilogy, *Hiding Place, Sent for You Yesterday* (1983) and *Damballah* (1984), which records the bravery and disintegration of his childhood community, the Homewood area of Pittsburgh, Pennsylvania. *Hiding Place* opens with a family tree, thus emphasizing continuity and community, but the title, from a spiritual, ironically reflects on what place cannot offer: '*Went to the rock to hide my face/ Rock cried out, No hiding place*'. The loving relationships his characters heroically construct cannot remain immune from the tremendous destructiveness of the white world that defines the community's boundaries and effectively limits its possibilities. The family experience from which Wideman drew the novel is explored from a different perspective in the memoir *Brothers and Keepers* (1984), where he passionately muses on his imprisoned brother's attempt to find some measure of identity in delinquency and drugs. Wideman himself was a college basketball star and a Rhodes Scholar, his own distinction putting him into the recurrent African American double bind of an impossible choice between what is envisioned as 'white' education and success as opposed to black communal identity. The theme is in black writing from the Harlem renaissance on where 'funky' (i.e. plain-spoken, tough-minded, disrespectful of middle class mores) characters upstage 'dicty' (i.e. prissy, pretentious, ridiculously respectable) ones but is given a special twist by a perverse result of the civil rights revolution. Whereas the African American middle class used to find its main economic role within the black community as doctors, preachers, undertakers, insurance salesmen, shopkeepers, etc., opportunity there has diminished in ratio to increased possibilities of entry into the lower and middle levels of the white economic world, draining the ghetto of its best talent. Wideman wrote about Homewood while teaching at the University of Wyoming, a western state about as homogeneously white as can be found in the United States. He is now at the University of Massachusetts at Amherst, somewhat less homogeneous but light years from the world of Homewood. He lives out the opposition on the nerve ends of his prose.

A similar opposition is central to Naylor's *Linden Hills* though with an original variation: an entire African American community, Linden Hills, is seduced into upward mobility, becoming in the process a replica of Dante's Inferno, complete with a series of circles spiralling downward to the domain of the Nedeed men, part house, part mortuary. The Nedeeds offer a Satanic bargain, asking in exchange for relative prosperity only the soul of the black community: 'Linden Hills wasn't black; it was successful. The shining surface of their careers, brass railings, and cars hurt his eyes because it only reflected the bright nothing that was inside them.' The model of the community concept of success is a character whose 'entire life became a race against the natural . . . '. In the

Nedeed world, wives once having replicated another froglike Nedeed patriarch become superfluous. A young man in the novel who is a folk poet intuitively grasps the position of the latest wife-victim: 'There is a man in the house at the bottom of the hill. And his wife has no name.'

Gender conflicts already glimpsed in the the novels of Hurston, Wright and Petry have become exacerbated in recent African American fiction, perhaps reflecting the breakdown of the institution of marriage in black ghetto areas. In a conversation with Toni Morrison, Naylor recounts her concern that *The Women of Brewster Place* might be misunderstood as an attack on black men: 'I worried about whether or not the problems that were being caused by men in the women's lives would be interpreted as some bitter statement I had to make about black men.'[21] It would be difficult to avoid such an interpretation of Gayl Jones's ironically titled *Eva's Man* (1976), which centres on Eva's murder and sexual mutilation of her lover. Gender conflict is a major theme in David Bradley's *The Chaneysville Incident*. The protagonist of this novel traces the historical roots of his Pennsylvania African American community and of his own ancestry. Only in so doing can he overcome the barrier separating him from the white woman he loves but cannot bring himself to trust. The subtext of the novel presents an African American world deeply divided by gender: a 'funky', hunting and drinking fellowship of men and a primly respectable one of women. The protagonist's breakthrough with his white lover does not bridge this gap. The protagonist of John A. Williams's *!Click Song* (1982) finds himself in antagonistic relations with white publishers and reviewers because he is a black writer and in antagonistic relations with black women because he has a white wife. He feels 'general vibrations and vapors from the bitches' brew directed by the black women against her whiteness'. The solidarity black writers ought to have in the face of publishers and reviewers is undermined by the distrust of those who work alone and inside their heads for group thinking and their paranoid suspiciousness of the smallest measure of success as evidence of a sellout. In the outcome of the novel the protagonist is sustained by the only true friend he has found among the African American intelligentsia and by his wife and children, a small bunker community.

Alice Walker's *The Colour Purple*, published the same year as Williams's novel, surveys the gender divide from what Walker calls a 'womanist' (a term she prefers to feminist) perspective. Walker's novel has a fine first-person colloquial energy reminiscent of Salinger but, like Salinger, the novel sometimes descends into bathos in its construction of an African American world where all women are models of perfection and all men models of wickedness except when they accede to matriarchal domination by the women. Male African American anger about the sexual politics of the novel was expressed in Ishmael Reed's 1986 novel *Reckless Eyeballing*, in which the hero kidnaps an African American feminist writer who resembles Alice Walker, imprisoning her until she recognizes the true virtues of African American manhood, a response that goes some distance towards making credible Walker's own caricature. There may be a sign of reconciliation in Charles Johnson's historical comedy *Middle Passage* (1990), in which the protagonist, a freedman, flees the threat of marriage and responsibility in typical American Adam style but by the outrageous expedient of stowing away on a slave ship going to Africa. After such adventures as a slave revolt patterned after that in Melville's *Benito Cereno* (in *Piazza Tales*, (1857)), he again encounters his determined lady and willingly chooses a life of exemplary domesticity, clearly a comic turn on both white (Adamic) and black codes of gender conflict. But the writer who most convincingly rethinks the conflict between individual and community and between male and female is Toni Morrison, whose major contribution to American fiction is focused on in Chapter 9.

Notes

1. David Levering Lewis, *When Harlem was in Vogue* (New York, 1982), Chapters 8 and 9.

2. Ralph Ellison, 'Recent Negro Fiction', *New Masses*, 5 August 1941, 22.

3. See Deborah E. McDowell, 'Introduction' to Nella Larsen, *Quicksand and Passing* (New Brunswick, 1986).

4. Mary Helen Washington, ' "Taming All That Anger Down": Rage and Silence in Gwendolyn Brooks's *Maud Martha*' in Henry Louis Gates (ed.), *Black Literature and Literary Theory* (New York, 1984), p. 249.

5. Richard Wright, 'Between Laughter and Tears', *New Masses*, 5 October 1937, 25.

6. June Jordan, 'Notes toward a Balancing of Love and Hatred', *Black World* (1974), p. 5.

7. Richard Wright, 'How "Bigger" was Born', 'Introduction', *Native Son* (New York, 1940), p. xxvii.

8. Lewis Gannett, *New York Herald Tribune*, 1 March 1940 in *Richard Wright: The Critical Reception*, ed. John M. Reilly (New York, 1978), pp. 40–41. In fact, Wright excized some passages that presented Bigger's sexual aggressiveness too overtly for the Book of the Month Club to accept. These passages are restored in Richard Wright, *Early Works*, ed. Arnold Rampersad (New York, 1991) in the canonizing Library of America series. See also Rampersad, 'Too Honest For His Own Time', *New York Times Book Review*, 29 December, 1991, pp. 3, 17–18.

9. Laura Tanner, 'Uncovering the Magical Disguise of Language: The Narrative Presence in Richard Wright's *Native Son'*, *Texas Studies in Literature and Language* **29** (1987), 412-31.

10. See Melvin J. Friedman, 'To "Make it New": The American Novel since 1945', *Woodrow Wilson Quarterly* **2** (1978), 136. *Lolita* was second, *Catch-22* third, followed by *Gravity's Rainbow, The Catcher in the Rye, Herzog, All the King's Men, The Naked and the Dead* and *An American Dream*.

11. Ralph Ellison, *Shadow and Act* (1964; repr. New York, 1966), p. 121.

12. Ellison, *Shadow and Act*, p. 181.

13. Ellison spells out the initials in *Shadow and Act*, p. 71. See also Robert Jay Lifton, 'Protean Man' in *History and Human Survival* (1970; repr. New York, 1971).

14. Ellison, 'Introduction', *Invisible Man* (New York, 1972), p. x.

15. Ellison, *Shadow and Act*, pp. 180, 70.

16. James Baldwin, *Notes of a Native Son* (Boston, 1955), p. 23.

17. James Baldwin, *Nobody Knows My Name* (1961; repr. New York, 1962), p. 145.

18. Robert A. Bone, *The Negro Novel in America* (New Haven, 1965), pp. 157, 189, 160.

19. Bernard W. Bell, 'Ann Petry's Demythologizing of American Culture and Afro-American Character' in *Conjuring: Black Women, Fiction, and Literary Tradition*, ed. Marjorie Pryse and Hortense J. Spillers (Bloomington, 1985), pp. 105, 111.

20. Ann Petry, 'The Novel as Social Criticism' in *The Writer's Book*, (ed.) Helen Hull (New York, 1950), p. 32.

21. Gloria Naylor and Toni Morrison, 'A Conversation', *The Southern Review* **21** (1985), 579.

Chapter 3
Southern Fiction

Institutionalizing Southern fiction

A major consequence of the rise of New Criticism in the 1950s was a
reversal in the assessment of Southern literature. From early on the
South had failed to develop literary institutions equivalent to New England and New York. After the Civil War the South became marginalized
economically and politically as well as culturally. By the 1920s H. L.
Mencken could describe the South as 'The Sahara of the Bozart' (i.e.
beaux arts) and as late as the 1970s Sacvan Bercovitch could write a
book, *The Puritan Origins of the American Self*, the title of which assumes
Puritan New England as the fount and origin of American Identity. In
fact the first permanent English colony was that of non-Puritan James-
town, Virginia in 1607 and the first American book was John Smith's
1608 account of this colony. It is arguable that there is a Chesapeake
Bay origin of the American self, a Southern, relatively secular and materialistic self that was at least as much a model for future American
identity as the Puritan version.[1] It is true that the religious evangelicism
that swept over America from the 1730s on ultimately left its strongest
imprint on the South, leading to its displacement of New England –
itself increasingly tending towards religious liberalism – as the stronghold
of Calvinistic religious intensity, yet a Southern fascination with hard
materialism and cultural lowlife persists from Ebenezer Cooke's *The
Sotweed Factor* (1708) and William Byrd's *The History of the Dividing Line*
(1728) through such nineteenth-century Southern humorists as Augustus
Baldwin Longstreet and George Washington Harris, and from them on
to contemporary Southern fiction. If the cultivated narrative voices of
Cooke, Byrd and Longstreet maintain a condescending superiority to the
vulgarities they portray, a certain relish in the piquancy of 'poor white
trash' behaviour and locution is equally apparent. Indeed Cooke's narrator is unreliable, easily duped by some of the Marylanders to whom he

condescends and oblivious to the good-humoured hospitality of others while Harris openly sides with his character Sut Lovingood's contempt for the moral code of respectable society. From Cooke on, Southern writing poises values of ethical cultivation and civility against those of raw materialism and self-assertion, sometimes privileging one side of this opposition, sometimes the other and sometimes playing both ends against the middle. Ellen Glasgow, especially in *The Sheltered Life* (1932), and Allen Tate in *The Fathers* (1938) poise family traditions of civility and restraint against the new, expressed as unmediated, *uncivilized* desire, a theme that carries over to the work of Katherine Anne Porter and Eudora Welty.

This tradition of Southern fiction lacked cultural visibility until the 1950s when, in an extraordinary reversal, it became valorized and institutionalized, a status still apparent in the culturally custodial *Harvard Guide to Contemporary American Writing* (1979), the chapters of which categorize American literature in terms of race and ethnicity – Black and Jewish, gender – Women's Fiction, and mode – 'Realists, Naturalists and Novelists of Manners' and 'Experimental Fiction', exalting only 'Southern Fiction' of any regional literature into a literary category, which raises the question of how it suddenly went from marginal to central – even as Southern history remained marginal. One answer is that there was simply a flowering of talent, a 'Southern Renascence' that began in the 1920s, flourished through the 1940s, and continues to this day. But what accounts for this emergence in a region so educationally impoverished that the Southern joke about Mississippi writers was 'They can't read but they sure can write'? The usual answer and that of the *Harvard Guide* is that Southerners were shocked into literature by the emergence of modernism.[2] Southern fiction used the techniques of modernism to explore the tension between traditional values based on a local, relatively static world and the new conditions resulting in a more urbanized and dynamic but also more anomic world order – in short, Southern economic backwardness coupled with literary modernism to allow the articulation of a morally traditionalist critique of the dehumanization supposedly consequent upon the ever-expanding economic modernism of American society.

Of course, the institutionalization of Southern literature was as much a critical construction respondent to the social and political conditions of the 1940s and 1950s as it was a literary phenomenon. By 1950, as we have seen, the 'New Criticism', a university-centred, formalist critical practice, had displaced such journalistic criticism as H.L. Mencken's as a source of cultural authority. This mode of criticism had been developed largely by a group of writers who in the 1930s had collaborated in the 'Southern Agrarian' manifesto, *I'll Take My Stand*, titled after a line of 'Dixie' ('In Dixieland I'll take my stand'), which called for a rejection of northern industrial economic modernism in favour of a traditional, Southern, agrarian and orthodoxly religious mode of life. However, the

'Agrarians' acute critique of the spiritual ravages of economic modernism was vitiated by a historically naive idealization of the Southern past and by a smug acceptance of social and racial injustice. It soon became clear that for Southerners generally the main problem with economic modernism was how to get hold of some capital and join in. Thus there was no ideological market for 'agrarian' ideas, least of all in the South. But as Southern Agrarians became New Critics they became adept at finding their traditionalist values conveniently placed in the centres of great works of literature. Southern literature, they could argue, was the sole meaningful regional American writing because in fact universal in its values, values recycled from Southern Agrarian doctrine, though with some of its more obviously reactionary features subordinated or quietly dropped. Such critics eventually discovered the greatest example of their construction of the South as the heart's universal homeland in the work of William Faulkner, though few critics were historically prepared to notice this before 1946 when Southern fiction and New Criticism helped fill the void left by the repudiation of radical politics and its literary reflections. Southern literature provided a godsend: a critique of the modern sociopolitical order but from a conservative and traditionalist as opposed to a radical Marxist perspective, thus shifting attention from social conflict to the heart in conflict. This is not to say that the perception of Southern literary brilliance was solely a political construction; rather, the flowering of Southern talent conveniently keyed into the Cold War ideology of the 1950s.

The two Faulkners

Faulkner's greatest writing years were behind him by 1943 without having brought him much financial reward or critical respect. By 1944 *Sanctuary* was his only novel in print, primarily because of its notorious scenes of sex and violence. Faulkner's rise to canonization began with a major publishing event not of a new work but of Malcolm Cowley's strategic selection and commentary in *The Portable Faulkner* in 1946 and was consolidated by the Nobel Prize in 1950. Cowley and the Nobel Prize gave the reading public a new Faulkner, one implicit in all his writings but perceived by only a few, a morally traditionalistic but state of the art modernist writer centred in a region but universal in vision and theme. This perceived universality was, however, to some degree a critical construction of the 1940s and 1950s. Lawrence H. Schwartz shows how critics adapted Faulkner to the Cold War, presenting him 'as an emblem of the freedom of the individual under capitalism, as a chronicler of the plight of man in the modern world. Faulkner was seen to exemplify the same values that Western intellectuals saw in capitalism that made it morally superior to communism. He came to represent American literary modernism.'[3] Paradoxically, it was Faulkner's alienation from the commercial and mechanical values of modern culture that critics used to certify his independent free world point of view. Faulkner's complexities of point of view paralleled him with Henry James while his irony and experimentalism aligned him with James Joyce to produce a fiction that criticism was belatedly prepared to appreciate by the 1950s.

This criticism gives us the version of Faulkner consolidated in a book by one of the original New Critics, Cleanth Brooks's excellent, somewhat pious study *William Faulkner: The Yoknapatawpha Country* (1963). But there is another side to Faulkner which carries over into his great 1940 novel, *The Hamlet*. This is the sly, cynical, blackly humorous novelist, allied less to the pieties of the New Critical construction of Southern culture than to the nihilistic tendencies of Southern humour, a Faulkner who armed his impotent rapist in *Sanctuary* with a corn cob and responded to an interviewer's question about art versus morality with 'If a writer has to rob his mother, he will not hesitate; the "Ode on a Grecian Urn" is worth any number of old ladies.'[4] (This was literary posturing; Faulkner routinely took on extraordinary family obligations.) Of Faulkner's 1940s writings, the 'universal' future Nobel Prize winner is most apparent in *Go Down Moses* (1942) and the subversive comedian in *The Hamlet*.

Go Down Moses is a set of stories grouped chronologically around the famous novella 'The Bear'. All but one of the stories revolve around the McCaslin clan and their relations with the African Americans who are slaves then tenants on their land. The other story, 'Pantaloon in Black', also makes an important contribution to the racial thematics of the book and even mentions the McCaslins. There are fine moments of comedy, horror and pathos in *Go Down Moses* but the book has dated more than most Faulkner critics admit, especially where it is most concerned with 'universal' values.

'The Bear' should be the test case of how well Faulkner's book still holds up. This novella has two plots: one a mythical seasonal hunt for a particular bear, powerful, canny and elusive, 'an anachronism indomitable and invincible out of an old dead time, a phantom, epitome and apotheosis of the old wild life' (1); the other Isaac McCaslin's discovery of his family complicity in a dreadful racial tragedy, a heritage he attempts to disown. Faulkner skilfully interrelates these themes and what no longer convinces is not the novella's structure or technique but its values.

The double plot is united by a double initiation. In the first plot Isaac is initiated into the wilderness and the values of the hunt, and it is these very values that allow him in the second plot to perceive the evils of slavery and the tenant system that succeeded it. So his initiation into nature prompts his initiation into the underlying reality of the social order, motivating his refusal to accept the guilt stained legacy of the McCaslin land and the income derived from it. Isaac's discovery of a family secret of 'miscegenation' and incest through his reading of the plantation ledgers is a brilliant invention, one that forces the reader into a role parallel to Isaac's as interpreter of the ledger's cryptic signs. The resonances with the hunting plot are continuous. Just as the hunting ground is diminished each year as the wilderness is violated by commerce and industry, so are human boundaries by enslavement, a violation compounded by the power it gives the McCaslin patriarch to combine incest with rape by sexually claiming his own daughter by 'his' slave woman. If the incest prohibition can be taken as second nature, both instances represent the violation of 'natural' boundaries.

But there is a problem with Faulkner's construction of the parallel. His wilderness mythology is a variation of the American Adam archetype described in the Introduction. The Adamic hero can find authentic identity only by refusing the roles offered by an intrinsically corrupt social world, turning rather to nature as restorative of original innocence and uncompromised individuality. The Adamic myth in 'The Bear' is resonant, misogynistic and socially simplistic as is apparent in Isaac's wife's attempt to blackmail him sexually into accepting his legacy which, not unreasonably, she had assumed she would share in. Though Southern white women were certainly co-conspirators in a viciously racist system, the central role Faulkner assigns to them is ludicrously out of scale. Southern white women hardly *needed* to try to persuade their husbands not to do the right thing. Moreover, Isaac's refusal is merely perverse since he passes on his legacy to his cousin, who is well able to handle the guilt, leaving the exploitative tenant system unchanged. There are even hints within the text that Isaac's reasons for divestiture of his legacy are more psychological than moral; he thus escapes the complications of social and sexual identity. Faulkner's ambivalence towards his protagonist even carries outside the text, as when in March 1957 he ascribes 'serenity' and 'wisdom' to Isaac whereas in April 1958 he specifies Isaac's withdrawal as a moral defeat: 'He says this is bad, and I will withdraw from it. What we need are people who will say, This is bad and I'm going to do something about it, I'm going to change it.'[5] In 'The Bear' the wilderness theme structurally rhymes with Isaac's empty idealism as Faulkner identifies the very ownership of land as a kind of original sin. But since neither Faulkner nor his readers were prepared to abjure land ownership this left very little to do about institutionalized economic injustice other than to participate in it with whatever degree of ironic distaste, a posture which became a standard intellectual mode in the 1950s, the era in which 'The Bear' became a critical icon. Finally, in the deeply flawed moral economy of the story women conveniently take the rap since tending more towards householding than hunting. The discontents of civilization are given a feminine coding.

Despite Faulkner's acknowledgement of the flaws in his protagonist's perspective, this flawed perspective still centres 'The Bear'; without it the story loses the universality and transcendence critically claimed for it. In fact, what once seemed universal now seems provincial. One might save the phenomena of 'The Bear' by seeing it as a send-up of the version of the eternal verities celebrated in it, but there are insufficient cues to such a pervasive thematic irony. As a hunting story, however, 'The Bear' is marvellous. Moreover, Go Down Moses has a story, 'Pantaloon in Black', whose African American protagonist's authenticity and intensity of grief liberate him from patronizing pity or amused condescension.

Faulkner is at his most original when working in the modes of, first, pure phenomenological pathos where he reveals a character's immediacy of perception and response to the world of desire, rage and grief, as in 'Pantaloon in Black' and the Joe Christmas sections of Light of August; and, second, in the mode of pure irony, where he plays with and against literary and moral conventions, commiting outrages of misogyny and misanthropy, outflanking the reader's reasonableness, as in The Sound and the Fury, Sanctuary and As I Lay Dying. Faulkner's 1940 novel The Hamlet was to be his last fully successful adventure in the second mode; the comedy of its two sequels, The Town and The Mansion, and of the late work The Reivers, is entertaining but lacks Faulkner's characteristic provocation.

Inevitably some critics sublimate The Hamlet into the traditionalist paradigm of Faulkner, reading it as another affirmation of the eternal verities. The verities do, in fact, have their place in the novel, which is to frame its hard comedy. This frame exists as external and mostly invisible to the characters of the novel who have their separate agenda, the code of possessive individualism and the pursuit of honour and power, these two codes contradicting the 'natural' verities, as well as, at times, each other. The Hamlet, indeed, presents a world of contradictions: rural but not innocent, agrarian but capitalistic to a fault, pettily individualistic but shot through with demonic energies and undergirded with archetypal identities. The plot of the novel revolves around small-scale machinations endowed with an odd sublimity by a narrative perspective that views its world sub specie aeternitatis and by the depiction of obsessive and self-destructive desires elevated by their analogy to the mythic acts of gods and heroes. The consistently oppositional structure parallels the binary oppositions that the structural anthropologists Claude Lévi-Strauss and Mary Douglas argue as the basis for categorical thought: culture/nature; male/female; cooked/raw; purity/danger. Out of such oppositions Faulkner elaborates a personal mythology of men, women, horses and cows, a mythology which centres on the perversities of exchange, whether economic or sexual.

A major theme of the novel is trades in which men try to prove their superiority in cunning and deception by 'deals', mostly for horses and land, motivated less by avarice than pride: 'the pleasure of the shrewd dealing which far transcended mere gross profit' (1:2). The art of the deal is a zero-sum game in which pride is the major exchange value; one can augment one's stock only by depleting another's, most usually by a clever use of fraud. The basic code of such transactions is what C. B. McPherson in his analysis of the capitalistic value system terms 'possessive individualism': the individual is considered free 'inasmuch as he is proprietor of his own person and capacities. The human essence is freedom from dependence on the wills of others, and freedom is a function of possession. Society becomes a lot of free equal individuals related to each other as proprietors of their own capacities and of what they have acquired by their exercise. Society consists of relations of exchange between proprietors.'[6] Though not totally definitive of the world of *The Hamlet*, possessive individualism sets its boundaries. A character comments 'It aint right. But it aint none of our business' while another is seen as having gone 'as far and even further than a man can let himself go in another man's trade' (1). Later, as a man insists on carrying through a foolishly self-destructive trade and responds brutally to his despairing wife's attempt to intervene, his peers are described as 'lounged along the fence in attitudes gravely inattentive, almost oblivious' (4:1). They observe and silently judge but intervention would violate the group ethos.

The traditionalist critical view that Flem Snopes's rise to power in Frenchman's Bend corrupts an innocent community has been corrected by recent critics who observe that Flem is no more exploitative and possibly less dishonest than the Varners whom he displaces. Before Flem, Will Varner 'owned most of the good land in the country and held mortgages on most of the rest' (1:1). Flem's distinction is not to increase exploitation but to rationalize it. The moment of economic rationalization in Frenchman's Bend is beautifully caught in the scene where Will Varner comes into his own store and orders the clerk, Flem, who has displaced Varner's own son Jody, to get him a plug of tobacco. Flem does. Then:

> Still talking, Varner took the plug and cut off a chew and shut the knife with his thumb and straightened his leg to put the knife back into his pocket, when he stopped talking and looked sharply upward. The clerk was still standing at his elbow. 'Hey?' Varner said. 'What?'
> 'You aint paid for it,' the clerk said. (1:1)

Varner, for the first time ever, pays for tobacco at his own store and Frenchman's Bend sidles towards a rationalized, as opposed to semi-feudal, economic system. David Minter's comment on Flem is precise: 'He differs in part because he takes so little delight in the process of swapping, his interest being only in the result. . . and in part because his deals are large, interrelated, consuming. The epitome of the coolly efficient trader, he is even stingier with words than money.'[7]

Flem has the *last*, the determinative word. His laconic utterances have a sinister resonance as, in the last lines of the novel, he heads for Jefferson, the county seat, a new financial world to conquer: 'Snopes turned his head and spat over the wagon wheel. He jerked the reins slightly. "Come up," he said' (4:2). Moreover his narrative value is supplemented by all the talk about him. The other characters are fascinated by the enigma of Flem's perfect emptiness which they mythologize into a form of negative grandeur with Flem displacing not merely Will Varner from Frenchman's Bend but the devil from Hell (2:2). A traditional view of evil is that it is absence, lack, and Flem triumphs over the devil by a superior lack. Next to Flem the Prince of Evil appears a pettily scrupulous bureaucrat, undone by his supposition that there are *some* moral boundaries. Flem's total lack of feeling, a lack built into the pun of his name, is the condition of his success as the hero of the tribe of possessive individualists; he has no interest in creation nor any distractions from accumulation. The more ambivalent members of the tribe, writer and reader, thus regard him with an mixture of awe and repulsion. Flem is, in a fashion, a hero of our time. Yet V. K. Ratliff, who as observer and storyteller about Flem becomes surrogate for reader and writer, paradoxically exploits Flem by converting this character incapable of exhilaration into a narrative cause of it. He cashes Flem in by converting his human lack into narrative plenitude with storytelling coming out as a long-term gainer.

Loss itself is a value in Faulkner due to the human feeling and striving inevitably expended in it; loss affirms the spirituality of human desire by its very gratuitousness, its negation of economic rationality. Thus in the 'spotted horses' episode the assurance that the horses are not only useless but dangerous is their selling point: 'You couldn't buy that much dynamite for just fifteen dollars' (4:1). It is honour and manhood the buyers are attempting to purchase, dubious but certainly spiritual goods. Neither are women in Faulkner, although more practical, completely immune; Ab Snopes's wife, fixated on her desire for a cream separator, forces her husband to sell their only cow to buy it. He then *buys* milk for her to recycle endlessly through her machine, all the more a symbol of her domestic feminine identity through its lack of functionality. But Faulkner values women not despite but as a mode of his self-evident misogyny. The paradox of male possessive individualism is that men constantly compete to prove their manhood, thus proving that it is external to them, a symbolic quality impossible ever to substantiate permanently and unquestionably. Thus alienation and frustration are intrinsic to

Faulknerian male identity or rather for Faulkner the non-identity of being male. It is logical that the male imagination in Faulkner constructs women as the polar opposite, in tune with, even an expression of the natural world, below but also transcendent of rationality because too self-possessed to need it. If the novel's legend-like heroine, Eula Varner, seems almost as phlegmatic as Flem himself it is for opposite reasons: Eula does not need to show passion because she embodies it. Flem is economic and linear whereas Eula's natural circularity subverts even the institutional hierarchical rationality of the classroom.

> She was neither at the head nor at the foot of her class, not be-
> cause she declined to study on the one hand and not because she
> was Varner's daughter on the other and Varner ran the school,
> but because the class she was in ceased to have either head or foot
> within twenty-four hours after she entered it. Within the year
> there even ceased to be any lower class for her to be promoted
> from, for the reason that she would never be at either end of any-
> thing in which the blood ran. It would have but one point, like a
> swarm of bees, and she would be that point, that centre, swarmed
> over and importuned yet serene and intact and apparently even
> oblivious, tranquilly abrogating the whole long sum of human
> thinking and suffering which is called knowledge, education, wis-
> dom, at once supremely unchaste and inviolable: the queen, the
> matrix. (2:1)

Given that Eula's very presence subverts hierarchies of value, the only man who can afford her is Flem Snopes, who knows the cost of every-thing but the value of nothing and is interested in her only as the means to an alliance with Varner wealth. That is, he can afford her because he is the only man to whom she has no value.

Flem and Eula have a like function in the novel. We have no access to their inner lives, feelings, thoughts or motivations. Neither even does very much, but as unmoved movers they cause the frantic actions of others. They are not characters but figures, archetypal versions of Pluto, god of wealth and the underworld, and Persephone, the principle of fertility. Psychological motivation is irrelevant to their marriage which has the mytho-logic of the subversion of desire by economic rationality. In Faulkner's inverted fairy tale the Princess marries a frog – Flem is so analogized – who stays one.

In realistic fiction character is ethically articulated; by comparing fine shades of difference in character the reader works towards a tacit con-ception of an ethical norm, defined not abstractly but dramatically as a collaborative moral creation of writer and reader. Faulkner has little in-terest in such articulation, going above it to the realm of mythic arche-type and below it to the phenomenological moment. Here too Faulkner exploits the margins; his phenomenology is always sliding towards pathology. In *The Hamlet* Faulkner delineates phenomenological pathos most intensely in his representation of the responses of an idiot and a killer. The idiot, as with Benjy Compson in *The Sound and the Fury* (1929), captures a sort of phenomenological purity. Philosophers must strive to bracket their conceptual categories and especially their preconceptions based on logical expectation, but idiots, at least Faulkner's, live in a world of pure experience. Thus Ike Snopes to whom the concept of 'season' is unknown can sensuously distinguish different qualities of dawn: 'by April it was the actual thin depthless suspension of false dawn itself, in which he could already see and know himself to be an entity solid and cohered in visibility instead of the uncohered all-sentience of fluid and nerve-springing terror alone and terribly free in the primal sightless inimicality' (3:1). Ike is also the one selfless true lover of *The Hamlet*, Faulkner complicating his phenomenological moment by locating it in the genre least hospitable to it, the courtly romance wherein an ideal lover quests after an ideal lady, proving himself by tests of courage. In this instance the lady is, literally, a cow. But Faulkner complicates his blatant perversion of the romance by showing Ike's loyalty and heroism as, in their fashion, genuine. For him fording a creek is an act of courage: 'he began to cross it, lifting his feet high out of the water at each step as he expected each time to find solidity there, or perhaps at each step did not know whether he would or not'. His consideration is exquisite when after receiving 'the violent relaxing of her fear-constricted bowels' (in attempting to push her up a bank from a creek) he did his best to assure her 'how this violent violation of her maiden's delicacy is no shame, since such is the very iron imperishable warp of the fabric of love'. Some critics have interpreted the cow episode as important to Faulkner's exposure of the degeneracy of the Snopeses, a high moral lesson, but it is hard to imagine readers who need to be sermonized against bestiality. Moreover, Faulkner rather blurs the lines by describing most females in the novel as bovine. Rather than affirming boundaries Faulkner is testing them.

There is, however, a privileged point of perspective in the novel, that of Nature which crosscuts human doings in a kind of choral commentary. The absurd cultural activity of the great spotted horses episode takes place against the background of a lambent natural world, efficiently going through its cycles: 'The moon now high overhead, a pearled and mazy yawn in the night sky, the ultimate ends of which rolled onward, whorl on whorl, beyond the pale stars and by pale stars surrounded. . . . Then the pear tree came in sight. It rose in mazed and silver immobility like exploding snow; the mockingbird still sang in it' (4:1). The mockingbird offers one commentary on the futility of the quest for the wildness and danger that the farmers of Frenchman's Bend project on to the wild horses they buy but never manage to possess as the horses explode from the corral, inflicting mayhem as they go. The other commentary is implied in Mrs Littlejohn's periodic errands, expressive of her acceptance of the duties and gifts of the everyday and scorn for the postures of masculine transcendence. Her only overt comment comes as she surveys the wounded: ' "I'll declare," she said. "You men." '

The most extraordinary thing about this bizarre novel in which one character displaces the devil and another romances a cow is how well it works. The last scene, it is true, is the least credible – a character previously depicted as shrewd seems far too easily duped by an uncompelling fraud as if Faulkner at this point had run out of mystifications. But even this scene ends perfectly with Flem's 'Come up.' It is no wonder that Faulkner was an influence on Latin American magic realism for he creates a world in which myth exudes as naturally as the smell of honeysuckle and leather harness from a completely realized rural Southern landscape. Eula Varner is both bovine country girl and goddess of love, Flem Snopes both saturnine country slicker and newly crowned Prince of Evil. Eula speaks only nine sentences in the novel but they are the right ones to maintain the dual focus of a character believable in her appearances but essentially legendary. Sexist and conservative, *The Hamlet* is also a send-up of traditional masculine values and a penetrating parable of possessive individualism, a way of being Faulkner understands so well precisely because of his deep allegiance to it – his most interesting letters are outraged responses to violations of privacy, of personal space. Faulkner's collusion with Southern and more generally American values enables his subversively undermining perception of them.

Distinct moral visions: Katherine Anne Porter and Eudora Welty

Katherine Anne Porter and Eudora Welty had defined literary voices before Faulkner's influence was strongly felt. There is a different world of feeling in these writers who focus as much on the values of family as on the extreme family dysfunction and violence that was Faulkner's theme from *The Sound and the Fury* (1929) to *Absalom! Absalom!* (1936). In her stories about the autobiographically based Miranda, 'Old Mortality' and 'Pale Horse, Pale Rider' in the collection *Pale Horse, Pale Rider: Three Short Novels* (1939) and 'The Old Order' in *The Leaning Tower* (1944), Porter balances the need for freeing the creative self from the constrictions of family and tradition with a severe vision of the dangers of relying on ego and impulse. Her powerful novella 'Noon Wine' in *Pale Horse, Pale Rider* presents the oddly moving predicament of a

shallow and foolish man who in an impulsive and at least partly accidental act, that yet implicates the entirety of his character, destroys any basis
for continuing to live. His failure to sustain the narrow but adequate
code proper to the unforgiving landscape of south Texas destroys him.
In 'Pale Horse, Pale Rider' Miranda survives a near-fatal disease, the
death of her lover and, most dangerously, an enticing out-of-the-body
vision of a lucent world just beyond the border of life only to have to
return to and settle for the artifices of everyday social performance. Di-
recting a friend to buy her cosmetics, clothing and a walking stick, Miranda sees herself as restored to the song and dance act of life: 'Lazarus,
come forth. Not unless you bring me my top hat and stick.' But her
performance thereafter will never lack the frame of a vision of ultimate
value. An even more haunting story is 'Flowering Judas' from *Flowering
Judas and Other Stories* (1930) where the the protagonist's guilt and dread
are locked into the frozen moment of the historical present tense. It is
important to see that the harsh judgement on this character derives not
from the reader's or even writer's moral evaluation but from the character's own consciousness, her residual sense of integrity, deriving from
family tradition, and that her dilemma results from her idealism in a
world that offers little ground for authentic moral action. This story of
insurgent Mexico, written in 1929, anticipated the political disillusion of
the 1940s and 1950s before most writers had got as far as the political
idealism of the 1930s. Porter's character, trapped between two absolutes,
the Catholicism of her upbringing and the communism of her political
choice, finds neither meeting the rigorous demands of her intelligence
but fears the loneliness of unsupported personal vision. Readers should
regard this character with fear and trembling rather than with the presumption to moral superiority many critics pretend to – she has more
integrity than most and her failure is threateningly implicative.

In her essays and interviews Porter could be obtuse about people of a
different race and class, even retroactively upgrading the class circumstances of her own childhood. What matters is that the moral vision of
her stories is precise. The little-discussed story 'Magic' is a *tour de force* of
ironic first-person narration that depicts in the starkest terms the bru-
talities of racial and economic exploitation. Part of the irony is that the
hearer of the story, herself an exploiter, quite fails to comprehend the
true meaning of the story and its underlying accusation.

In Porter situations are ambiguous but the writer's moral stance is
clear and authoritative – to the careful reader. Eudora Welty, in contrast,
tends to plunge readers into situations and leave them on their own.
This is so both in novels such as *Delta Wedding* (1946) and *The Optimist's
Daughter* (1972) and in short stories such as 'The Petrified Man', 'Why I
Live at the PO' and 'Powerhouse' (collected in *A Curtain of Green*,
1941). Like the English novelist Henry Green, whom she greatly admired, Welty creates structures of evanescence that are not without

strong moral and cultural implication. Welty aspires to transcend convenient abstraction: 'There is absolutely everything in great fiction but a
clear answer. Humanity seems to matter more to the novelist than what
humanity thinks it can prove.'[8] *The Optimist's Daughter* sets up an initially schematic opposition between Laurel, representative of traditional
values of consideration, taste and decency, and Fay, Laurel's father's second wife, younger than she, selfish, vulgar and morally stupid, 'a person
whose own life had not taught her how to feel' (4). No modern American novel so convincingly shows the crudity and meanness of life without family and community standards. The bumper sticker on Fay's
brother's pick-up truck is indicative: 'Do Unto Others Before They Do
Unto You' (2:3). Fay exceeds the bounds of common humanity when
she slaps her critically ill husband's face and later exceeds those of public
propriety by making a scene at his funeral. Welty seems to overload the
moral oppositions in making Laurel's husband, who died in the Second
World War, an architect and Laurel herself a fabric designer whereas
Fay's family owns a 'wrecking concern'. Yet Fay's funeral scene is within
a tradition of sorts; her mother comments approvingly: 'When I had to
give up her dad, they couldn't hold me half so easy. I tore up the whole
house, I did' (2:4). And Fay's striking of her husband was an attempt to
shock him out of giving in to death. On one level Fay allegorizes the
triumph of incivility – 'I belong to the future' she all too convincingly
tells Laurel – yet her survival-oriented values are not entirely negated
and she lives on the page with her 'round country-blue eyes and a little
feisty jaw' (1:3). By the conclusion of the novel the simplicity of its initial
oppositions have been thoroughly complicated though never reversed.

The characters of the splendid early stories 'The Petrified Man' and
'Why I Live at the PO' are so obviously awful that moral judgement
seems superfluous. For that matter, the characters' talk is more interesting than their actions. Welty's perfect pitch in her notation of Southern
vernacular focuses, as in Ben Jonson's comedies, on vigorously selfish
characters enunciating themselves in the vulgarest of tongues. As Porter
comments in her Introduction to Welty's first short story collection,
'The Petrified Man' is 'a fine clinical study of vulgarity – vulgarity absolute, chemically pure, exposed mercilessly in its final subhuman depths'.[9]
Set in a Jackson, Mississippi beauty shop, this horror comedy of sexual
antagonism is perfectly transparent yet in its evasion of glib categories it
refuses the reassurance of easy response. Two passages from the end indi-
cate Welty's play with tone. In one Mrs Fletcher is told that the petrified
man in the circus is really a fugitive wanted in California for four rapes:
' "Not really petrified at all, of course," said Mrs Fletcher meditatively.'
In the other the beautician, Leota, reflects on the five-hundred-dollar reward her former friend Mrs Pike received for exposing him: 'Four women.
I guess those women didn't have the faintest notion at the time they'd be
worth a hunnerd an' twenty-five bucks a piece some day to Mrs Pike.'

While admiring such hard edged stories as the two above, Porter preferred Welty's stories of subjective nuance, such as 'A Memory'. These are indeed finely crafted within the predominant subjectivist tradition of the modern short story but the 'objective' stories are *sui generis*. A masterpiece in the 'objective' mode is 'Powerhouse', inspired by a concert in Jackson by the African American musician Fats Waller, and written in jazz syncopation, each verbal exchange becoming a kind of riff, negotiating melancholy and mischief.

O'Connor: Catholic comedy

Faulkner, Porter and Welty were well along in their careers before Southern writing became an honorific critical category but by Flannery O'Connor's time Southern self-consciousness was unavoidable. In 1960 O'Connor wrote to John Hawkes that she was 'going to an art festival thirty miles from here where Katherine Anne Porter, Caroline Gordon, and Madison Jones are going to be paid (well) to swap clichés about Southern culture. An old lady left her sizable fortune for an Arts Festival . . . with the stipulation that the guests had to be Southerners and discuss Southern culture. The money goes on whether the culture does or not. I think it's programs like this that are going to hasten the end of it.'[10] At the conference Porter disposed of the inevitable question of definition with a crisp tautology: 'being a Southerner, I happen to write so I suppose you combine the two and you have a Southern writer, haven't you?' O'Connor topped this irreverence by pointing out what Southern identity of her own time was not: 'Walker Percy wrote somewhere that his generation of Southerners had no more interest in the Civil War than in the Boer War.' Language rather than nostalgia is the basis: 'I know if I tried to write stories about credible Japanese they would all sound like Herman Talmadge' (a folksy, racist Georgia politician); 'Southern writing' is an 'idiom': 'people in Princeton don't talk like we do. And these sounds build up a life of their own in your senses.'[11]

Her themes, as opposed to her language, derive less from her region than from her religion. A Roman Catholic, she described the major dimension of her fiction as 'anagogical', that is, allegorically figuring 'the Divine Life and our participation in it'.[12] Rarely, however, are her characters Catholic. O'Connor scorned the made-to-order piety of popular American Catholic writing while admiring the intensity of Southern Protestant fundamentalist faith. Her fiction empowers its anagogical implications by its absolutely specified Southern speech.

O'Connor's fiction is very funny and very violent for another Southern quality in her writing is its affinity with the nihilist and materialist tendencies in Southern humour. But in O'Connor the violence is strategic; it shows the world as it is as a way of emphasizing the need to see beyond the world. Moreover, O'Connor believes that the necessary supplement of grace is so far distant from the perspective of her readers that they must be strategically outflanked and then bashed by it: 'You can't clobber any reader while he's looking. You divert his attention, then you clobber him, and he never knows what hit him.'[13] She cares less how her characters live than how they die – in what state of the soul. Thus in 'A Good Man is Hard to Find' (collected in *A Good Man is Hard to Find*, 1952) she casually kills off four members of a family to concentrate on the spiritually relevant one, the grandmother. O'Connor's characterization of The Misfit, the antagonist of the story, exemplifies her brilliance at melding disparate realms of discourse – she derived his cognomen from the mass media, a story in the *Atlanta Journal*; his speech from rural Georgia; and his philosophy from existentialism. The Misfit's remembrance of prison is O'Connor's parody of the recently translated and popularized existentialist writings of Camus and Sartre: 'Turn to the right, it was a wall. Look up, it was a ceiling, look down it was a floor. I forget what I done, lady. I set there and set there trying to remember what it was I done and I ain't recalled it to this day. Oncet in a while, I would think it was coming to me, but it never came.' (In 'Good Country People' from the same collection, a countrified and seemingly naive bible salesman utterly defeats the protagonist, a PhD in philosophy given to quoting Heidegger to support her self-proclaimed nihilism, assuring her: 'you ain't so smart. I been believing in nothing ever since I was born!') O'Connor also throws in a play on Swift, allusions to *The Mikado*, Kafka, and a sneer at Freud. All this is perfectly functional. Freudianism competes with Catholicism as an all-purpose explanation for the vagaries of humanity by grounding all desire in materiality. So O'Connor leads in with an allusion to Kafka's 'The Hunger Artist' whose protagonist admits he fasted not out of heroic self-denial but only because he never found the food (clearly spiritual) that he really wanted. The Misfit responds to the grandmother's suggestion that he must have been sent to the penitentiary for stealing in like fashion: 'The Misfit sneered slightly. "Nobody had nothing I wanted. . . . It was the head-doctor at the penitentiary said what I had done was kill my daddy but I known that for a lie. My daddy died in nineteen ought nineteen of the epidemic flu and I never had a thing to do with it. He was buried in the Mount Hopewell Baptist churchyard and you can go there and see for yourself." ' The Misfit has literalized and materialized the psychoanalytic concept of the Oedipus complex in much the same fashion Freud used to discredit religious concepts.

O'Connor prefers Swift to Freud as an unmasker of vanity. Among other experiences The Misfit mentions 'I even seen a woman flogged', echoing Swift's dreadful metaphysical joke in *A Tale of a Tub*: 'Last week I saw a woman *flay'd*, and you will hardly believe how much it altered her Person for the worse.' Swift plays on surface/depth, flesh/spirit, appearance/reality; in O'Connor the grandmother's attitudes are grounded in cliché and appearance until The Misfit shocks her into grace. Some critics see in O'Connor a vision more Manichean than Catholic of an inherently corrupt material world, populated primarily by the shallow and the wicked and presided over by a punitive God. O'Connor vigorously denied this assessment but the protagonists of her two novels, *Wise Blood* (1952) and *The Violent Bear it Away* (1960), commit unpunished and unrepented murders in their pursuit of spiritual reality, and in all her work she seems to show vicious relations between people as negligible in the face of the quest after personal salvation. Does her version of religion dismiss charity? Perhaps it is a question of emphasis. Both novels centre on protagonists seeking spiritual validity in a world of pervasive, unreflective nihilism. Reacting violently against the falsity of merely external religiosity they proclaim a nihilism meant to shock their world as much as it profoundly shocks them. In the event they learn that they shock no one since the nihilism they furiously preach is what the world blithely practises. So there is nowhere to go except back to the faith they never really lost. The structure of the books having been built around bringing them to this, the books logically end, with no space for charity (in the religious sense of unconditioned love) and, admittedly, an open contempt for secular humanism. But several O'Connor short stories clearly turn on the presence or denial of charity. In 'The Displaced Person' an absent-minded priest memorably exemplifies the quality of charity and the story – one of O'Connor's best – implies nihilism as the logical alternative to it, which is just the solution the protagonists of the novels attempt to embrace. One of O'Connor's greatest moments comes in 'Revelation' when Mrs Turpin, one of her prototypical shallow, respectable protagonists, sees a streak in the sky as she is watering the hogs and experiences a vision.

> She saw the streak as a vast swinging bridge extending upward from the earth through a field of living fire. Upon it a vast horde of souls were rumbling toward heaven. There were whole companies of white trash, clean for the first time in their lives, and bands of black niggers in white robes, and battalions of freaks and lunatics shouting and clapping and leaping like frogs. And bringing up the end of the procession was a tribe of people whom she recognized at once as those who, like herself and Claud, had always had a little of everything and the God-given wit to use it right. She leaned forward to observe them closer. They were marching behind the others with great dignity, accountable as they had always been for good order and common sense and respectable be-

havior. They alone were on key. Yet she could see by their
shocked and altered faces that even their virtues were being
burned away.

O'Connor, who died in 1964, is the first writer emerging after the Second World War to have been canonized by publication of her work in a
Library of America edition.[14] How could a writer so fiercely Catholic
and so flagrantly Southern have reached a readership that was predominantly neither? Her writing had no special appeal to the literary gate-
keepers of the 1950s such as the New York intellectuals, and has even
less to the emergent critical powers of the 1990s, the feminists and neo-
Marxists. The Southern literary establishment endorsed her but no more
than other writers who have not shown similar staying power. Though a
conspiratorial theory of O'Connor's canonization is certainly imaginable,
it seems at least possible that the inventiveness of her imagination in
devising highly original ways to clobber the reader may have as much to
do with it as various ideological currents. Presumably, few readers converted to Catholicism after their clobbering but O'Connor's power,
nevertheless, may be in how her work cuts against the grain of contemporary ideology, causing us alarm as well as delight. Her writing was so
traditional in its values, those of the twelfth century, as to be outré.

This is one way in which she differs from a very good writer, William Styron, whose work never quite transcends the limits of sensibility
inherent in the 1940s and 1950s fiction noted in Chapter 2. Styron's first
and best novel, *Lie Down in Darkness* (1951), also runs into a difficulty
Flannery O'Connor nicely describes: 'The presence alone of Faulkner in
our midst makes a great difference in what a writer can and cannot
permit himself to do. Nobody wants his mule and wagon stalled on the
same track the Dixie Limited is roaring down.'[15] Distracting Faulknerian
echoes raise the question whether Styron had quite got out of the way
of the Dixie Limited. His heroine, especially, seems an extended but less
powerful variation on Caddy Compson, the doomed and poignant central figure of Faulkner's *The Sound and the Fury*. Though Styron's novel
is moving and sorrowful it lacks implicativeness, failing to attain the
unmistakable voice that arrests the reader in Porter, Welty and O'Connor. His best known work after *Lie Down in Darkness* is *The Confessions
of Nat Turner* (1967), a fictional version of the slave rebellion of 1831 led
by the historical Nat Turner. The hostile response of most African
American writers and critics to what they regarded as an appropriation
and falsification of their own history may not have been fair to Styron's
intensely imagined and painfully sympathetic novel but it is understandable. What was upsetting *was* the sensitivity, the lyrical, rather
murky emotional enmeshment of the characters, rather like that of a
dysfunctional family, akin to the 1940s and 1950s fiction of Carson
McCullers and James Baldwin, indeed as if James Baldwin had been

re-imagined *as* Nat Turner. Styron recodes the rebellion from political and active to psychological and passive, even the violence becoming an acting out of ambivalent love–hate family romance, thus giving an already – in 1967 – somewhat dated 1950s rereading of the past.

Contemporary Southern fiction

Though I found some important Southern writers more relevant to the concerns of other sections of this book – McCullers, Warren, Capote, Walker Percy, Peter Taylor – they should be thought of as contributing to the richness of Southern literary expression. But there is a question as to whether recent Southern fiction is still regionally distinctive and culturally central. Current critical theory, with its radical political orientation, seems bent on remarginalizing Southern writing in reaction to the traditionalism and conservatism so valued by the New Criticism. However, non-academic readers and newspaper reviewers have not abjured an interest in Southern writers who explore, in a morally traditionalist fashion, the complications of love, marriage and family. And academic interest is maintained in Southern universities and literary quarterlies. This humanist mode, aligned more with Porter and Welty than with Faulkner or O'Connor, shows the influence also of Reynolds Price. Price testifies that Rosacoke Mustian, the heroine of *A Long and Happy Life* (1962), 'had stood up, live from her first paragraph – in my mind at least and those of a few friends who dealt with her at once like a palpable creature, warm to the touch'. As a character of 'radiant energy' with 'a generous heart'. Rosacoke embodies Price's narrative credo: '*The world exists. It is not yourself. Plunge in it for healing, blessed exhaustion and the risk of warmth.*'[16] This credo is evident in the work of writers for whom Price served as mentor in his teaching at Duke University in North Carolina, most notably Anne Tyler and Josephine Humphreys whose work will be considered in my chapter on women's fiction. Also in Price's realist humanist mode are Kaye Gibbons, Gail Godwin and Lee Smith who have written their own versions of hearts in conflict – or even, amazingly, in concord.

Another Southern literary tradition, less favourably reviewed and less frequently read, derives from the explorations of violence and nihilism in Southern humour and has some affinities with Faulkner, O'Connor and the early comic stories by Welty. Cormac McCarthy, a lapsed Catholic, reveals in *Suttree* (1979) a world bleaker than O'Connor's because insusceptible to grace. McCarthy's protagonist sits outside a church listening to hymns, 'for even a false adumbration of the world of the spirit is better than none at all'. What makes the novel memorable, however, is not its despairing protagonist but his one-time jail-mate Harrogate, poor, white and trashy, combining low cunning with a basic cretinous degeneracy. At one point in the novel we find Harrogate trying to sell what he calls 'scobs' (i.e. squabs) to local restaurants though they are in fact defeathered and eviscerated pigeons. Barry Hannah's *Airships* (1978) renders Southern lowlife in surrealistic terms. If McCarthy with his abstruse latinate diction and Hannah with his surrealism are in the Longstreet tradition of mediating gross subject matter with notably literary style, the equivalent to George Washington Harris's insider perspective in this 'blood and grits' school of fiction is Harry Crews, whose phrase this is.[17] *A Feast of Snakes* (1976) is interesting precisely because of the flagrancy of its misanthropic and misogynistic vision, one that, in Southern parlance, does Sut Lovingood (see p. 55) proud.

Contemporary Southern fiction, then, exhibits the opposing tendencies of the tradition of civility, focused on family and relationship, and the tradition of grotesque humour, focused on violence and rejection. Although Southern fiction is now in critical disfavour, Southern writers, especially of the traditional group, contribute to the cultural conversation precisely their *unfashionable* emphasis on personal integrity, family tradition and the sense of the heart in an era where intellectual orthodoxy holds such values to be mere bourgeois mythology. But one of the most engaging Southern novels is less in either tradition than that of Jonathan Swift, deriving its title, *A Confederacy of Dunces*, from a Swift essay. John Kennedy Toole's novel was published in 1980, eleven years after his suicide, as the result of his mother dragooning Walker Percy into reading the manuscript which, to his surprise, was a comic delight. Its triumph is its protagonist, Ignatius J. Reilly, who rebels against the modern world as a reactionary rather than a radical, a Thomist rather than a Marxist. He is, as Percy says, 'an Aquinas gone to pot' who conducts a 'one-man campaign against everybody – Freud, homosexuals, heterosexuals, Protestants, and the assorted excesses of modern times'.[18] Unlike the anarchistic protagonists of Southern humour, Ignatius seeks order though his quest for it leaves massive disruption in its wake. Perhaps we could see him then as a paradoxical bridging figure between the traditionalists and the anarchists. Perhaps tradition is now the disordering element in a postmodern society.

Notes

1. Jack P. Greene, *Pursuits of Happiness* (Chapel Hill, 1988).

2. Lewis P. Simpson, 'Southern Fiction' in *Harvard Guide to Contemporary American Writing*, ed. Daniel Hoffman (Cambridge, Massachusetts, 1979).

3. Lawrence H. Schwartz, *Creating Faulkner's Reputation: The Politics of Modern Literary Criticism* (Knoxville, 1988), p. 4.

4. Jean Stein, 'William Faulkner: An Interview' in *William Faulkner: Three Decades of Criticism*, ed. Frederick J. Hoffman and Olga W. Vickery (Michigan State Press, 1960), p. 68.

5. Frederick L. Gwynn and Joseph L. Blotner (eds.), *Faulkner in the University* (New York, 1965), pp. 54, 246.

6. C. B. Macpherson, *The Political Theory of Possessive Individualism: Hobbes to Locke* (Oxford, 1964), p. 3.

7. David Minter, *William Faulkner: His Life and Work* (Baltimore, 1980), p. 181.

8. O'Connor, *The Eye of the Story: Selected Essays and Reviews* (New York, 1978), p. 149.

9. Katherine Anne Porter, 'Introduction' to Eudora Welty, *Selected Stories of Eudora Welty* (New York, 1954), p. 20.

10. Flannery O'Connor, *The Habit of Being: Letters of Flannery O'Connor*, ed. Sally Fitzgerald (New York, 1980), pp. 412-13.

11. 'Recent Southern Fiction: A Panel Discussion' in *Conversations with Flannery O'Connor*, ed. Rosemary M. Magee (Jackson, Mississippi, 1987), pp. 61–78.

12. O'Connor, *Mystery and Manners* (New York, 1969), p. 72.

13. *The Habit of Being*, p. 202.

14. O'Connor, *Collected Works*, ed. Sally Fitzgerald (Library of America, 1988).

15. *Mystery and Manners*, p. 45.

16. Reynolds Price, *A Common Room: Essays 1954–1987* (New York, 1987), pp. 345, 347.

17. Harry Crews, *Blood and Grits* (New York, 1979).

18. Walker Percy, 'Foreword' to Toole, *A Confederacy of Dunces* (New York, 1980), p. 12.

Chapter 4
Jewish American Fiction

The ethos of *menschlikeit*

Many critics cite the Yiddish concept of *menschlikeit* as what qualitatively differentiates Jewish American literature. A *mensch* in Yiddish connotation is not just a man as a man, the literal meaning, but a man as a man should be. Not necessarily a smarter man, he may even be a bit of a *schlemiehl*, that is, a fool, or a *schlimazel*, that is, a magnet attracting bad luck. (The usual distinction is that when the *schlemiehl* drops his bowl of soup it lands in the *schlimazel*'s lap though it is not uncommon to find a *schlemiehl* who is also a *schlimazel*). To be a *mensch* it is essential only that he be a man of heart and ethical responsibility, that he pursue ideals but never beyond human limits. A *mensch* is neither a creature reduced to its material needs nor a divinity able to alter a world to its heart's desire. Instead, a *mensch* must fulfil his obligations in the world as it is though sometimes striving to better it, frequently with somewhat ludicrous results. There are, as we shall see, problems with the concept, an obvious one being that, by definition, it leaves out women, unless Cynthia Ozick's Puttermesser could be considered a *mensch* or at least an example of *fraulichkeit*. The concept also has a certain reactive quality; as Ruth Wisse points out, the cultural function of the European Yiddish version of the *schlemiehl* was to dramatize the persistence of faith in the most adverse circumstances whereas the Jewish American *schlemiehl* is

> an expression of heart, of intense passionate feeling, in surround-
> ings that stamp out individuality and equate emotion with
> unreason. The schlemiehl is used as a cultural reaction to the
> prevailing Anglo-Saxon model of restraint in action, thought, and
> speech . . . . The American *schlemiehl* declares his humanity by
> loving and suffering in defiance of the forces of depersonalization
> and the ethic of enlightened stoicism.[1]

It is no wonder, then, that the 1950s was the Jewish decade since the heart was in, responsibility was in, and Jews were specialists in both, emotionally expressive but ethically restrained. Irving Howe notes that one man's sentimentality is another's *menschlikeit*: 'in Yiddish culture there is a greater emotional permissibility, a greater readiness to welcome tears or laughter, than in American culture. The desperate reliance upon blandness and composure, the cult of understatement, the assumption that it is good to feel but bad to show one's feelings – these attitudes are quite alien to the Jewish ethos.'[2] The 1950s construction was, that though the South might be the heart's true home, the Jew was its natural spokesman, an interrelation argued as late as 1972 by a Southern writer: 'Insofar as the twentieth-century novel in this country has consisted of the South and the Jews . . . it has been the product of two profoundly similar cultures – God-and-family centred . . . gifted with unashamed feeling and eloquence, supported by ancient traditions of sorrow and the promise of justice, a comic vision of ultimate triumph.'[3] Whether or not this is so, it is certainly significant that a number of Southern and Jewish writers think it to be and there is an approximate equivalence in the critical fortunes of the two literatures.

The theme of *menschlikeit* has given critics a way of resolving the recurrent dispute over who is to be considered a Jewish American writer. As Robert Alter comments, 'It is by no means clear what sense is to be made of the Jewishness of a writer who neither uses a uniquely Jewish language, nor describes a distinctively Jewish milieu, nor draws upon literary traditions that are recognizably Jewish.'[4] Moreover, Saul Bellow, Bernard Malamud and Philip Roth, three writers considered so prototypical as to be termed – with reference to a well-known suit company – 'the Hart Schaffner and Marx of our trade', have all at some time explicitly refused the label of 'Jewish writer'.[5] But each has invested in the theme of *menschlikeit* though Roth satirizes it in a postmodernist fashion. Closer to Malamud and Bellow is Cynthia Ozick, who uses postmodernist techniques *against* the postmodernist ethos in a wry defence of traditional Jewish values. Malamud, Ozick and Bellow present Jewish American identity as problematic but it is the issue in much of their fiction. There are writers who are in some way or another Jewish but who do not use Jewish protagonists or centre on Jewish themes and so are treated in different sections: Mailer, Salinger and Heller. Philip Roth's self-conscious play on Jewish American identity is in the context of postmodernism and will later be considered in that light.

The Jewish emergence

Jewish American fiction became a major critical category in the 1950s, 'the Jewish decade' as it has been described.[6] There was an emergence of highly talented and original writers matched by a support group of gifted critics centred in New York City of whom Irving Howe and Alfred Kazin have proved the most enduring. It almost seemed in the 1950s that if a critic was not Southern, then he (usually – feminism was not yet on the scene) must be Jewish and Howe, like Price, drew parallels.

> In both instances, a subculture finds its voice and its passion at exactly the moment it approaches disintegration. This is a moment of high self-consciousness, and to its writers it offers a number of advantages . . . . It offers the emotional strength that comes from traditional modes of conduct – honor for the South, 'chosenness' for the Jews – which the writers struggle to regain, escape, overcome, while finding through this struggle their gift of tongue. . . . And it offers a heritage of words, a wonderful rich mess of language, for the Southern writers everything from Ciceronian courtroom rhetoric to the corrupt vividness of redneck speech, and for the Jewish writers everything from the high gravity of Yiddish declamation to the gutter sparklings of the street.[7]

But the Southern writers developed a bit ahead of the critics, thus the belatedness of Faulkner's recognition. The Jewish American critics arrived just in time for the writers, thus the relative rapidity with which the writers reaped the institutional rewards of emergence: Bellow's National Book Award in 1953, Malamud's in 1958, Philip Roth's in 1959. The climate was ripe. The need for a major expansion of college faculties to serve the enrolment boom fuelled by the GI Bill shattered the existent barriers in English departments against hiring Jews. The casual, sometimes vicious anti-Semitism of the 1920s, reflected in Fitzgerald, Hemingway, Eliot and Cummings, gave way to a post-holocaust 'Philo-Semitism'. A Kentucky woman, Elizabeth Hardwick, come to New York to be a critic, could even opt against identification with the Southern New Criticism to become a volunteer secular Jew, a remarkable turn in cultural history: 'I do not consider myself a Southern writer. Even when I was in college "down home," I'm afraid my aim was . . . to be a New York Jewish intellectual.'[8] By the 1950s, then, readers could choose whether to be volunteer Southerners or volunteer Jews. Both, happily, had been critically constituted as universal categories.

The redefinition of Jew as universal came to some degree as a response to the Nazi denial of humanity to Jews. A delayed reaction to pre-war prejudices and to the 1945 photographs and accounts of the death camps led to an American wish to dissolve racial and cultural difference into 'The Family of Man', as an influential 1950s book of photography termed it. That the Jew had been seen as a 'specialist in alienation' added to the perception of universality since in the post-war era of Camus's *The Stranger* and Riesman's lonely crowd, alienation seemed representative. Even the Jewish type-character of the *luftmensch*, the man who lives by words, unattached to tradition or community, as light as air, seemed to reflect the circumstances of a growing sector of the American middle class, specialists in self presentation and the persuasive language of advertising, promotion, political imagery. As a Malamud character puts it, 'Believe me, there are Jews everywhere.'

Malamud and the universal Jew

Malamud's fiction is based on his image of the Jew as universal man: 'Personally, I handle the Jew as a symbol of the tragic experience of man existentially. I try to see the Jew as universal man. Every man is a Jew though he may not know it.'[9] This declaration points towards both the originality as well as the peculiar limitations of Malamud's fiction, both apparent in 'Angel Levine', a story in *The Magic Barrel* (1958) which ends with the famous 'Jews everywhere' line. The protagonist, Manischevitz, is an American Job: his son dies, his daughter runs off with a lout, his wife becomes terminally ill, his business burns to the ground, he has excruciating backaches. He prays in the Yiddish-inflected voice that Malamud and Bellow helped establish as a recognizable style: 'Give Fanny back her health, and to me for myself that I shouldn't feel pain in every step. Help me now or tomorrow is too late. This I don't have to tell you.' This is perhaps too endearing, a quality that increases exponentially when an African American, Levine, introduces himself, explaining that he is Jewish and an angel and can save Manischevitz if only he will have faith in Levine's profession of angelhood. The test is really whether Manischevitz can see his faith *as* universal, transcending race and culture. Since Levine, as a probationary angel, lacks wings or other evidence, to credit him demands a belief in generalized transcendence, 1950s style. Manischevitz finally summons belief, hears a winglike swoosh as Levine disappears, returns to his flat to find his wife up from her deathbed dusting, and delivers the memorable punchline. The language and plot of this fable are surprising and engaging but Malamud borrowed his angel from Frank Capra's *It's a Wonderful Life* (1946), without motivating its appearance nearly so convincingly. As Cynthia Ozick argues, Malamud's racial message seems unreal and the fantasy in the story clashes with rather than reinforces its religious and racial theme.[10] Here and elsewhere in Malamud universality seems an unearned premise, a 1950s cultural assumption of the writer that is not constructed into a felt reality for the reader. Later, in *The Tenants*, Malamud somewhat more convincingly imagines race war between a black and a Jew, mixed with the more literary dispute of the naive romantic writing from the heart (but in clichés) with the sophisticated formalist writing with craft (but not about anything).

Jewish characters and Jewish language rhythms are central in Malamud's work and there is play on Jewishness but critics question just how Jewish a world he presents. The strength of *The Assistant* in 1957, its essentialization of the Jew as universal suffering saviour, is its weakness in a time suspicious of claims of essence and universality. Moreover, the novel offers no more historically specific depiction of Jewish identity. There is so little external reference that it is not clear what decade, even what period, it is set in. When Frank Alpine, Morris Bober's 'assistant' in his marginal inner city grocery, questions Bober about his Jewish identity, noting that Bober sells and eats ham and keeps his store open on Jewish holidays, Bober responds that 'to be a Jew all you need is a good heart' and 'to do right, to be honest, to be good. This means to other people.' This seems overly general and Bober's poverty and suffering seem gratuitous in the lack of an external context. By 1957 American Jews were doing pretty well – *Making It*, in the deliberately provocative title of Norman Podhoretz's memoir. Even Morris Bober's daughter thinks he might have managed better and a reader may conclude that the underlying tragedy of *The Assistant* is that Bober did not move to a nicer neighbourhood. What Philip Roth calls the 'myth of Ethical Jewhood' has not worn well and Roth's sardonic reading of the final passage where Frank Alpine has himself circumcised and becomes a Jew so as to atone for his rape of Bober's daughter makes a certain sense: 'So penance for the criminal penis has been done.'[11]

Even more than *The Assistant* is Malamud's first novel, *The Natural* (1952), open to Alfred Kazin's 1958 complaint that American writers were overly eager 'to be freed of certain painful experiences through the ritualistic catharsis of modern symbolism. The Jewish or Negro writer, far from being mired in his personal pathos as of yore, is now so aware that his experience is 'universal' that he tends to escape out of the experience itself, to end up in the great American sky of abstractions.'[12] *The Natural* mixes baseball lore and Arthurian mythology to produce an inventive but curiously humourless novel, populated by archetypes rather than characters. The moral significances of the allegory come out as clichés to the point where the novel seems really allegory for its own sake, providing an air rather than a specific substance of deep meaning.

A New Life (1961), Malamud's most realistic novel, draws on his teaching experience at Oregon State University. Set in 1950 – though 1950s politics is curiously unapparent – the novel's originality is in its juxtaposition of two stereotypes, the Jewish character-stereotype of the *schlemiehl*, embodied in the protagonist S. Levin, and the American myth-stereotype of regeneration in the West, a myth previously undercut in Jack Burden's trip west in *All the King's Men*. The originality is in the combination: The *Schlemiehl* Goes West. After a series of academic and sexual misadventures Levin backtrails east, encumbered with someone else's wife, her two adopted children, no job, no prospects, but loads of responsibility. This fate is a great joke not only on the Adamic myth of going west to escape from social constraints, but as well, perhaps, on Malamud's own patented myth of ethical Jewhood: Levin ends up with a woman he does not love and children two removes from his own to suffer for, a kind of *reductio ad absurdum* of Jewish universality and the family of man. (Most critics, it should be mentioned, take the ethical Jewhood theme entirely seriously, although disagreeing in their evaluation of it.)[13]

The Fixer (1966) plays out Malamud's stock of conventions but has a historical grounding lacking in his previous fiction. He draws on the notorious Beiliss case, a conspiracy in pre-revolutionary Russia to frame an obscure Jew for the mythical crime of ritual murder of a Christian child. The tsarist government clearly intended Beiliss as a scapegoat to divert the populace from growing revolutionary discontent. Malamud names his protagonist Bok, Hebrew for goat, showing how he responds to absurd injustice by gradually transforming himself from a self-seeking individualist into one of the last just men.

Bok's refusal to end his torture with a false confession effectually keeps the truth alive and further exposes the Tsar – who appears symbolically naked in an extended dream fantasy in which Bok previsions the Tsar's eventual death though with himself as the killer. The Tsar appeals for pity as the loving father of a haemophiliac but Bok sees the irrelevance of the Tsar's claim for himself as a benevolent family man, responding that the Tsar too has something missing in the blood: 'In you, in spite of certain sentimental feelings, it is missing somewhere else – the sort of insight, you might call it, that creates in a man charity, respect for the most miserable. You say you are kind and prove it with pogroms.' He then puts a bullet in the Tsar's heart, reflecting, 'Better him than us.' Though *The Fixer* lacks the verbal and thematic surprises of Malamud's earlier fiction, its version of his central theme of *menschlikeit* matches up more convincingly with moral and historical reality.

Cynthia Ozick: postmodernism against itself

Robert Rauschenberg exemplified the creed of the contemporary avant garde in his famous telegram to Iris Clert: 'This is a portrait of Iris Clert if I say so', the telegram being the art work.[14] Is one a Jewish American writer if one thinks one is? One critic declares it is when 'a *feeling* of difference impinges upon the imaginative quality of the writer'.[15] There is a question of the limits of such tautology. Indeed, most of the limitations of self-reflective postmodernist fiction come from its involvement in the logic, the metaphysics really, of tautology. Some Jewish American writers define themselves primarily against this logic, maintaining the validity of the particular and the historical, of existences not essences, of that which we cannot create by the fiat of our imperial self. What matters really is the work a writer can do with the feeling of difference. Cynthia Ozick manifests her oppositional difference by turning post-modernism against itself, using postmodernist techniques to undermine postmodernist values and reaffirm traditional Jewish moral values of conscientiousness and respect for the limits of the self, in a word, *menschlikeit*.

In 'A Mercenary' from *Bloodshed and Three Novellas* (1976) she takes on the postmodernist doctrine of identity as a fictive construct, that who you are is the series of the roles you play. The novella begins 'Stanislav Lushinski, a Pole and a diplomat, was not a Polish diplomat.' Lushinski, when still a child, had escaped from Poland during the Second World War, finding eventual refuge in a small African country which he now represents in the United Nations. He is the ultimate *luftmensch*, living in New York and representing an African country but not an American, not an African, not even, as eventually becomes clear, unequivocally a Pole. He anticipates contingencies by keeping several bags permanently packed along with several passports offering a choice of identities and nationalities. Not surprisingly, he becomes a popular New York television personality.

> And somehow – because he had mocked and parodied, sitting under the cameras absurdly smiling and replete with contradictions, the man heard telling the boy, Pole putting himself out as African, candor offering cunning – an uneasy blossom of laughter opened up in his listeners, the laughter convinced: he was making himself up. He had made himself over and now he was making himself up, like one of those kind of comedians who tell uproarious anecdotes about their preposterious relatives.

Lushinski is not merely a person who frequently talks ironically. Rather he is ontologically ironic, this being his power and his limitation.

> Sometimes he wished he could write out of imagination: he fan-
> cied a small memoir, as crowded with desires as with black leafy
> woods, or else sharp and deathly as a blizzard, and at the the same
> time very brief and chaste, though full of horror. But he was too
> intelligent to be a writer. His intelligence was a version of cynicism.
> He rolled irony like an extra liquid in his mouth . . . . It gave
> him power.

Lushinski's lightness of being mostly takes harmless forms, as with the
officer's uniform of high rank but no specific nationality he orders from
a Paris tailor and uses to get the best table in European restaurants. But
Lushinski's main ironic as well as diplomatic triumph is to contrive a
brief 'war' so as to raise the price of his country's main export. 'A
month after the "war" – the quotation marks were visible in Lushinski's
enunciation: what was it but a combination of village riots and semi-
strikes? only two hundred or so people killed, one of them unfortunately
the Dt' poet L'Duy – the price of the indispensable cuttings rose sixty
per cent, increasing gross national income by two thirds.' It is possible
that L'Duy, about whom no more is heard, was not an ironist and thus
unable to appreciate the joke of his real death in a fictitious war. Eventually we discover that Lushinski's evasion of ultimate destiny is part of a
lifelong flight from the historically determinate identity of a Jewish boy
who by luck and cunning escaped the holocaust. His evasion of Jewish
identity is concomitant to his moral failure, both based on the emotional
coldness Wisse and Howe consider antithetical to Jewish identity.

   'A Mercenary' targets a Jewish writer who repudiated Jewish themes,
that is, Jerzy Kosinski, who was even known to use an army uniform in
exactly the fashion of Lushinski and whose novel *The Painted Bird* (1965)
is clearly the 'small memoir' that Lushinski does not write.[16] 'A Mercenary', then, is in a sense Ozick's usurpation of Kosinski's story and implicitly a judgement of its cold irony as a form of ethnic denial. Another
story in *Bloodshed* links with 'A Mercenary' in playing on usurpation of
other people's writings (or selves). This is 'Usurpation (Other People's
Stories)'. The protagonist of 'Usurpation' declares 'all stories are rip-offs
. . . . Shakespeare stole his plots, Dostoevsky dug them out of the
newspaper. Everybody steals. The *Decameron's* stolen. Whatever looks
like invention is theft.' In her preface to *Bloodshed* Ozick carefully notes
how 'Usurpation' itself draws on and conflates Bernard Malamud's 'The
Magic Crown', an anecdote in a story by S. Y. Agnon, a story about
Agnon by David Stern and a Yiddish poem by Tchernikovsky. Though
Ozick's story has a remarkable number of plot turns in its small space
her basic principle is illustrated in the story within the story that the
devout Jewish writer Agnon, tells to the ghost of the pagan Jewish
writer Tchernikovsky and in the latter's response. The story actually
derives from Agnon but Ozick gives it another layer of significance by

making Tchernikovsky its auditor, contrasting his postmodernist cynicism to Agnon's *menschlikeit*. In Agnon's story the Messiah decides to appear in a synagogue when called by the prayer 'I believe in the coming of the Messiah, and even if he tarry I will await his coming every day.' But the congregation has its mind on other things so that 'the prayer is obscured, all its syllables are drowned in dailiness, and the Messiah retreats; he has not heard himself summoned'. Tchernikovsky praises the story but for the wrong reasons, as Agnon discerns: 'It was clear to me that what he liked about the story was mostly its climactic stroke: that the Messiah is prevented from coming. I had written to lament the tarrying of the Messiah; Tchernikovsky, it seemed, took satisfaction in exactly what I mourned.' Ozick thus attacks postmodernist cynicism with postmodernist devices. In 'A Mercenary' she subverts postmodernist identity and in 'Usurpation' she employs the postmodernist plot device of multiple literary reflections to favour a traditional Jewish religious humanism.

The most engaging of Ozick's stories are the two about Puttermesser in *Levitation: Five Fictions* (1982). 'Puttermesser: Her Work History, Her Ancestry, Her Afterlife' introduces Ruth Puttermesser, a bureaucrat in New York City government, the sort of highly competent and undervalued professional who does the work for which an incompetent political appointee receives credit. She has daydreams not of self-advancement nor even erotic fulfilment but of municipal progress, New York as Eden – a self-indulgence Ozick significantly links with her passion for chocolate fudge. What seems to keep Puttermesser properly earthbound is her relation to her Uncle Zindel, who is teaching her not only Yiddish but *menschlikeit*, the Jewish wisdom of the heart. But this is Ozick's joke precisely on the lack of such roots for present-day Jewish Americans. The narrator calls a halt: 'Stop. Stop, stop! Puttermesser's biographer, stop. Disengage please.' We find that Uncle Zindel died four years before Puttermesser was born. She embodies in her fantasy of him a world now lost, precisely the irony Robert Alter examines in his essay 'Sentimentalizing the Jews': 'Ironically, what most American Jewish writers are outsiders to is that very body of Jewish experience with which other Americans expect them to be almost completely at home.' Ozick herself noted that John Updike's invented Jew, Bech, though ersatz, was hardly more so than some actual Jewish American intellectuals.[17] Yet there is a validity in Puttermesser's earnest yearnings for an identity both ethically meaningful and historically rooted.

Her fine and foolish ideals get wondrously out of hand in the sequel, 'Puttermesser and Xanthippe'. The first Puttermesser story ends with a challenge: 'Hey! Puttermesser's biographer! What will you do with her now?' What she does is allow Puttermesser to act out her utopian daydream. First there is a delicately comic reprise of the dream, honouring its decency but not missing its absurdity.

Every day, inside the wide bleak corridors of the Municipal Building, Puttermesser dreamed an ideal Civil Service: devotion to
polity, the citizen's sweet love of the citizenry, the light rule of
reason and common sense, the City as a miniature country
crowded with patriots – not fools and jingoists, but patriots true
and serene; humorous affection for the idiosyncrasies of one's distinctive homeland, joy in the Bronx, elation in Queens, O happy
Richmond! Children on roller skates, and over the Brooklyn
Bridge the long patchwork-colored line of joggers, breathing hard
above the homeland-hugging green waters. (1)

Forced out of her job by a political shark, abandoned by her lover –
who is angered at her insistence on finishing Plato's *Theaetetus* before
making love – Puttermesser is driven back to her fantasies and discovers
to her shock that somehow, without remembering it, she has created the
first female golem – in Jewish folklore a creature made of mud, enliv-
ened by a magic spell and sent on missions of revenge by its creator. She
becomes Puttermesser's means of putting into practice her 'PLAN' to re-
suscitate, reform, reinvigorate and redeem the city of New York. With
the golem's indispensable aid, Puttermesser is elected mayor, expels the
politicians from the municipal temple and, for a time, brings joy to the
Bronx and elation to Queens. But the failure of the utopia is inherent in
its sources, as when the golem insists on being named Xanthippe after
the shrewish wife of the idealist Socrates. In *Theaetetus* Plato tells the
story of the philosopher who falls down a well because too absorbed in
contemplating the stars. Puttermesser's idealism has led her into imagining an eighteenth-century republican Eden, an idyllic realm too neat and
rational to exist in any time or place, much less New York in the twentieth century. Moreover, in creating the golem she has violated the second commandment, against idolatry, which Ozick believes is the major
temptation of our time, our updated version of golden calves being ideologies. Ozick is imaginatively playing with the ethical limits to imagination, using fantasy against itself. Puttermesser finally proves a good
enough Jew to recognize that she has become the golem's golem and
destroy the extravagant creature of her imagination.

Saul Bellow: high principles and low facts in Chicago and New York

Saul Bellow is the most resourceful American novelist since Faulkner in
his use of his historical situation. The son of Russian Jewish immigrants,

Bellow was born in Montreal in 1915 but soon transplanted to Chicago and a life oppositional in its very structure: the subculture of traditional orthodox Jewish piety on the one hand, and the streets of Chicago, 'that center of brutal materialism', on the other.[18] Jewish intellectuals in the 1920s and 1930s could find a form for their spiritual intensity in radical political ideology after their loss of faith in orthodox Judaism but Bellow, after an initial attraction, had already participated in the 1940s reaction from radical politics before his literary career began in earnest. With a college degree in anthropology, an autodidact's familiarity with the 'great books' of European thought as well as the canon of American literature that emerged in the 1940s, Bellow could put into oppositional play an intimate childhood experience of traditional Judaic piety along with an intense involvement with various powerful and mutually competitive ideological systems, to all of which Bellow responded and to none of which he was bound. In Bellow's capacious prose Plato and Emerson jostle Freud and Marx with a ritual chanting of Jewish prayers in the background. Though one could hardly imagine an environment less apparently conducive to cultural accomplishment than the Chicago of Bellow's young manhood – unless it be the Mississippi of Faulkner's – we can see now that for a writer alert to contradictory possibilities it was the key to the candy store.

From the beginning Bellow thinks *against* prevailing doctrine, as in his youthful response to the massive pressure of the Chicago world: 'Before I was capable of thinking clearly, my resistance to its material weight took the form of obstinacy.'[19] He has made a career out of resistance to the strongest cultural force of the moment. For an apprentice novelist this is usually the force of a regnant style, a style that dances out a culturally fashionable attitude. In Bellow's first novel, *Dangling Man*, this force was Hemingway.

> This is an era of hard-boileddom. . . . Do you have feelings?
> There are correct and incorrect ways of indicating them. Do you
> have an inner life? It is nobody's business but your own. Do you
> have emotions? Strangle them. . . . Most serious matters are
> closed to the hardboiled. They are unpracticed in introspection,
> and therefore badly equipped to deal with opponents whom they
> cannot shoot like big game or outdo in daring.
>
> If you have difficulties, grapple with them silently, goes one of
> their commandments. To hell with that! I intend to talk about
> mine, and if I had as many mouths as Siva has arms and kept
> them going all the time, I still could not do myself justice.

This defiant assertion of the right to full emotional self-expression is one of the earliest instances of what critics came to define as a specifically Jewish attitude. A minor character, Schlossberg, in his second novel,

The Victim (1947) wonderfully elaborates a dialectical version of *menschlikeit*.

> You shut one eye and look at a thing, and it is one way to you. You shut the other one and it is different. I am as sure about greatness and beauty as you are about black and white. If a human life is a great thing to me, it is a great thing. Do you know better? I'm entitled as much as you. And why be measly? Do you have to be? Is somebody holding you by the neck? Have dignity, you understand me? Choose dignity. Nobody knows enough to turn it down.

As early as his first two novels Bellow had a method – the dialectical play of ideas, and a theme – the quest for a *modus vivendi* both ethically responsible and open to possibility. But from Bellow's later perspective these two novels seem somewhat measly, *too* well made, too responsive to cultural constraint: 'I had good reason to fear that I would be put down as a foreigner, an interloper. It was made clear to me that when I studied literature in the university that as a Jew and the son of Russian Jews I would probably never have the right *feeling* for Anglo-Saxon traditions, for English words.' Consequently, he worked in relation to a formalist, Flaubertian perfection in these first novels, one which repressed his creative energy: 'A writer should be able to express himself easily, naturally, copiously in a form which frees his mind, his energies. Why should he hobble himself with formalities? With a borrowed sensibility?'[20] *The Adventures of Augie March* was Bellow's breakthrough novel, in which he elaborated at long novel length the emergent Yiddish-inflected voice anticipated by Schlossberg's monologue in *The Victim*. This voice specializes in juxtaposing the contrarities of a Chicago world in which one grew up with Emerson as precept and Al Capone as example: ' "Give all to love," they read in Emerson. But in City Hall there were other ideas on giving, and we had to learn (if we could) how to reconcile high principles with low facts.'[21] This reconciliation proceeds on the levels of style, structure and play of ideas.

Style and structure in *The Adventures of Augie March* reflect the quirky, primarily self-educated perspective of the first-person narrator, Augie. Unlike Bellow, who not only graduated from college but eventually became a university professor, Augie is a college drop-out. Yet Bellow remembers the best part of his education was random, what he was reading on the side always more useful to him than his formal courses. Augie's education is not only random but illicit. He earns his way through two years of college by stealing books, reading the more interesting ones before passing them on to his fence. His sometime employer, Einhorn, adds to his education by giving him a set of the Harvard classics, scorched from a fire Einhorn had arranged in an attempted insurance fraud. Thus, Augie's high principles derive from texts acquired by low means. There are advantages to this haphazard mode of education. The formally educated person is limited by his/her formal relation to ideas, the sense of their embeddedness in a bygone culture as well as in the ongoing culture of the academic establishment. While this enables perspective, it attenuates response in contrast to the self-educated person who rather than 'placing' an idea or a person, reacts to them immediately as fresh voices, as guides to behaviour. To the autodidact reading consists not of subject matter but of instruments of discovery and models of possibility. Augie reads the Harvard classics in the same manner in which sixteenth-century Englishmen read Plutarch. He finds perfectly reasonable Einhorn's casting of himself as an updated Socrates playing to Augie as the somewhat unreliable disciple, Alcibiades.

> We had title just as good as the chain mail English kings had to Brutus. If you want to pick your own ideal creature in the mirror coastal air and sharp leaves of ancient perfections and be at home where a great mankind was at home, I've never seen any reason why not. Though unable to go along one hundred percent with a man like Reverend Beecher telling his congregation, 'Ye are as Gods, you are crystalline, your faces are radiant!' I'm not an optimist of that degree, from the actual faces, congregated or separate that I've seen; always admitting that the true vision of things is a gift, particularly in times of special disfigurement and world-wide Babylonishness, when plug-ugly macadam and volcanic peperino look commoner than crystal – to eyes with an ordinary amount of grace, anyhow – and when it appears like a good sensible policy to settle for medium-grade quartz. I wonder where in the creation there would be much of a double-take at the cry of 'Homo sum!'

This passage illustrates Augie's characteristic associative structure and stylistic juxtaposition of formal and colloquial speech registers as British mythology combines with the transcendental idealism of Henry Ward Beecher, a nineteenth-century American minister, who is cited as if from yesterday's newspaper, then questioned by way of Spengler's concept of Babylonishness, a degenerate urban stage of history that disallows the crystalline look, with a possible allusion to Jonathan Edwards's Calvinist theory of perception that only those endowed with Grace see the true beauty of the world, the whole riff concluding a sentence that juxtaposes the American colloquialism 'double-take' with a quotation from the Roman playwright, Terence 'Homo sum!' History collapses in a galli-maufrey that suggests the unquoted conclusion to Terence's line, '*humani nil a me alienum puto*' – 'I am a man. I think nothing human alien to me.' Augie can compare his hapless mother to 'those women whom

Zeus got the better of in animal form and next had to take cover from his furious wife' though he qualifies that he cannot envision her as the victim of such 'classy wrath', the vulgarism of 'classy' counterposing the classical comparison.

In Emersonian terms, Augie is not a philosopher but man thinking. Augie is in the Emersonian mode in his eclecticism, his associative logic, his variation of stylistic registers. Bellow's novel is a calculated play on the American Adam romance tradition of evasion of fixated social identity, its title an obvious echo of *The Adventures of Huckleberry Finn*. Like Huck, Augie is less the actor in his narrative than a reactor to the busy plotting of the odd characters he encounters. Bellow discovers a convention central in most of his fiction from here on, the protagonist's encounters with a series of what Bellow, in *Herzog*, terms 'reality instructors', powerful personalities who try to proselytize the protagonist to accept their competing systems of 'reality'. Augie goes along with the schemes of 'those Machiavellis of small street and neighborhood' only to a point because though recognizing 'there was something adoptional about me' (9), he also has 'opposition in me, and great desire to offer resistance and to say "No!"' ' Ultimately, 'I never had accepted determination and wouldn't become what other people wanted to make of me' (7). Though it seems dubious that an identity or vocation can be found solely in evasion, Augie has a salient identity for the reader so long as he keeps talking, which is just what his very fluidity enables. In the novel's last passage, one that implicitly rebuts the melancholic conclusion of Fitzgerald's *The Great Gatsby*, Augie refuses the closure of disillusionment.

> Look at me, going everywhere! Why, I am a sort of Columbus of those near-at-hand and believe you can come to them in this immediate *terra incognita* that spreads out in every gaze. I may well be a flop at this line of endeavor. Columbus too thought he was a flop, probably, when they sent him back in chains. Which didn't prove there was no America. (26)

The Adventures of Augie March provided an agenda for Bellow's literary career, refining on the obtrusively artificial 'Spirit of Alternatives' of *Dangling Man* by the invention of reality instructors and opening up language and plot from the constraints of the well-made novel. Yet not only does Bellow keep coming at the same themes from different angles but each new novel tends to respond dialectically to the preceeding one. So *The Adventures of Augie March*, a brilliant free-form novel but too long by half, somewhat overcheerful and where the parts add up to more than the sum of the whole, is succeeded by Bellow's tightest, best-made novel, set in a twilight world of constricted possibility.

Indeed, Tommy Wilhelm, the protagonist of *Seize the Day* (1956), is so constricted that he has trouble breathing. Throughout the novel he feels congested, suffocated; he feels as if he is drowning, going down for the third time. He is, in fact, overweight but Bellow is also borrowing from the psychoanalyst William Reich the concept of 'character armour'. The purpose of character armour is to repress emotion and one of its physical manifestations is precisely the constriction of the chest from which Wilhelm suffers. Wilhelm is oppressed by what one of Augie March's Chicago friends calls *moha*, 'a Navajo word, and also Sanskrit, meaning opposition of the finite. It is the Bronx cheer of the conditioning forces. Love is the only answer to *moha*, being infinite. I mean all the forms of love, eros, agape, libido, philia and ecstasy' (22). Wilhelm is doubly oppressed, having invested in, of all finite items, lard in the commodities market. Bellow is playing on Karl Marx's analysis of commodity fetishism in *Capital*: as human agents mistakenly attribute agency and autonomy to the market process of commodity exchange, really their own collective invention, they lose any sense of their own agency and autonomy to the point where they retain value for themselves only insofar as they see themselves *as* commodities. Wilhelm has tried to be an actor, then become a salesman, two obvious instances of selling a commoditized image of self. He is trying to regain financial independence and social recognition by investing in the very market world which has devalued him. Moreover, lard is a poor investment for a man drowning in his own fat. Finally, he is becoming aware of a return of the repressed, that is, repressed spiritual needs. He remembers fragments of poems read in a college introduction to literature, passages from Shelley, Keats and, most significantly, from Milton's 'Lycidas', a poem in which a death by drowning leads to profound reflections on spiritual vocation and redemption. In Bellow's complex joke, Wilhelm's financial and spiritual dilemma can be summed up in what at first glance is Wilhelm's reflection only on the former: 'They had bought all that lard. It had to rise today' (1).

Though one of Bellow's darkest and most distressing novels, *Seize the Day* is also one of his funniest, this being what keeps it bearable. Vulgar expression offsets depressing observation, as in Wilhelm's horror at the 'cynicism of successful people'.

> Cynicism was bread and meat to everyone. And irony, too. Maybe it couldn't be helped. It was probably even necessary. Wilhelm, however, feared it intensely. Whenever at the end of a day he was unusually fatigued he attributed it to cynicism. Too much of the world's business done. Too much falsity. He had various words to express the effect this had on him. Chicken! Unclean! Congestion! he exclaimed in his heart. Rat race! Phony! Murder! Play the game! Buggers! (1)

Wilhelm ends up a heartfelt prayer with 'Let me out of this clutch and into a different life. For I am all balled up. Have mercy' (1).

Bellow's novel equivocates about one central theme: whether Wilhelm's sorrow is mere masochistic self-indulgence in a misery predictably resulting from his consistently bad choices. The question is explicit.

> But at the same time, since there were depths in Wilhelm not sus-
> pected by himself, he received a suggestion from some remote ele-
> ment in his thoughts that the business of life, the real business –
> to carry his peculiar burden, to feel shame and impotence, to taste
> these quelled fears – the only important business, the highest busi-
> ness was being done. Maybe the making of mistakes expressed the
> very purpose of his life and the essence of his being here. Maybe
> he was supposed to make them and suffer from them here on this
> earth. And though he had raised himself above Mr Perls and his
> father because they adored money, still they were called to act en-
> ergetically and this was better than to yell and cry, pray and beg,
> poke and blunder and go by fits and starts and fall upon the
> thorns of life. And finally sink beneath that watery floor – would
> that be tough luck, or would it be good riddance? (4)

Every feeling, thought and action of Wilhelm can be seen either as a pathological masochistic pattern deterministically working itself out, or as a sign of the authenticity of suffering and of the needs of the heart denied by a cynical and materialistic culture. This double coding is heightened in the ending where Wilhelm's chest armour dissolves into tears as he is caught up by a procession past the open coffin of a com-plete stranger. Wilhelm is either projecting his masochistic self-pity or intuiting the human community of suffering and death, Bellow leaving to the reader to decide. Thus a year before the publication of *The Assistant* Bellow had skated a complete circle around the theme of *menschlikeit*.

In *Henderson the Rain King* (1959), however, Bellow out-universalizes even Malamud in generalizing *menschlikeit* well beyond its Jewish sour-ces. Though represented as an Anglo-Saxon of aristocratic origins, Hen-derson *sounds* as Jewish as any other Bellow protagonist, more, in fact, than most. It is true that Bellow always uses characters didactically, as position papers, as it were. Yet in other of his novels the didactic func-tion of these characters is reinforced by their specific gravity as shrewdly observed, recognizable creatures of the city, their Chicago or New York speech and manners as visible as stigmata. The Africans of *Henderson the Rain King* are purely literary inventions though Bellow does play his last best trick with Reich's ideas by inventing a royal African reality instruc-tor, well educated in Europe, who attempts to cure Henderson's spiritual ills not with ancient tribal wisdom but with Reichian therapy.

The most popular of Bellow's protagonists is the title character of *Herzog* (1964). This novel is best remembered for a fresh narrative invention, Herzog's imaginary letters to seminal modern thinkers, living and dead. Herzog himself became the most 'adoptional' literary character since Holden Caulfield. In fact, he is too cuddlesome by half and some of the popularity of the book may derive from its implicit appeal to the reader to indulge the protagonist's masochistic narcissism. Despite major external differences, Herzog is essentially a reprise of Tommy Wilhelm and Wilhelm is the more convincing characterization. The following description, which is of Herzog, could apply to either.

> His face revealed what a beating he had taken. But he had asked
> to be beaten too, and had lent his attackers strength. That
> brought him to consider his character. What sort of character was
> it? Well, in the modern vocabulary, it was narcissistic; it was
> masochistic; it was anachronistic. His clinical picture was depressive –
> not the severest type; not a manic depressive.

Readers tend to identify directly with Salinger's Holden Caulfield, casting themselves as tender-hearted victims. Readers do not identify with Moses Herzog so much as adopt him, cherishing him as the mascot of *menschlikeit*: he suffers for our cynicisms. In contrast, readers want to stay as far away from Tommy Wilhelm as they can get lest some of his failure and misery rub off on them. If one is wary of the sneaky attraction of narcissism mixed with masochism, this makes Wilhelm's characterization the more interesting test of a reader. Bellow carefully reduces his appeal by making him lardy in physique, constricted in the chest, vulgar in his language and banal in his circumstances. He is too clearly needy for any reader to want to inhabit, as with Holden, or adopt, as with Herzog. Yet the quest for spiritual meaning is, if anything, stronger in *Seize the Day* than in *Herzog*, because presented not as the special wish of an alienated intellectual but as a cry from the city streets. Wilhelm struggles to conceive some possibility of community, 'a larger body', in a seemingly Hobbesian world where each is against all and all against God.

> The idea of this larger body had been planted in him a few days
> ago beneath Times Square, when he had gone downtown to pick
> up tickets for the baseball game on Saturday . . . . He was
> going through an underground corridor, a place he had always
> hated and hated more than ever now. On the walls between the
> advertisements were words in chalk: 'Sin No More,' and 'Do Not
> Eat the Pig,' he had particularly noticed. And in the dark tunnel,
> in the haste, heat, and darkness which disfigure and make freaks
> and fragments of nose and eyes and teeth, all of a sudden,

unsought, a general love for all these imperfect and lurid-looking
people burst out in Wilhelm's breast. He loved them. One and
all, he passionately loved them. They were his brothers and his
sisters. He was imperfect and disfigured himself, but what difference did that make if he was united with them by this blaze of
love? And as he walked by he began to say, 'Oh my brothers –
my brothers and my sisters,' blessing them as well as himself.

This is one pole of the dialectic; the other follows apace.

On that very same afternoon he didn't hold so high an opinion of
this same onrush of loving kindness. What did it come to? As
they had the capacity and must use it once in a while, people
were bound to have such involuntary feelings. It was only
another one of those subway things, like having a hard-on at
random. But today, his day of reckoning, he consulted his memory
again and again and thought, I must go back to that, that's the
right clue and may do me the most good. Something very big.
Truth, like. (5)

The idea recurs in *Herzog* but without such effective dialectical play of
turn and turn and turn again. Herzog's ideas seem preformulated, those
of the philosopher rather than of man thinking (or, in Tommy's case,
man groping for thought). The ideas in *Herzog* are plentiful but less
flexible, dramatic and dialectical. *Herzog*'s antagonists seem simplistic,
melodramatic villains of modernism. In contrast, never are the characters
in *Seize the Day*, not only Wilhelm but his chief antagonist, his father,
and his main reality instructor, Dr Tamkin, mere foils to Wilhelm;
rather, they are so convincingly themselves that the reader may have
trouble remembering that they are the creations of Bellow's imagination.
The main plot in *Herzog* reads uncomfortably like a *roman á clef* in which
some private revenge is being taken, the characters seeming in need of
some external referent for completion: who *really* is Herzog's wife
Madeleine, and is she really quite *that* dreadful? The most convincing
part of the novel is Herzog's letters, a running polemic against modernist
dogma. These are more interesting in themselves than as revelations of
Herzog's character. In fact, Herzog seems less a character who has these
ideas than a narrative device for releasing them.

Arthur Sammler, of *Mr Sammler's Planet* (1970), is a reaction to the
sentimentalized conception of Herzog. Devastated and angry, quite lacking Herzog's cuteness, Sammler is more convincing than his antagonists
who are even more clearly straw men (and women) than those in
Herzog. The result is a strong but grudging, unpleasant book.

Humboldt's Gift (1975) is more effectively dialectical and nuanced.
The main question in *Humboldt's Gift* was most concisely formulated in

Bellow's 1951 short story 'Looking for Mr Green'. The protagonist of this story, though well educated, can only, in depression America, find a job delivering cheques to a transient group of welfare recipients. He feels an ethical obligation to do this well and becomes obsessively concerned with finding the elusive Mr Green. Finally his exasperated supervisor asks him a characteristically Bellovian question: 'Were you brought up tenderly, with permission to go and find out what were the last things that everything else stands for while everybody else labors in the false world of appearances?' In the event, the protagonist compromises by delivering the cheque to a person who says she represents Mr Green, clearly a dubious claim in the fallen world of appearances. The mix of Christian ('last things', 'fallen world') with Platonic concepts represents Bellow's career-long quest for a convincing language of the spirit, one that tries to apprehend the last things everything else stands for *in* the fallen world of appearances.

In Bellow's earlier novels the quest is formulated in a predominantly modernist secular intellectual vocabulary, but in *Humboldt's Gift*, though there is Bellow's usual witty play with his Alexandrian library of modern ideas, a religious vocabulary fully displaces the psychological one, a trend apparent from *Seize the Day* on. In an interview, Bellow speculates that it is no longer sex but spirituality which our society represses.

> Probably the place left vacant by the movement of the Freudian unconscious upward has been occupied by religion. It is certainly hard to see how modern man could survive on what he gets now from his conscious life – especially now that there is a kind of veto against impermissible thoughts, the most impermissible being the notion that man might have a spiritual life he's not conscious of.[22]

In *Humboldt's Gift* such serious themes are negotiated with an engaging lightness of touch. Charlie Citrine, the narrator protagonist, has problems similar to *Herzog* – a malevolent ex-wife is attempting to destroy him financially, modern life oppresses him, reality instructors bully him – but somehow he manages to float all these difficulties in a tone of speculative bemusement. As always Bellow works by the principle of opposition, with the major conflict again between spiritual reality and the pressing weight of the material world. Citrine, like the persona of Shelley's 'Adonais', finds himself 'sunk in the glassy depths of life and groping, thrillingly and desperately, for sense, a person keenly aware of painted veils, of Maya, of domes of many colored glass staining the white radiance of eternity, quivering in the intense inane and so on'. 'And so on' reminds us that Citrine is an erudite intellectual able to spin out stuff like this on demand but also, as with Augie March, someone for whom these ideas are immediate and optional. Later he observes,

'The painted veil isn't what it used to be. The damn thing is wearing out. Like a roller-towel in a Mexican men's room.' Citrine, largely speaking for Bellow, has the habit of mind of 'elevating. . . mean considerations to the theoretical level', as, when hearing the dial tone of a telephone, 'I identified this interminable squalling with the anxiety level of the disengaged soul.' As in *The Adventures of Augie March* and *Seize the Day*, such play against conceptual decorum makes for a comedy inclusive of moral and spiritual intimations. Corrupt and brutal Chicago presents an obvious obstacle to pure spirit yet has its own intoxicating, absurd vivacity. It contains such marvels as the patrons of the Russian Bath who, 'cast in antique form', are a vision of a gross materiality justified by its own irrefutable presence.

> They have swelling buttocks and fatty breasts as yellow as buttermilk. They stand on thick pillar legs affected with a sort of creeping verdigris or blue-cheese mottling of the ankles. After steaming, these old fellows eat enormous snacks of bread and salt herring or large ovals of salami and dripping skirt-steak and they drink schnapps. They could knock down walls with their hard stout old-fashioned bellies. Things are very elemental here. You feel that these people are almost conscious of obsolescence, of a line of evolution abandoned by nature and culture.

A more modernized representative of Chicago is the would-be Mafioso Rinaldo Cantibile who has carefully pounded every square inch of Citrine's Mercedes 280–SL with a baseball bat, a moving narrative invention. But even this hoodlum, aptly described by Citrine as 'smoky souled', has some intellectual pretensions, justifying himself by citations of Robert Ardrey and Konrad Lorenz: his criminal violence is just his mode of responding to 'the territorial imperative'. As Citrine notes, 'Nowadays the categories are grasped by those who belong to them and Cantabile, one of the new mental rabble of the wised-up world', has ideas that descend from thinkers like Sorel, who envisioned acts of exalted violence to shock the bourgeoisie: 'Although he didn't know who Sorel was, these theories do get around and find people to exemplify them. . . .'

Cantabile wants to show up Citrine's idealism partly because it attracts and threatens him. Citrine has, in a way, invited the aggression: 'It was only right that I should pay a price for coming on so innocent and expecting the protection of those less pure, of people completely at home in the fallen world. Where did I get off, laying the fallen world on everyone else!' For the world anterior to the fallen one Citrine's authorities are Plato, Shelley and, above all, Rudolph Steiner's anthroposophy, a blend of mysticism and spiritual philosophy. Bellow uses Steiner partly because he is an offbeat, unaccredited source, offering more possibilities for metaphorical development than some familiar, contextualized figure, the same advantage offered by Reich as opposed to Freud. The purpose is not parody or satire; Reich's concept of 'character armour' worked to reveal Tommy Wilhelm and Bellow has asserted his respect for Steiner's ideas. The method is apparent as Citrine explains Steiner's idea of our contact in sleep with supernatural beings.

> Through the vibrations and echoes of what we have thought and felt and said we commune as we sleep with the beings of the hierarchy. But now, our daily monkeyshines are such, our preoccupations are so low, language has become so debased, the words so blunted and damaged, we've said such stupid and dull things, that the higher beings hear only babbling and grunting and TV commercials – the dog-food level of things. This says nothing to them. What pleasure can these higher beings take in this kind of materialism, devoid of higher thought or poetry? As a result, all we can hear in sleep is matter creaking and hissing and washing, the rustling of plants, and the air conditioning. So we are incomprehensible to the higher beings. They can't influence us and they themselves suffer a corresponding privation.

This lovely imagining of higher beings interpenetrating the everyday world is an instance of the 'lifelong intimation' that Citrine – and, clearly, Bellow – pursues. It is true that, as Citrine recounts, another writer, Franz Kafka, hit Steiner on a bad day. Suffering from a bad cold Steiner 'kept working his handkerchief deep into his nostrils with his fingers' as the ultra-fastidious Kafka, come in quest of a new articulation of *his* intimation of pure spirit, looked on in horror, an instance of the anomalies of the spiritual quest in a material world. But, as Augie March would remind us, Columbus's flop did not prove there was no America. Once again Bellow manages the equilibrium of *menschlikeit*, high idealism balanced against the comedy of the material life.

Are there Jews in America?

Jewish American identity and literature may have become a victim of its own success. We have seen how the universalizing of Jewish identity in the concept of *menschlikeit* leads to various complications: if suffering is intrinsically Jewish, is everyone who suffers a Jew? Frank Alpine, it is true, supplements suffering with circumcision but since the 1930s most Americans have been circumcised, thus removing another ground of distinction. For that matter, is the Jewish embrace of suffering rather perverse, open to the suspicion of masochism? Bellow's novels do an elegant toe-dance around this question. How to take Tommy Wilhelm's suffering heart is the central dilemma in *Seize the Day* whereas Augie March is more of an American Adam, evading the pain almost gratuitously shouldered by Wilhelm and a host of Malamud characters. But then, is what makes Augie Jewish primarily his Yiddish-inflected patter? And if even this identity marker goes the way of the fast-disappearing Southern accent, what then will distinguish a specific Jewish quality to American fiction? Of course, there will continue to be Americans of Jewish ancestry who write notable fiction but if the books were anonymous, could we tell? Could we tell, in fact, about Salinger, Mailer or Heller? Heller did write a novel about a Jewish American diplomat and a historical novel about the biblical King David, but the former, the hero of *Good as Gold*, seems no *more* Jewish than Updike's Bech. Moreover, besides the problems of a dubious essentialism and an overextended universalism in grounding Jewish identity in *menschlikeit*, there is a limiting factor as well – the now embarrassing gender-specificity of it. Perhaps Ozick supplies the lack in her comic and judicious version of it in Puttermesser, but Puttermesser's desire for civility, however ardent, does not seem adequate as an ethnic differentiating trait.

All this leaves the question open to the postmodernist deconstructions of Philip Roth, who, as we shall see in Chapter 6, is dubious about any form of integral identity. Moreover most American Jews have become so socially assimilated, so intermarried, as to disappear into the American blend. Leslie Fiedler claims to have parlayed his identity as 'literary Fiedler on the roof of academe' to an assimilative success that threatens to cancel out its origins.[23] Perhaps Jewish American literary identity will continue to find a motive simply in trying to prove it exists. Moreover, there are signs of a renewed interest in their Judaic heritage among the younger generation of Jewish Americans. But in the apparent absence of an emergent figure with the force of Malamud, Bellow or Ozick, the question remains open.

Notes

1. Ruth R. Wisse, *The Schlemiehl as Modern Hero* (Chicago, 1971), p. 82.

2. Irving Howe, 'Introduction to Yiddish Literature' in Irving Malin and Irwin Stark (eds) *Breakthrough: A Treasury of Contemporary American Jewish Literature* (Philadelphia, 1964), p. 300.

3. Reynolds Price, *A Common Room: Essays 1954–1987*, (New York, 1988), p. 169.

4. Robert Alter, *After the Tradition: Essays on Modern Jewish Writing* (New York, 1959), p. 18.

5. P. Shiv Kumar, *Tablet Breakers in the American Wilderness* (Delhi, 1981), p. xviii.

6. There was, of course, a signifcant body of Jewish American fiction before the 1950s breakthough. The first notable Jewish American novel was Abraham Cahan's *The Rise of David Levinsky* (1917) which established the enduring convention that worldly rise equates to spiritual fall from essential Jewish values. In the 1930s Michael Gold's *Jews Without Money* examined life in the urban ghetto from a revolutionary perspective and Daniel Fuchs wrote pungent novels about Jewish low life in Brooklyn before departing for Hollywood to make his fortune as a screenwriter. Henry Roth's *Call It Sleep* (1934), now acknowledged as the classic Jewish American novel of the pre-Bellow era, was, however, too unseasonable to have an impact and remained largely unread and unrecognized until the 1960s. Published in the midst of the depression, Roth's novel concentrates with lyric intensity on the subjective vision of its protagonist, a boy whose quest is psychological and spiritual rather than political and economic. Perfect for the 1950s, *Call It Sleep* was thought self indulgent and irrelevant in 1934, another illustration of the influence of reigning paradigms of critical reception. The only Jewish American writer of the time who would now be considered on a par with Roth was Nathaniel West, born Nathan Weinstein, but though West was a Jew, an American and a writer, he is generally not considered a Jewish American writer, given that in his two finest novels, *Miss Lonelyhearts* (1933) and *The Day of the Locust* (1939), neither the characters nor themes are Jewish.

7. Irving Howe, *World of Our Fathers* (New York,1976), p. 586.

8. Leslie Fiedler, *Waiting for the End* (New York, 1964), p. 47; Louis Harap, *In the Mainstream: The Jewish Presence in Twentieth-Century American Literature, 1950–1980* (New York, 1978), p. 19.

9. Leslie A. Field and Joyce W. Field, 'Malamud, Mercy and Menschlikeit' in Field and Field (eds) *Bernard Malamud: A Collection of Critical Essays* (Englewood Cliffs, New Jersey, 1975), p. 7.

10. Cynthia Ozick, *Art and Ardor* (New York, 1983), pp. 90–112.

11. Philip Roth, 'Imagining Jews' in Joel Salzberg (ed.) *Critical Essays on Bernard Malamud* (Boston, 1987), p. 100.

12. Alfred Kazin, *Contemporaries* (New York, 1982), p. 208.

13. See Sam B. Girgus, 'In Search of Real America' in Harold Bloom (ed.), *Bernard Malamud: Modern Critical Views* (New Haven, 1986), p. 213; Leslie Fiedler, 'The Many Names of S. Levin: An Essay in Genre Criticism' in Astro and Benson, *The Fiction of Bernard Malamud* (Oregon, 1977), p. 153.

14. Lucy Lippard, *Pop Art* (London, 1970), p. 23.

15. Josephine Zadovsky Knopp, *The Trial of Judaism in Contemporary Jewish Writing* (Urbana, 1975), p. 28.

16. For a biographical sketch of Kosinski, who committed suicide in 1991, see John Taylor, 'The Haunted Bird', *New York* **24** (1991), 24–37.

17. Alter, p. 39; Ozick, p. 171.

18. Saul Bellow, 'The Civilized Barbarian Reader' *The New York Times Book Review*, 8 March 1987, 38.

19. Bellow, 'The Civilized Barbarian Reader', p. 1.

20. 'Interview' in George Plimpton, (ed.), *Writers at Work: The Paris Review Interviews, Third Series* (New York, 1967), pp. 182–183.

21. Saul Bellow, 'The Writer as Moralist', *Atlantic Monthly* (March 1963), 58.

22. Quoted in D. J. R. Bruckner, 'A candid Talk with Saul Bellow' *The New York Times Magazine*, 15 April 1984, 62.

23. See Morris Dickstein, 'Rebel with a Thousand Causes', review of Fiedler, 'Fiedler on the Roof', *New York Times Book Review*, 4 August 1991, 27.

Chapter 5
Postmodernism as Black Humour

How postmodernism differs from modernism

Postmodernism has come to be the accepted term for the experimental literature written in the United States, Europe and Latin America since the end of the Second World War. The early term used by American critics of the 1960s to describe this kind of fiction, however, was 'black humour', and this now superseded term is still appropriate for the emergent fictions of what later critics constructed as postmodernism. The cutting edge of what seemed an aggressive, cynical, even nihilistic humour was what first caught the attention of readers and critics, alerting them to the emergence of a new mood as well as a new mode. In the 1970s postmodernist fiction was redefined as 'metafiction', indicating a change in fiction and in criticism such that some works considered originally as black humour were reconsidered as metafiction. I shall distinguish metafiction from black humour in Chapter 6 but here I need to give some sense of postmodernism generally, especially in its differences from modernism. Postmodernism, however, is a notoriously slippery concept, it being on principle against principles and centrally defining itself as resisting centralizing definition. Ihab Hassan, one of its critical originators, reflects that 'the time has come to theorize the term, if not to define it, before it forges from awkward neologism to derelict cliché without ever attaining to the dignity of a cultural concept'. To Jean François Lyotard, the postmodern condition consists precisely in the lack of a framing narrative, whether grounded in religious tradition or the enlightenment idea of progress, that serves broadly to legitimize a social order. In art, as Frederic Jameson argues, this disappearance of foundation leads to 'the eclipse of all of the affect (depth, anxiety, terror, the emotions of the monumental) that marked high modernism and its replacement by what Coleridge would have called fancy or Schiller aesthetic play, a commitment to surface and the *superficial* in all the senses of the word'. Indeed, to define postmodernism is in postmodernist terms an inherently paralogical and paradoxical undertaking. But since paralogy (that is, anti-logical reasoning) and paradox are, as Lyotard claims, the argumentative modes of postmodernist discourse, a definition is called for.[1] It will, however, be a highly provisional definition extended through two chapters, with as many qualifications as can be crowded in.

One difficulty is that postmodernism is not quite the same thing in architecture, painting and sculpture, photography and so on as it is in fiction though there are some common attributes. The scope of this book does not permit a close examination of these differences and similarities, nor could I improve on Steven Connor's persuasive *Postmodern Culture*. However, the case with architecture is illustrative. Postmodernist architecture, like postmodernist fiction, notably employs the techniques of allusion, parody and pastiche, envisioning the past as a warehouse of styles. The result in both cases may be a cultural collage, a new object created out of old conventions in a mix and match fashion. Both clearly depart from the unified hieratic modernist vision. Yet the modernism each departs from is quite different. The only common quality, as Connor demonstrates, is the aesthetic formalism of attempting to make the work an autonomous artefact, reflecting only the essence of its formal material, be it steel or language.[2] But architectural modernists reject the past in an essentially optimistic embrace of the machine age whereas literary modernists more usually reject the present in a pessimistic loathing of the machine age, frequently expressing the nostalgia for a lost traditional culture so apparent in the poetry of Eliot and Yeats. Whereas modernist architecture allies with the modern economy, modernist literature tries to stand outside it in a posture of aloof resentment, more an aristocratic than a radical perspective. Thus easy correspondences between various artistic modernisms and postmodernisms should be resisted.

Nor, even limiting the field to fiction, is it easy to draw a clear line between modernism and postmodernism. Thomas Pynchon and Donald Barthelme have been convincingly argued for in either category. However, a generally agreed on distinction between modernism and postmodernism can be drawn although the more it gets down to particulars the more it is disputable. The difference is in the general attitude towards selfhood, subjectivity and essence. The postmodernists write *against* the heroic modernism that invests heavily in subjectivity whether in the form of Virginia Woolf's attenuations of sensibility or D. H. Lawrence's quest for blood knowledge. For postmodernists the self consists of a collage of picked up pieces, derived from the culture, mass as well as elite. Selfhood is not individual and original but a cultural echo chamber. The apparently integral self is merely dysfunctional; character, a critical theorist asserts, 'has the factitious coherence of all obsessions'.[3] The protagonist of a postmodern work, whether of black humour or metafiction, is, as Robert Alter says of Melville's Confidence Man, 'less a realized character than a continuous performance, embodying the principle of protean deception'.[4]

The postmodernist use of myth and symbol is similarly disintegrative. Philip Stevick observes that whereas modernist works use myth as a unifying device, the mythic resonances in postmodern fiction are 'unelaborated, unsustained, dubious in their values', never crystallizing into 'epiphanic illumination'. Postmodernists lack the heroic modernist 'belief in the possibility that an intuitive self-knowledge can cut through accumulations of social ritual and self deception, a belief so firm, that it permits the intuitive act to serve as dramatic end point and structural principle, indeed as the very moral justification for the fiction'. The texture of memory, as in Proust's Madeleine, is a central resource of modernism whereas postmodernism 'revises the conventions by means of which memory is represented on the page, rejecting the access to the consciousness claimed by the moderns – rich, dense, heavy with myth and symbol, full of sensibility, nuance, epiphany – in favour of a different artifice, no less persuasive, in which memory operates rather like Kodachrome slides of an old vacation'.[5] The modernism relevant to postmodernism is that which abjures the quest for authenticity and depth: the Gide of *Lafcadio's Journey*, the Joyce more of *Ulysses* than *The Portrait of an Artist* and more of *Finnegans Wake* than either, the Faulkner of *The Hamlet* rather than 'The Bear', the Eliot of 'Sweeney Agonistes' rather than *The Waste Land* or *Four Quartets*. As this list suggests, postmodernism is an impulse within modernism. From a postmodernist perspective, Woolf's greatest work was *Between the Acts* (1941), a work in which, as Alan Wilde argues, sensibility is bracketed so that 'things seem to exist, as they do not in the earlier work, in their own right' rather than as conduits to transcendent vision, and gaps and discontinuities open possibility rather than threaten psychic destruction.[6] Our perception of the relationship between the two works in reverse: we see the postmodernist aspects of modernism not by tracing modernist influences forward but by rereading modernist works from a postmodernist vantage, as if Beckett and Barthelme were influencing Gide and Woolf.

Black humour and the rejection of existential pathos

The term 'black humour' literally translates '*humour noir*', a French mode eventuating in certain forms of surrealism, its origins and outcomes collected in André Breton's *Anthologie de l'humour noir*. Despite the identity of terms, the American mode differs from the French[7] and there are more parallels with *humour noir* and metafiction than with *humour noir* and black humour. For Hawkes and Heller, the major French influence was Céline who stood apart from surrealism and literary movements generally. Of American writers, Heller cites Nathanael West as important to him and for Hawkes not only West but the obsessive and black humour aspects of Faulkner were seminal. Hawkes also felt affinities between Flannery O'Connor's work and his own. There are obvious anticipations of black humour in Jane Bowles's *Two Serious Ladies* and Kenneth Patchen's comic surrealist novels *The Journal of Albion Moonlight* (1941) and the unjustly forgotten *Memoirs of a Shy Pornographer* (1945), though later writers seem unaware of Bowles and Patchen. Ralph Ellison's *Invisible Man* is a prototype black humour text.

The primary target of this first wave of postmodernist fiction, running from 1955 to 1965, was what the sociologist Max Weber termed 'rationalization': the reduction of all spheres of life – economic, social, psychological – to a rational, bureaucratized, predictable routinization and uniformity. Politically and economically, rationalization was reflected in the growth of business and government bureaucracy. Socially and psychologically it was reflected in the popular appropriation of a social science vocabulary that tended to displace the traditional moral and religious vocabulary as a way of explaining what people do and why they do it. Though, as we have seen, a neo-orthodox religious sense had become fashionable among the literary intellectuals of the 1940s and 1950s, religion on the popular level tended to merge with pop psychology as a mode of what a best seller of the 1950s called the Power of Positive Thinking. The mind and feelings themselves could be efficiently rationalized; one could learn procedures for, as Dale Carnegie's book claimed, Winning Friends and Influencing People. Sociologists, by and large, apprehended individuals as functional units in a social system and tended to take that system as self-justifying. Psychiatry aimed at helping individuals 'adjust' to their society, this being their definition of health. (That the 1950s saw a boom in the use of tranquillizers is no accident.) Mass media routinized emotional and aesthetic response to formula, with canned laughter preprocessing personal response. Everything and everyone seemed categorized, placed, explained. But as the world became, to use Weber's term, 'disenchanted' from religious superstition – and mystery – it became also ungraspably remote and abstract. The public had faith that the scientists understood the cosmos but who, without an advanced degree in mathematics, understood the scientists? Moreover, if technology was the modern marvel, it seemed often to be used for trivial or even destructive ends. Psychologists helped the advertising industry to develop its highly sophisticated stimulation of primitive responses. The new efficiency of society seemed destructive of community. In sum, the process of rationalization began to appear inimical to the possibility of community, the survival of mind and the fulfilment of spirit.

If the above is something of a historical caricature, it all the more summarizes the picture of the world held by most culture critics from the 1950s on. It has obvious oversimplifications, as for instance of a mass culture that, as now seems apparent, had creative and subversive as well as conformist expressions. But it reflects a still persuasive sense of an official world, rational, predictable, well organized and possibly insane which a novelist of any integrity must instinctively oppose. However, this opposition could be only an individual gesture, confined to the energy of language within the book and having little enough political resonance since, as existentialist individualism replaced radical social thought, there was no available vision of an alternative world, just a choice of attitudes toward this one. Besides the culture critiques cited in the Introduction, there was the existentialist analysis of how mass society negates personal authenticity. But by the mid 1950s, existentialism itself was being absorbed and rationalized by mass culture. Though still useful as a form of negative critique, the positive ethos of existentialism, its hero of authenticity, looked increasingly dubious and writers like John Barth saw 'romantic existentialism as old hat, really a concealed "yes" posing as a "no" in thunder'. The defiant self of existentialism had come to seem somewhat ludicrous.[8]

With hardly anywhere to go, a recurrent strategy in black humour became to use the culture's movement against it, judo style. The hero of such a novel is apt not to resist cultural force but to go with it, even exaggerate it, pump it up to monstrous proportions, intensify it to the point of implosion. The de-spiritualized social scientific vocabulary of the rationalized culture could be resisted by a spiritually rich literary vocabulary, as primarily by modernists, or it could be postmodernistically appropriated, lovingly catalogued and extended, a new language for art directly expressive of the 'real' world of professional expertise and bureaucratic management. You could fight them by joining them. Yet there is an ethical as well as aesthetic danger in this strategy. The black humorists do hint at a more valid world than the one they parody but there is always a potential in parody as well as satire to become a kind of complicity, for the parody to end up reinforcing more than transcending the society's tendencies. For that matter, some black humorists had no real quarrel with religious disenchantment or social scientific reductiveness towards what had been interior mysteries of the self, seeing possibilities for creative play rather than foreclosure of human potential in these developments. Much of the interest of black humour comes from the way each writer manoeuvres through these contradictions, making opportunities of them.

Barth: sexual cynicism and the undermining of authenticity

Barth's first two novels, *Floating Opera* (1956) and *End of the Road* (1958), deploy most of what came to be the conventions of black humour: a reduction of action to mechanical process and of self to role; the eventuation of such reductions in a comic eroticism; a detached, cold-blooded tone especially in relation to concerns conventionally treated with seriousness and pathos; a conceptual play with the arbitrariness of events and the infinite regress of attempts at explanation and evaluation, all of which are apparent in an early passage in *End of the Road*, its protagonist, Jacob Horner, giving a long, carefully precise description of why certain positions of the legs are impossible when one is sitting in the Progress and Advice Room of his therapist's Remobilization Farm.

> The Doctor sits facing you, his legs slightly spread, his hands on his knees, and leans a little toward you. You would not slouch down, because to do so would thrust your knees virtually against his, neither would you be inclined to cross your legs in either the masculine or the feminine manner: The masculine manner, with your left ankle resting on your right knee, would cause your left shoe to rub against the Doctor's left trouser leg, up by his knee, and possibly dirty his white trousers; the feminine manner, with your left knee crooked over your right leg, would thrust the toe of your shoe against the same trouser leg, lower down on his shin. To sit sideways, of course, would be unthinkable, and spreading your knees in the manner of the Doctor makes you actually conscious of copying his position, as if you hadn't a personality of your own. (1)

An exact description of how one does sit follows but the point is that an action as simple and 'natural' as sitting in a chair has been reconstrued as complex, conventional, even tactical – tactical, that is on the part not of the patient but of the Doctor, another point being that motivation is usually external, a response to the pressure of another actor or of a situation. Both parties are indeed actors, performers, their body language a set of signs, a performance. Though leg position in this performance is pre-scripted, the upper body has options for improvisation, Horner answering a question as follows.

> 'Oh, I suppose' – I made a suppositive gesture, which consisted of a slight outward motion of my lapel-grasping left hand, extending simultaneously the fore and index fingers but not releasing my

lapel – the hand motion accompanied by quickly arched (and as quickly released) eyebrows, momentarily pursed lips, and an on-the-one-hand/on-the-other-hand rocking of the head.

The performance should not be taken as self-expression. Horner here may really be supposing or he may be elaborately evading the question (which was, in fact, only rhetorical). Gestures are not necessarily expressive of any deep interiority.

The sociologist Erving Goffman, in the *Presentation of Self in Everyday Life* (1959), analysed social situations as drama calling for certain conventional scripts and the 'self' as actor in this drama, performing with linguistic and gestural signs. Barth was a year ahead of Goffman, elaborating his own comic performance out of a reductive externalization of human behaviour. Thus, Horner's story is anything but a quest for identity. He has never had one and has no future expectation of finding one. He does have moods but these change and Horner believes, like certain contemporary philosophers, that there are as many discontinuous selves as there are moods: 'My moods were little men, and when I killed them they stayed completely dead' (3). Horner sees the self as merely the plurality of its roles.

In more traditional theories of the self one of the most crucial formative experiences is that of sexual relations for here the self is faced with a test of surpassing its limits through intimacy and commitment or of psychologically failing through a fear of commitment or even of experience generally – as in Jack Burden's failure to make love to Anne Stanton – or of morally failing by selfish, exploitative responses to the other. Jake Horner has no interest in intimacy or commitment, and sees sexual relations as necessitating a particularly disengaged, sometimes even irksome form of role playing. He is irritated when Peggy Rankin, the lonely pick-up he has started to undress protests the offhand briskness of his seduction. From Horner's perspective she, as much as he, is playing a role but the conventional and boring one of sincerity. The sexual relation he believes more natural is expressed in his reverie as he confronts his first class.

> I assigned texts and described the course; that was all, and that was enough. My air of scholarly competence, theirs of studious attention (they wrote my name and office number as frowningly as if I'd pronounced the key to the Mystery) were so clearly feigned, we were all so conscious of playing school, that to attempt a lesson would have been preposterous. Why, confronted with that battery of eager bosoms and delicious behinds, a man cupped his hands in spite of himself; the urge to drop the ceremonious game and leap those fine girls on the spot was simply terrific. The national consternation, if on some September morn

every young college instructor in the land cried out what was on his mind – 'To hell with this nonsense, men: let's take 'em!' – a soothing speculation! (7)

It may help us to understand what has become problematic about black humour to consider how differently readers now respond to this passage as opposed to those of 1958. In 1958 the passage seemed daringly risqué, a breakthrough from sexual hypocrisy and repression. This was reinforced in the 1960s by the 'sexual revolution' enabled by superior contraceptive technology and instanced in the disappearance of girdles; a shrinkage in size of women's undergarments and bathing suits, eventuating in the 'bikini'; the increasing use by women of such vocables as the one Mailer was forced to euphemize his male soldiers' use of in *The Naked and the Dead*; and the publication in the United States of previously banned works, Vladimir Nabokov's *Lolita* (1958), D. H. Lawrence's *Lady Chatterley's Lover* (1959), Henry Miller's *Tropic of Cancer* (1961) and William Burroughs's *Naked Lunch* (1962). Barth, we can see, was on the leading edge of a major revision of sexual proprieties, and indeed, he later did a revised edition of *The Floating Opera* that restored passages deleted at the insistence of his publishers in 1956, though these had as much to do with the cynical as the sexual passages of the novel. A reader now, however, affected by the emergence of feminism, will notice that the legal definition for what Horner fantasizes is rape.

Roger Sale, though impressed by the imaginative force of postmodern American fiction, sees it as scandalously piggish in its treatment of women.[9] Two novels originally published by the Olympia Press in Paris, which published both experimental and pornographic novels, sometimes without clear differentiation, are illustrative: J. P. Donleavy's *The Ginger Man* (1955, Paris; 1958) and Terry Southern and Mason Hoffenberg's *Candy* (1958, Paris; 1964). Donleavy's hero is an arrogant trickster who exploits women, his wife among them, but also everyone else whenever he can get away with it. The book is vigorous, consistently cynical and sometimes very funny, a guilty pleasure (for male readers) that, though using the same formula, Donleavy was never able to duplicate. *Candy* is a sexual fantasy, structured as a series of skits based on the concept of a teenage girl as naive as she is nubile, seducible by any man with a plausible line. *Candy* is so frankly dirty, so openly prurient that it seems oddly innocent. Its women are caricatures of naivety or sexual predatoriness (Aunt Livia boasts of her special sexual technique, ' the snapping turtle'), treated with an affectionate condescension. Southern later wrote *The Magic Christian*, a series of satirical skits, some ineffective but others outrageously funny, organized by a wealthy trickster out to subvert American middle class culture in its various forms. Interestingly, only the English edition contains a skit on the 'anticommunist' witch hunt of the 1950s.[10] Southern's last work of note was the screenplay that transformed Peter George's apocalyptic Cold War novel into the bizarre comedy *Dr Strangelove*. His later writing escalates bad taste and obscenity but lacks humour.

By 1978 Roland Barthes could accurately declare that 'it is no longer the sexual which is indecent, it is the sentimental'.[11] If, as argued by Saul Bellow in the preceding chapter, the contents of the Freudian unconscious have moved upward and it is now spiritual impulses that are repressed, black humour could be seen as aiding and abetting in this revolution. In one of the best scenes in *The Catcher in the Rye* Holden Caulfield is sickened by seeing a college boy feel up his weakly protesting date's thigh in a restaurant. Holden empathizes with the woman's victimization, her penalty for having more feeling, while the man's enjoyment is his reward for cynical manipulation. In contrast, the best scene in Terry Southern's *Flash and Filigree* (1958) is a precise process analysis, almost a how-to manual on undressing a not altogether willing woman in a parked car. The kind of diffuse love that pumps up Salinger's work, the love that Gore Vidal protested was the new *deus ex machina* of American fiction, is, beginning with a smack at W. H. Auden's line 'We must love one another or die', vigorously repudiated in John Barth's polemic 'Afterword' to Tobias Smollett's *Roderick Random*.

> However true it may be, in our time at least, that we must love
> our fellow man or perish, that fact in itself doesn't make the
> wretch a bit more lovable; indeed one failing of the love-boys in
> our current literature is that they're inclined to understand the
> phrase *Love or perish* as an ultimatum instead of a fair statement of
> alternatives. If Smollett chose to perish, he's not the first or grea-
> test man who ever did. If he found life mainly exasperating even
> when comfortable, and his neighbor generally tiresome even
> when pacific, we're not likely to kiss him for telling us so, or give
> him the Nobel Prize, but we might be impressed by his unsen-
> timental candor. In fact, if one has had a bellyful of Erich Fromm
> and J. D. Salinger, one may find Roderick Random's orneriness
> downright bracing.[12]

Barth's comment was bracing in 1964 but now seems rather callow since cynicism and aggression have so thoroughly replaced sensitivity and compassion as the dominant convention. Indeed, in the same year that Barth was pistol whipping sentimentality, Bellow, in *Herzog*, was attempting a resuscitation of humane feeling.

Humane feeling is not prevalent in Horner's re-encounter with Peggy Rankin, a scene which mocks both conventional and existential morality. By this time Horner has encountered Joe Morgan, his opposite and likeness, who proceeding from similar premises arrives at a quite different

THE LIBRARY
GUILDFORD COLLEGE
of Further and Higher Education

conclusion. In Morgan's ideas, Barth parodies the existentialist concept of responsibility and authenticity. Horner's therapist suggests he read Sartre and become an existentialist as a way of keeping him moving until he finds something more suitable: 'Be engagé' (6). Sartre argues that since existence precedes essence, man has not only the freedom but a duty to choose who to be. To fall, however, into a prefabricated social identity, a role, will not do since it exhibits 'false consciousness' and 'inauthenticity'. 'Authenticity' also entails a certain consistency; a self chosen and then discarded on the next deal hardly meets the highest existentialist criteria. But for Horner's therapist, existentialism is merely another temporary role. Horner, similarly, is bemused by the seriousness and consistency with which Joe Morgan takes his adopted role, knocking his wife cold for apologizing since for a principled existentialist apology inauthentically denies our previous free choice. She then apologizes for apologizing and, consistently, he knocks her out again, teaching her authenticity. Morgan, it is true, sees himself more as a pragmatist than an existentialist, explaining that it takes energy to carry on living without objective values and that 'Energy's what makes the difference between American pragmatism and French existentialism – where the hell else but in America could you have a cheerful nihilism, for God's sake?' (4) But 'cheerful nihilism' better describes Horner's outlook than Morgan's and Horner is more pragmatic, at least in the sense of looking to results, not meanings.

But Horner can make a practical use of Morgan's version of existentialism precisely because he believes, as he tells Morgan's wife, that 'Nobody's authentic' (5). She sleeps with Horner as a reaction to his demonstration that Joe Morgan himself is inconsistent, silly and thus 'inauthentic', as shown when, at Horner's instigation, they eavesdrop on him. Horner's triumph is to re-seduce Peggy Rankin by convincing her of his authenticity in refusing to use romantic conventions. He even hits her for laughing at him, explaining how this demonstrates his authenticity, and as they proceed to bed he makes 'a mental salute to Joseph Morgan, il mio maestro. . . ' (7). At times, Horner does say what he truly believes, which is always both sides of any proposition at issue. This, in fact, is the illness his therapist is treating. This therapist discovered Horner at a bus terminal in a paralytic trance from indecision about what direction to travel in. When asked a crucial question, Horner responds: ' "I don't have any opinion," I said. "Or rather, I have both opinions at once" ' (8). The opening sentence of the novel is 'In a sense, I am Jacob Horner' (1), his name an allusion to Mother Goose's little Jack Horner who sat in a corner and couldn't make up his mind. He comes closest to making up his mind not in an answer to his dilemma but rather in an aesthetic and logical play with its form.

However much Barth subverts the convention of the integral self, any rebelliousness in his writing is personal, not social. His protagonists have too much difficulty convincing themselves to attempt persuading others. As Todd Andrews of *The Floating Opera* questions, 'Having eithered, will I or?' (5) Horner spells out the political logic of the position.

> 'But the greatest radical in any society is the man who sees all the arbitrariness of the rules and social conventions, but who has such a great scorn or disregard for the society he lives in that he embraces the whole wagonload of nonsense with a smile. The greatest rebel is the man who wouldn't change society for anything in the world.' (10)

This makes me wonder if one source of the appeal of Barth's fiction is its essential narcissism. Freud notes that 'It seems very evident that one person's narcissism has a great attraction for those others who have renounced part of their own narcissism and are seeking after object-love. . . . In literature . . . even the great criminal and the humorist compel our interest by the narcissistic self-importance with which they manage to keep at arm's length everything which would diminish the importance of their ego.'[13] Jacob Horner's rebelliousness is perfectly narcissistic, making him feel superior without commiting him to action or trouble. Todd Andrews, in The *Floating Opera*, plans a suicide that will take a boatload of people with him and in the original manuscript that Barth later restored this is not softened by the concern he suddenly feels for his mistress's ill daughter (the ending his less tough-minded publishers insisted on). In both versions the suicide plus mass murder is aborted by sheer chance. Andrews is not wicked by his own lights because he really feels himself a member of a different species.

> I unconsciously began to regard my fellow men variously as more or less pacific animals among whom it was generally safe to walk (so long as one observed certain tacitly assumed rules), or as a colony of more or less quiet lunatics among whom it was generally safe to live (so long as one humored, at least outwardly, certain aspects of their madness). (14)

Jacob Horner does feel a certain regret and guilt at his qualified responsibility in the graphically described death of Joe Morgan's wife and the last line of the suggestively titled *End of the Road* is Horner's direction to the cab driver he has called to take him to the bus station: 'Terminal' (12). Perhaps we are to see this as the grim outcome of Horner's cynicism. But if so, so what? There are in Barth's first two novels only the alternatives of either and or, and both eventuate in 'Terminal'. In an interview, Barth comments that as a private citizen he worries about politics and civil rights but as a novelist his argument 'is with the facts of life, not the conditions of it'. This seems to put any blame on a higher level than, say, the state or federal government, and indeed in the same interview he plays out a rather euphoric narcissistic impudence: 'God wasn't too bad a novelist, except he was a realist'; 'reality is a nice place to visit but you wouldn't want to live there, and literature never did very long'. But there is a certain constricting reality even in nihilism and though Barth considered *The Sot Weed Factor* (1960) the last of a nihilistic trilogy, he notes that in it 'I had thought I was writing about values and it turned out I was writing about innocence, which I found to be a more agreeable subject anyway. . . .'[14] In *The Sot Weed Factor* Barth turns towards metafiction though carrying over most of the conventions of black humour, as will be shown in Chapter 6.

John Hawkes and William Burroughs: the mass-mediated self

In John Cheever's 'A vision of the World' (in *Collected Stories of John Cheever*), a man returns from work to find his wife in tears. She has a postmodern problem: 'I have this terrible feeling that I'm a character in a television situation comedy . . . . I mean I'm nice-looking, I'm well-dressed, I have humorous and attractive children, but I have this terrible feeling that I'm in black-and-white and that I can be turned off by anybody.' The feeling rather than the story is postmodern; Cheever is a realist recording the way people now feel, that is, unreal. If the primary content of a contemporary consciousness derives from mass media – the Pepsi-Cola jingle that runs through Jacob Horner's head when he is looking most reflective, political catch phrases, gossip about celebrities, memorable television moments – the modern self can be summed up as the trash bin into which all this has been emptied. The writer-critic Ronald Sukenick notes, without disapproval, that 'individuals' person-alities are becoming less and less important and less defined'. He com-pares his grandfather's generation of 'very august, aggressively rigid personalities' (what Riesman would call 'inner-directed') and contrasts this to a contemporary 'more flattened out, flowing, less rigidly defined personality that is still not necessarily uninvolved in its own terms'. This is related to the information revolution: 'It's just very difficult to absorb and respond to so much information while having a hardened, brittle personality circumference, as opposed to one that is porous.'[15] But Sukenick does not take this idea to its logical outcome, which would be to eliminate the self as a superfluous middle man, an epiphenomenon, and go direct to its source, the media discourse. Some postmodernist fiction tends this way.

Postmodernist writers are fascinated by the power of media discourse to appeal directly to fear and desire, bypassing rational intellect, though sometimes ambivalent about whether they wish to expose or appropriate this power. This fascination is especially apparent in John Hawkes and William Burroughs, who follow different strategies to the same end of breaking down perception into stimulus and character into response. Hawkes 'began to write fiction on the assumption, that the true enemies of the novel were plot, character, setting, and theme . . .'.[16] He distinguishes his writing from 'transparent' fictions in which the reader is cued to be 'interested not in the fiction but in the "life" the fiction seems to be about'. 'Such writers think they are reflecting or reproducing reality. They must think they know what reality is; they must think that "out there" is reality, which I don't think at all. As a writer, I'm not interested in "life". Fiction that insists on created actuality is its own reality, has its own vitality and energy.' But Hawkes's created actuality takes the risk of becoming so far removed from a world and a moral order with which readers connect as to become unconvincing, if not unintelligible. Hawkes does believe in the reality of evil; he wishes 'never to let the reader (or myself) off the hook . . . never to let him think that the picture is any less black than it is or that there is any way out of the nightmare of human existence'. His writing is a way of 'persuading the reader that even he may not be exempt from evil'.[17] But the bizarre and grisly events and images of his first novel, *The Cannibal* (1949), are too far removed to be threatening and implicating. However, as Flannery O'Connor testifies, *The Lime Twig* (1961) works.

> You suffer *The Lime Twig* like a dream. It seems to be something that is happening to you, that you want to escape from but can't. The reader even has that slight feeling of suffocation that you have when you can't wake up and some evil is being worked on you.
> This . . . I might have been dreaming myself.[18]

The Lime Twig has plot, character, setting and theme but in the key of nightmare fantasy rather than realistic reproduction. The order of reality derived from the world in the novel is the collective dream of mass-mediated desire. Hawkes borrows his protagonist's name, Michael Banks, from the boy hero of the children's book *Mary Poppins*, who has moments of glory in entering a world of fantasy, both demonic and innocent, that transcends the rational world of his parents. Hawkes's character, a timid lower-middle-class young man, living in a greyed-out version of post Second World War England, has a moment of factitious glory as he enters into a pop fantasy of sex and violence, its dream logic differing from realistic narrative logic in that links of desire rather than links of action are its organizing principle. As Leslie Fiedler observes,

Hawkes's 'characters move not from scene to scene but in and out of focus'.[19] As a dream world it has a reality very like the world of mass-mediated desire analysed in Marshall McLuhan's *The Mechanical Bride* (1951).

> The ad agencies and Hollywood are always trying to get inside the public mind in order to impose their collective dreams on that inner stage . . . . One dream opens upon another until reality and fantasy are made interchangeable. The ad agencies flood the daytime world of conscious purpose and control with erotic imagery from the night world in order to drown, by suggestion, all sales resistance.

Besides advertisements and films there are 'sadistic sex novels' in which 'The reader is to be habitually soused with sex and violence but at all times protected from the harsh contact of the critical intellect.' There is a visceral immediacy in these fantasies. Urban man gets daily 'beaten into a servile pulp by his own mechanical reflexes', responding to the barrage of media hyperstimulation: 'The average male educated in and by this environment tends to be not so much conscious of distinct physical and intellectual objects as he is of a variable volume of registered excitement within himself.' It takes a hero of rational reflectiveness to remain 'in detachment from the visceral riot that this sensational fare tends to produce. The reader has to be second Ulysses in order to withstand the siren onslaught.'[20]

McLuhan's analysis reads like a point for point gloss of *The Lime Twig* except that Banks cannot even manage to project himself as the hero of the fantasy he lives out. McLuhan notes that thriller heroes tend towards the brutal and 'smoothly metallic' precisely because they are the compensatory fantasies of 'the weak and confused who worship the pseudo-simplicities of brutal directness'. Banks projects this invulnerability on to the leader of the gang, Larry, who wears a smoothly metallic bullet protector, while casting himself in the passive, mainly spectatorial role that inspired it in the first place. Banks does manage a more direct enactment of his sexual fantasies with a series of teasing sexual images, culminating in an orgiastic night scene. In this fantasy, 'the women were ganging up on him, doing a job on him' (7). When he is told that 'there's someone wants to see you. A lady, mister', he responds with his new-found sexual smugness, 'I should imagine so!' The lady is his next-door neighbour, a coincidence explainable only as an incorporation of voyeuristic daydreaming: 'She was twenty years old and timeless. . . . At three o'clock in the morning she was a girl he had seen through windows in several dreams unremembered, unconfessed. . . .' And even the sex, especially with Banks's main temptress Sybilline, is displaced into the fetishism of lingerie advertisements: 'her legs, friendly and white and long, were the legs he had seen bare in the undergarment ads', Sybilline's sex is mostly an affair of suggestion and stockings: 'In Syb's voice he heard laughter, motor cars and lovely moonlit trees, beds and silk stockings in the middle of the floor.' (5) Banks's most intimate desires are those most mass-mediated.

The Lime Twig works because Hawkes not only conveys a sense of evil but specifies its mass-mediated sources. The convincingly nightmar-ish quality is evinced in images throughout, a splendid example being the appearance of Larry and his gang, fully clothed, in a steam bath where they commit a murder, a virtuoso surrealistic passage. In the extraordinary conclusion Banks commits his one act of courage by sabo-taging his own fantasy.

In *Second Skin* (1964), published the same year as Bellow's *Herzog*, Hawkes's protagonist represents himself as a lovable *schlemiehl* surrounded by 'reality instructors' affronted by his innocence and determined to validate their darker vision by brutalizing him into it, but the protagonist seems far too much in imaginative complicity with his victimizers for his version to be credible. The moral ambiguity of *Second Skin* is not to my mind a flaw though I can see how some readers might find it tending towards amorality. But Hawkes's novels after *Second Skin* are for me too far removed from both the reality 'out there' and the conventions of morality, both of which have at the least a certain accumulated weight of human experience behind them. The risk of overstepping the readers' boundaries, whether the fault be that of the readers or the writer, is intrinsic to novels whose world is primarily internal, open more to the subconscious and its constructions of the surreal than a less private re-ality.

William Burroughs's *Naked Lunch* portrays the public world as a mon-strous construction of fantasy. Published in the United States in 1962, a year after *The Lime Twig*, Burroughs's novel was published in Paris by Maurice Girodias's Olympia Press in 1959. Girodias printed in English as well as French works of pornography under such pseudonyms as Akbar del Piombo along with books by Samuel Beckett and Henry Miller. *Candy*, *The Ginger Man* and *Lolita* as well as *The Naked Lunch* (the orig-inal title) were available in America and England only when smuggled in from Paris until the censorship breakdown of 1958 (*Lolita*) to 1962 (*Naked Lunch*). *Naked Lunch* and *Candy* reflect their origin, both being, on one level, parodies of pornography with a certain equivocation be-tween the parody and the pornography. In structure, *Naked Lunch* resembles a set of vaudeville routines. It is not a single story but a series of skits: pornographic movie scenes, manic monologues of nonce characters, and Marx Brothers routines. The book is more an asssemblage than a narrative; Burroughs and his friends, Allen Ginsberg among them, selected out of a thousand-page manuscript what went into *Naked Lunch*, some of the rest spilling over into later Burroughs publications: *The Soft*

Machine, The Ticket that Exploded, Nova Express. This is not to say *Naked Lunch* lacks coherence. The streetwise narrative voice, that of a carnival pitch man luring 'marks' into various freak shows, provides continuity as do recurrent characters such as Dr Benway, a more sinister version of the anarchistic con-man Groucho Marx played. There is also a central theme, that of 'sending'. 'Sending' is a form of brainwashing that works by transferring images to others so powerfully as to put the receiver under the sender's rhetorical control. Burroughs envisions the Word as a virus that infects the reader so that the relation between sender and receiver becomes that of a shared disease. It is also a narcotic to which the receiver can become addicted, a convincing image for mass media imagery as in the centrefolds of pornographic magazines, an image fix that apparently lasts for exactly one month. Burroughs's archetype of narrator is Coleridge's ancient mariner, and his archetype of reader the wedding guest. But the narrator's sinister seduction of the reader is on another level a model of the sinister seduction of the audience by mass-media discourse. Burroughs offers a disenchantment from 'sending' by what the Marxist German playwright Bertolt Brecht called 'baring the device', that is, making the rhetorical devices of persuasion the subject, the topic of discourse, rather than the means of slipping a propaganda message by reader/audience perceptions. But at the same time Burroughs is baring his device he is using it, clearly attempting to implicate his reader in his own paranoid misanthropic and misogynist construction.[21]

Joseph Heller: the absurd logic of the rationalized world

In 1961 Philip Roth contributed the seminal essays 'Writing American Fiction' to *Commentary*, the Jewish American cultural periodical in which Roth became *persona non grata* after *Portnoy's Complaint*. The essay begins with an account of the murder of two teenage girls, Pattie and Babs Grimes, in Chicago and the grotesque media circus generated by the event. Among other bizarreries, donations are showered upon the bereaved mother.

> A stranger steps forward, by the name of Shultz or Schwartz – I don't really remember – but he is in the appliance business and he presents Mrs Grimes with a whole new kitchen. Mrs Grimes, beside herself with appreciation and joy, turns to her surviving daughter and says, 'Imagine me in that kitchen!' Finally, the poor woman goes out and buys two parakeets (or maybe another Mr

Schultz presents them as a gift); one parakeet she calls Babs, the other Pattie. . . . Shortly thereafter I left Chicago . . . and so far as I know, though Mrs Grimes hasn't her two girls, she has a brand-new dishwasher and two small birds.

The most horrifying thing about this anecdote is how funny it is. It is disturbing that it is more funny than horrifying. The media culture seems to have effectively reduced the most dramatic stories we tell ourselves from high tragedy to demented farce. This presents a literary dilemma: 'that the American writer in the midst of the twentieth century has his hands full in trying to understand, describe, and then make *credible* much of American reality'.[22] Writers, however, have always created out of their impediments, as certainly became the case with Roth's later Zuckerman novels. And at a certain point, readers found their own experience mirrored in the writers' vision.

Joseph Heller's *Catch-22* (1961) was the black humour novel most reflective of the increasing unreality of the public scene. Heller was in the Air Force in Italy during the Second World War and this is the setting of *Catch-22*, but not its true subject. Heller, who had a relatively good time during the war and no real quarrel with how it was fought, acknowledges his actual subject as 'the contemporary regimented business society depicted against the background of universal sorrow and inevitable death that is the lot of all of us'. The Cold War and the political situation of the 1950s is more to the point than the Second World War: 'Most of the polemic that is there, and the topical humor, relates to events occurring after World War II, during the McCarthy period. Deliberate anachronisms.'[23] These include farcical versions of the loyalty oaths required for various federal and state positions, the corporate philosophy of President Eisenhower's Secretary of Defence, 'Engine Charlie' Wilson, a former executive of General Motors famous for proclaiming 'What's good for General Motors is good for the country', echoed in Milo Minderbinder's 'what's good for the syndicate is good for the country' (22), etc. An example of the kind of thinking found in the notorious House Committee on Unamerican Activities 'investigations' is in the inquisition of the novel's most innocent and decent character, the Chaplain, who on affirming his belief in God is faced with a damning contradiction.

'Then that really is very odd, Chaplain, because I have here another affidavit from Colonel Cathcart that states that you once told him atheism was not against the law. Do you recall ever making a statement like that to anyone?'

The chaplain nodded without hesitation, feeling himself on very solid ground now. 'Yes sir, I did make a statement like that. I made it because it's true. Atheism is not against the law.'

> 'But that's still no reason to say so, Chaplain, is it?' the officer
> chided tartly. . . .' (36)

The comic technique of the passage is *reductio ad absurdum* yet it is not
far from conventional political logic: 'There is a tradition of taboo
against submitting to examination many of our ideological beliefs, religious beliefs; many things that become a matter of traditional behavior, or
habit, acquire status where they seem to be exempt from examination.
Or even to suggest that they do be examined becomes a form of here-
sy.'[24] Heller most effectively mocks this ideology by concentrating more
on its formal structure than its content. In fact, *Catch-22* is a novel based
on logic rather than on character, a classic illustration of Ron Sukenick's
belief that postmodernist writers have displaced ego psychology with an
emphasis on 'the whole cognitive faculty and just how we make sense of
patterns'.[25] The major rhetorical devices of the novel along with *reductio
ad absurdum* are *non sequitur* and logical inversion because these reflect the
public logic of an absurd world. Thus on the refusal of the protagonist,
Yossarian, to fly a dangerous mission to Bologna we have the following
exchange.

> 'That crazy bastard.'
> 'He's not so crazy,' Dunbar said. 'He swears he's not going to fly
> to Bologna.'
> 'That's just what I mean' Dr Stubbs said. 'That crazy bastard may
> be the only sane one left.' (10)

In the world of *Catch-22* everything is rationalized and nothing makes
sense. When Doc Daneeka is listed on the flight crew of a plane that
crashes he becomes bureaucratically dead and his complaints about feeling cold are met with impeccable institutional logic: 'You're dead, sir .
. . That's probably the reason you always feel so cold' (31). Thus even
death can be subordinated to the structure of institutional rationality
though the facts of death are the nearest things to absolute, existentially
grounded realities to be found in this inverted world. Death is the ultimate refutation: 'Clevinger was dead. That was the basic flaw in his
philosophy' (10).

The satirical power of the novel is in its inverted logic. This is what
reached readers, especially when paperback sales of *Catch-22* took off
from 1964 to 1968. Set during the Second World War, about the Cold
War politics and institutional rationalization of the 1950s, *Catch-22*
answered most to an audience that saw the novel's structural logic as a
perfect reflection of the American engagement in Vietnam. The rhetoric
of body counts, the proclamation of an American general that he had
destroyed a Vietnamese city in order to save it – this and other aspects
of Vietnam seemed a Heller invention, an extension of the logic of

Catch-22. The absurdity of the war was as evident to the soldiers there as on the home front. A soldier who was at the My Lai massacre is quoted by Robert Jay Lifton.

> But you feel like it's not all real. It couldn't possibly be. We couldn't still be in this country. We've been walking for days . . . . . You're in Vietnam and they're using real bullets . . . . Here in Vietnam they're actually shooting people for no reason . . . . Any other time you think, it's such an extreme. Here you can go ahead and shoot them for nothing. . . . As a matter of fact it's even . . . smiled upon, you know, good for you. Everything is backwards. That's part of the kind of unreality of the thing.

As Lifton analyses it:

> The predominant emotional tone here is all encompassing absurdity and moral inversion. The absurdity has to do with a sense of being alien and profoundly lost, yet at the same time locked into a situation as meaningless and unreal as it is deadly. The moral inversion, eventuating in a sense of evil, has to do not only with the absolute reversal of ethical standards but with its occurrence in absurdity, without inner justification, so that the killing is rendered naked.[26]

Vietnam novels, such as Tim O'Brien's *Going after Cacciato* (1978) and Gustav Hasford's *The Short Timers* (1979 – the basis for the film *Full Metal Jacket*), catch this sense of absurdity but Heller *anticipated* it.

What made Yossarian a 1960s hero was not his humanism but his recognition of absurd logic. He knows who the enemy is: 'anybody who's going to get you killed, no matter which side he's on. . . ' (12). The flaw in Clevinger's logic was that he did not know, though Yossarian does his best to explain.

> Yossarian had done his best to warn him the night before. 'You haven't got a chance, kid,' he had told him glumly. 'They hate Jews.'
> 'But I'm not Jewish,' answered Clevinger.
> 'It will make no difference,' Yossarian promised and Yossarian was right. 'They're after everybody.' (8)

Paranoia, that is to say, is the reality principle, not a clinical condition in individuals but a structural attribute of society, a conclusion some psychiatrists later endorsed, having come to see paranoia as a valid response to certain attributes of contemporary rationalization. An article on paranoia points out that it is supported 'by a complex, rigorously logical system' and that its occurrence as a common mental disorder 'follows the adoption of rationalism as the quasioffical religion of Western man. . .'. It is an interpretative not a perceptual dysfunction, not infrequently reinforced by self-fulfilling prophecy. For instance, the usual person 'does not worry that somewhere, without his knowledge, a secret tribunal is about to order him seized, drugged, and imprisoned without the right of appeal'. When a person does so worry, 'the probable next step is for a secret tribunal to convene, and, without his knowledge, order him to be seized, drugged, and imprisoned without the right of appeal'.[27] Readers responded to a novel that argued that they were less crazy than their society. Thus, any move away from alienation and paranoia is a move away from the specific reality check the novel offers, which leads to problems when Heller goes soft towards the end. Yossarian, whose charm is in the validity of his cynicism, starts saying things like 'There's a young kid in Rome whose life I'd like to save if I can find her, so it isn't all selfish, it it?' (42). But the young kid, known to us only as Nately's whore's sister, has not been made real enough to warrant this heartfeltness. It is as if someone had switched reels of a Marx Brothers film with *It's a Wonderful Life*. Sentimentality anomalously replaces absurdist logic. In this respect Heller's novel does not hold together as well as what Heller acknowledged as a major influence upon it, Louis Ferdinand Céline's *Voyage au bout de la nuit* (1932), a novel which never compromises its alienation and rejection. Though it should be remembered that Céline's resentments, expressed with a rhetorical brilliance that impressed Hawkes as well as Heller, eventually led him into collaboration with forces more evil than any he had denounced. Perhaps Heller's irrepressible liberal optimism was a saving grace after all.

For that matter, Heller does a kind of reversal of *Catch-22* in his other major novel, *Something Happened* (1974), a less popular, more threatening and ultimately more convincing work. Bob Slocum, the first-person protagonist, is as paranoid as Yossarian but his paranoia is clinical as well as structural and he is more a willing participant in the system of structural paranoia than a victim of it. The second section begins with the sentence that popped into Heller's mind as the originary germ of the entire novel. It is there elaborated into a classic passage of modern American fiction, a flow chart of paranoia.

> In the office in which I work there are five people of whom I am afraid. Each of these five people is afraid of four people (excluding overlaps), for a total of twenty, and each of these twenty people is afraid of six people, making a total of one hundred and twenty people who are feared by at least one person. Each of these one hundred and twenty people is afraid of the other one hundred and nineteen, and all of these one hundred and forty five people are afraid of the twelve men at the top who helped found

and build the company and now own and direct it. ('The office in which I work')

This is structural paranoia and there is no reason to believe the protagonist's fears are unreasonable. But the book opens with his clinical paranoia.

> I get the willies when I see closed doors. Even at work, where I am doing so well now, the sight of a closed door is sometimes enough to make me dread that something horrible is happening behind it, something that is going to affect me adversely; if I am tired and dejected from a night of lies or booze or sex or just plain nerves and insomnia, I can almost smell the disaster mounting invisibly and flooding out toward me through the frosted glass panes. My hands may perspire, and my voice may come out strange. I wonder why.
> Something must have happened to me sometime. ('I get the willies')

Yossarian has external enemies and his shiftiness, verbal and physical, is a strategy to evade the consequences of their stupidity and malice. Slocum's main enemy is far more dangerous and quite unavoidable; he has met the enemy and it is him. In the early stages of writing *Something Happened*, Heller thought he was creating 'possibly the most contemptible character in literature' but began feeling a certain sympathy before he was finished.[28] The reader's similar and disturbing ambivalence is intended: 'It was meant to be a first-person, present-tense, uncomfortably intimate book.' Slocum's account intentionally lacks the vivacity of *Catch-22*; indeed, *Catch-22* provided the security for Heller to risk keeping *Something Happened* 'as inert as I intended to do'.[29] No reader will wish to identify with Slocum but many will feel implicated by him.

Slocum's desolation of spirit is representative and keyed in a rhetoric of cynicism that resembles that of *Catch-22* but is performing a quite different cultural work. Cynicism in *Catch-22* is a defence against institutional deceit, a way of freeing up perception from absurdly false and harmful premises, as in Orr's explanation of the flies in Appleby's eyes.

> 'Oh, they're there, all right. . . although he probably doesn't even know it. That's why he can't see things as they really are.'
> 'How come he doesn't know it?' inquired Yossarian.
> 'Because he's got flies in his eyes,' Orr explained with exaggerated patience. 'How can he see he has flies in his eyes if he's got flies in his eyes?' (5)

Slocum *knows* he has flies in his eyes. His cynicism is a defence of his willing participation in institutional and personal deceit, basically a defence of a desperately ill state of being. Much of his irony is directed at himself, as when he worries that he may lose control and say aloud the awful things he continually thinks: 'If that happens, I will blend my inner world with my outer world and be disoriented in both.' He is aware that 'much of my waking life is composed of defenses against behavior I am not aware of and would find difficult to justify. ("My little boy is having difficulties").' His inverted clichés do not, as did Yossarian's, subvert a sick rational order; they are sick jokes about his complicity with it: 'When I grow up I want to be a little boy'; 'I can't fall in love. That's probably what holds my marriage together'; 'I was never sure I wanted to get married. But I always knew I wanted a divorce.'

The reason Slocum cannot allow himself to love is that without some conception of transcendence the things of the world are simply too much for him. In contrast to Yossarian who faces fear, which is determinate, Slocum faces dread which is indeterminate because relating not to presence but absence. Slocum fears death not because life is all there is but because life is not there either, being nothing but the empty space deferring death. Slocum lives an emotionally dead life as his strategy for evading death. Thus his 'aversion to hospitals and misgivings and distaste for people I know who fall ill. I never make hospital visits if I can avoid them, because there's always the risk that I might open the door of the private or semiprivate room and come upon some awful sight for which I could not have prepared myself.' ('I get the willies.') Slocum knows perfectly well for whom the bell tolls but has no cultural forms for dealing with such contingency as it affects others or himself. So he pursues a quite conscious course of denial. He fears and hates the ill and the crippled because they signify for him loss of control over the presentation of self in everyday life, a counterfeit mode of being but the only one he trusts.

Slocum works at convincing himself of his hatefulness, for the alternative is more frightening and painful. Thus:

> It is not true that retarded (brain-damaged, idiot, feeble-minded, emotionally disturbed, autistic) children are the necessary favorites of their parents or that they are always uncommonly beautiful and lovable, for Derek, our youngest child, is not especially good-looking, and we do not love him at all. (We would prefer not to think about him. We don't want to talk about him.) ('It is not true')

The rhetoric of this protestation pushes against its content as Slocum thinks and talks about whom he prefers not to think or talk about and savours his self-lacerating list of synonyms for 'retarded'. Slocum tries to survive by smothering any threat of uncontrollable, spontaneous feeling:

'I dislike anything unexpected' ('I get the willies'). Because he loves him
most his greatest fears are for his 'normal' son. In a section entitled, with
a terrible irony, 'My son has stopped talking to me', something happens
to his son, an automobile accident. Slocum encloses him in a protective
embrace that literally, as it turns out, smothers the boy. The final section
is 'Nobody knows what I've done'. In *Catch-22* Heller backed off from
Yossarian's amiable cynicism in an ill-considered attempt to re-establish
humanist credentials that were never really in doubt. In *Something
Happened* the logic of Slocum's cynicism is carried through to a devastating
conclusion. The most awful thing about this cynicism is that it is recognizable, even representative. In one of Slocum's litanies of complaint he
notes that none of the adolescents he knows (and especially his own
daughter) are well adjusted and then adds with a narrative leer, 'I am
well-adjusted, which is not exactly the best recommendation for adjust-
ment, is it?' He reflects, 'I am a shit. But at least I am a successful one'
('My daughter's unhappy').

Sensitive, in a hostile fashion, to everyone, he is no one, an essentially negative version of another type-character of postmodern fiction,
the protean man, who will be considered in the next section. The last
sentence in the novel shows where Slocum's inauthenticity, bad faith,
denial and malice get him in his world: 'Everyone seems pleased with
the way I've taken command' ('Nobody knows what I've done').

Heller's later novels lack the inventiveness of style that allowed him
to find an expressive form for the anxiety and dysfunction of American
society from mid-century through to the 1970s in *Catch-22* and *Something Happened*, which are, so far, his works of enduring value.

Berger's protean man and Vonnegut's shrug: the politics of black humour

'The whole ethical system' of Captain Simon Suggs, the hero of Johnson
Jones Hooper's classic 1845 work of Southern humour, is expressed in
his favourite aphorism – 'IT IS GOOD TO BE SHIFTY IN A NEW
COUNTRY'. Suggs's shiftiness is exemplified in the many roles he plays:
state legislator, Kentucky drover, prosperous slave buyer. Though Suggs
is an anti-hero, a horrible example of unprincipled roguery, his creator,
in the fashion of Southern humour, clearly participates in the *brio* of his
colloquial pungency and even the artistry of his confidence schemes.[30]
The new country is Alabama, part of the moving frontier of the 1830s,
the temporal setting of the work. In the first volume of *Democracy in
America*, published in 1835, Alexis de Tocqueville observed that 'In these

states, founded off-hand as it were by chance, the inhabitants are but of yesterday. Scarcely known to one another, the nearest neighbors are ignorant of each other's history.'[31] So the relative fluidity of social identity in America was exponentially increased on the frontier, the perfect setting for 'a new kind of man – a "protean man" ', as characterized in Robert Jay Lifton's seminal essay. Drawing on research with escapees from the communist regime in China and with young Japanese in the 1960s, Lifton discovered an emergent 'style of self-process', a self that was exploratory, in flux, open to possibility, responding to the rapid pace of social, technological and ideological change with a 'polymorphous versatility'. Lifton 'found that Chinese intellectuals of varying ages had gone through an extraordinary array of what I . . . called identity fragments – of combinations of belief and emotional involvement each of which they could readily abandon in favor of another'. Protean man lacks the classical superego, 'the internalization of clearly defined criteria of right and wrong transmitted within a particular culture by parents to their children. Protean man requires freedom from precisely that kind of superego – he requires a symbolic fatherlessness in order to carry out his explorations.' Thus protean man is recognizable less by any content in his fluctuating beliefs than by his attitude towards systems of belief: 'Intimately bound up with his flux in emotions and beliefs is a profound inner sense of absurdity, which finds expression in a tone of mockery. The sense and the tone are related to a perception of surrounding activities and beliefs as profoundly strange and inappropriate.' Protean man, then, has affinities to the Adamic hero with his evasion of social identity and Lifton commends Bellow's Augie March as 'a picaresque hero with a notable talent for adapting himself to divergent social worlds', as well as J. P. Donleavy's Ginger Man and the black humorists generally. Finally he notes as another feature of protean man a 'suspicion of counterfeit nurturance' whether from institutions or even 'intense individual relationships'. Ellison's Invisible Man, Barth's Jacob Horner and Heller's Yossarian match up with Lifton's definition. All have the protean man's 'sensitivity to the inauthentic'.[32] Even Heller's Bob Slocum has this, though it is overbalanced by his deep dread of authenticity. But the possibilities of the picaresque hero as protean man were most completely explored by Thomas Berger in *Little Big Man* (1964), a novel about a character who illustrates every nuance of a truth not universally acknowledged, that it is good to be shifty in a new country.

Berger wrote good novels both before and after *Little Big Man*, as with the series of novels centred on the non-Jewish *schlemiehl* hero Reinhart (*Crazy in Berlin*, 1958, *Reinhart in Love*, 1962, *Vital Parts*, 1970, *Reinhart's Women*, 1981). In *Neighbors* (1980) a drab suburbanite finds his life taken over by a bizarre couple, more mortal enemies than liberating friends but not quite either. His triumph as a novelist, however, has been *Little Big Man*.

Jack Crabb, Little Big Man, is by his own claim 111 years old and, besides being the sole survivor of Custer's last stand, was in a shootout with Wild Bill Hickok and knocked cold by Wyatt Earp. Of course, as Ralph Fielding Snell, the prissy amateur historian who frames the novel with his foreword and epilogue, comments, it all may be a hoax: 'Jack Crabb was either the most neglected hero in the history of this country or a liar of insane proportions' ('Editor's Epilogue'). But from a literary perspective, the latter possibility is equally heroic and Crabb's fictional reality is established in the one sure way, by his voice. It is a colloquial voice deriving its precepts from experience rather than tradition, pragmatic, not without feeling but unillusioned, its first words directed to a doctor at the home for the elderly where Crabb is incarcerated: 'Boy . . . I took a slug in the ham once near Rocky Ford and cut it out myself with a bowie and a mirror, and the sight of my hairy behind was a real pleasure alongside of looking at what you carry on the top of your neck' ('Foreword by a man of letters').

In a 1961 afterword to James Fenimore Cooper's *The Pathfinder* Berger sees Leatherstocking as 'a kind of early Margaret Mead in buckskin' who 'identifies but never judges the variations among cultures', even in relation to individuals, 'finding delinquent only those who cross the boundaries of their proper role. . . . To get the better of him morally you must leave his universe altogether and consider the man who stays in the right place but cannot make a go of it – say an Indian who faints at the sight of blood, or a cowardly frontiersman.'[33] This anticipates Berger's creation of a character who bounces back and forth between roles within cultures and between cultures themselves. As Jack Crabb reflects, 'God knows I thought enough about it and kept telling myself I was basically an Indian just as when among Indians I kept seeing how I was really white to the core.' Roles are dropped and picked up with equal abruptness: 'Within a month after I stopped being Mrs Pendrake's pampered son, I was a dirty old bum sleeping in the back of the stables.' This gives Crabb a certain freedom from systematized morality: 'Most all troubles come from having standards' (12). What Crabb falls back on in lieu of standards is 'a brainy opportunism'; he presents 'an image of human vitality holding its own in the world amid the surprises of unplanned coincidence'. He is 'neither a good man nor a bad one, but is genuinely amoral – now triumphant, now worsted and rueful, but in his ruefulness and dismay he is funny, because his energy is really unimpaired and each failure prepares the situation for a new fantastic move'. This is to say that he is an archetypal comic figure in the terms of Suzanne Langer's brilliant general description of the comic *persona*, from which I have quoted.[34] Certainly Crabb lacks the classical superego, losing his family early as a consequence of a cultural misunderstanding with a group of Indians. He is not terribly agonized: 'No, my Ma was wellmeaning but ignorant. My Pa was crazy and my brother was a traitor. .

. . They weren't much of a family, I guess, but then I was not with them long' (1). Later Crabb helps to respectability a prostitute who pretends to be his niece; when she confesses her deceit he comments that the relatives he really cares about were 'elected to the position' (23). One such is Old Lodge Skins, his elective Indian father. The novel's play with relative values is evident in Crabb's relating of the standard definition of sin by another claimant to the paternal role, Reverend Pendrake, who adopts Jack, to the behaviour of Old Lodge Skins.

> 'The works of the flesh are manifest, which are these: adultery,
> fornication, uncleanness, lasciviousness, idolatry, witchcraft,
> hatred, variance, emulations, wrath, strife, seditions, heresies, env-
> yings, murders, drunkenness, revelings, and such like.'
> It was a funny thing, the most important years of my rearing so
> far had been handled by my second father, who was Old Lodge
> Skins. Now take away 'envyings' from that list – for he didn't
> covet much, owing to his belief he had everything of importance
> already – and you had a perfect description of that Indian's charac-
> ter. Yet he was as big a success among the Cheyenne as a man
> could be. (9)

Clearly, in the antinomian 1960s, the comparison favours Old Lodge Skins. By 1970 counterculture values had become so institutionalized as themselves to demand the satirical jabs of Berger's *Vital Parts*. Berger's strength is that he has no position except on the edge where he can observe chips fly as systems collide.

Such detachment opens him to the critical complaint that black humour politically cops out, as in Carl Oglesby's 1968 attack: 'Irony becomes now, in the hands of the black humorists and their critics, the supremely *political* device by means of which the horror is to be lived with instead of destroyed. . . .'[35] It is impossible to say how much, if at all, the demystifications of power and authority in novels such as *Naked Lunch* and *Catch-22* actually influenced political events. There is some evidence, as in the response to *Catch-22* earlier cited, that such novels did, in fact, crystallize scepticism about establishment values, a modest but not negligible contribution.

A case in point is the deromanticization of Custer in *Little Big Man*. In the 1941 film *They Died with their Boots On*, Errol Flynn could play General George Custer as a romantic hero. As Max Schulz notes, Berger's versions of Hickok and Custer are so convincing that 'no one reading the novel will be able to assent easily to the previous legends, except as they and Berger's coincide'.[36] Custer is Berger's model of The Hero but heroism is constructed as a mode of vanity compounded with blatant lying and a truly monstrous solipsism. Crabb, in Custer's tent, loses control momentarily and says, quite distinctly 'You bastard, I should have knifed you when I had the chance.' For this he could be shot but 'Custer had not heard my comment, spoke directly to his face! As regards the outside world, he was like a stuffed bird under one of them glass bells. His own opinion sufficed to the degree that he had no equipment for detecting exterior positions. That's the only way I can explain it' (25). This deglamorization of military heroics seems a real contribution – although the success of the awful Rambo films suggests that it may have worn off.

Kurt Vonnegut, more than Berger, has been attacked for his tone of coolness and apparent lack of indignation, taken as evidence of political and moral indifference. But the very intensity of this antagonism, and especially the *ad hominem* form it takes of presenting Vonnegut as a frivolously amoral person who sniggers at the horrors of our time, seems to contradict the claim that Vonnegut arouses no moral response, not to mention that Vonnegut's public life is politically engaged and exemplarily humanitarian. In *Slaughterhouse-Five or The Children's Crusade, A Duty-Dance with Death* (1969) the protagonist, Billy Pilgrim, a sometime prisoner of war survivor of the Dresden fire bombing and space traveller to the planet Tralfamadore, explains that Tralfamodorians believe that all moments, past, present and future, have a continuous existence so that grief is irrelevant: 'Now when I myself hear that somebody is dead, I simply shrug and say what the Tralfamodorians say about dead people, which is "So it goes" ' (2). Some critics take this as representing Vonnegut's own shrugging off of modern horror. But clearly Vonnegut is not exhibiting but examining cool disengagement from horror. As he comments, 'World War Two had certainly made everybody very tough' (1). The Tralfamadorian subplot, however, is too frivolous a device to carry the moral weight Vonnegut attempts to put on it.

There are, however, moral as well as political questions to be asked of black humour. The brainy opportunism of its protean protagonists may well model a sane evasion of various political stupidities but no new political idea emerges from these individualist withdrawals and in the 1990s economic rationalization continues apace. Since 1970 rock music and television situation comedy can claim more of a transforming influence on American consciousness than literature. The Barthian *either* to this *or* is that black humour at least anatomized mass-mediated consciousness, providing a certain resistance to it. Perhaps the real question should be the quality of consciousness *in* black humour fiction, its narrowing of emotional range in which desire diminishes to a one-dimensional lust, a sexual revolution for men only with representations of women varying from the patronizingly chauvinistic to the savagely misogynistic. Sentiment seems as much repudiated as sentimentality and there may be a certain complicity with the emotional (not sexual) repression against which Bellow protested. But then the most telling representation of such emotional failure, Heller's *Something Happened*, comes from within black humour. And a quickly forgotten masterpiece of moral acerbity, Alexander Theroux's *Three Wogs* (1975), now out of print, excoriates racism with a theologically based rigour, its absolute coldness of tone a necessary formal restraint upon a Swiftian savage indignation. Linda Hutcheon notes that the paradox of postmodernism is that 'it works within the very systems it attempts to subvert'.[37] These paradoxes and these questions carry over into postmodernism constructed as metafiction.

Notes

1. Ihab Hassan, quoted in Linda Hutcheon, *A Poetics of Postmodernism* (New York, 1988), p. 3; Jean-François Lyotard, *The Postmodern Condition*, trans. Geoff Bennington and Brian Massumi (Minneapolis, 1979), p. 60; Frederic Jameson, 'Foreword' to Lyotard, *The Postmodern Condition*, p. xviii.

2. Steven Connor, *Postmodern Culture* (Oxford, 1989), pp. 65–102.

3. Leo Bersani, *A Future for Astyanax* (Boston, 1976), p. 313.

4. Robert Alter, *Partial Magic* (Berkeley, 1975), p. 135.

5. *Alternative Pleasures: Postrealist Fiction and the Tradition* (Urbana, 1981), pp. 36, 38, 90.

6. Alan Wilde, *Horizons of Assent* (Baltimore, 1981), pp. 48-9.

7. Matthew Winston, '*Humour Noir and Black Humor*' in Harry Levin, (ed.), *Veins of Humor* (Cambridge, Massachusetts, 1972), pp. 269–84.

8. Mark Winchell, 'Beyond Existentialism; or the American Novel at the End of the Road' in Thomas Daniel Young (ed.), *Modern American Fiction: Form and Function* (Baton Rouge, 1989), pp. 225–36.

9. Roger Sale, *On Not Being Good Enough* (New York, 1979), pp. 116–17.

10. Jerome Klinkowitz, *Literary Disruptions: The Making of a Post-Contemporary Fiction* (Urbana, 1980), pp. 190–92.

11. Roland Barthes, *A Lover's Discourse*, trans. Richard Howard (New York, 1976), p. 177.

12. (New York, 1964), p. 476.

13. Sigmund Freud, 'On Narcissism: An Introduction' in Freud, *General Psychological Theory* (New York, 1963), p. 70.

14. 'Interview' in L. S. Dembo and Cyrena M. Podrom (eds), *The Contemporary Writer* (Madison, 1972), pp. 23, 26.

15. 'An Interview with Ronald Sukenick' in Tom LeClair and Larry McCaffery (eds), *Anything Can Happen* (Urbana, 1988), pp. 295–96.

16. 'Interview', *The Contemporary Writer*, p. 11.

17. 'Interview', p. 7.

18. O'Connor quoted on back cover of *The Lime Twig* (New York, 1961).

19. Leslie Fiedler, 'The Pleasures of John Hawkes', *The Lime Twig* (New York, 1961), p. x. The reader may note how institutionally authorized are Hawkes's transgressions!

20. *The Mechanical Bride: Folklore of Industrial Man* (1951; Boston, 1967), pp. 23, 79, 97, 141.

21. Anthony Channell Hilfer, 'Mariner and Wedding Guest in William Burroughs's *Naked Lunch*', *Criticism* **22** (1980), 252–65.

22. Philip Roth, *Reading Myself and Others* (New York, 1975), pp. 117–35.

23. Quoted in Thomas Blues, 'The Moral Structure of *Catch-22*' in Robert M. Scotto (ed.), *Joseph Heller's 'Catch-22': A Critical Edition* (New York, 1973), p. 544.

24. 'An Impolite Interview with Joseph Heller' in Joseph Heller's *Catch-22*, p. 457.

25. Sukenick, p. 286.

26. Robert Jay Lifton, *Home from the War* (New York, 1973), pp. 36–37.

27. Hendrik Hertzberg and David C. K. McClelland, 'Paranoia' in Arthur M. Eastman (ed.), *The Norton Reader* (New York, 1977), pp. 73, 178–79.

28. *Writers at Work*, pp. 238–39.

29. *Conversations with American Writers*, pp. 160, 153.

30. Johnson Jones Hooper, *Adventures of Captain Simon Suggs* (1845; Chapel Hill, 1969), p. 8.

31. Alexis de Tocqueville, *Democracy in America*, trans. Henry Reeve, Vol. 1 (New York, 1960), pp. 53–54.

32. Robert Jay Lifton, 'Protean Man' in Lifton, *History and Human Survival* (New York, 1971), pp. 316–31.

33. Thomas Berger, 'Afterword' in James Fenimore Cooper, *The Pathfinder* (New York, 1961), p. 432.

34. *Feeling and Form* (New York, 1953), pp. 331, 342.

35. 'Bagging It', *Ramparts*, 24 August 1968, 53–54.

36. Max F. Schulz, *Black Humor Fiction of the Sixties* (Athens, 1973), p. 73.

37. Hutcheon, *A Poetics of Postmodernism*, p. 4.

Chapter 6
Postmodernism as Metafiction

By the 1970s the critical construction of postmodernism had shifted from black humour to fabulation and metafiction. Literature was being considered less in thematic, more in formal terms. In fiction, character, already diminished in black humour, is even more completely absorbed into narrative voice and reflexively displayed as a vehicle of formal inventiveness. William Gass insouciantly defines character as 'any linguistic location in a book toward which a great part of the rest of the text stands as a modifier'. 'Some of the most famous characters in the history of fiction are in the great novel called philosophy. . . . Substance is more interesting than most of my friends.'[1] Yet at times postmodernist characters, despite screaming their fictionality, come eerily to life, not excluding some of Gass's.

There is, however, a considerable carryover from black humour into metafiction: offhand, even flip treatment of the dreadful; apocalyptic themes; mass-mediated characters. Nor is there an absolute chronological division. Metafiction, that is to say fiction about its own fictionality, overlaps with as well as incorporates black humour. Barth's *Sot Weed Factor* appeared in 1960; Pynchon's *V.* in 1963; Donald Barthelme's *Come Back, Dr Caligari* appeared in 1964 along with two works earlier discussed as black humour but with strong metafictional elements, *Second Skin* and *Little Big Man*. The master of metafiction, Vladimir Nabokov, wrote *Lolita* in 1955 and *Pale Fire* in 1962. Yet the different terms point to significant differences of emphasis and origin.

For one, the influences and parallels for metafiction are distinct. Barth, whose 1960s novels moved to this mode, cites Cervantes, Rabelais, The *1001 Nights*, Machado de Asis, Joyce (*Ulysses* and *Finnegans Wake*), Beckett and Borges. These authors are inventors of elaborate, sometimes fantastic plots; experimentalists with form; parodists of genres and styles; writers self-conscious of their writing sometimes to the point where it becomes theme and subject, as when Part II of *Don Quixote* reflects upon the imagined author of Part I, Cidi Ben Hamete, and offers a critique of *Don Quixote*. The main parallels with French fiction are with writers like Michael Butor whose *L' Emploi de temps* (1956) is an inconclusive detective novel, undercutting the rationality and closure of that form, and Raymond Quenau, the language experimentalist and creator of such pyrotechnically reflexive novels as *Zazie dans le métro* (1959) and *Le Chiendent* (1933). The American predecessor is Melville whose *Confidence Man* (1957) began to make sense to critics in the 1960s when it could be seen in the light of Barth, Barthelme, Burroughs and Nabokov.

Moreover, metafiction has a more problematic relation to modernism than most black humour. Black humour remained predominantly realistic in technique, though a calculatedly flattened form of realism. Realism is, at the least, what black humour writes *against*. Metafiction, in contrast, specialized in one direction of modernism, taking it as far as it could go, more completely disputing the basis of any 'reality', even, in contrast to the modernists, that of the art work. Metafiction reduces all to discourse while doubting the validity of that discourse. Signs no longer moored to reference point only to other signs, creating a vertiginous spin. As Patricia Waugh notes, metafiction locates meaning 'in the relations between signs *within* a literary text, rather than in their reference to objects *outside* that text'. This differentiates metafiction from black humour, where though subjects are diminished, there is still some residual belief in objects. Waugh nicely distinguishes between two types of postmodernist fiction,

> one that finally accepts a substantial real world whose significance
> is not entirely composed of relationships within language; and one
> that suggests that there can never be an escape from the prison-
> house of language and either delights or despairs in this. The first
> sort employs *structural* undermining of convention, or parody,
> using a specific previous text or system for its base. . . because
> language is so pre-eminently the instrument that maintains the
> everyday. The second is represented by those writers who con-
> duct their fictional experiments even at the level of the *sign*. . .
> and therefore fundamentally disturb the 'everyday.'[2]

To the postmodernist of either sort, the self is the sum of its roles (or its locutions) and the world is the sum of our constructions of it. This postmodernist world is empty of presence – though replete with false signs of it. Any apparent essence, any 'natural' being or feeling or presence, is really a mere social construction, a sign of culture trying to pass itself off as a scene of nature. 'Nature' itself (*sic*) is a cultural convention.[3]

There is certainly much to admire in this grand sweep of negation though not necessarily the logic or evidence offered to support it. More to the purpose is what kind of fiction results from such beliefs, and here

there are both gains and losses. In its jettisoning of representational realism as well as modernist metaphysical pathos, postmodernism risks being
merely shallow, merely illustrative of that unbearable lightness of being
so acutely delineated by Milan Kundera. Postmodernist metafiction
needs a certain *resistance* from the reality it presumes to deny and it is
arguable that the best metafiction is that which most compromises its
anti-representational principles. Robert Alter, commenting on Nabokov,
argues that Nabokov's less powerful novels

> tend in various ways to press matters of design in a fashion that re-
> strictively flattens the characters. The patterns of parody and ob-
> truded artifice are cunningly devised but the constructed fiction
> world, however ingenious, is hardly allowed sufficient vitality to
> give the dialectic between fiction and 'reality' the rigorous to-
> and-fro energy which it requires: a play of competing ontologies
> cannot fully engage us when one of the competitors, the invented
> world of the fiction, too often seems like intellectual contriv-
> ance.[4]

When there is a sense of that resistance, postmodernism reflects the tension of contemporary experience. When there is not, it may well be in
collusion with the frequent emptiness of that experience.

John Barth's passionate virtuosity

In his second phase Barth moved from black humour to metafiction, a
transition discernible within *The Sot Weed Factor* (1960). The title derives
from Ebenezer Cooke's 1708 Maryland poem noted in Chapter 3. Since
practically nothing is known about Cooke, Barth was free to imagine
him into being as his protagonist. Unlike the cynical protagonists of
Barth's first two novels, Ebenezer is an idealist and an innocent, in keeping with the persona if probably not the actual author of the poem.
Ebenezer's moral flaw is to reify and fetishize his innocence, even deciding to remain a virgin as a self-conscious emblem of it. But this is an
American literary convention in itself, evidenced in Faulkner's Isaac and
Warren's Burden. Barth's plot parodies these instances of the theme of
the evasion of the always already morally compromised world of sexual
and political relations, his variation on the theme showing more interest
in irony than moral pathos. Less successful is Barth's laboured travesty of
colonial Maryland history, the difficulty being that his fantasy version of
history is less fantastic, less surprising than the rich historical *actuality* of

contradiction and paradox. In *Giles Goat Boy* Barth interweaves social and political allegory of Cold War America with the archetypal myth of the hero quest and here too the archetype holds up better than the historical allegory.

He does better with writing about writing and with mythologizing mythology, adding rather than subtracting complication and parodox. Here is where his prose is at its best, a prose that continually backs up on itself, subverting content by commenting on form: 'God, but I am surfeited with clever irony! Ill of sickness! Parallel phrase to wrap up series!' Manipulative rhetorical style is caught in the midst of its devices: 'to acknowledge what I'm doing while I'm doing it is exactly the point'. These passages are from 'Title' in *Lost in the Funhouse*, a book of short fictions experimenting with various possibilities of self-reflection. The title story has a protagonist who is to some degree autobiographical though with the qualification suggested in 'Autobiography: A Self-Recorded Fiction' which is designed to be played before an audience as a tape recording with Barth standing silently beside it: 'When I see myself as a halt narrative: first person, tiresome. Pronoun sans ante or precedent, warrant or respite. Surrogate for the substantive; contentless form, interestless principle; blind eye blinking at nothing. Who am I. A little *crise d'identité* for you.' The next line announces the principle that does interest Barth: 'I must compose myself.' The self of 'Lost in the Funhouse', an adolescent from the eastern shore of Maryland, Barth's home ground, similarly loses substantiality in self-reflection while the fiction finds substantiality in reflecting on *itself*.

> Stepping from the treacherous passage at last into the mirror-maze, he saw once again more clearly than ever, how readily he deceived himself into supposing he was a person. He even foresaw, winking at his dreadful self-knowledge, that he would repeat the deception, at ever rarer intervals, all his wretched life, so fearful were the alternatives. Fame, madness, suicide; perhaps all three. It's not believable that so young a boy could articulate that reflection, and in fiction the merely true must always yield to the plausible. Moreover, the symbolism is in places heavy-footed.

The use of mirrors to image self-consciousness is, of course, heavy-footed symbolism. Barth then tells us 'two important things happened', the use of a list, however abbreviated, being a device subversive of subjective pathos. The second item further loses the protagonist in self-reflection: 'Second, as he wondered at the endless replication of his image in the mirrors, second as he lost himself in the reflection that the necessity for an observer makes perfect observation impossible, better make him eighteen at least, yet that would render other things unlikely. . . . ' In the midst of the protagonist's musings his creator (or

more precisely his creator's characterization of his creator) slides into the
narrative to worry about the plausibility of these musings in a character
too young to be familiar with Heisenberg's principle of uncertainty, that
is, the rule that there can be no pure observation because observation
alters the observed to the point that you can see only the behaviour
brought about *by* observation. Applied to literature this becomes
the impossibility of reflection on oneself as one is in a natural, that is
unreflective, state. Moreover, a problem with self-reflectiveness is that it
cannot be grounded outside itself since any reflection on it is a reflection
on reflection and so on into the infinite regress that is another convention of metafiction.

It is arguable that Barth's anti-realism enables a 'real' representation of
the workings of *his* consciousness, his reality, and that his models ours.
Alfred Appel argues that there could hardly be a more primary text than
one which catches up the writer in his writing and the reader in his
reading.

> . . . the creative process is fundamental, perhaps nothing is *more*
> personal by implication and hence more relevant than fictions con-
> cerning fiction; identity, after all, is a kind of artistic construct,
> however imperfect the created product. If the artist does indeed
> embody in himself and formulate in his work the fears and needs
> and desires of the race, then a 'story' about his mastery of form,
> his triumph in art is but a heightened emblem of all our own ef-
> forts to confront, order, and structure the chaos of life. . . .[5]

For that matter, attacks on the self-consciousness of the writing are anticipated and are a resource to the writer: 'Oh God comma I abhor
self-consciousness' ('Title'). 'Life-story' is the story of a writer bored
with the conventionality of his own anti-realism.

> The prose style is heavy and somewhat old-fashioned, like an Eng-
> lish translation of Thomas Mann, and the so called 'vehicle' itself
> is at least questionable: self-conscious, vertiginously arch, fashion-
> ably solipsistic, unoriginal – in fact a convention of twentieth cen-
> tury literature. Another story about a writer writing a story!
> Another regressus in infinitum! Who doesn't prefer art that at
> least overtly imitates something other than its own processes?
> That doesn't continually proclaim 'Don't forget I'm an artifice!'

The answer to the supposedly rhetorical question is John Barth, who is
writing a story about a writer writing a story about a writer. Not Barth
but his character is the one in trouble: 'It's particularly disquieting to
suspect not only that one is a fictional character but that the fiction one's
in – the fiction one is – is quite the sort one least prefers.'

The question of preference is crucial: 'For whom is the funhouse fun?' ('Lost in the Funhouse') For a writer considered by some as basically cold, the answer may seem odd: 'Perhaps for lovers.' If narcissism and a kind of cynical erotic energy charge Barth's first two novels, a more general and generous eroticism floods the work of his second phase. His most self-reflective text is 'Menelaid' in which Menelaus is the ground narrator of a story with seven frames. Two-thirds of the way through this story the frames top up as Menelaus demands of Helen through the various layers of storytelling why she ever wed him.

> " ' " ' " ' "Speak!" Menelaus cried to Helen on the bridal bed,' I reminded Helen in her Trojan bedroom," I confessed to Eidothea on the beach,' I declared to Proteus in the cavemouth," I vouchsafed to Helen on the ship,' I told Peisistratus at least in my Spartan hall," I say to who-ever and where- I am. And Helen answered:
> " ' " ' " ' "Love!" ' " ' " ' "

In 'Dunyazadiad,' the first story in *Chimera* (1972), narrated by Scheherazade's sister, Scheherezade discovers that 'the key to the treasure is the treasure', that is, that her stories give no single key to survival but that to tell them is to stay alive, Barth's ultimate justification for his fiction.

> We tell stories and listen to them because we live stories and live in them. Narrative equals language equals life: to cease to narrate, as the capital example of Scheherezade reminds us, is to die – literally for her, figuratively for the rest of us. One might add that if this is true, then not only is all fiction fiction about fiction but all fiction about fiction is also fiction about life.[6]

As an answer to those who believe sociopolitical relevance justifies fiction, Barth has Scheherezade come up empty in her search through all political science and psychology for a way to end the Shah's gynocidal frenzy. At the point of her discovery a genie who looks exactly like John Barth appears to confirm the rightness of it and discuss aesthetics with her. The two agree that while 'Heartfelt ineptitude' and 'heartless skill' each have their appeal, the true medium of story telling is 'passionate virtuosity'. As an example Dunyazade tells us that the genie imagines 'a series of say, *seven* concentric stories-within-stories, so arranged that the climax of the innermost would precipitate that of the next tale out, and that of the next, et cetera, like a string of firecrackers or the chains of orgasms that Sharyar could sometimes set my sister catenating'. This is, of course, the structure of 'Menelaid'. An erotics of literature is extrapolatable.

The genie declared that in his time and place there were scientists of the passions who maintained that language itself, on the one hand, originated in 'infantile pregenital erotic exuberance, polymorphously perverse,' and that conscious attention, on the other, was a 'libidinal hypercathexis' – by which magic phrases they seemed to mean that writing and reading or telling and listening were literally ways of making love. Whether this was in fact the case, neither he nor Sherry cared at all; yet they liked to speak *as if it were* (their favorite words), and accounted thereby for the similarity between conventional dramatic structure – its exposition, rising action, climax and dénoument – and the rhythm of sexual intercourse from foreplay through coitus to orgasm and release.

This would seem to be as direct an experience as literature could offer! Within his revisionary myth of Bellerophon, 'Bellerophoniad', the final story in *Chimera*, Barth claims primacy for his ventures into mythology as well: 'Since myths themselves are among other things poetic distillations of our ordinary psychic experience and therefore point always to daily reality, to write realistic fictions which point always to mythic archetypes is in my opinion to take the wrong end of the mythopoeic stick, however meritorious such fiction may be in other respects. Better to address the archetypes directly.' So he turns to myth as black humorists did to media.

Barth is his own best defender but a qualification is in order. Barth is an inventive plotter but like most postmodern fiction his work depends on the vitality of its voice. His ultimate postmodernist protagonist in *Lost in the Funhouse* is Echo, who 'becomes no more than her voice'. Subject or topic matters less than sustained performance. This performance reaches the level of passionate virtuosity in *Lost in the Funhouse*, especially 'Night Sea Journey', a tale of a self-reflective sperm suffering an identity crisis, and in the three stories of *Chimera*. But *Letters* (1979), *Sabbatical* (1982) and *Tidewater Tales* (1987) are less successful. *Sabbatical* is passionate but lacks the virtuosity, the one second-phase Barth work that falls into a relatively conventional realism and even sentimentality, neither of which Barth carries off very well. For a Barth novel, it is too well intentioned. *Letters* and *Tidewater Tales* have their moments but tend to run them into the ground. In these books there is an insufficient resistance to the sweep of fantasy. They draw on the usual play of narrative frames, self-reflections, etc. but the devices have become a conventional dog and pony act. It is possible that Barth's long struggle with *Letters* was due not to inherent complexity but to the lack within the novel of a vitalizing principle, an inbuilt opposition to which the work answers.

In 'The Literature of Exhaustion' (1967) Barth emphasized that the seeming exhaustion of traditional forms of fiction presented opportunities to inventive writers, one of which was to write about the problem itself – as in *Lost in the Funhouse*. Some misunderstood the essay to be another declaration of the death of the novel so in 1979 Barth wrote 'The Literature of Replenishment' to re-emphasize that he was talking about what novelists *could* do, not what they could not. The original essay, while vigorously justifying experimental writing, also expresses a reservation. He has no fondness for the experimentalism that repudiates technique and virtuosity: 'Now personally, being of the temper that chooses to "rebel along traditional lines", I'm inclined to prefer the kind of art that not many people can *do*; the kind that requires expertise and artistry as well as bright aesthetic ideas and/or inspiration.' The distinction, he explains, 'is between things worth remarking – preferably over beer, if one's of my generation – and things worth doing. "Somebody ought to make a novel with scenes that pop up, like the old children's books," one says, with the implication that one isn't going to bother doing it oneself.'[7] To some readers the works of such experimental writers as Raymond Federman and Ronald Sukenick will fall into this category. Sukenick's work has a scrappy energy but the self-conscious experimentalism seems finally a veneer over the relatively realistic first-person accounts of an egoistic protagonist whose ideas and experiences have a limited interest. Walter Abish's *Alphabetical Africa* (1974) is the very model of a thing worth remarking as it progresses from a first chapter in which all words must begin with A to a second where they can begin with A or B through to Z and then Z to A again. However, Abish's *How German Is It* (1980) is a postmodernist political thriller which holds up rather well.

Nabokov's underlying reality

Vladimir Nabokov's best novels are virtuoso performances with built-in resistances. A novelist of ultimate duplicity, Nabokov comes by his artifices naturally, having had, in the course of his career, to change nationalities and languages, a heightened version of the situation of protean man. Though early classified as a black humorist, Nabokov was writing masterworks of metafiction well before the 1960s.

Nabokov was born in Russia in 1898, the son of a liberal aristocratic jurist, V. K. Nabokov, who, having distinguished himself by his courageous opposition to the Tsar's pogroms and his Beiliss persecution, fled the equally tyrannical communist regime and was murdered in 1922 in Berlin by a reactionary white Russian who later became a Nazi official. Vladimir Nabokov and his Jewish wife Vera went from Germany to

France to the United States in flight from various forms of totalitarianism, experiences which instilled in Nabokov the devotion to personal and literary freedom and the militant individualism so aggressively expressed in *Strong Opinions*, a collection of Nabokov interviews. Nabokov became an American citizen, and in 1955 wrote his extraordinary novel *Lolita*.

Lolita was originally published by Maurice Girodias's Olympia Press in Paris in 1955 and was republished in the United States in 1958 by G. P. Putnam, due to the changing censorship situation. Girodias and Nabokov have contentiously different accounts of the original publication and the novel remains controversial despite having attained classic status. Interpretations of *Lolita* range all over the map but evaluations generally take one of three tacks: Nabokov is complicitous with his paedophiliac protagonist and his novel is morally opprobrious; Nabokov is comically exposing his protagonist and his novel is morally alert; Nabokov is playing an aesthetic game and moral considerations are irrelevant to his artistic design. I shall try to demonstrate the validity of the second view while showing what in the novel made it possible for intelligent readers to arrive at the first and third.

The crux results from Nabokov being an idealist and somewhat of a narcissist, who writes about solipsists, a type easily confused with the first two. Moreover, Nabokov lends his most solipsistic protagonists some of his opinions and, most importantly, his voice: 'Psychoanalysts wooed me with pseudoliberations of pseudolibidoes'; 'Let the credulous and vulgar continue to believe that all mental woes can be cured by a daily application of old Greek myths to their private parts.' The first voice is that of Humbert Humbert, the protagonist of *Lolita*, the second Nabokov's in *Strong Opinions*. The voices express identical opinions of Freudian psychology in similarly salient fashion. Moreover, Humbert's solipsism has much in common with Nabokov's aesthetic idealism.

Nabokov's adherence to subjective idealism is a motif of *Strong Opinions*: 'Your use of the word "reality" perplexes me. To be sure, there is an average reality, perceived by all of us, but that is not true reality: it is only the reality of general ideas, conventional forms of humdrummery, current editorials . . . average reality begins to rot and stink as soon as the act of individual creation ceases to animate a subjectively perceived texture.' 'Your term "life" is used in a sense which I cannot apply to a manifold shimmer. Whose life? What life? Life does not exist without a possessive epithet.' 'I tend more and more to regard the objective existence of all events as a form of impure imagination – hence my inverted commas around "reality". Whatever the mind grasps it does so with the assistance of creative fancy, that drop of water on a glass slide which gives distinctiveness and relief to the observed organism.' 'You can get nearer and nearer, so to speak, to reality; but you can never get near enough because reality is an infinite succession of steps, levels of perception, false bottoms, and hence unquenchable, unattainable.' *Lolita* was written, Nabokov declares, because 'It was an interesting thing to do. Why do I write any of my books, after all? For the sake of pleasure, for the sake of the difficulty.'[8] In his afterword, 'On a book entitled *Lolita*', Nabokov further disclaims moral intention: 'I am neither a reader nor a writer of didactic fiction, and . . . *Lolita* has no moral in tow. For me a work of fiction exists only insofar as it affords me what I bluntly call aesthetic bliss, that is a sense of being somehow, somewhere, connected with other states of being where art (curiosity, tenderness, kindness, ecstacy) is the norm.' Yet to create such a connection would seem to be a moral transaction and thus not so far from Nabokov's claim, in another mood, that 'one day a reappraiser will come and declare that, far from having been a frivolous firebird, I was a rigid moralist kicking sin, cuffing stupidity, ridiculing the vulgar and cruel – and assigning sovereign power to tenderness, talent, and pride'.[9]

The danger in subjective idealism is that idealists in pursuit of aesthetic or political bliss may coerce others into their ideal design, thus violating the quite different designs of these others. The strongest response to this danger comes from the idealist philosopher Immanuel Kant: 'man and generally any rational being *exists* as an end in himself, *not merely as a means* to be arbitrarily used by this or that will'. Human beings are '*objective ends*, that is things whose existence is an end in itself: an end moreover for which no other can be substituted, which they should subserve *merely* as means'.[10] This is the subjective idealist golden rule. From the legal point of view Humbert Humbert has committed child abuse and statutory rape; from the subjective idealist point of view he has used others as means. The reader's judgement of him would seem self-evident. Yet a number of readers have read the book as attempting to justify *Humbert's* perverse perspective. How could this be?

A book in which the protagonist was an unequivocal villain would be too easy and self-evident for Nabokov who writes, as he says, 'for the sake of the difficulty'. The difficulty and brilliance of the novel come from variations on two literary conventions – first, the seductive effect of first-person narrative voice, and second, the compelling plot and theme conventions of romantic love, endorsed by Humbert, parodied by Nabokov.

Humbert Humbert as first-person narrator begins by parodying his own role as antihero, undercutting the reader's predictably valid responses. His style is both outrageously lyrical and outrageously jokey as he plays on the whole literary history of dubious antiheroes and duplicitous first person protagonists from the dual protagonists of Diderot's *Le Neveu de Rameau* through Dostoevsky's versions. Of Dostoevsky, Nabokov said, 'his sensitive murderers and soulful prostitutes are not to be endured for one moment' (*Strong Opinions*, 42) and in *Lolita* he trumps Dostoevsky by combining into one character a sensitive murderer, as in Raskolnikov, and a duplicitous narrator, as in the underground man. The reader's response to all this is built into the narrative: Humbert mock apologizes for his fancy prose style, excusing his self consciousness by noting 'I am writing under observation. . . ' (1:2). Within the narrative, this is literal – the whole of the novel is represented as Humbert's retroactive account written in a cell with an observation window in a psychiatric ward of a prison. But Humbert is additionally aware of being under the the reader's observation as well. He attempts to tease the reader out of appropriate responses by anticipating and undercutting them: 'But let us be prim and civilized. Humbert Humbert tried hard to be good. Really and truly, he did. He had the utmost respect for ordinary children, with their purity and vulnerability, and under no circumstances would he have interfered with the innocence of a child, if there was the least risk of a row' (1:5). The shameless switch from moral imperative to social expediency plays on our modern temptation to redefine morals as social conventions besides exploiting the comic archetype that Suzanne Langer delineated: Humbert is a 'brainy opportunist'. Humbert even contrives to represent normal sexual intercourse as an elephantine absurdity appropriate only to the supremely gross.

> The human females I was allowed to wield were but palliative agents. I am ready to believe that the sensations I derived from natural fornication were much the same as those known to normal big males consorting with their normal big mates in that routine rhythm which shakes the world. The trouble was that those gentlemen had not, and I *had*, caught glimpses of an incomparably more poignant bliss. (1:5)

After such rhetoric, the reader may be hard put to recall that the ideal of the nymphet is a euphemism for paedophilia. But then Humbert has got in his pre-emptive strike on the therapeutic categories, playing on our conventional fear of those who attempt to change our minds and on the subversions of word play: 'the psychotherapist as well as the rapist. . . ' (1:27). The verbal conflation (psycho*the/rapist*) is meant to suggest an underlying identity. Humbert adopts a moral convention of our 'age of suspicion' (in Nathalie Sarraute's designation): that since corruption and duplicity are universal, the person who shamelessly confesses to the worst has a moral edge.

It is also difficult to resist Humbert's construction of his desire in the terms of romantic love, with allusions to Poe's Annabel Lee and Catullus's Lesbia, and even a resuscitated version of the long-obsolete catalogue of charms, a convention so hackneyed that Shakespeare memorably mocked (and renewed) it in Sonnet 30, 'My Mistress' Eyes Are Nothing Like the Sun.' The conventional catalogue cites the lady's golden hair, cherry-red lips and pearl-like teeth whereas Humbert worships a given nymphet for her 'axillary russet', 'iliac crests' and 'her lovely uvula, one of the gems of her body' – that is, red armpit hair, the upper bones on the two sides of the pelvis, and the pendent fleshy part of the soft palate, none of which had been properly celebrated in previous catalogues. The climax to this celebration of neglected parts turns the usual catalogue inside out: 'My only grudge against nature was that I could not turn my Lolita inside out and apply voracious lips to her young matrix, her unknown heart, her nacreous liver, the sea-grapes of her lungs, her comely twin kidneys' (2:2).

In addition to specific rhetorical conventions, the very perversity of Humbert's desire is central to the tradition of romantic love. As Lionel Trilling points out, Humbert is 'The Last Lover' within a tradition in which passion is an emotion before which we are helpless, passive and suffering, a tradition that measures the reality and intensity of passion by the social conventions it flouts, the scandal it provokes. To revivify this tradition in an age in which adultery had become routine necessitated Nabokov's finding a new and still charged taboo.[11]

Trilling reads Nabokov's use of perversion as a metaphor for the intensities and subversions of passion, a way of getting a new literary charge out of an apparently exhausted theme. But this brings us back to the evaluation of the novel as a literary game in which moral and emotional response is evoked only to be undercut, since what matters is a self-referential aesthetic design. Certainly much in the novel seems radically self-referential, a verbal design in which words connect only illusorily with persons or things, their ultimate reference being to other words. This motif reaches its apex in the allusive trail of aliases with which Humbert's antagonist, Quilty, who has appropriated Lolita, taunts him in his futile pursuit through various motel registers. Some are fairly obvious such as the reference to a fine French dictionary: 'N. Petit, Larousse, Ill.' – Nouvelle Petit Larousse Ill. ('Ill. standing for both Illinois and Illustré). But Humbert may be overly sanguine in his view that 'one hardly had to be a Coleridgian to appreciate the trite poke of "A. Person, Porlock, England" '. 'A person from Porlock' is who Coleridge said interrupted his envisionment of 'Kubla Khan', leaving the poem incomplete. And few readers would get 'Dr Kitzler, Eryx, Miss'. 'Miss.' is for Mississippi on one level. But Dr Kitzler? Eryx? *Kitzler* is German for clitoris and Mount Eryx had ritual prostitutes, one of whom would then be an Eryx miss. The elucidations in Carl Proffer's *Keys to Lolita* are necessitated by the complexity of allusion and verbal play in the novel. The literariness of the novel is carried so far that Humbert even changes physical appearance in accordance with literary convention: as seducer he had 'clean-cut jaw, muscular hand, deep sonorous voice, broad shoulders' (II:11), while as loser in love he is 'fragile, *frileux*, diminutive, old-world, youngish but sickly. . . ' (II:29). Humbert himself mentions 'the stability of type that literary characters acquire in the reader's mind' (II:27), clearly with the purpose of undercutting the convention. The postmodern convention *is* to remind us of the fictionality of fiction, to divert us from the novel as referential to the external world, to the novel as referential to its internal world.

The moral question of a crime done to a child seems to be submerged in all this narrative artifice but the trick of the novel is that artifice is precisely where it continually resurfaces before becoming overtly and explicitly thematized in the second half of the novel. The moral theme surfaces precisely in bits of word play as when Humbert, buying Lolita a new wardrobe, drops in among cute plays on colour names – 'glans mauve'; verbal plays with internal rhyme and alliteration – 'Slips? No slips. Lo and I loathed slips'; a quite sinister exactitude – 'pumps of crushed kid for crushed kids' ; concluded by an excruciatingly valid recognition – 'We rounded up the deal with some prim cotton pajamas in popular butcher-boy style. Humbert, the popular butcher' (I: 25). Popular with whom else but the reader, it is suggested. *Brute Force* and *Possessed* are playing at the movie theatre of the town where Humbert first possesses Lolita.

There is as much pain as there is comedy and artifice in *Lolita*. Nabokov's overinsistence on the purity of his aestheticism can be understood as a form of denial, a self-protective pose of moral insouciance. I suspect that two factors worked to overdetermine such denial: Nabokov's reaction to the moral posturing that reduces moral response to stock response, analysed by Nabokov as *poshlost* and by Milan Kundera as *kitsch* and seen by both as common to the bourgeois and the totalitarian mentality, and Nabokov's need for distance from his own sense of exile, desolation and loss. The passage in the last chapter in which Humbert responds to the sound he hears coming from the valley below is not an authorial irony.

> And I soon realized that all these sounds were of one nature, that no other sounds but these came from the streets of the transparent town, with the women at home and the men away. Reader! What I heard was but the melody of children at play, nothing but that, and so limpid was the air that within this vapor of blended voices, majestic and minute, remote and magically near, frank and divinely enigmatic – one could hear now and then, as if released, an almost articulate spurt of vivid laughter; or the crack of a bat, or the clatter of a toy wagon, but it was all really too far for the eye to distinguish any movement in the lightly etched streets. I stood listening to that musical vibration from my lofty slope, to those flashes of separate cries with a kind of demure murmur for background, and then I knew that the poignant thing was not

Lolita's absence from my side, but the absence of her voice from that concord. (II: 36)

That some readers do not see this is understandable. Humbert Humbert has picked his pseudonymous name because it 'expresses the nastiness best' but he had considered 'Mesmer Mesmer' and his narrative mesmerizes the reader into 'umber and dark Humberland' (II:3) where Lolita herself is captivated. The European tradition of courtly and romantic love was analysed by Denis de Rougemont's *Love in the Western World* (1939) as a form of pathology and this pathological tradition is what Nabokov invites us into and exposes for us and in us once we are there. He reconstructs this tradition more thoroughly to deconstruct it. Humbert's early construction of his perversion into a self-justifying mythology of romantic passion is a classic instance of psychological denial. On the philosophic level, when Humbert has Lolita 'safely solipsized' (I:12), he commits the ultimate idealist sin of imprisoning another self within one's own fantasy, denying, specifically, Lolita's right to be an ordinary vulgar obnoxious and charming but not charmed or enchanted or mesmerized child. Of course, this all happens to characters in a book, verbal constructions of an author, as postmodernist aestheticians tediously reiterate. Of course, none of it is 'real'. Which reminds one of the scene in *Through the Looking Glass* when Alice finds the Red King sleeping, and is informed by Tweedledum and Tweedledee that she is merely 'a sort of thing in his dream'. She is, in fact, worse off since the King is in Lewis Carroll's dream and Lewis Carroll is in Charles Luttwidge Dodgson's dream. Alice, protesting her reality, begins to cry, provoking this exchange.

> 'You won't make yourself a bit realler by crying,' Tweedledee remarked: 'there's nothing to cry about.'
> 'If I wasn't real,' Alice said – half laughing through her tears, it all seemed so ridiculous – 'I shouldn't be able to cry.'
> 'I hope you don't suppose those are *real* tears?' Tweedledum interrupted in a tone of great contempt.' (4)

Carroll is joking on the solipsistic tendencies in Bishop Berkeley's philosophy but we can also extrapolate from this passage four approaches to reading: the sentimentalist who valorizes the tears but not the laughter; the cynic who valorizes the laughter but not the tears; the postmodernist theorist who knows there are no real tears in texts (or in life since that also is a text); and the realist who knows somehow Alice's tears make her real: she cries, therefore she is. All these approaches are correct. The triumph of *Lolita* is that, as Patricia Merrivale shows, Lolita's 'real' nature, needs and loss show through the chinks of the narrative.[12]

The all but Dickensian image of a child in pain appears in *Bend Sinister* (1947), Nabokov's second novel in English, and in his other

masterwork, *Pale Fire* (1962). Taking Nabokov too simply on the level
of fantasy and artifice has led to some critical confusion on this latter
novel which certainly is dazzling in its play with 'levels of perception,
false bottoms' but has its secret centre in a character, Hazel Shade, whose
name even is a literary allusion (to Sir Walter Scott's line 'In lone Gle-
nartny's hazel shade'). Nevertheless, her pain is at the apex of the novel's
hierarchy of reality. That much of the criticism on the novel fails to
discern this suggests that some academic criticism parallels the novel's
narrator, Charles Kinbote, in his structure of emotional denial.

   Ada (1969), Nabokov's last long fiction, lacks the power of voice so
compelling in most of Nabokov's work. Here the verbal ingenuity
becomes truly autonomous, even hermetic. The disappearance in this
novel of the pole of a reality not *completely* confined within Nabokov's
head leaves it a nugatory and solipsistic text. Solipsism always may have
been Nabokov's temptation yet in his best work, which is most of his
work, Nabokov uses the writer's trick of converting his worst tendencies
into his best writing. *Ada* is stylistically clever but fails to effect this
conversion, Nabokov's patented magic trick.

Gass's, Gardner's and Coover's questionable versions

The interrelation between formalist aesthetics and emotional denial is
fascinatingly articulated by William Gass, who is, along with Barth, Barthelme and Nabokov, the most inventive and vivacious of the self-conscious metafictional postmodernists. Gass's dismissal of realistic
characterization was cited in the first section of this chapter. In the same
interview, he asserts his interest in 'disarming the almost instant com-
municability of language' and in the creation of a work of literature not
as communication to the world but as a new object in it, an object of a
peculiar sort 'made of signs' that point not to things but to other signs.
As with Barth, such creation is an act of love: 'I would like to add
objects to the world worthy of love. I think that the things one loves
most, particularly in other people, are quite beyond anything they com-
municate or merely "mean". Planting these objects is a moral activity, I
suppose.' Later Gass comments that 'Very frequently the writer's aim is
to take apart the world where you have very little control, and replace it
with language over which you can have some control.' In another interview, Gass reveals how his need for verbal control over an imagined
world to which objects of love have been added derives from a family
background lacking in control, prolific in anger and deprivatory of love.

A powerful motive for inventing a world was Gass's rejection of the one he was born into. Unable to handle his mother's alcoholism and his father's crippled body and character, Gass 'decided, as one of my characters says, to pick another cunt to come from'. Although influenced by formalist New Criticism, Gass chose formalism primarily as a response to a major emotional danger.

> I am basically a closet romantic, a tame wild man. When I was in college, I closed the closet door behind me. Then, for all sorts of reasons, some artistic if you like, but at bottom personal as bottoms are, I became a formalist. I became detached; I emphasized technique; I practiced removal. I was a van. I took away things. And I became a toughie, a hard-liner.

In a single day, Gass changed his handwriting, deciding 'with the greatest deliberation and thought how I would make each letter of the alphabet from that time on'. As he later sees it, 'that change of script was a response to my family situation and in particular to my parents. I fled an emotional problem and hid myself behind a wall of arbitrary formality.' He went as far as anyone could go in consciously rejecting the self derived from a specific background and consciously inventing a new self and a new world for it: 'The alphabet, for Christ's sake, I would have changed that, if I'd been able.' In this interview Gass claims all this as 'a cowardly thing to do, but I simply would not have survived. I still hate scenes unless I make them.' In *The Tunnel*, a manuscript of a novel he has been working on for decades and which is still uncompleted as I write, though sections of it have appeared in various literary magazines, Gass is attempting to come to terms with his family trauma: 'What is perhaps psychologically hopeful is that. . . I am turning back to inspect directly that situation, and that means I have not entirely rejected it. On the other hand, I am taking a damn long time to write the book.'[13] This extraordinarily perceptive and honest account is dubious only in Gass's assessment of his decision to formalize himself as a cowardly rather than desperately heroic act. It helps explain the brilliance as well as limitations of his unique body of work. In *Omensetter's Luck* (1966) a basic flaw in the conception is counterbalanced by a spectacular play of ideas and language. The theme of the novel is simple but finely elaborated, counterpointing Jethro Furber, a conniving, extremely hysterical and self-conscious character, ill in body and in mind, against Bracket Omensetter, a natural, extremely serene and unreflective character, strong in body and so instinctive in his actions as hardly to need a mind. Omensetter is clearly a version of the Adamic hero and Furber plays a kind of Claggart to his Billy Budd.

The flaw in the novel is that Omensetter's characterization is quite unequal to the intensity of Furber's and thus fails to represent a forceful counterpoise to Furber's perversely inverted values. Yet in Gass's original conception, worked out in a manuscript stolen by a university colleague and never recovered, Omensetter was the sole protagonist, Furber not yet having been invented. Furber crept into later versions of the novel, eventually displacing Omensetter in a way that retrospectively seems inevitable for a novelist too emotionally as well as intellectually committed to self-conscious rhetoric to lend much sympathy to a character so 'natural' that he 'lived by not observing – by joining himself to what he knew' (2:4). As Gass later recognized, 'Omensetter is certainly not the major figure because he is basically a person without language. He is a wall everybody bounces a ball off. Now anybody who emerges in my work with any strength at all is somebody who has a language. . . . ' In contrast, language is Furber's sole defence against a world that appears actively hostile, allying him with the young Gass who chose language as the reality he could control. Furber's narrative is replete with 'jokes and poetry', the poetry usually obscene or scatalogical reflections on members of his congregation: 'Samantha Totty. . . grew her nose. . . in her potty. . . like a rose' (3:1). Moreover, Gass composes, as he says, in a state of tenseness on the verge of illness and his writing 'proceeds almost always from a sense of aggression'. A performative writer, writing for the voice, Gass is less interested in verisimilitude than in establishing 'the legitimacy of the verbal source'.[14] This source in *Omensetter's Luck* could only be Furber as opposed to the all but voiceless Omensetter.

The problem with the novel is that the ineffectiveness of Omensetter's non-verbal naturalness and innocence seems to justify Furber's neuroticism and malice, whereas if there were no figure offsetting Furber, the horror of his condition would show all the more clearly, a performance self-revealing and self-concealing. Though Gass has reservations about his idiosyncratic novella *Willie Masters' Lonesome Wife* (1968), it is a more integral performance than *Omensetter's Luck*, dominated as it is by the obsessive single voice of its titular heroine, Babs Masters. Gass comments that the appearance of obsessional solipsism comes from his compositional method of locating his work in a single consciousness: 'Solipsism is one of the risks of the letter "I." If we were really listening in on any person's subconscious talk, it would sound pretty obsessional. One is consumed by one's self.'[15] But Gass's power as a writer comes from his creative sublimation of emotional injury, a strategic retreat that incorporates pain while disarming it into a vivid comic malice. The voice in the novella creates its own resistance, doubling back on itself in mockery of self as well as others. Moreover, the protagonist takes an emblematic presence in photographs interspersed through the text, besides a front cover that shows her nude front and a back cover that shows her nude rear. The (male) reader is thus introduced to the naked reality of the book at the beginning, enjoys it at some length, then sees it depart. The book plays graphic games throughout with a variety of type faces and graphic layouts, – a page in the shape of a Christmas tree, sections of different coloured pages, simulated glass rings on the same pages, a giant announcement proceeding a word at a time down the page, lapping a paragraph, informing the reader 'You've/been/had/ [paragraph] from/ start/to/finish' and within a glass ring at the conclusion declaring 'YOU HAVE/FALLEN/INTO ART/ – RETURN TO LIFE.' The book rejects the reader as consumer seeking vicarious satisfaction for egoistic desires. 'Babs' mocks her male exploiters, the last page of the blue section showing her lying in nude profile while above her floats in large curved type '00–000–00/my Mister/Handsome/how could you?' Caught in the act of reading! What is surprising is that somehow despite the verbal and graphic jazz, the self-consciously fictionalized voice of Babs takes on a kind of reality, becomes a legitimizing verbal source, supplying what Gass himself could not later see in it: 'Too many of my ideas turned out to be only ideas – situations where the reader says, "Oh yeah, I get the idea" ' but that's all there is to get, the idea. I don't give a shit for ideas – which in fiction represent inadequately embodied projects – I care only for effective effects.'[16] In fact these effects work in *Willie Masters' Lonesome Wife*.

Gass had a personally friendly and aesthetically antagonistic relationship with John Gardner, whose best novel *Grendel* (1971) does not entirely conform to the views expressed in his notorious *On Moral Fiction*. Gardner's other novels, the best of which is *The Sunlight Dialogues*, fail quite to come together, their cross purposes productive more of muddle than tension. But his retelling of *Beowulf* from Grendel's updated point of view, that of a monster who anticipates the bleaker aspects of the existential philosophy, is a *tour de force*. Trained as a medievalist and author of an article on *Beowulf*, Gardner plays with medieval notions of psychology and numerological symbolism and counterposes a Christian and heroic world view against Grendel's materialism, nihilism and existentialism, all of which Gardner is opposed to as a moralist looking for sustainable values and attracted to as a writer looking for an edge. Grendel is a model of the self-conscious postmodernist narrator: 'I cry, and hug myself, and laugh, letting out salt tears, he he! till I fall down and gasping and sobbing. (It's mostly fake.)' He dislikes natural creatures, deer and rabbits, because they lack tortuous self-consciousness: 'they see all life without observing it. They're buried in it like crabs in mud' (1). He carries on a continual self-dramatization motivated primarily by spite, as, when hearing the mead hall poet's exaggerated praise of King Hrothgar, he responds by snatching up a snake and whispering to it, 'I knew him *when*!' Yet he recognizes that the poet's ideal vision in fact reshapes reality by changing the audience's aspirations. His own postmodernist solipsistic internal monologues seem futile in contrast. Yet Gardner cannot help but let Grendel win the argument from a literary point of view. Hrothgar, the Geats and Beowulf may be right but are all also unconvincing and uninteresting; Grendel may be wrong but has the best lines. In his battle with postmodernism, Gardner, even within his own work, lost.

Robert Coover is a writer who sometimes exemplifies the postmodernist occupational hazard of writing that is more interesting in its narrative concepts than in its stylistic execution of them, as with *The Universal Baseball Association* where the criticism of the book is somewhat more interesting than the book itself. The book's archetypes resonate less with a sense of reality than an attunement to the explications to come. Both it and *The Origin of the Brunists* (1966), Coover's first novel, play with systems of belief, drawing, as did Barth in *Giles Goat Boy* and *Chimera*, from Lord Raglan's anatomy of the mythic hero. *The Origin of the Brunists* holds up better but Coover's masterwork is his short story 'The Babysitter' in his postmodernist story book *Pricksongs and Descants* (1969). This story resembles Alain Robbe-Grillet's experimental novel *La Maison de rendezvous* in playing out a set of bifurcating alternative scenarios of its basic situation and has an exemplary narrative complexity without losing its eerie intimations of contemporary forms of desire and consciousness. These are derived from mass media but are far from unrealizable or implausible as they play out into possibilities of rape and murder. We are never quite sure how much of the sex and violence of this story – the babysitter is raped and murdered by various characters in the various scenarios – is to be taken as vivid representation of the characters' fantasy lives or as actuality, Coover's idea being that media fantasy is in perverse complicity with contemporary reality. It is like Hawkes's *The Lime Twig* set up to a jazzier beat and as with Gass and Gardner as well as Hawkes the story's hook is in the guilty involvement of the (male) reader with fantasies of sex and violence.

The Public Burning (1977) is the most ambitious of Coover's later fictions. Though the political anger of this book carries conviction and the use of a fictionalized 'Richard Nixon' as a somewhat sympathetic narrator is oddly effective, this account of the 1950s trial and execution of the Rosenbergs, the 'atomic spies', presents the usual problem of fictionalized history – the failure to match the bizarreness of the real.

The Paranoids: Pynchon, Gaddis, De Lillo and McElroy

Thomas Pynchon has attained a cult status, paradoxically by avoidance of celebrity. Not only does Pynchon avoid the lecture circuit, television interviews and public literary ceremonials but his present whereabouts and even appearance are unknown – the last known photograph of him dates from the 1950s. Though his social invisibility is probably the result of a rational decision to avoid the lures and distractions of the American publicity/celebrity racket, it also adds to the mystique that his fiction projects. This projection is of a world on the verge of apocalypse, doomed by a massive conspiracy whether against or directed by the established power elite. The conspiracy is apparent in a series of arcane signs though these signs demand interpretive decoding according to the rules of structural paranoia, one of which is that structural paranoia is impossible to distinguish from clinical paranoia so that interpretation itself may be a symptom rather than a diagnosis.

Explication of Pynchon has been a growth industry, an understandable response to the plethora of interpretable signs and explicatable references his works abound in. A thirty-page article on *Gravity's Rainbow* acknowledges help from an electrical engineer, a biologist, a physicist, a mathematician, a German professor and two librarians, one an expert in Hermetic lore. Moreover, the novel has complex internal self-reference: a critic notes: '*Gravity's Rainbow* is an extraordinary web of links among characters and actions, doubles, role-playing and role-reversing. Images of coordinating systems, parallel ideas, cross it at every point and at every level of theme and plot.'[17] His work is then both esoteric and interpretable, a winning combination. But though Pynchon is certainly one of the most original as well as erudite novelists since the 1960s there are, as some critics have noted, serious flaws in his fiction. The most unsparing critique is Pynchon's own introductory essay to his early stories, *Slow Learner* (1984).

Pynchon sees his basic early problem as a tendency 'to begin with a theme, symbol or other abstract unifying agent, and then try to force characters and events to conform to it'. The lesson is that if you 'get too conceptual, too cute and remote . . . your characters die on the page'. But in drawing much of the story 'Under the Rose' (1959) from the 1899 Baedeker guide to Egypt, he was still 'beginning with something abstract – a thermodynamic coinage or the data in a guidebook – and only then going on to try to develop plot and characters. This is simply, as we say in the profession, ass backwards. Without some grounding in human reality, you are apt to be left with only another apprentice exercise, which is what this uncomfortably resembles.' What substituted for this grounding were some ready-made ideas and attitudes. Pynchon's exhaustively explicated play with entropy, the second law of thermodynamics on how energy gradually becomes randomized and unavailable in a closed system, derived from Norbert Wiener's *The Human Use of Human Beings* and the sacred text of 1950s intellectuals, Henry Adams' *The Education of Henry Adams* (1918). The use of entropy as a metaphor for civilization running down became a popular fiction motif from the 1960s on and Pynchon was one of the first to take it up. In retrospect Pynchon finds the theme questionable: 'A pose I found congenial in those days – fairly common, I hope, among pre-adults – was that of a sombre glee at any idea of mass destruction or decline. The modern political thriller genre, in fact, has been known to cash in on such visions of death made large scale or glamorous.'

Pynchon also acknowledges the influence of 1950s formalism.

. . . the notion that one's personal life had nothing to do with fiction, when the truth, as everyone knows, is nearly the direct opposite. Moreover, contrary evidence was all around me, though I chose to ignore it, for in fact the fiction both published and un-published that which had been made luminous, undeniably auth-entic by having been found and taken up, always at a cost, from deeper, more shared levels of the life we all really live.[18]

Since characterization is not Pynchon's gift as a novelist it is not the best ground on which to evaluate him. It is, however, reasonable to inquire into the 'grounding in human reality' of Pynchon's writing, its participa-tion in deeper, more shared levels of the life we all really live and whether certain weaknesses in this area derive from the conceptions of character operative in his novels.

Taking all this into account, Pynchon's first novel, *V.*, though a *tour de force* of ideas about entropy, dehumanization and the like, is, except for one powerful episode, a rather slight book. The book is heavily populated by the shades of ideas, abounding with mechanical brides, running down in entropy, etc. *ad infinitum* but lacks affective power because the characters are not so much threatened as already subdued by these malevolent forces. There is a half-Jewish *schlemiehl* in the book but he is too thin a character to evoke the picaresque vitality of Augie March or the pathos of the losing game of Tommy Wilhelm. The book's comedy has an undergraduate aura to it, some of it all the same funny, some of it definitely dated, as topical humour tends to become. Yet a bizarre Parisian sequence catches some of the quality of 1912 European decadence and there is the one powerful and haunting episode of the German murder campaign of 1904 in Southwest Africa (now Namibia). One source for this episode may be Hannah Arendt who, although she does not specifically take up the instance of Southwest Africa in *The Origins of Totalitarianism*, interprets the 'administrative mas-sacres' of Africans by European armies as an educational experience in dehumanizing power, training for the holocaust. Throughout her book, Arendt traces the process by which Germans especially learned the de-lights of abandoning civilized constraints for a different kind of orderli-ness: that of bureaucratically organized mass murder. In *V.* a former soldier in the Von Trotha campaign nostalgically reminisces.

'It's impossible to describe the sudden release; the comfort, the

luxury; when you knew you could safely forget all the rote-lessons
you'd had to learn about the value and dignity of human life. I
had the same feeling once in the Realgymnasium when they told
us we wouldn't be responsible in the examination for all the
historical dates we'd spent weeks memorizing. . . .
'Till we've done it, we're taught that it's evil. Having done it,
Here's the struggle: to admit to yourself that it's not really evil at
all. That like forbidden sex it's enjoyable.' (5:2)

Unfortunately, Pynchon's attempt at an alternative to dehumanization is
risible. McClintic Sphere, a black jazz musician in the 'cool' modern jazz
quartet style, delivers what is clearly authorized by Pynchon as a value:
'keep cool but care' (4:6). This period attitude, unconvincing to anyone
under fifty, comes from a character so thinly created as hardly to exist.
Thus the sentence has a certain historical value as an example of 1950s
to 1960s attitudinizing but otherwise floats in the air, unattached to a
person and inapplicable to a mature conception of a world.

Pynchon is dismissive of his second novel, *The Crying of Lot 49*, but
within his limitations this is arguably his best novel to date. It is also his
most metafictional. All Pynchon's novels play against the conventions of
realistic characterization by giving their characters outlandish, frequently
allegorical names: Benny Profane, McClintic Sphere, Roger Mexico and
the like. But Pynchon outdoes himself in *The Crying of Lot 49* with his
protagonist Oedipa Maas, her husband Mucho Maas and such secondary
characters as the lawyer, Manny Di Presso. The basic question of this
text, foregrounded as a text by such devices as the antirealistic character
names, is whether its protagonist can correctly interpret the text which
she confronts, that is, a fictional world made up of what look like signs
but may not be. Oedipa stumbles across what seems a major conspiracy:
a secret organization known as the Tristero is seeking to undermine
official systems of communication by substituting its alternative mail system. Any sign found by Oedipa might be a genuine clue to the conspiratorial pattern; or deliberately planted as part of an elaborate posthumous
practical joke by Oedipa's deceased lover, Pierce Inverarity; or a mere
coincidence forced into the semblance of relationship by Oedipa's clinically paranoid construction of it. Hertzberg and McClelland note in an
essay on paranoia that '*The Crying of Lot 49* . . . is a story whose plot
is a plot – a fiction with the structure of a paranoid delusion.'[19] The
normal way of reading any complex text is to infer links between the
signs of the text even when they are not self-evident as in, Jonathan
Culler argues, taking contiguity to imply relationship. The reader, in
effect, creates textual pattern and meaning.[20] Readers, especially critics,
'are fond of patterns, and they abhor confusion or uncertainty. For them
there are no accidents, and nothing is coincidental.' This last quote
might have been from Culler on readers but is actually from Hertzberg

and McClelland on paranoids and the resemblance is not accidental. To read Pynchon carefully is to be in Oedipa's dilemma: is one uncovering a structurally paranoid world or participating in a clinically paranoid perceptual process? Finding clues in a particularly bloody Jacobean revenge play, *The Courier's Tragedy*, Oedipa must become a textual critic, tracking down textual variants, some of which seem to have been suppressed because of too direct references to the centuries-old conspiracy. The conspiracy, if it exists, also implicates the second law of thermodynamics since it communicates via messages left in WASTE baskets. Pynchon's implication is that interpretation of complex texts may be an essentially entropic, solipsistic and paranoid activity, a premise reinforced by Hertzberg and McClelland's analysis of paranoia and Culler's of the reading process. If what passes for 'reality' is merely an interpretative construction, the line between fiction and fact becomes blurred to the point of disappearance, as also in the social text of a Southern California society defined by role mobility, as celebrated by Oedipa's lawyer, Metzger.

> 'But our beauty lies,' explained Metzger, 'in this extended capacity for convolution. A lawyer in a courtroom, in front of any jury, becomes an actor, right? Raymond Burr is an actor, impersonating a lawyer, who in front of a jury becomes an actor. Me, I'm a former actor who became a lawyer. They've done the pilot film of a TV series, in fact, based loosely on my career, starring my friend, Manny Di Presso, a one-time lawyer who quit his firm to become an actor. Who in this pilot plays me, an actor become a lawyer reverting periodically to being an actor. The film is an air-conditioned vault at one of the Hollywood studios, light can't fatigue it, it can be repeated endlessly.' (2)

Such an infinite regress of roles seems to crowd out the possibility of identity. Yet Pynchon's protagonist, Oedipa Maas, comes the nearest of any character in his fiction to having one. In a genuinely poignant passage, Oedipa recalls a moment of perception that seems to encapsulate her reality:

> In Mexico City they somehow wandered into an exhibition of paintings by the beautiful Spanish exile, Remedios Varo: in the central painting of a triptych, titled 'Bordando el Manto Terrestre,' were a number of frail girls with heart-shaped faces, huge eyes, spun-gold hair, prisoners in the top room of a circular tower, embroidering a kind of tapestry which spilled out the slit windows and into a void, seeking hopelessly to fill the void: for all the other buildings and creatures, all the waves, ships and forests of the earth were contained in this tapestry, and the tapestry was the world. Oedipa, perverse, had stood in front of

the painting and cried. No one had noticed; she wore dark green
bubble shades. (1)

Oedipa is Pynchon's most realized character for two reasons: (1) She
cries, therefore she is, and (2) her adventure in decoding the novel's text
is the mirror image of her creator's adventure in coding it. She is the
only Pynchon character who has a full share in his consciousness. This
consciousness is literarily constituted primarily by its voice, a predominantly comic one in this novel, and its quest, central in all of Pynchon's
fiction, for political possibility and religious revelation.

Politically, the quest is for the lost America of spirit, enunciated by
Whitman, perhaps forever lost in the land of General Electric, Dow
Chemical and Pynchon's own invented corporation, Yoyodyne. As
Oedipa first approaches the flagrantly named Southern California city of
San Narciso, home of Yoyodyne, she has an epiphany of rationalized,
corporate America.

> She looked down a slope, needing to squint for the sunlight, onto
> a vast sprawl of houses which had grown up all together, like a
> well-tended crop, from the dull brown earth; and she thought of
> the time she'd opened a transistor radio to replace a battery and
> seen her first printed circuit. The ordered swirl of houses and streets,
> from this high angle, sprang at her now with the same unexpected,
> astonishing clarity as the circuit card had. Though she knew even
> less about radios than about Southern Californians, there were to
> both outward patterns a hieroglyphic sense of concealed meaning,
> of an intent to communicate. There'd seemed no limit to what
> the printed circuit could have told her (if she had tried to find
> out); so in her first minute of San Narciso, a revelation also trem-
> bled just past the threshold of her understanding. Smog hung all
> round the horizon, the sun on the bright beige countryside was
> painful; she and the Chevy seemed parked at the center of an
> odd, religious instant. As if, on some other frequency, or out of
> the eye of some whirlwind rotating too slow for her heated skin
> even to feel the centrifugal coolness of, words were being spoken.

There is a question to be asked of Pynchon's religious meanings. These
have been traced to their sources and excellently interpreted by Pynchon
critics, especially Edward Mendelson in 'The Sacred, The Profane, and
The Crying of Lot 49'. As Mendelson points out, Pynchon draws on the
notion of 'hierophany', the manifestation of the sacred, from the com-
parative religionist, Mircea Eliade, and his title plays on the Pentecost
(Acts:2), when the Holy Ghost, the Paraclete, descended on the elect to
enable them to 'speak with other tongues, as the Spirit gave them utterances', yet 'every man heard them speak in his own language'. On one

level, the crying of Lot 49 is an auctioneer's calling of the lot number of a collection of stamps which Oedipa believes may provide a crucial clue to Tristero. But as Mendelson explicates, 'the word Pentecost derives from the Greek for the "fiftieth". The crying – the auctioneers calling – of the forty-ninth lot is the moment before a Pentecost revelation, the end of the period in which the miracle is in a state of potential, not yet manifest.'[21] Pynchon not only withholds his revelation but implies that it might encode an epiphany of nothingness. Despite major differences in tone and technique there is an affinity between Pynchon's novel and that of Paul Bowles. The text of the world, as of Pynchon's novel, may be a sheltering sky, protecting the reader from 'the terrible nakedness' that Tristero figures. The Tristero's graphic logo is a muted post horn, symbolizing the silencing of the official mail service but perhaps also ultimate silence, absolute entropy, heat death. Yet in another passage Oedipa's speculations are at least marginally more hopeful: 'Each clue that comes is *supposed* to have its own clarity, its fine chances for permanence. But then she wondered if the gemlike "clues" were only some kind of compensation. To make up for her having lost the direct epileptic Word, the cry that might abolish the night' (5). Here it is at least assumed that the cry, if only accessible, *might* abolish the night, a slim, highly qualified hope but a step up from none at all. Pynchon's novels, however, more generally hint at a revelation, 'some pitiless advent' as figured in *Vineland*, that seems more likely to establish than abolish the night.

The same tilting towards nihilism is found in the implied politics of the novels. Pynchon is in the Puritan tradition of the American Jeremiad, as analysed by Sacvan Bercovitch, a set of denunciations of Americans for backsliding from their chosen status as God's model theocratic or democratic or economic society. The underlying assumption is that if America is not the type of Heaven, then it is headed for Hell. As Bercovitch and others have noted, the Jeremiad has both right- and left-wing political possibilities, justifying imperialistic bullying and demands for civil rights, empowering Ronald Reagan, who was given to citing Jonathan Winthrop's famous 'City on a Hill' sermon, a Puritan definition of the new world formulated before Winthrop had set eyes upon it, and Martin Luther King, whose 'dream' derived from the same sources. Bercovitch, however, may be too ingenious in arguing that even the most apparently despairing accounts of failure of the mission reaffirm its possibility, thus reaffirming the status quo.[22] With Pynchon it is hard to tell. That Pynchon's politics are of the left is not in doubt but the general sense his work conveys is of a world so given over to the rationalized control of a death-loving fascist corporate conspiracy that there is hardly a space for political alternatives. Control is so total that even protest may serve its purpose – which conforms to Bercovitch's model, as well as the influential one of Michel Foucault. Tristero itself seems as sinister as the power it is attempting to subvert. In a nightmarish profusion of signs relating to Tristero, Oedipa finds AC–DC. This could stand for two types of electric current. Or it could stand for sexual preferences. But here it stands for 'Alameda County Death Cult, along with a box number and a post horn' (5). The nearest thing in the novel to a positive vision of political community is the musicless dance of the deaf that Oedipa wanders into, in which each couple dances whatever they please yet somehow without colliding: 'The only alternative was some unthinkable order of music, many rhythms, all keys at once, a choreography in which each couple meshed easy, predestined.' But this 'anarchist miracle' (5) seems a metaphor that leads no further. Nearer to a possible answer is that

> here were God knew how many citizens deliberately choosing not to communicate by US Mail. It was not an act of treason, nor possibly even of defiance. But it was a calculated withdrawal from the life of the Republic, from its machinery. Whatever else was being denied them out of hate, indifference to the power of their vote, loopholes, simply ignorance, this withdrawal was their own, unpublicized, private. (5)

It is possible, within the parameters of Pynchon's plot, that these withdrawals are a joke or delusion, but even if 'real' the frankly corrupt effectiveness of Warren's Willie Stark seems a liver, and even a more honourable moral alternative.

Oedipa's own increasing withdrawal seems more authentic since really a forced option; she has nowhere to go. *The Crying of Lot 49* is more convincing than other Pynchon works because his verbal sallies crystallize around the central point of Oedipa. The novel adds to its metafictional trickiness fine observational moments, as in 'another three-in-the-morning phone call, its announcing bell clear cardiac terror' (1), the perfect description of a specific modern experience. This 1966 book also participated in the cultural work of demystifying governmental authority: 'Hanging in the air over her bed she now beheld the well-known portrait of Uncle that appears in all our post offices, his eyes gleaming unhealthily, his sunken yellow cheeks most violently rouged, his finger pointing between her eyes. I want you' (1). In a Tristero forgery 'The deep violet 3c regular issue of 1954 had a faint menacing smile on the face of the Statue of Liberty' (6).

Gravity's Rainbow (1973) is Pynchon's most spectacular and explicatable book. It has generated its own critical industry, attained cult status and there are places that do observances (annual readings and like ceremonies). A rich and interesting book, resourceful in ideas and themes, *Gravity's Rainbow* lacks the coherence that the central character of Oedipa provided in *The Crying of Lot 49*. It is not difficult to understand or overly complex. With the available wealth of commentary, it seems quite apparent what the book is saying, much of which is very bright. But to the degree that these ideas cohere into a central vision, it is the now familiar one of an increasingly rationalized world fatally attracted to the void. There are, as critics have pointed out, moments of grace, but Scott Sanders persuasively argues that the 'few interludes of tenderness and compassion' are 'so fragile and evanescent that they only accentuate by contrast the general drift toward brutality'. Sanders also finds Pynchon less an analyst than an exemplar of a solipsistic and privatist tendency which, however unintentionally, reinforces existent American power relations. Pynchon's conspiratorial and paranoid imagination 'tends to make our social organization appear even more mysterious than it is, tends to *mystify* the relations of power which in fact govern our society',[23] thus lending them an aura of omnipotence, though this is more the case in *Gravity's Rainbow* than in *The Crying of Lot 49*. Despite the countertendencies within it, the general effect of Pynchon's fiction seems to me to deliver his world up to the forces of rationalistic order and the swoon towards non-being, the modern version of chaos and old night. There is a rare 'happy ending' in Pynchon's latest novel, *Vineland* (1990), brought about by the ironic *deus ex machina* of Reagan budget cuts that stymie a putative federal invasion of a Northern California dropout druggie paradise. But this is Pynchon's least convincing work in both character and theme, its characters not so much unbelievable as uninteresting, its prose the least inventive of any Pynchon work to date. The problem with Pynchon is that even his best work seems located not before or during the rebellion against the rationalized death-world but after the surrender. This is not to deny the special sense of threat that just this positioning conveys.

The paranoiac fiction of William Gaddis, Don DeLillo and Joseph McElroy has frequently been compared to Pynchon. Gaddis, in fact, predated and possibly influenced Pynchon with his 1955 novel *The Recognitions*, praised by Tony Tanner as 'inaugurating a new period of American fiction in which the themes of fictions/ recognitions has come to occupy the forefront of the American writer's consciousness'.[24] These themes are indeed central to Gaddis, Pynchon, DeLillo and McElroy though that they occupy *the* forefront of *the* American writer's consciousness is dubitable, another instance of Tanner's overprivileging of the romance tradition in American fiction in its various avatars.

The Recognitions, over a thousand pages long, follows various characters from America to Europe in a complicated plot of art forgery and personal inauthenticity. The many characters break down, however, into two basic types: lost souls, authentic but (or because) inarticulate, alienated from a world of vulgarity and pretence and from the fakers and decadents who constitute this world. This relates to the American theme of The Confidence Man, especially as enunciated in Melville's novel, and, like Melville, it makes of fraud a metaphysical principle, but the

tone of contempt for a fake bourgeois world is closer to Flaubert. Ultimately the weight of the novel's contempt, of its Manichean rejection of
the human body and the humanly constructed social space, is oppressive,
and even, as in the poetry of T.S. Eliot, to which it also shows affinities,
arbitrary. The book seems as punitive to, as enlightening of, its readers.
Darkly ironic, its creepy comedy is finally dead serious, lacking the gamesmanship of Melville, West, Barth, Pynchon and Roth. Gaddis's most
accessible novel is *Carpenter's Gothic* (1985), told primarily but not completely in dialogue and notably economical in its development of character and theme. This novel has as protagonist the one really sympathetic
character of Gaddis's fiction, a character again inarticulate – like the
main character in *The Recognitions* she rarely completes a sentence – but
with such a convincing sense of value that she becomes valuable to the
reader. It is at this point that Gaddis arbitrarily and abruptly kills her off,
a fictional trick that goes back to E. M. Forster and Evelyn Waugh but
that seems here more egregious than functional.

Don DeLillo has experimented with a very literary form of science
fiction in *Ratner's Star* (1976) but more characteristic is a series of paranoid literary thrillers. *The Names* (1982) is a prototype postmodernist
work in many respects. Full of such canny local observations as how the
price of oil 'has become an index to the western world's anxiety', telling
us 'how bad we felt at a given time' (3), it works out a plot whose
meanings are finally purely formal and verbal. Signs that seem richly
implicative end up pointing only at other signs, as empty of final substantial referential significance as a Peter Greenaway film. A character
declares 'This is my vision, a self-referring world, a world in which
there is no escape' (12) and this rather well describes the world of Gaddis, DeLillo and McElroy, though Pynchon has various escape hatches.
The greatest disappointment in this novel, as in McElroy's *Lookout Cartridge* (1974), is that when we *do* find out the nature of the terrorist plots
both revolve around they do not live up to their portentous anticipations. Yet both writers do convey a sense of an aimless contemporary
world where systems operate and intersect to no great end and where
destructiveness is as rampant as it is random. Still, the conception of
formal systems functioning in a void seems to work less well as a resource for these than for more baroque inventors as Beckett, Borges,
Barth or Barthelme.

Philip Roth's literary recycling

One might argue for a specifically Jewish school of postmodernism, citing Cynthia Ozick's use of postmodernism against itself, Philip Roth's

postmodernist play with the possibilities – not infrequently the impossi-
bilities – of Jewish and literary identity and the verbal gamesmanship of
Stanley Elkin's writings. Elkin, however, avoids using Jewishness as a
theme, one of his many memorable characters identifying himself as an
Assyrian – not a Syrian but an Assyrian. Indeed, Elkin's works are less
interesting for idea or theme than in their extravagant verbal inventiveness. Here is the Assyrian, a bailbondsman, trying to sell advance bail to
the University of Cincinnatti.

> 'There's going to be sit-ins, break-ins, rumbles you could read on
> a Richter scale. The Black Students' Organization will fire the frat
> houses and sear the sororities. Weathermen in the meteorology
> lab, safety pins in the computers, blood on the blackboards. Pro-
> fessor's notes'll be burned, they'll rip off the railings in the cafe-
> teria and pour weed-killer on the AstroTurf. What, are you
> kidding me? Mass arrests are coming. The night school students
> are spoiling for a fight.'
>   'The night school students?'
>   'They want the professors to take naps. They ain't fresh in the
> evening classes. They need shaves, They say, their suits ain't
> pressed.'

Who wouldn't buy a used car from this man? Only William Gass is
Elkin's equal at building a verbal structure that can float on its own
grease. But Philip Roth is the postmodern master at elaborating whole
narratives built on the model of Russian dolls with a series of false bottoms. Roth needs his complexities; his career is illustrative of the need
writers have to generate sufficient resistance.

> You're looking as you begin *a novel*, for what's going to resist
> you. You're looking for trouble. Sometimes in the beginning un-
> certainty arises not because the writing is difficult, but because it
> isn't difficult enough. Fluency can be a sign that nothing is hap-
> pening; fluency can actually be my signal to stop, while being in
> the dark from sentence to sentence is what convinces me to go
> on.

The problem with England (where Roth, married to the actress Clare
Bloom, lives part of each year) is that it is too benign: 'Nothing drives
me crazy here, and a writer has to be driven crazy to help him to *see*. A
writer needs his poisons. The antidote to his poisons is often a book.'[25]
  Roth's career began with the self-created difficulties of his first published stories, especially 'Defender of the Faith'. In this story a Jewish
soldier manipulates a Jewish officer for special treatment based on their
ethnic solidarity. But the officer draws the line at protecting the private

from a combat assignment and instead makes sure he gets one. The publication of the story in *The New Yorker* inspired a controversy in which Roth was accused of anti-Semitism and underwent the ordeal of appearing at Yeshiva University before an audience which expressed active hatred of him. A devastating experience at the time, it became a literary opportunity, a model of Roth's inventive version of literary recycling. This recycling encompasses not only his writings but the reactions of their readers and critics in an ingenious spiral of metafictional self-reflectivity.

Roth's first swirl was a number of realistic novels, including *Letting Go* (1962) and *When She Was Good* (1967), though the best known of these was his first, *Goodbye Columbus* (1959), a story satirically presenting the crassness of an assimilated generation of affluent secularized Jews whose identity is more rooted in American commercialism and mass culture than in any specific Jewish traditions. Although these books are observant and effective, Roth, like Bellow, still felt constrained by the prevailing formalist standards, his own voice still too imitative. The breakthrough book was *Portnoy's Complaint* (1969). In *The Facts* (1988), Roth's mock memoir, he notes that the scandalous subject matter of this novel – Jewish mothers, masturbation, '*shiksas*' (gentile women) as lovers, introductory and advanced fellatio – was less significant than its style.

> It was a book that had rather less to do with 'freeing' me from my Jewishness or from my family (the purpose divined by many, who were convinced by the evidence of *Portnoy's Complaint* that the author had to be on bad terms with both) than with liberating me from an apprentice's literary models, particularly from the awesome graduate-school authority of Henry James, whose *Portrait of a Lady* had been a virtual handbook during the early drafts of *Letting Go*, and from the example of Flaubert. . . . ('Now Vee May Perhaps to Begin')

That is, Roth had turned from modernist realism to postmodernist black humour. *Portnoy's Complaint*, however, now seems a one dimensional book, intermittently funny, but tamer than it appeared in 1969, especially as compared with the earlier literary scandals of Henry Miller and William Burroughs. Its real importance is as subject matter for Roth's second and much more engaging turn from black humour to metafiction, a turn of Roth's screw which manages to recycle Henry James into the centre of a fictional world also accommodative of the lunatic version.

The best of this material is in what Roth in *My Life as a Man* (1974) calls the 'Zuckerman variations' (2:1). Nathan Zuckerman first surfaces in this novel as a character created by the fictional novelist Peter Tarnopol. But a recycled and revised Zuckerman, with a different family background, comes into his own as the protagonist of a cycle of five novels, *The Ghost Writer, Zuckerman Unbound, The Anatomy Lesson, The Prague Orgy* and *The Counterlife*, and then, in his most extravagant manoeuvre, refutes Roth's version of his own life in the last section of *The Facts*. What the Zuckerman variations are mainly about is the dysfunctional relationship of a writer to his muse. The relation is actually a triangle because it includes the audience which becomes another fictitious character modelled to some degree on a real one. In *The Anatomy Lesson* episode where Zuckerman decides to switch professions he explains that no one tells an obstetrician what he ought to be producing: 'He catches what comes out and everybody loves him. When the baby appears they don't start shouting, "You call that a baby? That's not a baby!" '(2)

The Ghost Writer cites the famous lines from Henry James's 'The Middle Years' on 'the madness of art'; Zuckerman learns the craziest part of it is how boring it is: 'When, some years later, he went to see a production of *Waiting for Godot*, he said afterwards to the woman who was then his lonely wife, "What's so harrowing? It's any writer's ordinary day. Except you don't get Pozzo and Lucky" ' *(The Anatomy Lesson*, 4). One gives up a lot of life to do art but readers are intrigued by the supposed identity between the two. A woman once told Roth that his sister had confessed to her how shattered she felt by brother Philip's portrayal of her in *Portnoy's Complaint*. But Roth, unlike Portnoy, has no sister.[26]

Roth's later work consists of elaborating these mostly non-existent identities and relationships. Zuckerman becomes famous for *Carnovsky*, which is to Zuckerman as *Portnoy's Complaint* is to Roth. As did Roth, Zuckerman gets into trouble for not writing about the right kind of Jews. In the *Writers* interview Roth comments that 'The moral atmosphere of the Portnoy household, in its repressive aspects, owes a lot to the response of persistent voices within the official Jewish community to my debut' *(Writers*, 286). So audience response to the early work helps generate *Portnoy's Complaint* and audience response to that helps generate the Zuckerman variations. Trying to evade a proselytizing Jew at Jerusalem's Wailing Walls, Zuckerman reflects, 'Here we go. One Jew is about to explain to another Jew that he is not the same type of Jew that the first Jew is. . . ' *(The Counterlife*, 2). But the Zuckerman variations focus less on whether Zuckerman gets the Jews straight than on his difficulties getting himself straight. Like most postmodernist characters, Zuckerman tends towards irony and paranoia and 'ironic paranoia is the worst' as Zuckerman realizes in *The Anatomy Lesson*, where it gets so beyond his control that he splits into two opposed roles in his attempt to contain his contradictions.

> In *The Anatomy Lesson* the discovery I made – having banged the typewriter with my head far too long – was that Zuckerman, in the moment that he takes flight for Chicago to try to become a

doctor, should begin to impersonate a pornographer. There had to be a willed extremism at either end of the moral spectrum, each of his escape-dreams of self-transformation subverting the meaning and mocking the intention of the other. If he had gone off solely to become a doctor, driven only by that high moral ardor, or, if he had just gone around impersonating a porno-grapher, spewing only that anarchic and alienating rage, he wouldn't have been my man. (*Writers*, 7, 274)

Roth needs the internal opposition. In the role of the pornographer Milton Appel, publisher of *Lickety Split*, Zuckerman exaggerates his sex-ual rebellion well beyond the complaints of his harshest critics, inter-spersed with claims that even pornographers have standards.

> 'Sure I had animals in my last film, but nobody there forced any-body to fuck them. Chuck Raw, my star, walked off the picture because of the dog. He says, "I love dogs and I won't be a party to this, Milton. Banging women fucks up their minds – they can't handle it. Any dog who fucks a woman is finished as an animal." I respected Chuck for that.'

This ultimate send-up of the misogyny basic to the pornography trade is funnier and more telling than anything in *Portnoy's Complaint*, though clearly Roth also participates in the sheer joy of outrage. Zuckerman, reflecting on his role of Appel, observes that 'Anti-Semitically speaking, if a Jew wants to make money running a brothel, he'll make it sound like an adult day-care centre', though this seems equally true of the non-Jewish publishers of *Penthouse* and even *Hustler*, who may have been models for 'Milton Appel'. Zuckerman in his role of pornographer has borrowed the name Milton Appel from a critic who had written a sca-thing attack on Zuckerman's fiction much like Irving Howe's on Roth's. In another variation on life versus art versus life Roth reveals in *The Facts* that a dialogue in which a young woman intelligently tries to dis-suade the enraged Zuckerman from delivering a counterattack on Appel is the precise inverse of a conversation in which he explained to a friend why he should *not* attack Howe. To complicate matters further, when Zuckerman calls up Appel to make a long distance complaint, Appel clearly comes off better in the exchange. It is left open whether Zucker-man's severe undiagnosable neck injury in the implicatively titled *The Anatomy Lesson* is something he caught from his muse.

The most interesting of the Zuckerman variations is *The Counterlife*, possibly Roth's best literary performance to date. *The Counterlife* picks up from speculations in *The Prague Orgy* about 'the ever-recurring story that's at once your invention and the invention of you', that is, 'mock autobiography'. *The Counterlife* is a fiction about the transformation of life into fiction. In the first section Zuckerman tells of his brother Henry's death from a heart operation undertaken to restore his sexual potency. In the second section, the brother has lived through the operation and decided to renew his life as the follower of a fundamentalist nationalist rabbi in Israel, a character obviously based on Meir Kahane. In the fourth section it is Zuckerman who needs the heart operation. Midway through the section he dies from it, and first Henry, then Maria, the English lady for the sake of whom Zuckerman decided to risk the operation, become the central consciousness of the narrative. Henry discovers Zuckerman's story about Henry's death and bitterly reflects on Zuckerman's typical transference of his own worst possibilities on to his brother. He even finds a heavily emended draft of the very eulogy Zuckerman's editor had given at the funeral: Zuckerman had written his own eulogy, the ultimate expression of literary narcissism. Worst yet, though Henry does not know it, is that Henry's thoughts and actions though different in content from Nathan's fictionalized version of him fulfil Zuckerman's basic outline of his limited, emotionally dishonest personality, giving Zuckerman the last laugh as we read this story of Henry destroying Zuckerman's stories so he does not have to be a character in them.

Maria's Zuckerman variation is more interesting. She finds a manuscript that Henry had spared since he was not a figure in it. Both Henry and Maria respond to this manuscript, which turns out to be section five of the novel we are reading. So we 'actual' readers have seen this section critiqued before we could read it, in effect reading a commentary on it by one of its characters. Maria no more than Henry likes Zuckerman's version of the two of them married, living in England and attempting to cope with her family's and England's snobbery and anti-Semitism. But Maria's reading is more generous and more acute. She recognizes that what animates Zuckerman's misrepresentation of her family is not malice nor self-justification but a somewhat demonic version of literary necessity.

> I dread going back to my family. They're not so disagreeable as Nathan described, but neither are they very intelligent, by any means. He both heightened their intelligence and lowered their conscience and their moral tone. They're just deeply boring people who sit and watch television, and that was too boring for him – to put in a book, I mean. (4)

Zuckerman needs them to be better at being bad. He needs more opposition from them in fiction than he could manage to provoke in life.

Maria is one of the most real seeming characters in the Zuckerman variations because of her recognition that she is a fiction – of Zuckerman's in *The Counterlife* and of Roth in *The Facts*. Maria's eroticism is intensified by its reduction to the literary terms of an erotic voice. Before his operation Zuckerman reflects 'Suppose all I have fallen in love with is that voice deliciously phrasing its English sentences? The man who died for the soothing sound of a finely calibrated relative clause.' But, of course, this and some description is what Maria consists of. Erotic writing is a form of extended foreplay, as Maria realizes: 'It's all become so hopelessly tender just because we don't make love – because everything is always trembling just on the edge we can't cross over. This endless talk that never reaches a climax. . . . ' It is a 'verbal infatuation' and the nearest to culmination that it comes is when Maria finally says Zuckerman's name: 'There is the climax to all our talk – Maria speaking my name' (4). Here, more implicatively than in *Portnoy's Complaint*, is the eroticization of language that is so much a feature of postmodernist writing. Gass's reflections on what he calls 'the verbal sexualization of the mind' which is 'not sex, it's the language of sex' and is symbolic of creativity, holds good for Barth, Nabokov and Roth as well: 'language becomes the object it displaces – not just for sexual impulses, but for everything'.[27]

Maria recognizes she is in a subordinate position not as woman to man, which is negotiable, but as character to author where only mock negotiations with the ultimately controlling authorial figure are possible. Zuckerman is frightened by Maria's threat to leave the marriage he has imagined. The threat, of course, is also imagined: 'Imagine Maria gone, my life *without* all that, imagine no outer life of any meaning, myself completely otherless and reabsorbed within – all the voices once again only mine ventriloquizing, all the conflicts germinated by the tedious old clashing of contradictions within' (5). But Maria and her family are already projections of this internal clashing of contradictions, already ventriloquized. What most upsets her is that even her rebellion is pre-empted.

> At the point where 'Maria' appears to be most her own woman,
> most resisting you, most saying I cannot live the life you have im-
> posed upon me . . . at this point of greatest strength, she is least
> real, which is to say *least* her own woman, because she has
> become again your 'character,' just one of a series of fictive prop-
> ositions. This is diabolical of you. (5)

Her rebellion against being a character in a Zuckerman novel is a device we see Zuckerman spontaneously invent:

> I'm leaving the book.
> That's it. Of course. The book! She conceives of herself as my
> fabrication, brands herself a fantasy and cleverly absconds, leaving
> not just me but a promising novel of cultural warfare barely writ-

ten but for the happy beginning. (5)

She is aware, as she writes to Zuckerman, that her rebellion is a literary convention, but she is not ashamed, as an English character, to behave in an intelligently conventional fashion: 'I know characters rebelling against their author has been done before, but . . . I have no desire to be original and never did.' Who has outflanked whom here? She has recognized the real danger that authors present to characters. 'And how do I know what's to happen to Phoebe? That terrifies me. You weren't beyond killing your brother, you weren't beyond killing yourself . . . what if you decide everything will be more interesting if my daughter steps off the towpath into the river?' It should be noted that such danger is not exclusive to postmodern fiction. Phoebe would be as much in harm's way in a novel by Dickens, Dostoevsky or Harriet Beecher Stowe.

Maria, although she knows she is a postmodernist fiction, has the values of a realist. It is in Zuckerman's plea to her that Roth's novel becomes most oddly eloquent. Thus, Zuckerman counters the usual conception of the integrity of self with the authenticity of performance.

> I realize that what I am describing, people divided in themselves, is said to characterize mental illness and is the absolute opposite of our idea of emotional integration. The whole Western idea of mental health runs in precisely the opposite direction: what is desirable is congruity between your self-consciousness and your natural being. But there are those whose sanity flows from the conscious *separation* of those two things. If there even is a natural being, an irreducible self, it is rather small, I think, and may be the skill itself, the innate capacity to impersonate.

Zuckerman's unwillingness 'to perpetrate upon myself the joke of a self' is a postmodern convention. Less conventional is his invitation to Maria to join him in the game of self-refraction:

> But it *is* INTERESTING trying to get a handle on one's own subjectivity – something to think about, to play around with, and what's more fun than that? Come back and we'll play it together. We could have great times as Homo Ludens and wife, inventing the perfect future. We can pretend to be anything we want. All it takes is impersonation. That is like saying it takes only courage. I know. I am saying just that.

Johan Huizinga's idea of play in *Homo Ludens* (1944) finds its highest form in a citation from Plato's *Laws*, vii, 803.

> I say that a man must be serious with the serious . . . . God

alone is worthy of supreme seriousness, but man is made God's plaything and that is the best part of him. Therefore every man and woman should live life accordingly and play the noblest games and be of another mind from what they are at present . . . . For they deem war a serious thing, though in war there is neither play nor culture worthy the name . . . which are the things *we* deem most serious . . . . What then, is the right way of living? Life must be lived as play, playing certain games, making sacrifices, singing and dancing, and then a man will be able to propitiate the gods, and defend himself against his enemies, and win in the contest.[28]

Roth has not played the *noblest* games nor has he altogether propitiated his gods – or demons. But it is certain that he has made sacrifices, done a song and dance, and outflanked his enemies – by incorporating them into his fiction – and done rather well in the contest, in a literary game intelligently played. In his final appeal to Maria in *The Counterlife* he argues that she would be foolish to wish to escape from his book: 'To escape into what, Marietta? It may be as you say that this is no life, but use your enchanting, enrapturing brains: this life is as close to life as you, and I, and our child can ever hope to come' (5). Yet Maria has a right to dread, at the conclusion of *The Facts*, which started as a memoir and ended as another Zuckerman variation, that Roth has further designs on herself and on the resuscitated Zuckerman, now 'really' married to her in yet another of Roth's false bottoms: 'What she's saying is, "Oh; Christ, here he goes again – he's going to fuck us up!" ' This is true; it is even a condition for being a character in a Roth novel, but the compensation is, as Zuckerman has convincingly argued, that the characters are more real than the author: 'Your medium for the really merciless self-evisceration, your medium for genuine self-confrontation, is me.'

Postmodernist claims and accomplishments

Postmodernism, despite its claims, has not 'really' disproved the traditional conception of the self or of the world. Putting the word 'real' into quotation marks does not keep the rent from coming due. But the extravagant political claims – made mostly by the critics rather than the novelists – outdistance the philosophical ones. These claims notably concentrate on form rather than content, the idea being that to disorient a reader's perception of reality demystifies a bourgeois world which passes off a historically contingent political economy as natural and ordained.

Discrediting the possibility of *any* truth or moral standard especially undermines the bourgeois version, leading, somehow, to a radicalization of consciousness. By deconstructing the integral self, the 'other' within us all is liberated, free-floating, polymorphously perverse desire, innately subversive of the status quo.

So goes the postmodernist critical paradigm, but as Steven Connor among others has shown, a strong case can be made that postmodernism goes with rather than counter to the energies of late capitalism, being indeed a helpful ideology for a consumer society captive to the fleeting sensations offered by the postmodern media of television and advertising.[29] Indeed, the postmodernist attack on traditional spiritual and family values helps undermine the few surviving sources of resistance to the complete dominance of media and market. But perhaps this overstates the opposite case.

There can be no doubt that postmodernism expanded the possibilities of literary play, rediscovered some lovely literary conventions, undermined some dangerous cultural mythology and increased the energy level of American fiction. But there is also a certain depreciation of the complexities of sexual and family relationship, an overeasy cynicism, a failure of appreciation of the obduracy as well as the possibilities of what we usually suppose real. At this time, however, it seems that the postmodernist impulse, so strong from the late 1950s through to the 1970s, is fading. The main energy in American fiction since the 1980s appears to be in realism, a realism not quite revived because, however marginalized by contemporary criticism, it had a quiet, parallel, neighbourhood life all the while the postmodernist party was emptying the champagne bottles. The next chapter will show the very qualities left out of postmodernism reaffirmed in a realist strain of fiction that carried on through and beyond the postmodern era, though not without picking up some postmodernist doubts – and tricks – on the way.

Notes

1. 'A Debate: William Gass and John Gardner' in LeClair and McCaffery, *Anything Can Happen*, p. 28.

2. Patricia Waugh, *Metafiction* (London, 1984), pp. 53, 100.

3. Roland Barthes, *Mythologies*, trans. Annette Lavers (New York, 1972).

4. Alter, *Partial Magic*, p. 182.

5. Alfred Appel Jr, 'Introduction' to Vladimir Nabokov, *The Annotated Lolita* (New York, 1970), p. lvii.

6. *The Friday Book*, (New York, 1984), p. 236.

7. *The Friday Book*, pp. 65–66.

8. *Strong Opinions* (New York, 1973), pp. 10, 118, 154.

9. *Strong Opinions*, p. 193.

10. *Fundamental Principles of the Metaphysics of Ethics*, trans. Thomas Kingsmill (London, 1926), p. 55.

11. *Encounter* **11** (1958), 9–19.

12. Patricia Merrivale, 'The Flaunting of Artifice in Vladimir Nabokov and Jorge Luis Borges' in L. S. Dembo (ed.), *Nabokov: The Man and his Work* (Madison, 1967), p. 221.

13. 'A Debate', pp. 23, 27; 'William Gass' in *Writers at Work*, Fifth Series, pp. 251–54.

14. *Writers at Work*, Fifth Series, pp. 273–74, 263, 254.

15. *Writers at Work*, Fifth Series, p. 263.

16. *Writers at Work*, Fifth Series, p. 258.

17. Marjorie Kaufman, 'Brunnhilde and the Chemists: Women in *Gravity's Rainbow*' in George Levine and David Leverenz (eds), *Mindful Pleasures: Essays on Thomas Pynchon* (Boston, 1976), p. 201.

18. Thomas Pynchon, 'Introduction' to *Slow Learner* (Boston, 1984), pp. 12–13, 17–18, 21.

19. Hertzberg and McClelland, 'Paranoia', *The Norton Reader*, p. 177.

20. Jonathon Culler, *Structuralist Poetics* (Ithaca, 1975).

21. Edward Mendelson, 'The Sacred, The Profane, and *The Crying of Lot 49*' in Mendelson (ed.), *Pynchon: A Collection of Critical Essays* (Englewood Cliffs, New Jersey, 1978), pp. 122, 135.

22. Sacvan Bercovitch, *The American Jeremiad* (Madison, 1978).

23. Scott Sanders, 'Pynchon's Paranoid History' in *Mindful Pleasures*, pp. 149, 157–58.

24. *City of Words*, (New York, 1971), p. 393.

25. 'Philip Roth' in George Plimpton (ed.), *Writers at Work*, Seventh Series (Harmondsworth, 1988), pp. 271, 290.

26. *Reading Myself and Others*, p. 40.

27. 'William Gass' in Jo Brans (ed.), *Listen to the Voices* (Dallas, 1988), pp. 211–12.

28. Johan Huizinga, *Homo Ludens* (1944; Boston, 1955), pp. 18–19.

29. Connor, *Postmodern Culture*, pp. 201–247. Frederic Jameson has similar doubts but waffles in 'Postmodernism, or the Cultural Logic of Late Capitalism', *New Left Review* **146** (1984), 53–92.

Chapter 7
The Sorrows of Realism: Anglo-Saxon Attitudes

Rethinking realism

A dismissal of realism is one of the unexamined axioms of current critical theory. As we have seen, it is an article of theoretical faith that realism presents a historically contingent social order as if an artifact of eternity, not so much endorsed as unquestionably and inalterably there. Even the *momentary* 'reality' of what is supposed to be the realist representation of this social order is illusory, largely a creation of smoke and mirrors, of a language game of the version of reality held by white, affluent, heterosexual males, relegating women, people of colour and of different sexual orientation into a silenced marginality. Even the techniques of realism work to this end, subordinating the cacaphony of the different voices of the culture to 'the dominant "voice" of the omniscient author'. As in modernism, contradiction is entertained only to be eventually recuperated: 'textual contradictions are always finally resolved, either at the level of the plot (realism) or at the level of point of view or "consciousness" '.[1]

This is said so often and with so little doubt that it is surprising to see how strongly the same case could be made against postmodernism. As the next chapter will argue, American women write predominantly in the realist mode whereas postmodernist fiction is primarily the creation of white heterosexual males. The notion that radical technique makes for radical politics seems a classic false analogy and receives little support from the expressed political views of actual postmodernist novelists. Moreover, the supposed chorus of marginal voices is rather less apparent in postmodernist fiction than in theories about it. Indeed, Roger Sales finds postmodernist American fiction characterized by the imperial voice of the dominant, even domineering, novelist: 'it is possessive of its imagination and experience and casual in its presumption that its readers go right along with the show. The single imagination is unredeemably single and isolated, but it is also everything.'[2]

It would be ludicrous to reverse the poles of the poststructuralist argument and proclaim realism as an inherently revolutionary form. No revolution will take place under realist any more than postmodernist auspices yet neither is there the supposed unquestioning acceptance of things as they are. In fact, the white males who write realist fiction express a pervasive discontent. Though supposedly they occupy the centre, these novelists clearly *feel* displaced and marginal, even rather forlorn. Moreover, American realist novels whether by men or women tend to be structured around contradictions that are never quite resolved, perhaps because they reflect the contradictions of the social structure. Finally, it is arguable that these novels persuade their readers not to confirm the status quo but to question why its most consistent product seems to be unhappiness. One of the most plaintive of these writers is John Cheever and he illustrates the need to rethink the papal bull poststructuralist criticism issued against realist fiction.

John Cheever: portents of the abyss

Cynthia Ozick's review of John Cheever's *The Wapshot Chronicle* (1957) accuses the novel of a fake nostalgia for the community of St Botolphs that its protagonists love and lose: 'The trouble is not just homesickness but meretricious homesickness.' Noting that the character in the novel whose viciousness most contrasts with the traditional values is named Bracciani, Ozick protests there is 'no St Botolphs any more and for most of us there never was. We too were born Bracciani.' Even Cheever's stylistic grace is a form of dishonesty; his actual disbelief in his created world 'must be *detected*, for he covers everything over with a burden of beauty and sensibility'. St Botolphs is 'a fabrication, a sort of Norman Rockwell cover done in the manner of Braque'. Ultimately, the problem is that American writers of English descent lack an authentic experiential basis: 'Oh, it is hard to be a Yankee — if only the Wapshots were, if not Braccianis, then Wapsteins — how they might then truly suffer! And we might truly feel'.[3]

Though Ozick's commentary is acute, her notion that what John Updike calls 'the deep melancholy peculiar to American Protestant males'[4] is somehow literarily inadmissible smacks of the claim to a Jewish emotional monopoly that Philip Roth so derided. Joan Didion's response to Ozick provides an instructive counterpoint, affirming, though from an obviously different perspective, just those qualities in Cheever's fiction that most irritated Ozick.

Some of us are not Jews. Neither are some of us Southerners, nor

children of the Iriquois, nor the inheritors of any other notably
dark and bloodied ground. Some of us are even Episcopalians. In
the popular mind this absence of any particular claim on the con-
science of the world is generally construed as a historical advantage, but in the small society of those who read and write, it
renders us 'different' and a little suspect. We are not quite ac-
credited for suffering, nor do we have tickets for the human
comedy. We are believed to have known no poverty except that
of our own life-force. We are seen by the more tolerant as carriers merely of an exhausted culture, and by the less tolerant as
carriers of some potentially demonic social virus. We are seen as
dealers in obscure manners and unwanted pessimism. We are
always 'looking back.' We are always lamenting the loss of our
psychic home, a loss which is easy to dismiss – given our present
history in this particular country – as deficient in generality and
even in credibility. Yet, in a very real way the white middle-class
protestant writer in America is in fact homeless – as absent from
the world of his fathers as he is 'different' in the world of letters –
and it is precisely this note of 'homelessness' that John Cheever
strikes with an almost liturgical intensity.[5]

The common observation in these oppositional assessments is of the
presence of absence in Cheever's fiction. St Botolphs is, as Ozick argues,
a historical myth but homelessness is a metaphysical more than sociological condition. Didion acknowledges that Cheever's lost world never
quite really existed: 'Life has somehow bewildered these Cheever
people, left them bereft of something – they forget just what it is – once
promised . . . . *Lost money, the recollection of better times, silver bells ringing
in children from play*; the twilit world of the old American middle class is
indeed a lost world, as lost as Czarist Russia or the Antebellum South,
and like both those countries of the mind it has become a dream that in
some respects never was, an imagined territory capable of paralysing its
exiles.'[6] Cheever himself was later bemused by reviewers of *Bullet Park*,
who complained he should have stayed with St Botolphs 'which, of
course, never existed at all. It was so odd to be told to go back to a
place that was a complete fiction.'[7] St Botolphs was, in fact, reactively
constructed, the concept of it coming to Cheever 'late one night in a
third-rate hotel on the Hollywood strip where the world from my windows seemed so dangerously barbaric and nomadic that the attractions of
a provincial and a traditional way of life were irresistible'.[8] The trouble
with referring to this world for standards is that these standards partake
of its ontological insubstantiality, therefore more paralleling than opposing the anomic emptiness of city and suburb. As Ozick perceives, there
is a difference between what Cheever's texts overtly proclaim and what
they covertly reveal. Cheever's fiction is a hide and seek game in which

the surface realism is the cover story designed to divert us from a subtext of obsessional psychological archetypes. These archetypal motifs, most visible in *The Wapshot Chronicle*, *The Wapshot Scandal* and *Bullet Park*, play out a dialectic of Cheever's personal obsessive oppositions: macho assertiveness opposed to bisexual intimation; suburban conventionality opposed to demonic impulse; and, as the supercode to which all the above are subcodes, overt denial opposed to covert revelation. Denial is the principle of Cheever's writing, inherent in his evasive style, fore-grounded frequently as theme. Denial was too essential to Cheever's peculiar strategy for psychological survival to forgo but glimpsing this strategy out of the corner of his eye, he delivers classic descriptions of the process.

At his worst Cheever liked to play the role of huffily conventional American Protestant male but he partly understood his own pretence: 'there has been a rush on the part of many writers, to insinuate them-selves into the middle class, to live like bank clerks and to eschew any outward sign of disorder; a splendid maneuver, it seems to me, as long as the writer realizes that this is an act of espionage, that this is intended to put him in a position to observe the mores of his natural enemies'.[9] The weaker parts of his writing are where Cheever himself forgets, when he tries to enchant himself into acceptance and complacency, as in the truly awful story 'The Worm in the Apple', wherein the rhetoric of accept-ance could not be more obviously false, or in his accusatory reactions to women who venture out of the housewife role, as in the equally awful 'An Educated American Woman'. Cheever's strength is in his awareness of 'the portents of the abyss' in New York City and its suburbs, where 'You hear the voices and glimpse the faces of the fallen', and in his recognitions of a personal *and* representative failure. 'What we take for grief and sorrow seems, often, to be our inability to put ourselves into a viable relationship to the world; to this nearly lost paradise.'[10]

St Botolphs, the New England village of *The Wapshot Chronicle* and *The Wapshot Scandal* (1963), does not bear up under the burden of rep-resenting paradise lost. Much of the problem is in Cheever's construc-tion of Leander, father of the dual protagonists, Coverley and Moses Wapshot. Leander is intended as a normative character, exemplifying sturdy if provincial New England values and an engaging lust for life and women. None of this works. The characterization is strained and uncon-vincing throughout, Leander's invented voice sounding forced and smug rather than salty and vital. As a result, the advice left by Leander to his sons that closes both Wapshot novels has too little behind it to provide either closure or ironic open-endedness. The poignancy in both passages comes only from our recognition of how desperately Cheever, imper-sonating Leander, wants to believe in the talismanic efficacy of his rhetoric: 'Let us consider that the soul of man is immortal, able to en-dure every sort of good every sort of evil' (*The Wapshot Scandal*, 32).

The sentence, striving for nobility, finds a more convincing context in Cheever's tortured journals than in this novel in which deprivation and doubt have a basis lacking to even the most qualified affirmation.

One obsessive subtext reiterates female irrationality, vindictiveness and treachery. This is an obvious pattern even in the first and less dark of the Wapshot novels. Moses Wapshot loses his security clearance and job when his mistress explains 'a man came to see me one afternoon and I told him this long story about how you took advantage of me and promised to marry me and took all my money but I had to tell them something because they would have thought I was immoral if I didn't and I'm sorry and I hope nothing happens to you' (23). Betsey, Coverly's wife, desperately needy for affection, rejects it from Coverley, the only one who feels it for her, and blames him for her inability to connect with anyone else in the world. Moses courts Melissa, a sleeping beauty enchanted by her wicked guardian, Justina, who puts him in a room at the diametrically far end from Melissa of the mouldering castle wherein she has psychically imprisoned her ward. In a parody of medieval courtly romance, Moses earns Melissa's favours by clambering naked over the rooftop to her room, once narrowly escaping a gunshot from the suspicious Justina who has been watching for him. Justina's marriage present is two uncomfortable twin beds to replace Melissa's double bed and though Moses and Melissa continue to live at the castle only at Justina's insistence, she begins to charge him an outrageous rent besides giving all his clothes away to a charity on the principle that everything in her house belongs to her. Eventually Melissa turns on Moses, taking to wearing drab, desensualizing clothes and assuring him, 'I sometimes think you don't love me at all . . . and of course you put much too much emphasis on sex, oh much too much. The trouble is that you don't have enough to think about. I mean you're really not interested in business . . . . Most men are too tired to think about love every morning and every afternoon and every night. They're tired and anxious and they lead normal lives.' This scene climaxes with a line from Moses that Cheever had to battle for with his 1957 publisher: ' "You've talked yourself out of a fuck," he said bleakly' (35).

These scenes are some of Cheever's most effective, but in the aggregate this female malevolence is overdetermined, more projected authorial obsession than autonomous behaviour of characters. The denial here, is of misogyny, a motif so obvious in Cheever that he was frequently questioned about it in interviews, once by his daughter.[11] The greatest literary energy in *The Wapshot Chronicle* is invested in this personal misogynistic mythology though at times, as in Coverly's musings on the putative curriculum of a 'school of love', Cheever almost sees through his own masquerade: 'There would be special courses for Coverly on the matriarchy and its subtle influence – he would have to do make-up work here – courses in the hazards of uxoriousness that, masquerading as love, expresses skepticism and bitterness' (34). Uxoriousness actually functions as an excuse for a lack of interest in the subjectivity of Cheever wives whose ideal role is to accept male worship, serve male sexual desire and keep still.

The Wapshot Scandal of 1963 verges towards the emergent style of postmodernist black humour. Though Cheever disliked the postures of postmodernism with its implicit elitism, nihilism, and aestheticism, black humour was a better fit to his compulsions and perceptions than he liked to acknowledge. The function of verisimilitude in his fiction is to provide a stage for the intrusion of contingency: 'Verisimilitude is, by my lights, a technique one exploits in order to assure the reader of the truthfulness of what he's being told. If he truly believes he is standing on a rug, you can pull it out from under him . . . . What I've always wanted of verisimilitude is probability . . . . This table seems real, the fruit basket belonged to my grandmother, but a madwoman could come in the door any moment.' The Wapshot Scandal, Cheever declared, was a book 'built around non sequiturs'.[12] Betsey looks out of her window while watching television and sees a man putting screens on his windows fall two storeys. She resumes watching television: 'Presumably her concern for security had led her to overlook the death of a neighbor' (4). Betsey reacts to the unfriendliness of the world in general by cutting off the buttons on Coverly's shirts. When Coverly tries to recover his garbage pail from a neighbour who has openly stolen it, the neighbour shrieks social Darwinist philosophy at him and bites him on the leg. The aforementioned Bracciani, his boss at the missile complex where he works, is a sadistic psychopath. But then practically all the characters in this novel are either sociopaths or solipsists. Melissa, no longer frigid, turns nymphomaniac, caressing her doctor in the midst of a gynaecological examination and deciding that a small scar on the belly of the boy who delivers her groceries 'was more precious to her than the enormousness of all of Moses's love' (34). But all of Moses's enormous love has little to do with any aspect of Melissa except her sexuality: 'Outside the dark circle of love they seemed almost like strangers, and glimpsing Melissa down a long dinner table he had once wondered who was that pretty woman with light hair' (5).

This is a world of denial and disappointment. Denial is a theme as well as quality of the novel: Coverly 'had developed an adroitness at believing that what had happened had not happened, that what was happening was not happening and that which might happen was impossible' (26). Denial is of a pervasive disappointment: 'Why, in this most prosperous and equitable world, should everyone seem so bored and disappointed?' (5) The non sequitur style registers the structural illogic of the world as Cheever enunciated it in his Journal.

A bigoted and anaesthetized world. But what I don't seem able to do is to pull up the vision: the feeling of what life can be without uncommon bigotry, censure, and repression. And I don't seem able to get the triangle, the balance between the niceties, the stress on the appearance of things, the natural violence that lies beneath all of this, and the vision of a world where the balance is more commodious; where the sense of tragedy is not lost in anaesthesia.[13]

There is no tragedy in Cheever but he does convey the darkly humorous sense of the anaesthesia.

Bullet Park (1969), Cheever's most maligned novel, is also the one that most interestingly plays out his dialectic of denial and its revelation. The suburb of Bullet Park is in a state of general anaesthesia, occasioned by denial. Cheever's protagonist, Nailles, 'thought of pain and suffering as a principality, lying somewhere beyond the legitimate borders of western Europe' (4). But he and his community are under threat as even the newspapers cataloguing their daily disasters 'seemed to be news from another planet': 'a hairdresser in Linden, New Jersey, had shot his wife, his four children, his poodle and himself' (5). In this world whimsy has turned lethal. The disorder, however Nailles denies it, is as internal as it is external. In a rage about his son Tony's television addiction Nailles destroys the set meanwhile commending his own temperance: 'I love my gin and I love my cigarettes but this is the fourteenth cigarette I've had today and this is only my fourth drink' (5). This is his world's version of discipline. Nailles so dreads his commuter train trips to New York that he can manage them only when stoned with illegal tranquillizers. He cannot understand why his son Tony decides one day not to get out of bed again, and neither can the reader until Cheever flashes back to the night before when Nailles takes his son out to play miniature golf and discuss his underachievement at school. When Tony questions the ultimate value of Nailles's own occupation of advertising mouthwash, Nailles tries to kill him with his putter. John Gardner correctly sees Tony's consequent malaise as the result of soul murder.[14] Hammer, Nailles's openly murderous double, nearly carries through the son's murder but the intervention of a curiously convincing African American swami allows Nailles to save his son from his shadow self and leads to a paradoxically 'happy ending': 'Tony went back to school on Monday and Nailles – drugged – went off to work and everything was as wonderful, wonderful, wonderful, wonderful as it had been' (17). How it had been and continues to be is exactly caught in a reflection of Hammer's dotty mother: 'we have set up whole artificial structures as acceptable reality and stubbornly refuse to admit the terms by which we live' (11).

In his next to last and best selling novel, Falconer (1977), Cheever broke through the barrier of his repressions to a relatively open homosexual theme – as, later, he confessed to his children who had half realized. Yet *Falconer* now seems a lesser novel than *Bullet Park* or the Wapshot books. Denial, almost outflanked in *Bullet Park*, returns in *Falconer* with another motivelessly malignant wife and a demonic brother on to whom the protagonist's dark side is projected. The protagonist's escape from prison at the end is, in fact, escapist. In sum, Cheever's most informative mode was not that of (nearly) open confession but of the shadow dance of denial carried to the point of disclosing its own choreography.

John Updike: maintenance culture and transcendence culture

As F.C. Crews asserts, the critical standing of John Updike, despite his being 'our most prolific and various man of letters remains curiously out of focus and resistant to consensus'. The most influential critics disagree about whether Updike is despicable or merely unimportant, Crews judging that after an ethically approvable beginning his 'sensibility, it appears, has appreciably calcified, leaving him at once morally obtuse, politically inflexible, and crabbedly protective of beliefs that boil down to me-first salvationism'. The usual charge is more that he is 'a minor novelist with a major style' (Bloom), having 'nothing to say' (Aldridge) but saying it beautifully in a 'style in search of a centre' (Rupp).[15] The ethical indictment of Crews and others is certainly true of one of the various John Updikes to be found in his books but not of another John Updike who is critically aware of the first and takes him for subject matter. But critics could more accurately complain of an excess of meaningful themes, a surplus of signifiers, than a paucity. If Updike's style and his implied ethos lacks a centre, it is because he puts ethical oppositions into free play, not centring them into a predetermined moral universe. Updike even allows morally disreputable characters to speak in what sounds very much like his own voice. But the opinions of these characters are not altogether Updike's own. The confusion may come from his being more a *moraliste* than a moralist, that is a writer who poses moral dilemmas rather than one who delivers the latest ten commandments.

Updike has been better understood by other novelists. Joyce Carol Oates describes 'that remarkably detached, rather elegantly ego-less ability to glance without judgment on all sides of a melodramatic event, a basic clownishness that seems to go largely unnoticed in his writing, but which gives it its energy, its high worth'.[16] This quality is especially apparent in the first and last of his four novels featuring Harry 'Rabbit' Angstrom and in his mock-postmodernist novel *The Coup*. The Rabbit books illustrate the persistence of realism as Updike's favoured fictional mode while showing the adaptability of that realism to contemporary themes and issues. *The Coup* is one of a number of Updike novels responsive to more experimental themes and devices.

Rabbit, Run, published in 1960, is in many respects an epitome of the 1950s American novel. Its protagonist, innocent of politics and for the most part of ideas, feels crowded by his world and seeks freedom in flight. Tony Tanner correctly assimilates Updike's protagonist to the romance pattern of male flight from social conditioning. At one point in the novel Rabbit flees south but finds 'the further he drives the more he feels some great confused system, Baltimore now instead of Philadelphia, reaching for him'. His road map, a system of systems, becomes part of the problem rather than its solution: 'The names melt away and he sees the map whole, a net, all those red lines and blue lines and stars, a net he is somewhere caught in.' Citing these and other passages, Tanner describes Rabbit as 'simply one of many modern Huck Finns wanting to quit society and avoid growing up but with no "territory" to light out to'.[17] The escape theme and the entropy theme Tanner also emphasizes are prominent in *Rabbit, Run* but Tanner, though recognizing that the theme works dialectically, does not give sufficient weight to the counterbalance. In fact, *Rabbit, Run* is more a response to than an illustration of the escape theme in American writing. Updike declares that 'to be a person is to be in a situation of tension, is to be in a dialectical situation'.[18] He intends to place his readers in just this situation.

> My books are all meant to be moral debates with the reader, and if they seem pointless – I'm speaking hopefully – it's because the reader has not been engaged in the debate. The question is usually, 'What is a good man?' or 'What is goodness?' and in all the books an issue is examined. Take Harry Angstrom in *Rabbit, Run*: there is a case to be made for running away from your wife. In the late Fifties beatniks were preaching transcontinental traveling as the answer to man's disquiet. And I was just trying to say: 'Yes, there is certainly that, but then there are all those other people who seem to get hurt.' That qualification is meant to frame a moral dilemma.[19]

Reacting to Kerouac's *On the Road*, Updike is closer to Robert Penn Warren's critique of American fantasies of moral innocence and untrammelled freedom. But not quite that either since, as Updike acknowledges, his work consistently says ' "Yes, but." Yes, in *Rabbit, Run* to our inner urgent whispers, but – the social fabric collapses murderously.' Indeed, he writes fiction 'because everything unambiguously expressed seems crass to me'.[20]

Rabbit twice leaves his wife Janice, the second time because she refuses to accede to his urgent sexual demand because still not recovered from having a child. Updike brilliantly describes the series of rationalizations by which Janice then enables herself to get extremely drunk while assuring herself that she is meeting her responsibilities. The scene concludes with her baby's drowning as she tries to bathe her. The drowning brings Harry to a second reconciliation. But in the final scene of the novel, Harry, feeling the pressure of silent accusation, blurts out *at the funeral*, 'Don't look at me . . . I didn't kill her.' Harry's intention is not malevolent; he 'just wants this straight', 'in tune with the simplicity he feels now in everything', which he has rediscovered from his high school basketball star days in the form of a perfect golf shot. But 'the mute dense presences' of others do not allow for the simplicity of the perfect arc. Harry's mistress had found it infuriating that 'he just lived in his skin and didn't give a thought to the consequences of anything' and Janice's mother responds to an endorsement of Harry as 'in some respects a special case' with the judgement that 'The only thing special about him is he doesn't care who he hurts or how much.' Within the dialectic of the novel, both are right, both are wrong. Updike does not editorialize, the novel's present-tense voice putting the readers into the action so directly that they must clear their own ground for judgement. One must remember that on the fatal evening Harry *persuades* the reluctant Janice into her first drink, trying to loosen her up sexually. This does not make him a killer but it clearly contradicts the simplicity of his moral weightlessness. In the final passage of the book, off and running from the funeral, Harry reflects 'Funny, how what makes you move is so simple and the field you must move in is so crowded.' His flight is unjustifiable and lyrical: 'His hands lift of their own and he feels the wind on his ears even before, his heels hitting heavily on the pavement at first but with an effortless gathering out of a kind of sweet panic growing lighter and quicker and quieter, he runs. Ah: runs: Runs.' As Updike later reflected, 'Kerouac's *On the Road* was in the air and a decade of dropping-out was about to arrive, and the price society pays for unrestrained motion was on my mind.' Yet 'the title is a piece of advice, in the imperative mode . . . '.[21]

Rabbit, Run is a novel that encodes social history; it is recognizably a book of the Eisenhower years. *Rabbit Redux* (1971) takes the protagonist through the 1960s, featuring as subsidiary characters a hippie and a black artist. *Rabbit is Rich* (1981) is the Reaganomic rabbit, making money selling, what else, Toyotas. Both these seem more interesting as social history than vibrant as fiction. The last of the Rabbit books, however, is one of Updike's strongest, the terminally titled *Rabbit at Rest* (1990). But it will help to place this book to consider first a very different type of novel, Updike's contribution to or perhaps fictional revocation of the third world, *The Coup* (1978). From the beginning of his career Updike played with formal and thematic possibilities, his first novel *The Poorhouse Fair* (1959) being realistic in style but set in a dystopian future. Among his novels are *Roger's Version* (1986), an updating of Hawthorne's *The Scarlet Letter* told from the point of view of that novel's most malevolent character; *The Centaur* (1963), both autobiographical and mythical; and *Bech: A Book* (1969) and *Bech is Back* (1982), imitation Jewish novels that irritated Cynthia Ozick.[22] *The Coup* is the most outrageous of these ventures yet its protagonist and themes reflect Updike's underlying contradictions as clearly as the historical hops of his Rabbit books.

The major dialectical contradiction in *The Coup* is between two versions of value, corresponding to what the art critic Dave Hickey distinguishes as transcendence culture and maintenance culture. Concentrating on Post-Reformation still lifes, Hickey contrasts those which arrange a few objects in starkly apparent geometric relation to those in which a rich melange of objects sprawl over the canvas, lacking a clear centre and formal hierarchical order. The former vision sees the world in transcendent religious terms: few things are of value and then only within a divinely ordained strict order. The latter vision sees the world in secular hedonistic terms: the world is full of a number of things, good to look at, eat and drink, non-competitive and self-justifying. The goods of the maintenance culture require no overarching spiritual purpose being merely what comfortably maintains life. The maintenance culture tends towards complacency and excess; the transcendence culture tends towards fanaticism and sterility.[23] As a literary example, T. S. Eliot's *The Waste Land* is a nightmare vision of a maintenance culture described from a transcendence perspective. *The Coup* satirizes transcendent pretensions; *Rabbit at Rest* is a terminal vision of maintenance culture.

On the narrative level, the first-person protagonist of *The Coup* is Colonel Ellellou and its setting is Kush, a fictional African nation, the northern half of which is Saharan. Just beneath this level, Ellellou is the transparent mask of Updike's contradictions and Kush is the Paradise or Hell of his religious imagination. Curiously most critics hostile to Updike see him as an exemplar of the maintenance culture, a shallow hedonist lacking transcendent intensities. F. C. Crews more alertly recognized an anti-humanist transcendent side to Updike in his 'me-first salvationism'.

In *The Coup* Updike mocks American consumerism, Marxist rhetoric, avant-garde literary attitudes and, not least, his own theological leanings. The novel is Updike's as well as Ellellou's 'war within himself' (5) and reflects an intonation Ellellou describes in his tribal language, 'what in Salu we call having-it-both-ways'. Ellellou mocks the American aid the well meaning emissary Donald X. Gibbs offers, pointing out, in an obvious reflection of Updike's research, that where this aid is not absurdly pointless, it is ecologically disastrous. Ellellou then torches the mound of cereal boxes – '*Kix Trix Chex Pops*' – Gibbs has ascended, an immolated martyr to consumerism. But Ellellou's anti-American and anti-consumerist diatribes are equally the target as he idealizes Kush as 'a land of delicate, delectable emptiness, named for a vanished kingdom', a kind of anti-humanist, deconstructionist Utopia, the ultimate absence as presence, whose 'form of government is a constitutional monarchy with the constitution suspended and the monarch deposed' (1). The satire is partly of third world radicalism: 'The pure and final socialism envisioned by Marx, the theocratic populism of Islam's periodic reform movements: these transcendent models guide the council in all decisions' (1). This satire hardly exceeds verifiable political realities – even Ellellou's shocking discovery that colonialism was unprofitable, though obviously not what the 'politically correct' person is supposed to think is not necessarily *historically* incorrect, originating as much from Updike's research as did his satire on American aid.

Ellellou, however, also reflects Updike's own theological side as an admirer of Karl Barth's *Amselm: Fides Quaerens Intellectum*: 'There is no way from us to God – not even a *via negativa* – not even a *via dialectica* nor *paradoxa*. The god who stood at the end of some human way . . . would not be god.' Updike notes how what interested Barth in Anselm's argument was 'its rigorous negativity, its perfect independence of natural phenomena and the key it holds for him is, possibly, that it proves nothing – proves, that is, the nothingness from which rises the cry for god'.[24] Ellellou believes in 'a God without qualities', noting 'what can be purer than non-existence?' (3). The nearest to a visual icon of what he worships is the Sahara, which has 'a superior beauty, the beauty of the minimal, the changeless, the unpolluted, the necessary'. Though he takes a trip to the barren north in a quest to remove the curse of drought, he later logically recognizes the drought as the objective correlative of his religious faith: 'the drought is a form of the Manifest Radiance, and our unhappiness within it is blasphemy' (6). This implicates, besides Updike's own transcendent impulses, those of avant-garde art, looking back to the resonances of *The Sheltering Sky* and John Hawkes's nihilistic *Lunar Landscapes* (1969). Ellellou judges by 'lunar perspectives' (4). Transcendent gestures of art, politics and theology are implicated in Ellellou's ideal of Kush, the map of which suggests 'an angular skull whose cranium is the empty desert' (1).

But another side of Updike is found in the deposed king Edumu, one of the representatives of the maintenance culture, a character who displays 'the smiling obscurantism of the hopeless cynic' (2). One of Ellellou's consorts persuades him to execute the imprisoned king as a 'sky criminal'. 'She used here a technical Sara term referring to an offender not against his fellow men but against the overarching harmony of common presumptions: "political criminal" might be our modern translation' (2). But just what these presumptions are becomes a central issue in the novel. To Ezama, his chief minister, Ellellou declares his suspicion of a conspiracy meant to undermine the dreams of the people. Ezama, a maintenance type, replies: 'or is it the dreams of the people that are doing the undermining?' (2). On his trip to the northern badlands Ellellou thinks he sees, if it is not a mirage, 'two golden parabolas show[ing] above a distant deckled ridge'. Later he discovers the dreadful truth: Mcdonald's has indeed come to Kush. The most benevolent of his consorts protests against Ellellou's faith in 'a no-God, an eraser of gods; He cannot be believed in, for he has no attributes and is nowhere'. In short, the transcendence God. She believes in 'the little gods that make the connections, that bring love and food and relief from pain.' (3). In the trip north Ellellou, in a disguise that fools no one, joins a caravan whose unprincipled eclecticism of goods represents the values of the little gods, maintenance values: 'hallucinogenic khat, firearms of Czech and Mexican manufacture, plastic sandals from Japan, transistor radios assembled on such low-wage platforms as Singapore and Hong Kong, and boxes of Bic pens, Venus pencils, and Eberhard Faber typewriter erasers' (4). Ellellou is ideologically distressed less by the exploitativeness of capitalism than by its obscene profusiveness; its fruits spill over the page like the mix of objects in a still life: 'the gimmicky, plasticky, ball-and-jacky, tacky, distinctly dusty abundance of these toys, tools, hobby helps, and cardboard games – agitated Ellellou's breast with the passion to destroy, to simplify, *to make riddance of* . . . . This excrescence in the heart of Kush was not lava, it was an artifact, a plurality of artifacts, that had been called here by money' (6). Money as a means of exchange, a form of communication, violates Ellellou's quest for the abstract purity of the solipsism he finds in a political extremism in which 'I was free to imagine myself in an absolute form' (4). Yet as narrator Ellellou is complicitous in the verbal profusion obvious in the alliteration, assonance and internal rhyme of the artifact passage above. The wicked secret he has kept from his people is that the missing years of his early life were spent at a college in Wisconsin, where, indeed, he fell in love at the Oasis pharmacy. In a passage whose malice cuts both ways, Updike has an American emissary, Klipspringer, argue that 'A nation hates America because it hates itself'. The American Revolution has lasted two hundred years because 'All our Founding Fathers promised was the pursuit of happiness. Our people are still pursuing it, they'll never catch up to it; if they did, they'd turn right around and blame the Revolution. That's the secret, if you follow me' (6). Updike ironically uses Klipspringer to cite as a virtue of capitalism what conservative and Marxist critics alike denounce as the happiness trap of consumerism, but the implicit argument of the novel supports the ethos of the small gods and Ellellou is shown to hate America because he hates himself. His quest for purity founders on the obduracies of matter: 'Even the purity of water is a paradox, for unless it be chemically impure, it cannot be drunk' (7).

In *The Coup* the politics of high theory is undercut by particularities as when the 1957 homecoming football game at Ellelou's American

college, an occasion exemplary of conservative American mythology, is
won 'by a field goal kicked sideways, soccer style, from the forty-three-
yard line by a Peruvian general's degenerate son, who had gone out for
the team as a way of making homosexual contacts' (4). It would be
untrue to say that Updike discredits ideology, for *The Coup* wittily pro-
motes a maintenance ideology of promiscuous pluralism. At the end of
the novel, exposed as himself the curse on the land, Ellellou finds that
he has been quietly and formally deposed though still nominally ruling
Kush. In a kind of poetic justice, that is, his rulership has now attained
total abstraction. But the new, pragmatic rulers of Kush and their American allies are not unmerciful; Ellellou is deported to the south of France
to write his memoirs – that is, *The Coup*, financed by a Donald X.
Gibbs Travelling Fellowship.

The Coup might seem the last word in Updike's dialectic but if I read
him right there can be no last word and *Rabbit at Rest* is a low-keyed,
comic but quite grim indictment of a terminally entropic maintenance
world. It is a novel distinguished not by its complexities but by its re-
lentlessness, depicting a world whose structure is that of repetition, a
machine that keeps repeating the same movement until it wears down
and gives out. Harry Angstrom keeps on doing all the wrong things
until by the end of the novel he is dying of it. The novel's apt epigraph
comes from *Life and Times of Frederick Douglass*, Douglass's account of
how he freed himself from American slavery. Noting how the idleness
of his white masters had its own implicit penalties, Douglass observed
that 'food to the indolent is poison, not sustenance'. In *Rabbit at Rest* we
see Harry Angstrom eat himself to death. Harry is enslaved metaphysi-
cally, to be sure, to his body which must eventually wear out, but he
hurries along the process with his addiction to junk food. It is not that
Harry has no sense of the death's head on the desk; the novel is replete
with reminders of death, none of which Harry misses. But thinking of
death makes him want to eat and eating – peanut brittle, corn chips,
hamburgers, scallops wrapped in bacon – brings death closer. Watching a
television laxative commercial he 'can't help picturing the world filling
up with our Smiling American excrement, we'll have to pay poor third
world countries to dump it pretty soon, like toxic waste' (3). Seeing his
image reflected, he cannot justify his own superfluous presence.

> [Harry] is startled by how big he is, by how much space he is tak-
> ing up on the planet. . . . Though his inner sense of himself is
> of an innocuous passive spirit, a steady small voice, that doesn't
> want to do any harm, get trapped anywhere or ever die, there is
> this other self seen from the outside, a six-foot-three ex-athlete
> weighing two-thirty at the least, an apparition wearing a sleek
> gray summer suit shining all over as if waxed and a big head
> whose fluffy shadowy hair was trimmed at Shear Joy Hair Styling

(unisex, fifteen bucks minimum) to rest exactly on the ears, a fear-some bulk with eyes that see and hands that grab and teeth that bite, a body eating enough at one meal to feed three Ethiopians for a day, a shameless consumer of gasoline, electricity, news-papers, hydrocarbons, carbohydrates. (3)

Updike manages to focus a number of central issues of the 1980s/1990s on the figure of Harry Angstrom as a walking ecological disaster, a one-man 'greenhouse effect' – which is, of course, referred to in the novel. The novel obviously indicts the excesses of American consumer culture but the implications are theological as well; Harry responds to his daughter-in-law's view of herself as white trash with an affirmation he knows to be dubious: ' "Hey, hey," he has to say. "Come on. Nobody's trash." But even as he says it he knows this is an old-fashioned idea he would have trouble defending. We're all trash really. Without God to lift us up and make us into angels we're all trash' (2). There is still a mem-ory of transcendence even in this prematurely obsolescent protagonist. In Updike the analysis of transcendence and maintenance is interminable.

Walker Percy: the highest moments of a malaisian's life

In realist fiction's dialectic of maintenance and transcendence, Cheever's protagonists yearn most for a lost paradise of conventional maintenance culture, thwarted by persistently perverse wives too shaken by demonic impulses to provide consistent domestic service; Updike probes the weaknesses in both cultural ideals, exploring thereby his own ambivalen-ces; and the Louisiana writer Walker Percy best represents the transcend-ent position.

In his first and best novel, *The Moviegoer*, Percy's protagonist, Binx Bolling, sees some value in maintenance culture, the way of the little gods affirmed in *The Coup*. Binx speculates that 'It is not a bad thing to settle for the Little Way, not the big search for the big happiness but the sad little happiness of drinks and kisses, a good little car and a warm deep thigh' (3.2). But this does not save him from the 'malaise' of 'everydayness'. Everydayness is Martin Heidegger's term from *Being and Time*, Percy's novel's epigraph is from Kierkegaard, and Sartre's *Nausea* is a major influence on it. In its existentialist echoes, its flat ironic style and its depiction of much human behaviour as the acting out of dead con-ventions, this 1961 novel might be seen as more a black humour than a realist novel except that its characters never quite descend into caricature and that Percy's intention is not to rest in but go beyond the absurd in quest of a faith that can revivify life in a world recognizably our own. Satisfaction with the now prevailing values of this world is not a live option; Cheever, who tried and failed, is cited in Percy's self-help book for spiritual survival: 'As John Cheever said, the main emotion of the adult Northeastern American who has had all the advantages of wealth, education, and culture is disappointment.'[25] Alienation is Percy's starting point: 'The common thread that runs through all my novels is of a man, or of a woman, who finds himself/herself outside of society, maybe even in a state of neurosis, psychosis, or derangement. . . . I try to design it so that it will cross the reader's mind to question the, quote, "normal culture", and to value his own state of disorientation.' Alienation for Percy is spiritual, rather than political or economic, deriving from 'ancient, orthodox Christian doctrine. Man is alienated by the nature of his being here. He is here as a stranger and a pilgrim . . . .' If alienation is a metaphysical condition the American romance solution of flight from society is beside the point, a mere instance of what Kierkegaard called rotation: 'There are more suicides in San Francisco [the limit of flight west] than in other cities; that is why the rotation has run out.' In this, Percy agrees with Southern traditionalists like Robert Penn Warren, but he does not define himself as a 'Southern writer': 'I stay away from the Southern novel . . . . I think that the day of regional Southern writing is all gone.' Yet 'without the Southern backdrop . . . the novel doesn't work – it doesn't work at all. Try to imagine Binx Bolling in Butte, Montana. There has to be a contrast between this very saturated culture in the South, on the one hand, whether it's French, Creole, uptown New Orleans, or Protestant. It's a very dense society or culture which you need for Binx to collide with.'[26]

The temptation of existentialism is towards a merely aesthetic scorn for bourgeois conventions, a philosophized cultural elitism. But Binx, (like Percy himself) lives by choice in a middle class suburb rather than the more aesthetic and exotic French Quarter or Garden District of New Orleans, and he enjoys his work as a stockbroker. Percy's target is the spiritual banality and inauthenticity manifested in a pervasive emotional deadness. Two by now famous passages instance Percy's perspective. The first comes when Binx meets a relative, Nell Lovell, at the library.

> Whenever I feel bad, I go to the library and read controversial periodicals. Though I do not know whether I am a liberal or a conservative, I am nevertheless enlivened by the hatred which one bears the other. In fact, this hatred strikes me as one of the few signs of life remaining in the world. This is another thing about the world that strikes me as upside down: all the friendly and likeable people seem dead to me; only the haters seem alive.

Nell boasts of reading Khalil Gibran's *The Prophet* aloud and the scene concludes, 'We part laughing and dead' (2:9). The other passage is when Binx and his emotionally troubled cousin, Kate, do their best to make love, Binx invoking the aid of his patron saint, the 1950s romantic film actor Rory Calhoun.

> The truth is I was frightened half to death by her bold (not really bold, not whorish bold but theorish bold) carrying on . . . . Kate too was scared. We shook like leaves . . . . I never worked so hard in my life, Rory. I had no choice. The alternative was unspeakable. Christians talk about the horror of sin, but they have overlooked something. They keep talking as if everyone were a great sinner, when the truth is that nowadays one is hardly up to it. There is very little sin in the depths of the malaise. The highest moment of a Malaisian's life can be that moment when he manages to sin like a proper human being. (4:2)

This engaging passage, however, brings up a problem in that at first glance it seems typically black humoristic, in the John Barth mode, and existential in the atheist, Heidigger–Sartrian rather than the Christian–Kierkegaardian mode. In fact Percy became a Catholic convert in 1947 and constructed Binx as an example of the flaws of the aesthetic mode, exposed by Kierkegaard in *Either/Or*. That is, Binx is at least aware of being in despair and thus open to spiritual possibility as Kierkegaard construes it in *The Sickness unto Death*. But he assuages his despair with irony, casual sex, and self-conscious play with his own experience, a variation on the inadequacy of the aesthetic as opposed to the essential spiritual mode. The problem is that sometimes Binx speaks for Percy in his perception of a spiritually devitalized world but at others he misperceives because operating from the perspective of 'aesthetic damnation'[27] and the reader must go outside the book to Percy's essays and interviews to be certain which is which. In a scene near the end of the novel, reacting to his crippled half-brother's death, Binx seems to have become a Christian in between passages. In succeeding books, most notably *The Second Coming* (1980), Percy also had trouble with endings and sometimes, as in *Lancelot* (1977), his spiritual intention was all but indiscernible.[28] Nevertheless, he is a moral and spiritual writer of integrity and wit. *The Second Coming*, another novel of spiritual quest, has a soft, wish-fulfilling ending but finely distinguishes between what Kierkegaard called Christianity, that is the religion of the New Testament, and christendom, that is the smug and philistine practices of contemporary churchgoers. Percy's is an excoriating depiction of the wealthy, mindless, born-again christendom of the North Carolina of the Reagan years.

Raymond Carver: the submerged population

John Barth, mocking critical categories, suggests that some of the best contemporary American writers belong to the school of 'Post Alcoholic Blue-Collar Minimalist Hyperrealism'.[29] The category has one member: Raymond Carver, a short story writer whose spare narrative style gave rise in the 1980s to a certain critical hysteria about 'minimalism', a term borrowed from art criticism where it was dubious enough. Carver's own explanation for keeping stories short and bypassing the novel is both economical and metaphysical: he was working too hard at various low-level jobs to have the time for sustained writing and he was in a state of despair.

> To write a novel, it seemed to me, a writer should be living in a world that makes sense, a world that the writer can believe in, draw a bead on, and then write about accurately. A world that will, for a time anyway, stay fixed in one place. Along with this there has to be a belief in the essential *correctness* of that world. A belief that the known world has reasons for existing, and is worth writing about, is not likely to go up in smoke in the process. This wasn't the case with the world I knew and was living in. My world was one that seemed to change gears and directions along with its rules, every day. Time and again I reached the point where I couldn't see or plan any further ahead than the first of next month and gathering together enough money, by hook or by crook, to meet the rent and provide the children school clothes.[30]

Carver's style, that is, was a reflex to lower-class exigency. When his spiritual – and economic – condition changed, so did his literary perspective.

> My life is very different now than it used to be; it seems much more comprehensible to me. It was previously almost impossible for me to imagine trying to write a novel in the state of incomprehension, despair, really, that I was in. I have hope now, and I didn't have hope then – 'hope' in the sense of belief. I think now that the world will exist for me tomorrow in the same way it exists for me today. . . . In this second life, this post-drinking life, I still retain a certain sense of pessimism I suppose, but I also have belief in and love for the things of this world.[31]

Carver died in 1989 but his last story collection, *Cathedral*, reflects his new horizon, one story, 'A Small, Good Thing', even revising to include new possibilities of hope and communion one of his bleakest previous stories, 'The Bath', collected in *What We Talk about when We Talk about Love*. The title story in this collection is targeted in a front-page attack on the 'minimalists' in a 1985 Sunday *New York Times Book Review*, Robert Dunn's 'Fiction that Shrinks from Life'. Dunn aptly quotes from Christopher Lasch's 'The Minimal Self': 'In a time of trouble, everyday life becomes an exercise in survival. People take one day at a time. . . . Under siege the self contracts to a defensive core armed against adversity.'[32] Lasch's description fits Carver's characters but Carver is witnessing, not shrinking from American life. The characteristic response to those who witness ugly truths is critically to prescribe a different point of view towards nobler topics, a mode of denial. Dunn attacks minimalists for having too much focus on the personal as opposed to the public but Carver's readers are hardly forbidden to extrapolate his characters' private difficulties into a highly disturbing revelation not only of the way some people live but the way things are in the society they live in. A story in the earlier collection, 'Tell the Women We're Going', is as chilling a revelation of everyday casual American sexist attitudes as could be found and it is appalling how convincing it is when Carver carries the logic of these attitudes into random and gratuitous murder. One does not want to look but it is out there. A quieter violence is in the strangulated failures of communication that end many of Carver's stories.

> He said, 'I just want to say one more thing.'
> But then he could not think what it could possibly be.
>   ('One More Thing')

Carver intimates the alienation and desperation underlying these characters' silences.

Critics shrink from Carver less because he focuses on the personal than because his protagonists are unpleasant and their dilemmas frequently banal. Thus a critic attacked 'Preservation' because the main plot incident was of a refrigerator that breaks down, scornfully suggesting the characters call a repair man. But Carver's characters are people on the economic margin who, as Carver noted in an interview, 'can't afford to bring in a repair man if it's going to cost them sixty bucks, just like they don't go for a doctor if they don't have insurance, and their teeth go bad because they can't afford to go to a dentist when they need one'. These characters suffer from a dread as authentic as that of Cheever's Nailles, Updike's Rabbit and Percy's Binx, a dread that takes material form: 'These were lives where people really *were* scared when someone knocked on their door, day or night, or when the telephone rang; they didn't know how they were going to pay the rent or what they could do if the refrigerator went out.' Like Chekhov, Carver focuses on a 'submerged population', giving voice to door to door salespeople, waitresses, out of work alcoholics, 'people who aren't so articulate and who are confused and scared. . .'.[33] *Cathedral* makes a turn in Carver's fiction but the change in perspective is not all that great and is unquestionably hard-earned. It includes as desolate a story as Carver has written, 'Careful', a brilliant and indeed careful showing of how an alcoholic manages to naturalize his growingly self-destructive behaviour, explaining why it no longer seems 'unusual' to have doughnuts and champagne for breakfast. It is the attitude not the incident which is sinister; this man is clearly sinking out of sight.

The turn in Carver's fiction is most evident in the change of 'The Bath' into 'A Small Good Thing'. The first story ends in a totally warped anti-communication, the second expands into a small moment of emotional communion, even venturing into the religious symbolism of communion, the offering of bread. The title story features one of Carver's most self-enclosed, malicious, mean-natured protagonists and shows him open up, if only for a moment, to a sense of awe, again one with obvious religious overtones. These are not forced moments and they have a significance all the more in coming from a writer for whom affirmation was so difficult.

Waiting for realism

During the era in which black humour, then metafiction, attracted the most critical attention, most serious novels published year by year continued to be in the realist vein, character and story foregrounded, narrative voice and artifice deliberately unobtrusive. The sum of this fiction could now be regarded as an important minor tradition in the American fiction of 1960 to 1990 though it is possible that a future perspective may revalue it as major. It is arguable even that the most interesting American fiction of the 1980s has been realist rather than postmodernist. At this time the American writers most often cited as exemplars by young writers are in the realist mode.

The critical dismissal of realism has blurred the continuity of the tradition. James Gould Cozzens, who had seemed headed for canonization in 1957 with his best selling but serious novel *By Love Possessed* has now all but critically disappeared, due partly to a backlash at the preciously elaborated style of *By Love Possessed* that quickly followed its acclaim and due partly to Cozzens's unapologetic right-wing politics. The American writers who come the closest of anyone to being the bridging figures between Fitzgerald and Cheever as chroniclers of the American upper-middle-class, John Marquand and John O'Hara, have

similarly disappeared from the main critical ring. Marquand is still remembered for his gentle but apt satirical portrayal of *The Late George
Apley* (1937) but his novels of the 1940s and 1950s now seem overly
predictable and rather tame. The same cannot be said of John O'Hara
whose 1934 novel *An Appointment in Samarra* is a neglected masterpiece
of dysfunction and decline, pointing the way towards recent fiction on
marital and family breakdown, and whose short stories caught various
nuances of middle-class behaviour on into the 1970s. It is conceivable
that O'Hara's position in the literary stock market is tied to that of the
realist mode and that his stock may rise when it does. J. F. Powers is a
realist who has received little critical attention, perhaps due to his narrow though brilliantly explored choice of subject matter, that is, the
difficulties, petty but ultimately soul threatening, of Catholic priests
struggling to maintain meaningful vocation in the most consumerist society in all history, explored in his two short story collections and the
novel *Morte D'Urban* (1962). Realist writers are apt to specialize in a
given milieu, as Powers does with the Catholic parish world. Indeed,
though critically marginalized, the nineteenth-century realist tradition of
local colour has never quite disappeared. There are, for instance, Wright
Morris's Nebraska novels, especially *The Field of Vision* (1960) and *Ceremony in Lone Tree* (1960) which show the extraordinarily obsessive inner
life of some ordinary appearing Midwesterners by continuously reverting
to a few key events refracted through variant points of view. Morris,
from Nebraska but a longtime resident of California, shows insight also
into the very different culture of the west coast, *Love among the Cannibals*
(1959) being one of the best Hollywood novels, not so powerful as
Nathaniel West's *The Day of the Locust* or so savagely funny as Evelyn
Waugh's *The Loved One* but on a par with Alison Lurie's good comic
novel *The Nowhere City*.

Certain writers in effect 'own' a region, as Peter Taylor does the
middle south of Tennessee, the setting of his superlative short stories and
of his low-keyed subtle novels *A Woman of Means* (1950) and *A Summons to Memphis* (1986). William Kennedy owns Albany and Larry
McMurtry the Anglo North Texas of *Texasville* (1987), a sequel to *The
Last Picture Show* (1966) that is superior to the original. Rolando Hinojosa, however, owns the Mexican American South Texas of the Rio
Grande Valley, as in the slice of life vignettes of *The Valley* (1983) and
others of his Klail City Death Trip series. Moreover, Hinojosa's fiction is
central in a canon of Mexican American writing that began to emerge in
the 1970s and includes Tomas Rivera's *y no se lo trago la tierra* (1971),[34]
Rudolfo Anaya's *Bless Me, Ultima* 1972), Sandra Cisneros's *The House on
Mango Street* (1984), Maria Helena Viramontes's *The Moths and Other
Stories* (1985), and Arturo Islas's *The Rain God* (1984). However, this
body of fiction has yet to receive clear recognition in the general book
market, being published primarily by minority presses in Houston and

Los Angeles, partly due to the community loyalties of the authors and partly to the negect by mainstream presses. However, in 1990 the late Arturo Islas's second novel, *Migrant Souls*, was published by the mainstream house, Morrow, while 1991 saw his *The Rain God* reissued in paperback by Avon and – an even more significant breakthrough – Sandra Cisneros's second book, *Women Hollering Creek and Other Stories* published by Random House.

The realist novel remains one of the best forms in which to examine political currents and undercurrents, as in E. L. Doctorow's *The Book of Daniel* (1971), based on the Rosenberg case and his more panoramic *Ragtime* (1975). Billy Brammer's *The Gay Place* (1961) is a primer of 1950s Texas politics and Robert Stone brought the Vietnam War home in *Dog Soldiers* (1974), one of several Stone novels that use adventure story plots to examine the causes and consequences of the American penchant for violence. Peter Matthiessen's main interest is in the encroachments of our dubious civilization on more 'natural' worlds, as in *At Play in the Fields of the Lord* (1965), while Paul Theroux similarly investigates the impingements of mad American idealism on a more 'primitive' environment (*The Mosquito Coast*, 1982). The subgenre of the realist detective and crime novel is rich in depictions of the politics of conspiracy and corruption, as in Edward L. Heath's completely convincing account of Byzantine political manoeuvrings in an Alabama town in *Ill Wind* (1957) and the intelligent thrillers of Elmore Leonard, graced by Leonard's wonderful ear for lowlife speech. *The City Primeval: Detroit at High Noon* (1980) sends up both feminist and macho clichés with comic *brio*. George Higgins drew on his experience as a lawyer for the Massachusetts Attorney General's office in convincingly nasty novels such as *The Friends of Eddie Coyle* (1971). Even darker is Hubert Selby's *Last Exit to Brooklyn* (1964) which reads something like a realist version of William Burroughs. Though Selby does not have Burroughs's verbal and thematic inventiveness, the savagery of his urban death world is all too memorably portrayed. Most recently, Tom Wolfe, best known for his 'New Journalism' reportage written with the style and, to a degree, the factual reliability of fiction, produced a novel examining the warped ambitions and everyday duplicities of urban journalism, politics, and law in *The Bonfire of the Vanities* (1987).

Perhaps the most vital realist theme in contemporary fiction is that of the decline or rupture of relationship. Richard Ford's *The Sportswriter* (1986), a book well known to beginning novelists, is a first-person account of a man attempting to cope with the loss of vital relationship by reassuring himself of the adequacy of a minimalist form of stoicism coupled with alertness to the small graces of everyday life. Frederick Exley's *A Fan's Notes* (1968) takes an opposite tack with its first-person narrator who can neither abandon the ideal of transcendent glory nor attain it except as reflected in a dubious hero-worship. Both these writers are better known to other novelists than to critics, but Richard Yates's *Revolutionary Road* is the classic family horror novel. It is an excruciatingly convincing account of two people whose whole structure of life is entirely built on the lies they tell themselves. Published in 1961, *Revolutionary Road* is an instance of a novel that a non-academic audience and other novelists have kept alive despite the relative indifference of academic criticism. The 1989 film *Mr and Mrs Bridge* restored to prominence Evan Connell, author of the 1959 novel *Mrs Bridge* and the 1969 novel *Mr Bridge*, works that anatomized a traditional supposedly happy marriage, showing its basic rootedness in cultural pathology. Writers becoming recognized in the 1990s are Frederick Barthelme, whose *Two Against One* (1988) manages quite eerie descriptions of the psychic peril of vacuuming a room or buying a steak, and André Dubus, who shows his characters attempting, with varying degrees of success, to hang on to the traditional verities in *We Don't Live Here Anymore*.

It would be premature to declare who the coming writers of the 1990s will be but there is reason to suspect that most will be realists. Indeed, this chapter and the following one on women realists probably leave out more writers deserving recognition than any other section of this book due to the fact that contemporary realist fiction has been where you find most writers and least critics. Some of the most affecting recent fiction has taken the form of realist exploration of family dynamics, examining the effects of divorce, alcoholism, mental illness, loss of a child, child abuse. It is possible that future critics will look back to Russell Banks's *Affliction* (1989), which develops three of these themes literally and one metaphorically, as a breakthrough novel in an emerging subgenre of fiction, centred on the family, and telling its story from the different perspectives of male and female writers, fathers and sons, mothers and daughters.

Notes

1. Waugh, *Metafiction*, pp. 6, 137.

2. Roger Sale, *On Not Being Good Enough*, p. 61.

3. Cynthia Ozick, 'Cheever's Yankee Heritage' in R. G. Collins (ed.), *Critical Essays on John Cheever* (Boston, 1982), pp. 64–65.

4. Quoted in Scott Donaldson, *John Cheever: A Biography* (New York, 1990), pp. 241–42.

5. Quoted in Collins, 'Introduction', *Critical Essays*, p. 4.

6. Joan Didion, 'The Way We Live Now' in *Critical Essays*, p. 68.

7. 'John Cheever' in George Plimpton, (ed.), *Writers at Work*, Fifth Series (Harmondsworth, 1981), pp. 122–3

8. Cheever quoted in Donaldson, p. 159.

9. *The Letters of John Cheever, ed.* Benjamin Cheever (New York, 1988), p. 116.

10. John Cheever, 'Journals: From the Late Forties and the Fifties', *New Yorker* (6 August 1990), 48, 54.

11. Susan Cheever Cowley, 'A Duet of Cheevers' in Scott Donaldson, (ed.), *Conversations with John Cheever* (Jackson, Mississippi, 1987), p. 124.

12. *Writers at Work*, p. 117; *Conversations*, p. 41.

13. 'Journals: From the Late Forties and the Fifties II', *The New Yorker* (13 August 1990), 56.

14. John Gardner, 'Witchcraft in Bullet Park' in *Critical Essays*, p. 260.

15. Frederick Crews, 'Mr Updike's Planet', *The New York Review of Books* **33** (December 4, 1986), 7, 12; Harold Bloom, 'Introduction' in Bloom (ed.), *John Updike: Modern Critical Views* (New York, 1987), p. 7; John W. Aldridge, 'The Private Vice of John Updike' in Bloom, p. 13; Richard H. Rupp, 'John Updike: Style in Search of a Center' in Bloom, p. 15.

16. Joyce Carol Oates, 'Updike's American Comedies' in Bloom, p. 67.

17. Tony Tanner, *City of Words*, p. 281.

18. 'John Updike' in George Plimpton (ed.), *Writers at Work*, Fourth Series (Harmondsworth, 1977), p. 441.

19. John Updike, *Picked-up Pieces* (New York, 1975), p. 483

20. *Writers at Work*, pp. 439–40; 427.

21. John Updike, *Hugging the Shore* (New York, 1984), pp. 850–51.

22. See Cynthia Ozick, 'Cultural Impersonation' and 'Bech Passing' in Ozick, *Art and Ardor* (New York, 1983), pp. 113–14 and 114–129.

23. For the concept of maintenance culture versus transcendence culture see Hickey, 'Jim Shaw, Stopping the Image Wheel', *Vision Magazine* (1989).

24. John Updike, *Assorted Prose* (New York, 1965), pp. 273, 282.

25. Walker Percy, *Lost in the Cosmos: The Last Self-Help Book* (New York, 1984), p. 178.

26. *Conversations with Walker Percy*, ed. Lewis R. Lawson and Victor A. Kramer (Jackson, Mississippi, 1985), pp. 281, 28, 86, 69.

27. *Conversations*, p. 66.

28. See the surprising and persuasive reading of this novel by Stephen R. Yarbrough, 'Walker Percy's *Lancelot* and the Critic's Original Sin', *Texas Studies*

in Literature and Language **30** (1988), 272–94.

29. John Barth, *The Friday Book* (New York, 1984), p. 256.

30. Raymond Carver, *Fires* (New York, 1989), p. 256.

31. 'An Interview with Raymond Carver' in Larry McCaffery and Sinda Gregory (eds), *Alive and Writing: Interviews with American Authors of the 1980s* (Urbana, 1987), pp. 67–8.

32. *The New York Times Book Review* (June 30, 1985), p. 24.

33. *Alive and Writing*, pp. 78–9.

34. Rivera's novel has been translated twice: by Evangelina Vinal as *and the earth did not devour him* in a bilingual edition and in a free, less literal rendition by Rolando Hinojosa as *This Migrant Earth*, both published by Arte Publico in Houston.

Chapter 8
Fiction by Women: Voicing the Unspoken

(Women) writers

Any consideration of 'women's fiction' should begin with the disputability of the category. Cynthia Ozick's short story 'Virility' mocks the idea that there is a recognizable woman's voice, taking it to be a male chauvinist critical construction used to marginalize and trivialize women who write. Joyce Carol Oates in *(Woman) Writer* proclaims that 'a woman who writes is a writer by her own definition; but she is a *woman* writer by others' definitions'.[1] Yet to some feminists it is the denial of a specific woman's voice in fiction that is seen as chauvinist marginalization, reducing storytellers who are women to mere adjuncts of a male defined and dominated literary canon. In fact, although the highly diverse individual voices of American women writers are reducible to no single measure, their recurrent themes and techniques reflect psychological and political dilemmas specific to contemporary American women. These writers spiritually witness routine social brutality, tell stories about and for those previously left out of the literary and social text, make claims for the powerless, and reveal the courage and resourcefulness of people generally believed to be unimportant and unheroic. Especially, they respond to a male American fixation on untrammelled individualism with the reminder that the freedom of the self is empty without relationship and responsibility. Women writers are concerned with what one needs to be free *for* rather than *of*.

Another problem in assessing contemporary American fiction by women is the lack of a clear canon. Feminist criticism, now a very powerful force in American academic criticism, has resurrected a number of writers from the past and articulated methods of criticism that enabled readers to see an intelligence and force previously overlooked or even denied in writing by women. Charlotte Perkins Gilman's 'The Yellow Wallpaper' (1892) was revived by feminist critics as a classic revelation of how the personal is the political and is now in American literature college anthologies. Feminists rediscovered Kate Chopin's *The Awakening* (1899) and elevated the stature of such already canonized writers as Edith Wharton and Willa Cather. But although I shall draw heavily from some acute feminist readings of some of the writers in this chapter, feminist criticism has not altogether taken up the challenge of contemporary fiction by American women. Classic writers such as Katherine Anne Porter are generally disliked or ignored by the more prominent and theoretically inclined feminist critics due to her some-times illiberal politics. Recently, however, theoretical approaches have been applied illuminatingly to Eudora Welty's short story sequence, *The Golden Apples* (1949), demonstrating precisely the diversity and otherness of voice supposedly absent in predominantly realist writers.[2] Writers like Mary McCarthy and Joyce Carol Oates tend to receive more attention from educated readers and newspaper reviewers than from the most aca-demically prestigious feminist criticism. Women readers may be some-what ahead of the critical theorists in their perceptions.

There are, it is true, a few postmodernist American women writers, most notably Susan Sontag and Kathy Acker, but Sontag's criticism more dramatically expresses the theories that her fiction seems designed to il-lustrate, while Acker's fiction is, to me, unreadably callow and narcissis-tic. The argument of some feminist theorists for there being an essential identification between women and postmodernism and between post-modernism and political radicalism appears to ignore the predilection of actual American women novelists for realism.[3] Other readers may judge differently but drawing on the responses of both readers and critics, I see Mary McCarthy and Joyce Carol Oates along with Katherine Anne Porter, Eudora Welty, Flannery O'Connor and Cynthia Ozick as having most clearly emerged as major contemporary women writers, with Toni Mor-rison in a class by herself. But a central feature of the current literary scene is the diversity and excellence of talent, especially among women writers.

Mary McCarthy: from wedding to funeral

Elizabeth Janeway's 1979 essay on 'Women's Literature' in *Harvard Guide to Contemporary American Writing* distinguishes between literature by and about women and women's literature: 'The women writers treated here, then, will be those who deal with women's experience from within; but clearly not all writing by women, about women, can be called women's literature. The touchstone used is the author's vision of the experience treated.' Janeway sees an objective, supposedly neutral outside view of women's experience as essentially masculine and therefore excludes 'Lillian Hellman's plays and Mary McCarthy's fiction because these writers base their interpretations of women's needs and desires on standards that are essentially masculine even if not conventionally so'.[4] This conjunction takes on a retroactive piquancy given Hellman's 1980 lawsuit against McCarthy for her comment in a television interview that 'every word [Hellman] writes is a lie, including "and" and "the" '.[5] To be sure, McCarthy in her rather ferocious concern for truth does write from the outside, as a witness, an accuser, even a spy of women's experience, her own included. It seems odd, however, to perceive as 'masculine' a daring, groundbreaking report on the condition of women, much of which can now be confirmed by various feminist critical, psychological and sociological analyses. Yet McCarthy, possibly because she told painful truths and abjured political cheerleading, has been very nearly shut out. Perhaps McCarthy's problem for modern criticism may be that she is overly lucid.

The satire in her first book, *The Company She Keeps* (1942), less a novel than a set of stories about the same protagonist, is notably ruthless and cold blooded. The protagonist lives in cliché and revels in false consciousness. Yet a certain growth is apparent. In the last stories the protagonist has learned to judge false doctrine – Stalinism, Freudianism – by the light of her own intellect and experience. The masterpiece of the collection, 'The Man in the Brooks Brothers Shirt', unremittingly explores the embarrassment of the protagonist in a sexual encounter. The protagonist, somewhat though not powerfully attracted to an older man, a businessman, in the course of a train trip to California wakes up to find herself naked in his bed. She is embarrassed to recognize that she was wearing 'a pair of white crepe-de-chine pants, many times mended, with a button off and a little brass pin in its place.' McCarthy later had to explain the historical existence of panties with buttons on the side but more importantly, this local detail has ideological significance: 'it was the kind of detail that a worldly man would regard as sloppy and bohemian.' The protagonist is embarrassed by how well her partner's cliché vision actually fits her, a characteristic McCarthy sally against received ideas from whatever source. Then, missing a garter, she agonizes over the prospect of having to walk through the train with one stocking hanging down. By 1942 men's feelings about sexual encounters had been so thoroughly explored as to be vaguely redundant but McCarthy's report of a woman's experience was unique and troubling.[6]

McCarthy's 1954 story 'Dottie Makes an Honest Woman of Herself' did it again. What occasioned the furore was not so much Dick Brown's offhand deflowering of Dottie Renfrew, though McCarthy went further than most male writers of the time had dared; rather it was the famous pessary scene.

'Get yourself a pessary.' Dick's muttered *envoi*, as he propelled her firmly to the door next morning, fell on Dottie's ears with the effect of a stunning blow. Bewildered, she understood him to be saying 'Get yourself a peccary,' and a vision of a coarse piglike mammal they had studied in Zoology passed across her dazed consciousness, like a slide on a screen, followed by awful memories of Krafft-Ebbing and the girl who had kept a goat at Vassar. Was this some variant she ought to know about, probably, of the old-maid joke. Tears dampened her eyes, though she tried to wink them back. (*The Group* (3))

This is not a joke for the sake of one but a revelation of the vulnerability inherent in the sexual ignorance and innocence of women of the time. Dottie does visit a doctor to get fitted for her diaphragm, waits to meet her lover in a park, and when he fails to appear, leaves the apparatus under the bench. McCarthy later commented, 'There was a terrible protest about the Dottie-going-to-the-doctor Chapter. It was considered the most outrageous thing – that I had betrayed feminine secrets.' Brendan Gill saw McCarthy as 'a pioneer taking big chances, and by doing so, increasing the range of permissible subject matter.' In 1959 Philip Roth's protagonist cites McCarthy to *his girlfriend* in persuading her to get a diaphragm.[7] Since the secrets McCarthy revealed were the kind that women had been keeping as much from themselves as others, the effect was empowering, allowing a taboo subject to become available for conscious thought and response. Dottie Renfrew is one of McCarthy's more sympathetic protagonists and the entire scene has as much pathos as comedy. Indeed, it is Dick Brown's cynicism and coldness that finally seem callow and naive.

In *The Group* McCarthy follows the fortunes of a group of Vassar women from the class of 1933, beginning with the first wedding among them in 1933 and ending with the first funeral in 1940. Although a best seller at its publication, *The Group* has not received much critical respect. Yet it is keenly intelligent and rather affecting, in some ways even a prototype feminist text. The preceeding chapter showed in recent male realists a concern for the submerged America, isolated and inarticulate, a problem of articulation compounded for women by the cultural dominance of a male-centred world view – what the French theorist Foucault calls an 'episteme' – and a public language reflecting that view. The result is that women, trying to match their experience with the dominant interpretive language, are coerced into self-doubt. In Carol Gilligan's formulation:

> Women come to question whether what they have seen exists
> and whether what they know from their own experience is
> true. These questions are raised not as abstract philosophical

speculations about the nature of reality and truth but as personal
doubts that invade women's sense of themselves, compromising
their ability to act on their own perceptions and thus their
willingness to take responsibility for what they do.[8]

McCarthy described the main theme of her book as the confrontation of
her female characters with prevailing social ideas.

No male consciousness is present in the book; through these eight
points of view, all feminine, all consciously enlightened, are
refracted, as if from a series of pretty prisms, all the novel ideas of
the period concerning sex, politics, economics, architecture,
city-planning, house-keeping, child-bearing, interior decoration,
and art. It is a crazy quilt of *clichés*, platitudes, and *idées reçues*.
Yet the book is not meant to be a joke or even a satire, exactly,
but a 'true history' of the times despite the angle or angles of
distortion.[9]

What needs to be added to this description is that the male consciousness is in fact ever present in the book much in the fashion of Aristotle's
unmoved mover. Point for point the eight characters become confused
and distanced from their own best perceptions as they try to bring them
into accord with the prevailing, male-centred systems of thought.
Though McCarthy, writing before the revival of feminism, never introduces a specifically feminist political voice in her novel, the absence is a
felt one. The novel cries for a perspective transcending the limitations of
the massive false consciousness it so brilliantly exposes, thus expressing
not only the 1930s but its own moment as well: the need in the 1950s
and 1960s for an as yet unformulated critique of the prevailing episteme.
What later feminist critiques argue is what McCarthy implicitly but
clearly enough *shows* in *The Group*.

She shows it especially in the story of Kay with whose marriage the
novel begins and with whose funeral it ends. In a crucial episode Kay
ends up in a hospital with a black eye inflicted by her husband. To her
shock, it turns out to be a mental hospital; her husband has committed
her, evidently for having been crazy enough to have been victimized.
Jacqueline Taylor's feminist critique of Grace Paley argues that 'The recognition that the craziness might be in the system rather than in the
perspective of an individual woman is the beginning of a radicalizing use
of humor',[10] an insight accurate though needing to be supplemented by
the remembrance that such recognition is a central device of satire and
black humour generally. McCarthy shows Kay caught in a number of
double binds as the crazy hospital system and her crazy husband define
her reality for her. Kay is shown as a reasonably intelligent woman yet
she continually defers to her mate, the dreadful Harald Petersen, whose

only real talent is for totally selfish manipulativeness. And yet we see Kay and other women excusing and rationalizing Harald's viciousness. They fall into the socialized tendency of women to take responsibility even for abuse inflicted upon them, while inventing convoluted excuses for ghastly male behaviour. As with Dottie and Dick, the woman overcommits, inventing a relationship where none authentically exists while the man undercommits, denying responsibility for sustaining relationship. What McCarthy shows is in precise accord with at least one version of contemporary feminist psychological theory.[11]

The structure of *The Group* is as woman-centred as its themes. Sharing the point of view among various protagonists, avoiding dramatic conflict and heroic action in favour of the emotional content of everyday experience, privileging characters over the plot have all been defined as feminist literary strategies that more generally reflect women's ways of telling stories[12] and these are the main structural features of McCarthy's novel. McCarthy for the most part stays out of the novel, writing in third person but in the voice and vocabulary of her characters, Helena Davison's morally aware voice, Libby McAusland's posturing and silly voice, a prime example of the diversity of voices, the 'heterology' supposed to be missing from such fiction. The ultimate failure of the group is that they insufficiently share their separate, sometimes accurate, perceptions. The reader of the novel is empowered because drawing up this pool of perception while being shown the folly of the social episteme deflecting the group from articulating their inchoate recognitions. The result is a novel both cleverly comic and unsentimentally sorrowful.

Joyce Carol Oates: 'violence can't be singled out from an ordinary day'

Conflict, violence and melodrama, abjured by some women writers, are prominent in the work of Joyce Carol Oates. Yet, despite Oates's warnings at being classified a 'woman writer', her work at its deepest levels encodes a primarily female vision of violence, not unlike that of Emily Brontë.[13] Like Raymond Carver and unlike most American writers, Oates comes from a working-class background, one less insulated from the harsher realities of American life. She taught in Detroit for some years and as the narrative voice in *them* declares, 'All of Detroit is melodrama, and most lives in Detroit fated to be melodramatic. . . ' (2:5). Oates has been continually exasperated by reviews and interviews questioning her concern for violence, as if an impropriety in a woman writer. Her best defence is in the 'Author's Note' to *them*: 'Nothing in the novel has been exaggerated in order to increase the possibility of drama – indeed, the various sordid and shocking events of slum life, detailed in other naturalistic works, have been understated here, mainly because of my fear that too much reality would become unbearable.' This indeed is the threat Oates's work presents to readers and critics – at its best, it enmeshes the reader into the structure of trauma, a nightmare of American history from which the reader cannot awake because it is the world to which one awakens.

Oates depicts this violence in a primarily realist and naturalistic technique, though she has experimented with various forms and genres in the course of her career. But even some of her uses of postmodernism ultimately serve other ends, as is the case with *Expensive People* (1968) and *them* (1969), novels that are quite dissimilar while exhibiting a significant convergence in how they play off against postmodernist conventions. They also confute, I think, Sacvan Bercovitch's influential thesis that even the most pessimistic American writing covertly embraces the notion of the glorious national manifest destiny of America to become the model society, appointed by God to be the beacon of the world. For Bercovitch, American despair at not having reached such a mythical height is a left-handed tribute to the enduring fantasy of its possibility. But the despair to be found in Oates and many American women writers, past and present, is firmly based on the historical and material conditions of their time and place as opposed to any utopian fantasy. The American dream shows up in *them* primarily as a fuel to the violence.[14]

In *Expensive People* violence is personal and private yet in these very terms implicative of 'the domestic American darkness' (2:8). Oates's narrator-protagonist proclaims himself a 'child murderer', explaining that he means a child who is a murderer rather than a murderer of children, though the novel implies some lurking equivocations of this definition. This self-conscious narrator is clearly intended to remind us of Nabokov's Humbert Humbert: 'if I were ever to dedicate this novel to anyone it would be to *that other unfortunate traveler* from whom I have stolen so much' (1:23). The allusion is multi-layered, to Thomas Nashe's 1500s novel *The Unfortunate Traveller*, an original, self-conscious fiction, and to Humbert and his equally expatriated creator, a sojourner, after exile from Russia, in Germany, England, the United States and Switzerland. Reinforcing the allusion, Nabokov is mentioned twice in the novel. Indeed, the weakness in *Expensive People* is that it is overderivative of Nabokov. Yet Oates uses the postmodernist convention of self-reflectivity to put into question the imperial selfhood of American postmodernist narration. The person the narrator murders (if anyone – some doubts are planted) is his mother, Natasha Romanov, for whom his pet name is Nada. The name is apt since she exists as his verbal creation, reflecting Humbert's boast about his literary immortalization of Lolita towards the close of his narrative. Yet Oates's protagonist himself exists by a lucky accident; he discovers that his mother was barely prevented from aborting him. Moreover, his mother, herself an author, resembles in her described appearance and in her writings their mutual creator, Joyce Carol Oates. Nada's short story 'The Molesters', a story published previously by Oates, is replicated in the novel, with a commentary on it by the narrator. From Nada's notebook he quotes the self-directive, 'Revise "Death and the Maiden" and change title.' 'Death and the Maiden' was the working title of Oates's classic story 'Where Are You Going, Where Have You Been?' There is also a structural note: 'There must be a thread of story somewhere but where? The climax will be the death of X, but one must get past. The trouble is getting there . . . and getting past. As in any first-person narrative there can be a lot of freedom. Certain central events – what the hell can they be? – leading up to the death' (2:2). This can only describe the structure of *Expensive People*, the narrative delay of Nada's own death. But then, who is ultimately writing about whom? Is it the narrative itself that has survived abortion, i.e. deletion, non-publication? Without Joyce Carol Oates it would be nothing, but who is Joyce Carol Oates for her readers but the creation of her narrative – and narrator? If the novel is a kind of child it has the precariousness of one born of dysfunctional parentage: the protagonist's response to a peer's complaint about his parents is 'They're all trying to kill us, it's nothing personal' (2:4). Later he decides that the meaning of 'The Molesters' is that '*Molesters are all about us*' (2:15). Even 'about' here is grammatically ambiguous: is postmodernist narration a form of molestation? Yet this narrator fails to transcend the world's menace by a sheer act of narration. He is, in contrast, the chief victim, destroyed by his mother's lack of love, murdering her (if he does) because she is once again about to leave him. The theme of the novel then is not the dream of freedom but the terror of abandonment. Insecurity, not transcendence, is the theme.

them is less finished but more powerful than *Expensive People*; indeed, its lack of finish is a calculated part of its literary strategy. The centre of the novel is a letter written by one of its protagonists, Maureen Wendall, to the author, Joyce Carol Oates. This is a fiction within a fiction, fictionalized as a reality within a fiction. The 'Author's Note' to the novel frames it as Oates's telling of the real story of her former night school student to whom she gave the name 'Maureen Wendall'. The story is represented as a transference of nightmare.

> Her remarks, where possible, have been incorporated into the narrative verbatim, and it is to her terrible obsession with her personal history that I owe the voluminous details of this novel. For Maureen, this 'confession' had the effect of a kind of psychological therapy, of probably temporary benefit; for me as a witness so much material had the effect of temporarily blocking out my own

reality, my personal life, and substituting for it the various nightmare adventures of the Wendalls. Their lives pressed upon mine
eerily, so that I began to dream about them rather than myself,
dreaming and redreaming their lives.

The letter turns out to be an attack on Oates, on criticism, on literature.
'You failed me' Maureen accuses, clearly implying the spirit as well as
the letter (that is, 'F'). In her earlier schooling Maureen had worshipped
fiction, feeling Jane Austen's protagonist to be more real than she herself.
Later, prostituting herself in a desperate attempt to get enough money
together to escape her dreadful home, she decides that though she cannot
understand or feel sexual desire, she can understand the money she obtains
from coldly exploiting it: 'it was something that could be counted again
and again: it was as real as a novel by Jane Austen' (1:16). Oates failed
her by demanding of Maureen what was not in her or the situation:
'*Lack of coherence and development*, you wrote at the bottom of the paper'
(2:9). Maureen's writing is at fault for expressing her experience: 'The
books you taught us didn't explain this. The jumble was hidden somehow.' Oates taught the value of 'form' but 'What is form? Why is it
better than the way life happens by itself?' What especially has been left
out is women's experience, so little susceptible to 'form'.

> The woman by the radiator gets to her feet. She is heavy, she
> seems pained when she stands: thick cream- colored fat marbled
> old legs, poor legs, veins cracking and rising to the surface, a
> woman of middle-age. Oh, we women know things you don't
> know, you teachers, you readers and writers of books, we are the
> ones who wait around libraries when it's time to leave . . . we
> are always wondering what will come next, what terrible thing
> will come next.

But what makes *them* a deeply disturbing novel is how much of just such
experience Oates brings into it. Her formal intention is to avoid those
overt, metafictional flourishes of form that protect the reader from confrontation with the pain, shapelessness and emptiness her characters experience. *them* is not the greatest of contemporary novels but, meeting
the terms of its contract, it has a painful validity.

This is true not only in the sections on Maureen but also in those on
her brother Jules, equally adrift in chaos and cognizant that 'Nothing
follows' (2:4). The novel concludes with Jules's involvement in the Detroit riot of 1967. Early in the novel Jules has read of the Indian activist
Vinoba Bhave saying 'My object is to transform the whole of society.
Fire merely burns . . . . Fire burns and does its duty. It is for others to
do theirs' (1:9). At its end, Jules, in a television interview he happens
into as gratuitously as anything else in his life, hysterically and lucidly

explains the riot: ' "Everything in America is coming alive. It's breaking out and coming alive," Jules said eagerly.' Jules has somehow got on the staff of a radical sociologist's poverty programme but he understands the riot better than his employer.

> 'I would like to explain to everyone how necessary the fires are, and people in the street, not as Mort says here – Dr Piercy – so that things can be built up again, black and white living together, no, or black living by itself, by themselves – no, that has no im-portance, that is something for the newspapers and insurance com-panies. It is only necessary to understand that fire burns and does its duty, perpetually, and the fires will never be put out –.'

The political motivations Dr Piercy ascribes parallels the irrelevance of the literary form that Professor Oates taught. There are political/econ-omic causes underlying the urban malaise that flared into riot but the riot itself is not a political expression. As Jules declares, 'Violence can't be singled out from an ordinary day!' The riot, as Oates shows in a perfectly unpalatable insight, expresses rather the free-floating violence of American conditions and is as much a form of participation in the cul-ture as a protest against it, a version of apocalypse less witty but more convincing than Pynchon's. Some other Oates novels tend towards the diffuse, but at her best she delivers stunning revelations of the underside of American life. Moreover, short stories such as 'Where Are You Going, Where Have You Been?' and 'How I Contemplated the World from the Detroit House of Correction and Began My Life Over Again' are among the best American short fiction of our time.

Realism and fantasy in women's fiction

If contemporary writing by American women is still relatively margi-nalized by the most prestigious schools of criticism, it is probably less out of gender than genre prejudice. Feminist high theory, like high theory generally, draws from the dematerialized Marxism of Althusser and the desubstantialized Freudianism of Lacan mixed with Foucault's generalized suspicion of social structure. From this perspective realism merely con-firms an oppressive patriarchal social order by depicting it as natural rather than historically contingent. This misreading of realism joins with the older traditional critical paradigm that privileged the American ro-mance and marginalized realism and naturalism. There are, however, signs of a reassessment of realism, even if it takes the form of rereading it in postmodern terms.[15] Moreover, feminist critics have begun to reaffirm some nineteenth-century women realists – Kate Chopin, Sarah Orne Jewett, Mary Wilkins Freeman – previously marginalized under what had become the opprobrious label of local colour realism. A critical reassessment of the genre of realism and even the subgenre of regionalism is overdue, not just for nineteenth- but for twentieth-century writers, especially given how many talented women writers are in fact in the realist tradition. It is difficult to think of a region or a subculture in the United States not being put on record by a woman writer of considerable talent. There is Joan Didion on Southern California, Carolyn Chute and Cathie Pelletier on Maine, a legion of Southern writers, Mary Gordon on sectarian Catholic culture, Louise Erdrich on the North Dakota Indian world, Maxine Hong Kingston and Amy Tan on Chinese American identity, not to mention the emergence of the African American woman writer Toni Morrison. It is true that some of these writers depart from realism in the direction of fantasy and myth, as did such foremothers as Hurston and Wharton (in her ghost stories and her ur-postmodernist joke 'Xingu'). Yet these departures are also in the direction of establishing a woman's perspective on American reality frequently out of accord with the official version. Indeed, the power of these writers both aesthetically and politically lies in their exploration of forms of subjectivity previously marginalized and ignored by the literary as well as larger culture. Some feminist critics in fact have recognized in these writers how their presentation of subjectivity becomes an enabling act, not without political implications.

Jean Stafford's *The Mountain Lion* (1947) and Marilynn Robinson's *Housekeeping* (1980) are in the mythical mode. As Dana Heller points out, they are feminizations of the quest romance.[16] Stafford's novella, as in her earlier, more traditionally realistic *Boston Adventure* (1944), shows the failure of a young woman to attain full identity in the face of a social world not yet opening to women's full potential. Robinson's eerily beautiful novel portrays a woman, Aunt Sylvie, who does not so much rebel against as simply fail to observe the conventions of female identity, eventually carrying with her one of her nieces, though losing the other to the world of conventional expectation. This novel clearly plays on the American romance convention of lighting out for the territory but significantly it is Sylvie and Ruth rather than Huck and Jim (or Holden or Rabbit) who light out, inverting not the convention but its gender specification.

McCarthy's kind of satirical social comment can be found in Alison Lurie's writings, especially comedies of sexual table turning such as *The Nowhere City* (1965) and the wittily titled *The War between the Tates* (1974) (the Southern designation for what is generally called the 'Civil War' is the 'War between the States') where betrayed women discover that they can outdo their mates at the same game. *The Nowhere City* is additionally distinguished as one of the better novels about the culture shock occasioned to Easterners transplanted to Los Angeles, especially in that Los Angeles, contrary to the usual cliché, gets somewhat the better of the cultural comparison. *The War Between the Tates* is the best academic novel since Randall Jarrell's *Pictures from an Institution* (1954) in which Jarrell's satirical caricature of a woman novelist who is herself writing a satirical academic novel was widely thought to point to Mary McCarthy and *The Groves of Academe* (1952), though Jarrell denied such intent and McCarthy was unperturbed.[17]

Oates's turning of postmodernism against itself is paralleled, though in her own unique fashion, in the stories of Grace Paley, a writer intensely admired by other writers for both her commitment and her craft. Jacqueline Taylor's excellent study of Paley shows how she uses the convention of self-reflectivity to reveal both the plotlessness and the intense interweaving of women's lives, the perceptual and emotional riches not so much of subjectivity as of intersubjectivity. Carol Gilligan argues that women predominantly see life not in absolute and linear terms as a path but in relative and relational terms as a web,[18] an insight richly illustrated in Paley's stories. Her characters are morally careful, not without a certain asperity but highly alert to alternative points of view. The stories they tell tend to branch off towards various possibilities rather than contrive a tidy and exclusive closure. Her most memorable stories are less likely to be of a woman's relation to a husband than to a father or to other women. These stories avoid high drama in favour of *The Little Disturbances of Man*, as Paley's first collection is entitled. The irony of the title is that these are the true tests of the self, a view common to nineteenth-century realists such as George Eliot, William Dean Howells, Sarah Orne Jewett and Mary Wilkins Freeman. The plotlessness, lack of closure, and avoidance of blatant symbolism are defended by the protagonist and authorial spokeswoman of 'A Conversation with My Father' who despises the kind of plot that creates an 'absolute line between two points'. Her dislike is ethically motivated: 'Not for literary reasons, but because it takes all hope away. Everyone, real or invented deserves the open destiny of life.' The father responds by objecting 'to people sitting in trees talking senselessly, voices from who knows where,' a clear reference to another story, 'Faith in a Tree', in this same collection, *Enormous Changes at the Last Minute*, which evidently the father has been reading. But as in Oates, the self-reference privileges not the postmodernistic primacy of fiction but the fluidity of a reality too rich and strange to limit by fictional convention. In the above books of stories and a third collection, *Later the Same Day*, Paley writes tales that seem random and inconclusive but never insignificant. Tillie Olsen in her 1950s stories belatedly collected in *Tell Me a Riddle* (1976) also wrote of little disturbances but in a darker tone, reflecting a sense of more obdurate circumstance, a vision tending somewhat, though never reductively, toward naturalism without the violence of Petry or Oates but without Paley's slight edge of hopefulness. What strikes one about all these authors is that they have 'been there', as the American phrase has it. They know things about commonplace endurance and courage.

The investment of women writers in relationship is especially apparent in the work of Ann Beattie, Ann Tyler and Josephine Humphreys. By no means is relationship uncritically glorified; women are generally more acutely aware of the costs as well as the rewards of relationship and there is always a question of a negative balance. Ann Beattie acknowledges being a specialist in 'the breakdown of relationships', though noting these usually result from character flaws preceding the original relationships. Indeed, the sense of Beattie's short stories and novels is of relationship always on the brink, partly because her people lack the personal density to sustain them. Some critics attack her characterization for this thinness while acknowledging how recognizable these characters are. Not interested in inventing better people, Beattie writes low-keyed accounts of those who exist, paralleling other women writers in her distaste for linear plots: 'One critic who wanted to put me down said that reading my stories was like watching a dog go round and round until it succeeded in catching its tail. He was saying that my writing lacked structure, and when I read that I thought, "Wow, he's right." But I took what he said as a compliment.' Her endings tend towards ambiguity. Readers of her first novel, *Chilly Scenes of Winter* (1976), liked the protagonist, Charles, and supposed the ending to be conventionally happy when he recovers the woman he has obsessively longed for. But Beattie, describing her character as 'neurotic, obsessive, extremely defensive', notes how readers missed the irony of the portrayal.[19] Charles does not so much win over his lover as wear down her resistance and there is little reason to suppose they will live happily every after; I give them six months. The happy ending is a narrative joke.

Relationship is problematic but sometimes more propitious in what John Updike aptly terms the 'emotional anthropology' of Anne Tyler's fiction. Tyler's 'paradoxes of the family' play out in various novels 'a fundamental American tension . . . between stasis and movement, between home and escape'. No one Tyler novel has stood out as her unquestioned masterpiece but, keeping in mind her Southern settings, Updike asks the canonical question: 'the only question remaining about her talent is: will it ever, in its scintillating display of plenitude, make a dent as deep in our national self-awareness and literature as that left by the work of O'Connor, and Carson McCullers, and Eudora Welty?'[20] Mary Robertson's brilliant analysis helps answer this by demonstrating how Tyler's emotional anthropology usually works to privilege exogamy: her characters and families best survive by incorporating new members who bring a saving difference into the family sameness. Tyler's constant 'oscillation between shedding and incorporation' gives full value to both impulses without endorsing 'the negative freedom of merely shedding' found in Robinson's *Housekeeping* or the contrived nostalgia of those presentations of extended families so popular on American television.[21] Thus Tyler brilliantly contributes to a central American theme as is confirmed, even overdetermined, by her novel *The Accidental Tourist* (1985). It is the business of its protagonist, Macon Leary, to reduce the contingencies of travel to the minimum in his Accidental Tourist guidebooks.

> He covered only the cities in these guides, for people taking business trips flew into cities and out again and didn't see the countryside at all. They didn't see the cities for that matter. Their concern was how to pretend they had never left home. What hotels in Madrid boasted king-sized beautyrest mattresses? What restaurants in Tokyo offered Sweet 'n' Low? Did Amsterdam have a McDonald's? Did Mexico City have a Taco Bell? Did any place in Rome serve Chef Boyardee ravioli? Other travelers hoped to discover distinctive local wines; Macon's readers searched for pasteurized and homogenized milk.(2)

As one would expect, Macon's own life is characterized by rigid habits and compulsive rituals. He fears life and has arranged his own around a series of defences so elaborate as to resemble medieval fortifications. Tyler develops all this with comic verve but the underlying situation has a profound pathos. Macon's lack of confidence in life had been horribly confirmed by the random, senseless murder of his son in a fast food store. When his wife leaves him, discouraged at his discouragement, he lapses into an even more rigidified routine then retreats to his extended family which has, even more than he, elaborated retreat into an art form. What differentiates Tyler is that she gives full value to Macon's need for safety and the eccentric charm of his family. The family's way of life is in fact viable, even moving, if ultimately deeply limiting. It carries its form of eccentricity, the retreat into ritual pattern, to one extreme as the wonderful dog trainer Muriel, who enters Macon's life in order benevolently to disrupt it, carries her manic disorderliness to another. Tyler herself is so stylistically composed a writer that readers sometimes miss her commitment to contingency and disorder, the choice of danger over purity that Robertson recognized as Tyler's basic design.

Robertson also points to Tyler's abjuring of the fashionable posture of alienation: 'A critic who believes that alienation is still the only authentic response to the world will not like Tyler. Her world makes room for the alienated moment, but it finally makes one wonder whether the alienated attitude does not rest on a secret, stingy resentment that the world and its many people are different from oneself.'[22] Here again Robertson anticipates *The Accidental Tourist* because besides being a plausible if odd character, Macon is surely intended as a parodic comment on alienation, an upside down version. The intellectuals experience angst at the sight of a McDonald's; Macon experiences it when he cannot find one. The Tylerian subtext of the newspaper story that led to Macon's Accidental Tourist series subtly parodies Heideggerian homelessness and Sartrean nausea (in *Nausea*) and viscosity (analysed in *Being and Nothingness*).

> [Macon] contributed a free-lance article to a neighborhood weekly. His subject was a crafts fair over in Washington. *Getting there is difficult*, he wrote, *because the freeway is so blank you start feeling all lost and sad. And once you've arrived, it's worse: The streets are not like ours and don't even run at right angles.* He went on to evaluate some food he'd sampled at an outdoor booth, but found it contained a spice he was unused to, *something sort of cold and yellow I would almost describe as foreign* . . . .

This alienation from alienation is a feature in a number of contemporary Southern writers, concerned, like Tyler, with the 'oscillation between shedding and incorporation' in marriage and family. Josephine Humphreys's *Dreams of Sleep* (1984) and *Rich In Love* (1987), set in her native Charleston, South Carolina, play out the dialectic, but what is most striking about her fiction is the charity of the characterization. No character is *reduced* in a Humphreys novel to make an ideological point or for the sake of a comic triumph. Yet feeling in these novels never degenerates into sentimentality and they are keenly witty throughout. *Dreams of Sleep* unquestionably has the finest scene ever set in a Piggly Wiggly supermarket. The ironically titled *In Country* (1985), by the Western Kentucky writer Bobbie Ann Mason, brings the war home ('in country' was American soldier slang for Vietnam), depicting post-traumatic shock disorder as both an individual and a social hangover from the war, a family inheritance. Such critical labels as 'hick chic' that have been tagged on Mason and other writers who deal with the America of K-Marts and Bruce Springsteen (whom Mason's heroine loves from afar) reveal more about the class attitudes of the critics than the qualities of the writers.

The Maine writer Carolyn Chute, of working-class, 'poor white' background, uncovers a world that *aspires* to the K-mart level. Somewhat reminiscent of Welty, Chute's sagas of the bizarre Bean and Le-Tourneau families, along with Cathie Pelletier's *The Funeral Makers* (1988), could be taken to constitute a Maine school of fiction, disputing Southern ownership of regional weirdness. But, as previously noted, it is difficult to find an American region not being explored in fiction of real quality. Central Texas has Beverly Lowry (*Breaking Gentle*, 1988) and Carolyn Osborn (*A Horse of a Different Color*, 1977) and had Shelby Hearon (*Owning Jolene*, 1988) before she moved east, all writers who originally explore relationship and loss. Though Joan Didion's razor-sharp essays somewhat overshadow her fiction, the languid hothouse

anomie of *Play it as it Lays* (1970) certainly captures something quintes-
sentially Southern Californian. Didion's husband, John Gregory Dunne,
concentrates on subculture rather than region in his thriller of Catholic
sin and guilt, *True Confessions* (1977), but to find why *women* can stand
so patriarchal and constricted a world one needs to read Mary Gordon's
Final Payments (1978). There is a certain patness in Gordon's feminist
counterpointing of the perfect male villain with the ideal mate − though
the villain is all too credible − but the portrayal of the rewards her
heroine experiences in what seems an impossibly constricting relation
with her rigidly orthodox father is unexpectedly convincing.

Louise Erdrich in *Love Medicine* (1984) and *The Beet Queen* (1986)
brings North Dakota American Indian life to powerful literary expression
but perhaps the most interesting development in women's fiction has
been the emergence of the Chinese American authors Maxine Hong
Kingston and Amy Tan. Tan's *The Joy Luck Club* (1989) is an account of
the usual generational complications of mothers and daughters compounded by the cultural double consciousness intrinsic to being Chinese
American. But who set out to and succeeded in writing a classic work
on this subject is Maxine Hong Kingston in *The Woman Warrior* (1976).
That *The Woman Warrior* is generally read as autobiography rather than
fiction is the consequence of an after-the-fact decision by the book's
editor at Knopf who thought it would market better in that form than as
a first novel. Indeed, although the main reason for the book's almost
instant canonization is the power of its intense, broodingly interior style,
it must be admitted that the enthusiasm of some early reviews owed
much to their belief that the book somehow definitively represented not
only Chinese American womanhood but also Chinese Americans and
even Chinese generally. Kingston herself complained of the profusion of
cultural misreadings, usually taking the form of ignoring the white
American racism shown in the book and exaggerating or misrepresenting
the Chinese attitudes towards women portrayed in it.[23] At the same
time, Kingston's book is clearly a daringly self-conscious canonical gesture. From her University of California education Kingston had learned
the new critical strategy of intensifying narrative through constructing it
around a densely symbolic subtext. Her extraordinary narrative invention
was to combine this technique with the Chinese conventions such as
'talk-story' so as to combine the symbolic with the vernacular in the
fashion of classic American literature: 'I am in the tradition of American
writers who consciously set out to create the literature of a new culture.
Mark Twain, Walt Whitman, Gertrude Stein, the Beats, all developed
ears for dialect, street language, and experimented with how to make
written language sound like spoken language. The content of that language is the ever- changing mythology. I am writing American mythology in American language.'[24] In *The Woman Warrior* she draws on two
Chinese poems, the story of the titular woman warrior and that of T'sai

Yen, the woman poet captured by barbarians, transforming the latter from the poem of anger and humiliation it actually was into a story of how the poet through her art negotiates her way into the centre of her new society. David Weilei Li shows how here, as with her complex play on the significance of Chinese women's names, Kingston enunciates her own literary identity.

> The recoded myth of T'sai Yen with the minority voice accepted by a majority audience becomes a self-fulfilling prophecy that signifies Kingston's own canonicity. 'It translated well,' as our narrator asserts in the last sentence of *The Woman Warrior*, as her book is indeed a translation *par excellence*. It translates a cross-cultural experience into words, a hyphenated Chinese-American into a non-hyphenated Chinese American, and a no-name woman into the woman warrior, Maxine Hong Kingston.[25]

Kingston's canonization is no more unmerited than Faulkner's but historical contingency in both cases was clearly involved. If Faulkner needed Malcolm Cowley, Kingston, like Ralph Ellison, another deservedly canonical figure, showed a Napoleonic daring in seizing the moment.

Canonization is a topic in my next chapter and suffice it to say here that I believe Toni Morrison to be not only the major American contemporary woman novelist but, along with Donald Barthelme, one of the two most impressive American talents from the 1970s to the present.

Kingston's work illustrates one writer's engagement with the problems of gender and ethnicity, and with the rules of the literary game, to seize the critical moment. The concerns of a woman's experience and the literary voice appropriate to that experience provide one dimension of the books identity, an avenue of approach into another concerned with issues of ethnic identity and, the voice appropriate to that. Her work demonstrates the way women's fiction enters into dialogue with other forms, styles and genres, defined more by the richness and variety of its products than by any single schematic identity. Such issues, and those of canonicity in such a diverse and unfolding field, are picked up in the next chapter in the work of Toni Morrison.

Notes

1. (New York, 1988), p. 27.

2. See Patricia Yaeger, 'Because a Fire was in my Head: Eudora Welty and the Dialogogic Imagination', *PMLA* **99** (1984), 955–73; Susan Donaldson,

'Recovering Otherness in *The Golden Apples*', *American Literature* **63** (1991), 489–506.

3. See Rita Felski's questioning of this equation in *Beyond Feminist Aesthetics* (Cambridge, Massachusetts, 1989).

4. Elizabeth Janeway, 'Women's Literature', *Harvard Guide to Contemporary American Writing* (Cambridge, Massachusetts, 1979), p. 345.

5. Carol Gelderman, *Mary McCarthy: A Life* (New York, 1988), pp. 332–42.

6. After the controversy over its original 1941 publication of the story the *Partisan Review* turned down another story about the same character. See Gelderman, p. 100.

7. Gelderman, pp. 252–53.

8. Carol Gilligan, *In a Different Voice: Psychological Theory and Women's Development* (Cambridge, Massachusetts, 1982), p. 49.

9. Quoted in Gelderman, p. 253.

10. Jacqueline Taylor, *Grace Paley: Illuminating the Dark Lives* (Austin, 1990), p. 47.

11. See Gilligan, *passim*; Nancy Chodorow, *The Reproduction of Mothering: Psychoanalysis and the Sociology of Gender* (Berkeley, 1978); Harriet Goldhor Lerner, *The Dance of Intimacy* (New York, 1989). Some feminists attack these writers as dire essentialists, not to mention that they draw on mere empirical evidence and women's experience as opposed to the more reliable *ex cathedra* pronouncements of French theorists. But as Diane Fuss, though herself an anti-essentialist, elegantly demonstrates, the most anti-essentialist theories always themselves smuggle in essentialism somewhere along the line. See Fuss, *Essentially Speaking* (New York, 1989).

12. See Taylor, pp. 92–96.

13. See Joyce Carol Oates, 'The Magnanimity of *Wuthering Heights*', *Critical Inquiry* **9** (1982).

14. *The American Jeremiad* (Madison, 1978).

15. This reading is brilliantly accomplished in Eric J. Sundquist (ed.), *American Realism: New Essays* (Baltimore, 1982). See also Yaeger and Donaldson, above, and Robertson, below.

16. *The Feminization of the Quest Romance: Radical Departures* (Austin, 1990).

17. Gelderman, pp. 138–39.

18. Gilligan, p. 148.

19. 'Ann Beattie' in Larry McCaffery and Sinda Gregory (eds), *Alive and Writing: Interviews with American Authors of the 1980s* (Urbana, 1987), pp. 52, 63, 49–50.

20. *Hugging the Shore* (New York, 1983), pp. 280, 287, 298.

21. Mary F. Robertson, 'Anne Tyler: Medusa Points and Contact Points' in Catherine Rainwater and William J. Scheick (eds), *Contemporary American Women Writers: Narrative Strategies* (Lexington, 1980), pp. 136–37.

22. Robertson, p. 137.

23. 'Cultural Mis-readings by American Reviewers' in Guy Amirthanayagam (ed.), *Asian and American Writers in Dialogue: New Cultural Identities* (London, 1982).

24. Quoted in David Leiwei Li, '*China Men*: Maxine Hong Kingston and the American Canon', *American Literary History* **2** (1990), 496.

25. David Leiwei Li, 'The Naming of a Chinese American "I": Cross-Cultural Sign/ifications in *The Woman Warrior*', *Criticism* **30** (1988), 511.

Chapter 9
Distinct Voices: Donald Barthelme and Toni Morrison

Canonical change

As the past recedes, its outlines configure into clarity. Much, of course, is lost and can be even approximated only with great effort. There is no way fully to recover the experience of a reader of 1855 opening *Leaves of Grass* for the first time. Except that few did. Whitman published the book at his own expense because reputable firms were not interested. One of the finest minds of the nineteenth century did have a shock of recognition in 1855 but even Emerson cooled off on Whitman and did not include him in the anthologies of American poetry he edited in his later years. Indeed, Whitman was not really canonized until the 1950s, even then with some objections from formalist critics. For a reader of 1884, the year of *The Adventures of Huckleberry Finn*, the important American poets were Longfellow, Bryant, Whittier and Holmes, not Whitman, much less the as yet unpublished Dickinson. Melville did not count as a novelist. The nineteenth-century canon of American literature emerged in the 1940s and 1950s and came under the challenge of feminists and leftists in the 1980s though this challenge seems to be resulting in an expansion – Frederick Douglass alongside Emerson, Zora Neal Hurston giving added verve to 1930s fiction – rather than an overthrow of the canon. What should be kept in mind is that the canon was never fixed and unalterable but itself a contingent, historical construct,[1] responding to political as well as aesthetic change, to luck as well as skill: Faulkner, through no fault of his own, was retroactively recognized; Zora Neal Hurston benefited posthumously from feminist politics and racial change; Ralph Ellison and Toni Morrison consciously played the literary market though never selling out to it and, like Maxine Hong Kingston, essentially crowned themselves.

Looking back to the 1950s the strongest canonical bets seem now to be Ellison, Bellow, Nabokov and O'Connor. From the 1960s, Pynchon's

stock is up in the literary market, Barth's somewhat down but holding at
its level, while the market has suspended trading on Terry Southern and
J. P. Donleavy. But no reputations of the 1960s and on seem even so
relatively securely canonized as those of Ellison, Bellow, O'Connor and
Nabokov. Even the important, much less the canonizable, writers are
difficult to select out from the 1970s on; perhaps we are reading the
Longfellow and Holmes of our day rather than the Melville and Whitman. Though individual critics have sometimes major influence on
canon formulation – Eliot bid up Donne as Cowley did with Faulkner –
the writer of this volume, though putting in a word for Jane Bowles and
Ann Petry and wishing he could have done more than space allowed for
Harriet Arnow, has no illusions of being an arbiter. It is his not unwel-
come task, however, to go out on a limb and from that perspective he
sees the two most interesting and enlivening voices to emerge from
1960 on as those of Donald Barthelme, born in 1931, whose first book
was published in 1964 and who died in 1990, and Toni Morrison, born
the same year, whose first book was published in 1970 and who continues (1991) her innovative work. What distinguishes these writers is an
originality and authority of voice, combined with an eye for what in our
cultural context disturbs, delights and appals. This combination gives
their writing a certain ultimacy as the last and most telling word on 'that
vision which most brilliantly exalts and vilifies the world' ('Hiding Man'
in Barthelme's *Come Back, Dr Caligari*).

It is indicative of the paradoxes of centrality and marginality in
American literary culture that it is Barthelme, a middle class white Texan
who moved to New York and quickly established himself as a writer for
the *New Yorker*, arguably the centre *of* the centre of the literary scene,
who seems the more alienated of the two, carrying the postmodernist
aesthetic logic of fragmentation to what seems its ultimate limit while
Morrison, an African American woman writer from the northern but
border state of Ohio, incorporates this sense of fragmentation into
a revitalized realism that quests after a restored coherency of self and
society, one which would move the African American world from the
periphery to a reconstituted centre. Thus, both represent in a heightened
and brilliant fashion literary modes – postmodernist and realist fiction –
and cultural patterns – the play between the margins and the unstable
centre – we have seen throughout this study.

Donald Barthelme: a student of the surfaces

It is appropriate that Donald Barthelme, one of the most self-conscious
of modern writers, should have enunciated his literary programme as it

just got under way. In 'After Joyce', an essay published in 1964, the same year as his first collection of short stories, Barthelme allies himself with the modernist art of James Joyce and Gertrude Stein, artists who 'modify the world by adding to its store of objects the literary object – which is then encountered in the same way as other objects in the world'. The writer is removed from this work, in effect displaced by it while 'the reader is not listening to an authoritative account of the world delivered by an expert (Faulkner on Mississippi, Hemingway on the corrida) but bumping into something that is *there*, like a rock or a refrigerator'. Except that the work is so odd that the reader is in the position 'of a voyager in the world coming upon a strange object. The reader reconstitutes the work by his active participation, by approaching the object, tapping it, shaking it, holding it to his ear to hear the roaring within.'[2]

Barthelme's work is verbally witty, formally elegant and representative in its fashion of the sociological, psychological and linguistic situation of his time. It is true that there is no subjective interiority in Barthelme, that he is, as he once declared, 'a student of surfaces.'[3] But these highly polished surfaces refract fragments of the modern self, its attitudes and language, especially the scientifically rational language with which we try to control our desire and disappointment, a language, moreover, whose reductiveness is partly the cause of our disappointment. Through odd juxtapositions and unpredictable swerves Barthelme recovers the irrational from this rationalized discourse, reopening a space for invention and possibility. This was why his early work had power for its small but ardent audience. Readers could walk around a Barthelme verbal object, seeing a model of how to free up language and feeling from stale associations. Along with Heller, Barthelme demonstrated the absurdity of the official version, its lifelessness, its low-grade concrete-block quality, getting out of this bind by going through it, using the most effective hegemonizing instrument of the official version, its language, against itself and evolving a new estranging poetry out of the shards of philosophic, sociological and bureaucratic discourse.

'The Balloon' in *Unspeakable Practices, Unnatural Acts*, which covers forty-five north–south blocks of (apparently) New York City, is a paradigm of the Barthelme art object.

> There were reactions, some people found the balloon 'interest-
> ing.' As a response this seemed inadequate to the immensity of
> the balloon, the suddenness of its appearance over the city; on the
> other hand, in the absence of hysteria or other societally-induced
> anxiety, it must be judged a calm, 'mature' one. There was a cer-
> tain amount of initial argumentation about the 'meaning' of the
> balloon; this subsided, because we have learned not to insist on
> meanings, and they are rarely even looked for now, except in
> cases involving the simplest, safest phenomena. It was agreed that

since the meaning of the balloon could never be known absolutely, extended discussion was pointless, or at least less purposeful than the activities of those who, for example, hung green and blue paper lanterns from the warm gray underside, in certain streets, or seized the occasion to write messages on the surface, announcing their availability for the performance of unnatural acts, or the availability of acquaintances.

Useful messages in art are parodied: 'The apparent purposelessness of the balloon was vexing (as was the fact that it was "there" at all). Had we painted, in great letters, "LABORATORY TESTS PROVE" or "18% MORE EFFECTIVE" on the sides of the balloon, this difficulty would have been circumvented.' The final joke of the story is the narrator-creator's critical explanation of what turns out to be *his* balloon, in terms of autobiographical and psychological criticism.

> I met you under the balloon, on the occasion of your return from Norway; you asked if it was mine; I said it was. The balloon, I said, is a spontaneous autobiographical disclosure, having to do with the unease I felt at your absence, and with sexual deprivation, but now that your visit to Bergen has been terminated, it is no longer necessary.

Oddest of all is that there is an autobiographical aspect; Barthelme was married to a Scandinavian woman.

After Joyce and Stein, the writer closest to Barthelme's ideal is Samuel Beckett whose pessimism Barthelme sees not as an ethical position but as an aesthetic heuristic: 'this pessimism is the premise necessary to a marvelous pedantic high-wire performance, the wire itself, supporting a comic turn of endless virtuosity'. Beckett's comedy elaborates the obvious; he 'painstakingly and with the utmost scholarly rigor retraces the rationales of simple operations, achieving comic shocks along the way by allowing language to tell him what it knows'. Beckett's is 'a search for the meanings to be gleaned from all possible combinations of all words in all languages. . . .'. Barthelme commends also another writer, the poet Kenneth Koch, for his 'pure linguistic play with abrupt changes of mood and intentionality' and how he contrives verbal environments in which 'Things lump themselves together in apparently random fashion with liberating effect. . . .'[4]

'After Joyce' may be the last thing Barthelme wrote or even said straight, that is, without parody, irony or conceptual quotation marks. Exemplary of his style is the opening passage of 'Henrietta and Alexandra' (in *Overnight to Many Distant Cities*) with its verbal riffs first, on the phrases 'young girl', 'had been told' and 'make [made] the most of it' and second, on the idiom, 'beyond the pale'.

Henrietta said: 'Once I was a young girl, very much like any
other young girl, interested in the same things, I was exemplary. I
was told what I was, that is to say a young girl, and I knew what
I was because I had been told and because there were other
young girls all around me who had been told the same things and
knew the same things and looking at them and hearing again in
my head the things I had been told I knew what a young girl
was. We had all been told the same things. I had not been told,
for example, that some wine was piss and some not and I had not
been told . . . other things. Still I had been told a great many
things all very useful but I had not been told that I was going to
die in any way that would allow me to realize that I really was
going to die and that it would all be over, then, and that this was
all there was and that I had damned well better make the most of
it. That I discovered for myself and covered with shame and shit
as I was I made the most of it. I had not been told how to make
the most of it but I figured it out. Then I moved through a period of depression, the depression engendered by the realization
that I had placed myself beyond the pale, there I was, beyond the
pale. Then I discovered that there were other people beyond the
pale with me, that there were quite as many people on the wrong
side of the pale as there were on the right side of the pale and
that the people on the wrong side of the pale were as complex as
the people on the right side of the pale, as unhappy, as subject to
time, as subject to death. So what the fuck? I said to myself in the
colorful language I had learned on the wrong side of the pale. By
this time I was no longer a young girl. I was mature.'

The motifs of 'young girl' and 'beyond the pale' unite at the end in a
triumphant closure of a pure linguistic elaboration. Yet as Barthelme
asserts in 'After Joyce' it is in the elaboration of form that 'social and
historical concerns re-enter the ambience of the work. Far from implying a literature that is its own subject matter, the work that is an
object is rich in possibilities. The intention of the artist may range in any
direction, including those directions which have the approval of socially
minded critics.' The first riff in 'Henrietta and Alexandra' comments on
the social construction of the identity of 'young girls', an identity that
proves inadequate to Henrietta because it has omitted existential
exigency. The second riff elaborates the dawning recognition of the
possibility of alternative identity as the inert idiom 'wrong side of the
pale' is reified into a live option. As the story proceeds it becomes clear
that Alexandra and Henrietta are lovers, a deviation from conventional
usage already naturalized and justified by the precedent linguistic devia-
tions while also impudently demonstrating the possibility of writing a
one-paragraph lesbian *bildungsroman*. The emergence of lesbianism in the

1970s becomes, characteristically for Barthelme, a linguistic event.

Like most comedians of the word from Mark Twain to Woody Allen, Barthelme risks an occasional slip into the inane but as Henrietta comments, 'I prefer the inane. The ane is often inutile to the artist.' Indeed, it is impossible to critique Barthelme in a way not anticipated in his self-reflective writing, a play on linguistic construction that continually doubles back on itself. The paradigm story for this tendency is 'Kierkegaard Unfair to Schlegel'. The story begins with a titillating sexual fantasy that is ironically undercut, a typical Barthelme manoeuvre. Then there is a reflection on the fantasy.

> Q: That's a very common fantasy.
> A: All my fantasies are extremely ordinary.
> Q: Does it give you pleasure?
> A: A poor . . . A rather unsatisfactory . . . .

The story then reflects on its own irony, on irony not merely as a tactical rhetorical device but as a strategy for living. 'A' has been reading Kierkegaard's *The Concept of Irony* and is disturbed by Kierkegaard's attack on the ironic posture as exemplified in Friedrich Schlegel's novel *Lucinda*. Kierkegaard sees this posture as the modern form of the sin of pride, a mask for solipsism and nihilism: 'Q: Solipsism plus triumphantism'. Irony enlarges the ironist by negating his world.

> The object is deprived of its reality by what I have said about it. Regarded in an ironical light, the object shivers, shatters, disappears. Irony is thus destructive and what Kierkegaard worries about a lot is that irony has nothing to put in the place of what it has destroyed. The new actuality – what the ironist has said about the object – is peculiar in that it is a comment upon a former actuality rather than a new actuality. This account of Kierkegaard's account of irony is grossly oversimplified. Now consider an irony directed not against a given object but against the whole of existence. An irony directed against the whole of poetry. The ironist, serially successful in disposing of various objects of his irony, becomes drunk with freedom. He becomes, in Kierkegaard's words, lighter and lighter. Irony becomes an infinite absolute negativity. Quote irony no longer directs itself against this or that particular phenomenon, against a particular thing unquote. Quote the whole of existence has become alien to the ironic subject unquote page 276.

After attacking Kierkegaard for attacking Schlegel, the narrator confesses that his reasons for thinking Kierkegaard is unfair to Schlegel are not very interesting: 'What is interesting is my making the statement that I think Kierkegaard is unfair to Schlegel.' A large blank square appears on the page before A. explains his real problem with Kierkegaard.

> Because that is not what I think at all. We have to do here with my own irony. Because of course Kierkegaard was 'fair' to Schlegel. In making a statement to the contrary I am attempting to . . . I might have several purposes – simply being provocative, for example. But mostly I am trying to annihilate Kierkegaard in order to deal with his disapproval.
> Q: Of Schlegel?
> A: Of me.

After a brief shift back to the sexual fantasy, the reflection on Kierkegaard is concluded.

> A: But I love my irony.
> Q: Does it give you pleasure?
> A: A poor . . . A rather unsatisfactory. . . .

This equates the pleasure of irony to that of masturbation except for the discomfiting period after the second ellipsis, implying an ultimately terminal dissatisfaction to the former indulgence. Out of the devices elaborated in 'After Joyce' Barthelme has invented a stylistic machine for producing estrangement and poetry, while self-reflecting the harshest critique imaginable upon this undertaking.

Like all great ironists, Barthelme is having his cake and eating it too. For the claim in 'After Joyce' that the formalist artist creates new objects anticipates Kierkegaard's protest against ironic negativism. *The Concept of Irony* and a standard sexual fantasy are equally found objects juxtaposed to create a new object called 'Kierkegaard Unfair to Schlegel'. Yet there are *intended* doubts as to whether this object transcends Kierkegaard's pre-emptive challenge of its ontological status. This irresolvable tension which has the structure of infinite regress – Kierkegaard doubting Barthelme doubting Kierkegaard doubting Barthelme – is the created object.

Clearly the story is as referential as it is self-reflective since it invites the reader to consider the history of romantic irony from Schlegel to Barthelme, the philosophical basis of irony, its moral adequacy and so on. Barthelme covers as much ground in his short story as Peter Sloterdijk in his long *Critique of Cynical Reason*. Sloterdijk observes 'Psychologically, present-day cynics can be understood as borderline melancholics, who can keep their symptoms of depression under control and can remain more or less able to work.' Barthelme exploits a borderline melancholia in his work. Sloterdijk sees modern nostalgia as collaborative with modern cynicism: 'Behind the capable, collaborative, hard facade, it covers up a mass of offensive unhappiness and the need to cry. In this,

there is something of the mourning for a "lost innocence" . . . Always
a bit unsettled and irritable, collaborating consciousness looks around for
its lost naiveté, to which there is no way back. . . .'[5] This last observation rather well describes the Anglo-Saxon attitudes of Chapter 7 and
the narrative voice in many Barthelme stories: unsettled, vaguely irritable, regretfully nostalgic. Though the comparison does not usually
occur to his critics, Barthelme was in his earlier days thought of as 'the
F. Scott Fitzgerald of Houston'.[6] The attitude is evident in Barthelme's
Snow White's response to the collective voice of the seven dwarfs as
they ask about the poem she is writing.

> 'The theme is loss, we take it.' 'What,' she said, 'else?' 'Are you
> specific as to what is lost?' 'Brutally.' 'Snow White,' we said,
> 'why do you remain with us? here? in this house?' There was a
> silence. Then she said: 'It must be laid, I suppose, to a failure of
> the imagination. I have not been able to imagine anything better.'
> *I have not been able to imagine anything better.*

These are Fitzgerald themes and even reverberations, albeit in a rather
different key. Another passage sounds like a variation on a Simon and
Garfunkel lyric, although *Snow White* slightly predates 'Mrs Robinson':

> *Emily Dickinson, why have you left me and gone*
> ah ah ah ah ah

And the plot of *Snow White* slightly alters its original by having the
'prince-figure' turn out, mixing in another fairy tale, *'pure frog'*. But is
not this *The Great Gatsby* with the gender roles inverted? Barthelme
even remystifies the fairy tale, restoring to it some of its original strange-
ness and violence by recoding its motifs as concrete poetry:

> WHAT SNOW WHITE REMEMBERS:
>
> THE HUNTSMAN
> THE FOREST
> THE STEAMING KNIFE

As Northrop Frye argues in *Anatomy of Criticism*, irony, logically the last
point in a literary cycle, circles back to myth, logically the first.[7] The
precedent is Joyce, whom Barthelme self-consciously comes after, in *Finnegans Wake*. Though Barthelme is an instance of Sloterdijk's 'declassed
urban intelligentsia' who adopt irony/cynicism as a protective mask, he
is as much the critic of this posture as Sloterdijk and shows greater
resourcefulness at hinting alternative possibilities.

Barthelme is a postmodernist partly in the sense that he is a post-

Freudian and a post-existentialist. Existentialism and psychoanalysis (and existential psychoanalysis) are for Barthelme not explanations of his environment but part of it, as much found objects as some junk in a dump might be for a sculptor. In 'Shower of Gold' (*Dr Caligari*) he invents an existentialist game show, *Who Am I*, where when a contestant gives a wrong answer, as in this game all answers are, the tote board spells out, in huge, glowing white letters, the words BAD FAITH. After seeing the first two contestants trashed, Barthelme's protagonist, Peterson, informs the television audience that 'Yesterday . . . in the typewriter in front of the Olivetti showroom on Fifth Avenue, I found a recipe for Ten Ingredient Soup that included a stone from a toad's head.' Having struck a blow for myth, he exhorts the audience: 'Turn off your television sets . . . cash in your life insurance, indulge in a mindless optimism. Visit girls at dusk. Play the guitar. How can you be alienated without first having been connected? Think back and remember how it was.' As the producers are trying to cut him off, he shouts his vita:

> 'My mother was a royal virgin . . . and my father a shower of
> gold. My childhood was pastoral and energetic and rich in experi-
> ence which developed my character. As a young man I was noble
> in reason, infinite in faculty, in form express and admirable, and
> in apprehension. . . .' Peterson went on and on and although he
> was, in a sense, lying, in a sense he was not.

Existential insights are as little help to Peterson as films such as *Les Parapluies de Cherbourg* and *A Man and a Woman* are to Snow White:

> 'My suffering is authentic enough but it has a kind of low-grade
> concrete block quality. The seven of them only add up to the
> equivalent of about *two real* men, as we know them from the
> films and from our childhood, when there were giants on the
> earth. It is possible of course that there are no more *real men* here,
> on this ball of half-truths, the earth. That would be a disappoint-
> ment. One would have to content oneself with the subtle falsity
> of color films of unhappy love affairs, made in France, with a
> Mozart score. That would be difficult.' (*Snow White*)

Barthelme is too sceptical for existentialism although he supplements Heidegger in 'Nothing: A Preliminary Account' with a helpful list of what nothing isn't.

> We are persuaded that nothing is not the yellow panties. The yel-
> low panties edged with white on the floor under the black chair.
> And it's not the floor or the black chair or the two naked lovers
> standing up in the white-sheeted bed having a pillow fight during

the course of which the male partner will, unseen by his beloved, load his pillowcase with a copy of Webster's Third International. We are nervous. There is not much time. Nothing is not a Gregorian chant or indeed a chant of any kind unless it be the howl of the null muted to inaudibility by the laws of language strictly construed. . . . It's not the ice cubes disappearing in the warmth of our whiskey nor is it the town in Scotland where the whiskey is manufactured nor is it the workers who, while reading the Bible and the local newspaper and Rilke, are sentiently sipping the product through eighteen-foot-long, almost invisible nylon straws.

This parody celebrates not nothingness but plenitude, illustrated by the power of drawing a fetishistic frisson from a realistic enough image that is then given context in a jolly erotic scene that unexpectedly switches codes into an intimation of the sinister. Barthelme then intimates his own ability, found at spots throughout his fiction, of bringing the howl of the null to audibility by playing with the laws of language strictly construed. Nothingness is then confuted by a sensory image traced back to a social origin, a community, imagined realistically enough again until we get to Rilke where it takes a surrealistic swerve. (Scottish distillery workers may read Rilke but I doubt the eighteen-foot straws.) 'Nothing' seems worth nothing after this.

The Dead Father (1973), Barthelme's best book after Snow White and City Life, stays on the surfaces yet again but refracts from there more troubling suggestions about the relation of fathers to sons than many deeply psychological novels. The father here is explicitly what psychoanalysts call a father-imago, that is the terrifying, grotesque, gigantic image of the father that lurks in the child's subconscious. Barthelme exaggerates this exaggeration:

> Jawline compares favorably to a rock formation. Imposing, rugged, all that. The great jaw contains thirty-two teeth, twenty-eight of the whiteness of standard bathroom fixtures and four stained, the latter a consequence of addiction to tobacco, according to legend, this beige quartet to be found in the centre of the lower jaw. He is not perfect, thank god for that. The full red lips drawn back in a slight rictus, slight but not unpleasant rictus, disclosing a bit of mackerel salad lodged between two of the stained four. We think it's mackerel salad. It appears to be mackerel salad. In the sagas, it is mackerel salad.

The father stands in for God, tradition, law, and rulership, and this is why his sons, led by Tom, are hauling him across country on a long cable as he floats behind them like a dirigible, supposedly in quest of the golden fleece but really to bury him in a gigantic hole being prepared by a team of bulldozers. The golden fleece, it turns out, has been travelling with them all along as Julie, Tom's consort, reveals by simply lifting her skirt – a calculated affront, given that Barthelme is well aware of the emergent feminism of the 1970s, having anticipated it in the dissatisfactions of Snow White. Here as there he both endorses, incorporates and flouts this new paradigm, seeing its validity but resisting the politically correct limits it would set for sexual feeling. The narrative moves from displaced psychological reality to unpredictable fantasy to dirty joke, in a fashion characteristic of Barthelme. But the most startling aspect of *The Dead Father* is that partway through it Barthelme interjects what amounts to a second book, *A Manual for Sons*, that itself includes three monstrous paternal voices engaged in the project of soul murder. The voices sound Southern redneck but the values are generally American, as in voice A's reassurances about starting school.

> We're right behind you son, your mother and I who love you.
> You'll be getting your sports there, your ball sports and your
> blood sports and watch out for the coach, he's a disappointed
> man, some say a sadist but I don't know about that. You got to
> develop your body, son. If they shove you, shove back. Don't
> take nothin' off nobody. Don't show fear. Lay back and watch
> the guy next to you, do what he does. Except if he's a damn fool.
> If he's a damn fool you'll know he's a damn fool 'cause every-
> body'll be hittin' on him. Let me tell you 'bout that school, son.
> They'll do what they do 'cause I told them to do it. That's why
> they do it. They didn't think up those ideas their own selves. I
> told them to do it. Behave yourself, kid! Do right!

Michel Foucault's grandly paranoid vision of every aspect of life and every system of ideas as an elaborated social mechanism designed for totalitarian control over thought, feeling and behaviour is here encapsulated. Barthelme shows the structure of pathological domination and it is his very abstraction from realistic texture that allows such structural revelation. Over the course of his career Barthelme found various techniques for deflecting nihilism but he never denied the prevalence of disappointment nor the possibility of horror.

Toni Morrison: breaking the silence

The most comprehensive critique of Barthelme is his essay 'After Joyce', written at the time of some of the fiction it enunciated. The most comprehensive critique of Morrison is her essay 'Unspeakable Things Unspoken: The Afro-American Presence in American Literature', written after the fact of five diverse and powerful novels. Morrison explains that she uses her own work to illustrate the culturally specific qualities of African American literature 'not because it provides the best example, but because I know it best, know what I did and why, and know how central these queries are to me'.[8]

Morrison's career has a shape very different from Barthelme's. Barthelme announced where fiction should go and went there. Morrison married, mothered, divorced, and was engaged in a publishing career before she began to write fiction. Moreover, like Oates and unlike Barthelme, she sees herself less as a creator of unique objects than as a witness to an abominable history: 'My work bears witness. . . .' Both Barthelme and Morrison employ cliché but to entirely different ends. Barthelme explodes cliché or pumps it up to the point where it embodies no longer a traditional heavy dullness but a modernist lightness of being. Morrison works into the heaviness of experience, the secret terror or unrealized hope, encoded within the cliché. She quests not after newness but recovery.

> I like to work with, to fret, the cliché, which is a cliché because the experience expressed in it is important: a young man seeks his fortune [Milkman Dead in *The Song of Solomon*]; a pair of friends, one good, one bad [Nel and Sula in *Sula*]; the perfectly innocent victim [Pecola in *The Bluest Eye*]. We know thousands of these in literature. I like to dust off the clichés, dust off the language, make them mean whatever they may have meant originally.[9]

Morrison is as crucially concerned with language as Barthelme but, again, at an opposite end of the pole. Barthelme uses language to express and outflank banality.

> 'OH I wish there were some words in the world that were not the words I always hear!' Snow White exclaimed loudly. We regarded each other sitting around the breakfast table with its big cardboard boxes of 'Fear,' 'Chix,' and 'Rats.' Words in the world that were not the words she always heard. What words could those be? (*Snow White*)

The human condition is the ultimate banality.

> Henry Mackie, Edward Asher and Howard Ettle braved a rainstorm to demonstrate against the human condition on Wednesday, April 2. . . . They began at St John the Precursor on 69th Street at 1:30 P.M. picketing with signs bearing the slogans MAN DIES!/THE BODY IS DISGUST!/COGITO ERGO NOTHING!/ ABANDON LOVE! ('Marie, Marie, Hold on Tight' in *Come Back, Dr Caligari*)

A priest emerges to defend the concern being picketed.

> The photographers made the churchman a little nervous but you
> have to hand it to him, he maintained his phony attitude of polite
> interest almost to the last. He said several rather bromidic things
> like 'the human condition is the *given*, it's what we do with it
> that counts' and 'The body is simply the temple wherein the soul
> dwells' which Henry Mackie countered with his famous question,
> 'Why does it have to be that way?' ('Marie, Marie, Hold on
> Tight')

Barthelme begins and ends with language for its own sake, rendering the
subject epiphenomenal though, as I have argued, apparent in a new
light. There is representation, in however fragmentary a form, but Barthelme programmatically displaces it by language. In contrast, Morrison's
'genuine criticism of most contemporary books is that they're not about
anything. Most of the books that are *about* something – the books that
mean something – treat old ideas, old situations.'[10] In postmodernist
fiction language is privileged and opaque; in Morrison it is powerful in
ratio to its transparency, in 'getting the sound without some mechanics
that would direct the reader's attention to the sound'.[11] She wants the
reader 'to feel dread and to feel the awfulness without having the language compete with the event itself'.[12] Morrison's fiction is highly indeterminate but in a fashion quite distinct from postmodernist
gamesmanship in its reflection of moral and existential as opposed to
epistemological and linguistic concerns.[13]
    Morrison's language represents and reconstructs a historically specific
black community in cultural jeopardy.

> For a long time, the art form that was healing for Black people
> was music. That music is no longer *exclusively* ours; we don't have
> exclusive rights to it. . . . So another form has to take its place,
> and it seems to me that the novel is needed by African-Americans
> now in a way it was not needed before – and it is following along
> the lines of the function of novels everywhere. We don't live in
> places where we can hear those stories anymore; parents don't sit
> around and tell their children those classical, mythological archetypal
> stories that we heard years ago. But new information has to get out,
> and there are several ways to do it. One is in the novel.[14]

The African American language difference is not a facile one, as in some
literary misrepresentations.

> I always hated with a passion when writers rewrote what black people
> said, in some kind of phonetic alphabet that was inapplicable to

any regional pronunciation. There is something different about that language, as there is about any cultural variation of English, but it's not saying 'dis' and 'dat.' It is the way words are put together, the metaphors, the rhythm, the music – that's the part of the language that is distinctly black to me when I hear it.[15]

Morrison's gloss on the phrase 'quiet as it's kept' in *The Bluest Eye* in 'Unspeakable Things Unspoken' eloquently instances her linguistic specificity.

> First, it was a familiar phrase, familiar to me as a child listening to adults; to black women conversing with one another; telling a story, an anecdote, gossip about some one or event within the circle, the family, the neighborhood. The words are conspiratorial. 'Shh, don't tell anyone else,' and 'No one is allowed to know this.' It is a secret between us and a secret that is kept from us. The conspiracy is both held and withheld, exposed and sustained. In some sense it was precisely what the act of writing the book was: the public exposure of a private confidence. (20)

Style reflects theme which in all Morrison's novels is that which is not to be spoken of. At the centre of all Morrison novels is race, 'still a virtually unspeakable thing', but there is also child abuse in *Tar Baby*, incest in *The Bluest Eye*, especially taboo forms of rape in *Beloved*, serial racial murder in *The Song of Solomon*, random and motiveless murder in *Sula* (committed by one co-protagonist and abetted by the other). These relatively universal taboos are reinforced by race-culturally specific ones: incest is a universal taboo and white fathers have raped their daughters, but not in American literature in 1970. Morrison compounded scandal by violating an African American dirty laundry prohibition, a prohibition understandable in relation to the white tendency to feel smugly horrified at dysfunction in the African American community while remaining carefully ignorant of parallel instances in their own. Morrison, however, disallows projection and evasion of white readers by showing, in *The Bluest Eye*, the complicity of the white community in the dysfunction of the black Breedlove family. Her most daring gesture, one which puts the reader at risk, is to show the humanity of the malefactor as well as his social determination by the massive conspiracy of the white world against the black. Morrison puts a kind of curse on this white world's fantasy of family innocence by the use of a passage from a reading primer. The primer features Mother, Father, Dick and Jane as the model white family, living in the model green and white house with the model cat and dog. But this picture is unframed when reiterated without punctuation and put further askew when repeated again without spacing, one segment taking on particularly sinister intimation: 'seefatherheisbigandstr-

ongfatherwillyouplaywithjanefatherissmilingsmilefathersmileseethedog'.
Tar Baby depicts a white family where Mother used to stick pins in baby
and the passage makes us eerily aware of the potential for horror in any
family. But in *The Bluest Eye* it is an African American family specifically
destroyed by the force of white racism. The primer passages are followed
by the phrase 'quiet as it's kept', which then reflects backward as well as
forward: the ultimate family secrets of Father, Mother, Dick and Jane, as
expressed in 'Unspeakable Things': 'Thus, the opening provides the stroke that announces more than a secret shared, but a silence broken, a
void filled, the unspeakable spoken at last' (22).

Each Morrison novel speaks aloud the family secrets, those of western
culture and of the African American community. Some of these secrets
are those of strength. *Sula* is misunderstood when seen as unequivocally
endorsing either Sula's unrestrained individualism or the community's
conservative traditionalism. These are oppositional strengths, rather than
the one a strength, the other a weakness. Moreover, because of the
relative tolerance of the African American community, the two are
oddly complementary.

> A woman who wrote a paper on *Sula* said she thought Sula's com-
> munity was very unnurturing for her. That's very strange to me
> because I found that community to be very nurturing for Sula.
> There was no other place in the world she could have lived with-
> out being harmed. Whatever they think about Sula, however diff-
> erent, they won't harm her. Medallion is a sustaining
> environment even for a woman who is very different. Nobody's
> going to lynch her or call the police. They call her bad names
> and try to protect themselves from her evil; that's all. But they
> put her to very good use, which is a way of manipulating her.[16]

As Robert Grant, a critic who does understand Morrison, demonstrates,
'This novel is one in which the relative social values of conservancy *and*
iconoclasm are exquisitely balanced and readers are hard put to determine
where the author's ultimate moral–thematic sympathies were directed.'[17]
But this is true of all Morrison's novels, except perhaps *The Bluest Eye*.

In *Song of Solomon* the tension focuses on a male protagonist, neither
so destructive nor so courageous as Sula but destructive enough in an all
too typical fashion and *ultimately* courageous. The novel has a patented
Morrison opener, matter of fact in tone, startling in content: 'The North
Carolina Mutual Insurance agent promised to fly from Mercy to the
other side of Lake Superior at three o'clock' (1). In the event he goes
down rather than up but the sentence introduces a theme of flight which
has the potential, just beyond the border of the page, of genuine ascent.
Morrison presents supernatural possibility on the same plane as scientific
law, yet another taboo violation: 'I could blend the acceptance of the

supernatural and a profound rootedness in the real world at the same time with neither taking precedence over the other.' The theme is also culturally specific.

> It is indicative of the cosmology, the way in which Black people looked at the world. We are very practical people, very down-to-earth, even shrewd people. But within that practicality we also accepted what I suppose could be called superstition and magic, which is another way of knowing things. But to blend those two worlds together at the same time, was enhancing, not limiting.

Finally, it is part of Morrison's recuperative mission: 'And some of those things were "discredited knowledge" that Black people had; discredited only because Black people were discredited therefore what they knew was "discredited." And also because the press of upward social mobility would mean to get as far away from that kind of knowledge as possible.' The flight theme also embodies a moral opposition, that between individualistic freedom and relational responsibility, the specific community secret being the tendency of African American men to take flight from family, encapsulated in Milkman's abandonment of Hagar. Morrison reminds us that Pilate in *Song Of Solomon*

> had a dozen years of close, nurturing relationships with two males – her father and her brother. . . . Her daughter Reba had less of that and related to men in a very shallow way. Her daughter [Hagar] had even less of an association with men as a child, so that the progression is really a diminishing of their abilities because of the absence of men in a nourishing way in their lives. . . . That is the duality we must guard against for the future – the female who reproduces the female who reproduces the female.[18]

Yet flight is also associated historically with the escape from slavery and spiritually with transcendence, thus transacting another indeterminacy, besides recapitulating the 'white' American romance theme of flight from society.

Tar Baby reverses the gender conflict with the man offering and the woman fleeing commitment. Jadine's rejection of Son brings into play the community secret of gender and class division – not between the African American and white community but within the former, as noted at the end of Chapter 2. Written in 1981, *Tar Baby* reflects underlying oppositions in the African American community intensified by 'black power' ideology. For Son, Jadine is the tar baby (out of the white Southern writer Joel Chandler Harris's Uncle Remus stories, themselves derived from African oral tales), trying to trap him into assimilation with respectable white culture. She can ultimately accept him only on the condition that he travel upwardly out of his black identity. For Jadine, Son is the tar baby, attempting to suck her down into a murky black world at the loss of the individualistic cultivated identity in which she has invested. In her own play on a traditional African American opposition Morrison clearly favours the funky (i.e. highly sexed, frankly physical, ghetto-style, obviously and unapologetically black) Son over the dicty (i.e. high-class, snobbish, demanding, upwardly mobile, white-oriented) Jadine. Ultimately, however, both positions are traps. Neither the northern ghetto nor the all-African American southern small town offers Jadine sufficient identity while her high fashion career offers only a transient and detached one. Jadine sees nothing for her in the African American community but is rootless outside it. Son reveres the Southern community he stemmed from but though he insists on their visiting it he can no more imagine living there than Jadine. It is a community more viable in terms of nostalgia than possibility. But in the northern ghetto world Son is as rootless as Jadine and, indeed, has no way to live except on her money which he has intelligent political objections to accepting. She tells him to stop loving his ignorance; he tells her that what she learned in college did not include *him* (that is black male identity). She wants him to make it. He wants 'to *be* it' (9). So the relation winds down to total deadlock: 'Mama-spoiled black man, will you mature with me?' 'Culture-bearing black woman, whose culture are you bearing?' (9). Both are right, both are wrong. Within the terms presented in the novel, the dilemma of finding a central relation to a marginalized community is 'literally a cul-de-sac', not least upsetting to the author: 'I was miserable and unsettled when I wrote the book, because it's a depressing and unlovely thought'.[19]

Recovering community and surmounting the repression of the past so as ultimately to exorcize it are the heroic tasks of *Beloved* (1987), a novel that takes up unfinished business from Morrison's previous works. *The Bluest Eye* powerfully explores Pecola's victimization by the massive social conspiracy of racism. But though Morrison brilliantly demonstrated the cause of Pecola's psychic disintegration, in 'Unspeakable Things' she expresses dissatisfaction with her handling of the effect.

> The shattered world I built (to complement what is happening to Pecola) . . . does not in its present form handle effectively the silence at its center. The void that is Pecola's 'unbeing.' It should have had a shape – like the emptiness left by a boom or a cry. It required a sophistication unavailable to me. . . . She is not seen by herself until she hallucinates a self. And the fact of her hallucination becomes a point of outside-the-book conversation, but does not work in the reading process. (22)

In *Beloved* Morrison depicts not the self who is disintegrating but the disintegration itself as an embodied psychic process. Beloved receives the individuation even of a name only after death, the name on the tombstone paid for by Sethe with her body: 'Ten minutes for seven letters. With another ten could she have gotten "Dearly" too?' (1) Beloved reappears eighteen years later, tall as an eighteen-year-old but as uncoordinated and needy as the infant she was when her mother killed her to prevent her reenslavement. As a literary invention, Beloved has two conjoined vital narrative functions: as a multiply implicative symbolic construct and as a phenomenologically intense figure for a psychological process. Both are allegories of disintegration and repression, the former pointing to the historical world, the latter to the interior self. History is a trauma that Sethe has repressed because too painful, too indecent really, to bear: 'every minute of her past life hurt. Everything in it was painful or lost. She and Baby Suggs had agreed without saying so that it was unspeakable' (1). Beloved is the repressed past of slavery and atrocity, an emblem of the unspeakable thing who becomes, in a stunning narrative device, the one person to whom Sethe can tell it. Beloved enables and embodies the return of the repressed. In 'Unspeakable Things Unspoken' Morrison declares, 'The trauma of racism is, for the racist and the victim, the severe fragmentation of the self, and has always seemed to me a cause (not a symptom) of psychosis. . . ' (16). The historical self is fragmented by repressing the history of pain which Morrison recovers in this story which, in fact, is less grim in outcome than the real story of Margaret Garner upon which it was based. Even Morrison's fragmentation theme is explicit in the historical incident. Asked whether she acted out of madness, Garner replied, 'No, I was as cool as I now am, and would much rather kill them at once and end their suffering than have them taken back to slavery, and be murdered piecemeal.' In the event, Garner and her other children were returned to their owner and sold down the river to New Orleans,[20] one of the children drowning en route. As in *The Bluest Eye* Morrison demonstrates how fragmentation is socialized. But the hole in the centre of Beloved has a shape like the emptiness left by a boom or a cry. This is because Beloved hallucinates a self that precisely represents deprivation and disintegration. Not understanding her loss of a baby tooth, Beloved fears it is the beginning of self-dissolution.

> Beloved looked at the tooth and thought, This is it. Next would be her arm, her hand, a toe. Pieces of her would drop maybe one at a time, maybe all at once. Or on one of these mornings before Denver woke and after Sethe left she would fly apart. It is difficult keeping her head on her neck, her legs attached to her hips when she is by herself. Among the things she could not remember was when she first knew that she could wake up and find herself in pieces.

The deep thematic concern of *Beloved* is the question of boundaries of self, where one self properly leaves off and another self or community of selves begins, and their presumptuous violation. On the social level, slavery is a massive and flagrant boundary violation, the presumption of one group of their right to own and totally control the selves of another group. Sethe's killing of Beloved is a parallel although far less morally culpable presumption. Death may be preferable to enslavement but Sethe is presumptuous to make this choice for another being – her child, yes, but also, in a sense, the child of the profoundly disapproving black community. It is part of Morrison's indeterminacy to show Sethe's proud separateness from this community as a weakness as much as a strength. Moreover, if Sethe draws too much of a boundary between herself and her community, she fails to draw enough of one between herself and Beloved, an aspect of that self that threatens to destroy the integrity of the whole, besides that Beloved died before achieving physical integration or separateness from her mother. So, naturally, the reappeared Beloved brooks no boundary and begins to engorge her mother. For her part, having previously repressed Beloved, with all her significations, Sethe now overfocuses on her, leading to the stunningly literalized image towards the end of the novel of a gigantic Beloved towering over a diminished Sethe. This is a model of a specific type of pathological relationship and of a specific personality disorder, both eventuating in a self given over whether to another self or a hypertrophied aspect of one's previously 'own' self. Indeed, these are one and the same since Beloved is, in psychological terms, a daughter image for Sethe, a projected image from the depths of self. Sethe has previously lost part of herself to repression, now in a destructive overcorrection she is losing her whole self to obsession. Sethe's memory and guilt demonically possess her.

To some contemporary high theorists, Sethe's position would be ideal. She has become authentic by disintegrating factitious self into demonic impulse and is properly alienated from community which can only be oppressive. But such is not Morrison's ethos. It is clear from all her novels that the integration of both self and community is her vital issue. In 'Unspeakable Things' Morrison declares her affinity to Greek tragedy with its 'heroic struggle between the claims of community and individual hubris' (2). Barthelme's postmodernism achieves its effects by cancelling out both community and individual though the fragments of both brilliantly glimmer in his carefully displaced prose. Morrison's career-long quest is to recover the individual-in-community without resorting to utopian simplification or sentimental evasion. In all her novels before *Beloved*, she demonstrates the ideal balance by how far her characters fall short of it, though Milkman Dead at the ambiguous end of *Song of Solomon* is closing fast. In *Beloved* Sethe's live daughter, Denver, acts for life, appealing to the community which then gathers itself to exorcize

Beloved and reclaim Sethe, an extraordinarily positive and convincing conclusion. Except that with Morrison's characteristic indeterminacy it is not quite the ending, tragic claims never being *ultimately* reconcilable. Midway through the novel Beloved has imaged her condition to Denver.

> Beloved drops her hand. 'I'm like this.'
>   Denver watches as Beloved bends over, curls up and rocks. Her eyes go to no place; her moaning is so small Denver can hardly hear it. (1)

This image is of the unaccommodated self, the self without integration or relation. The very last section of the novel, a kind of coda, returns to the 'disremembered and unaccounted for' Beloved: 'Although she has claim, she is not claimed.' Disremembered, she is also dismembered: 'the girl who waited to be loved and cry shame erupts into her separate parts. . . .'. Belying itself, the narrative declares, 'This is not a story to pass on' while doing so. What is left is not integral narrative but phantasmal traces, those at first of Beloved's footsteps in the stream behind the house she had haunted, then only the narrative trace of the absence of traces.

> By and by all trace is gone, and what is forgotten is not only the footprints but the water too and what is down there. The rest is weather. Not the breath of the disremembered and unaccounted for, but wind in the eaves, or spring ice thawing too quickly. Just weather. Certainly no clamor for a kiss.
>   Beloved.

In effect, though Sethe has earned her exorcism, the reader has this to prove and must first experience the ghost, undergo the disintegration, suffer the guilt, and empathize with the margin, only then to begin the movement to the centre.

Notes

1. See Wendell V. Harris, 'Canonicity', *PMLA* **106** (1991), 110–21.

2. Donald Barthelme, 'After Joyce', *Location* **1** (1964), 13–14.

3. 'An Interview with Donald Barthelme' in Tom LeClair and Larry McCaffery (eds), *Anything Can Happen: Interviews with Contemporary American Novelists* (Urbana, 1988), p. 43.

4. 'After Joyce', 16.

5. Peter Sloterdijk, *Critique of Cynical Reason*, trans. Michael Eldred (Minneapolis, 1987), pp. 5–7.

6. Richard Schickel, 'Freaked out on Barthelme', *The New York Times Magazine* 16 August 1970, p. 44.

7. Northrop Frye, *Anatomy of Criticism* (Princeton, 1957), p. 42.

8. Toni Morrison, 'Unspeakable Things Unspoken: The Afro-American Presence in American Literature', *Michigan Quarterly Review* **28** (1989), 19–20.

9. 'An Interview with Toni Morrison' in LeClair and McCaffery, *Anything Can Happen*, p. 254.

10. *Anything Can Happen*, p. 254.

11. *Anything Can Happen*, p. 257.

12. 'Interview' in Claudia Tate (ed.), *Black Women Writers at Work* (New York, 1983), p. 125.

13. See Catherine Rainwater, 'Worthy Messengers: Narrative Voices in Toni Morrison's Novels', *Texas Studies in Literature and Language* **33** (1991), 96–113.

14. Toni Morrison, 'Rootedness: The Ancestor as Foundation' in Mari Evans (ed.), *Black Women Writers (1950–1980)* (Garden City, 1984), p. 340.

15. 'Toni Morrison' in Charles Ruas, *Conversations with American Writers* (New York, 1984), p. 219.

16. *Black Women Writers at Work*, pp. 129–30.

17. Robert Grant, 'Absence into Presence: The Thematics of Memory and "Missing" Subjects in Toni Morrison's Sula' in Nellie Y. McKay, (ed.), *Critical Essays on Toni Morrison* (Boston, 1988), p. 91. See Deborah E. McDowell's essay in this collection for parallel insights.

18. 'Rootedness', pp. 342, 344.

19. *Conversations*, p. 237.

20. Philip S. Foner, *History of Black Americans: From the Compromise of 1850 to the End of the Civil War* (Westport, Connecticut, 1983), pp. 87–91.

Chronology

DATE	AMERICAN FICTION	OTHER WORKS	HISTORICAL/CULTURAL EVENTS
1940	Faulkner *The Hamlet*	Eliot *East Coker*	Forty-hour working week adopted nationally
	Hemingway *For Whom the Bell Tolls*	Winters *Poems*	First peacetime conscription
	McCuliers *The Heart is a Lonely Hunter*		US population over 131,000,000
	Stead *The Man Who Loved Children*		
	Wright *Native Son*		
1941	Schulberg *What Makes Sammy Run*	Agee *Let Us Now Praise Famous Men*	Japanese attack on Pearl Harbor and USA enters war
	Welty *A Curtain of Green*	Matthiessen *American Renaissance*	
1942	Faulkner *Go Down Moses and Other Stories*	Stevens *Notes for a Supreme Fiction*	Japanese Americans imprisoned in concentration camps

DATE	AMERICAN FICTION	OTHER WORKS	HISTORICAL/CULTURAL EVENTS
	McCarthy *The Company She Keeps* Welty *The Robber Bridegroom*	Wilder *The Skin of Our Teeth*	
1943	Farrell *My Days of Anger* Saroyan *The Human Comedy* Warren *At Heaven's Gate* Welty *The Wide Net*	Eliot *Four Quartets*	Zoot suit riots in Los Angeles Race riots in Detroit and Harlem
1944	Bellow *Dangling Man* Brown *A Walk in the Sun* Porter *The Leaning Tower and Other Stories* Winsor *Forever Amber*	Warren *Collected Poems 1923–43*	. GI Bill of Rights enacted Penicillin becomes a 'miracle drug' 'Paperback' book boom
1945	Himes *If He Hollers Let Him Go* Patchen *Memoirs of a Shy Pornographer* Steinbeck *Cannery Row*	Brooks *A Street in Bronzeville* Williams *The Glass Managerie* Wright *Black Boy*	World War II ends in Europe Roosevelt dies and is succeeded by Truman Japan surrenders after atomic bomb attacks

DATE	AMERICAN FICTION	OTHER WORKS	HISTORICAL/CULTURAL EVENTS
1946	McCullers *The Member of the Wedding* Petry *The Street* Warren *All the King's Men*	Lowell *Lord Weary's Castle* Williams *Paterson, Book I*	Churchill names 'Iron Curtain' Returning veterans greatly expand college enrolments First American computer operates Loyalty Program requires investigation of all government workers
1947	Bellow *The Victim* Burns *The Gallery* Powers *The Prince of Darkness and Other Stories* Spillane *I, The Jury* Stafford *The Mountain Lion*	O'Neill *A Moon For the Misbegotten* Williams *A Streetcar Named Desire*	Marshall Plan for European recovery Baruch names 'Cold War' Captain Yeager breaks 'sound barrier'
1948	Capote *Other Voices, Other Rooms* Cozzens *Guard of Honor* Faulkner *Intruder in the Dust* Mailer *The Naked and the Dead*	Pound *The Pisan Cantos* Roethke *The Lost Son and Other Poems* Trilling *The Liberal Imagination*	Berlin blockade and airlift Eliot awarded Nobel Prize President Truman bans segregation in the armed forces Long-playing record introduced
1949	Algren *The Man with the Golden Arm* Bowles *The Sheltering Sky*	Frost *Complete Poems* Miller *Death of a Salesman*	American communist leaders convicted of conspiracy 'Bikini' bathing suits introduced from France

DATE	AMERICAN FICTION	OTHER WORKS	HISTORICAL/CULTURAL EVENTS
	Clark *The Track of the Cat* Hawkes *The Cannibal*	Williams *Selected Poems*	
1950	Faulkner *Collected Stories* Hemingway *Across the River and into the Trees* Taylor *A Woman of Means*	Eliot *The Cocktail Party* Riesman et al. *The Lonely Crowd* Smith *Virgin Land* Williams *Collected Later Poems*	US population 150,000,000 Faulkner awarded Nobel Prize Senator McCarthy claims to find 'communists' in government Korean War begins
1951	Jones *From Here to Eternity* Salinger *The Catcher in the Rye* Styron *Lie Down in Darkness* Wouk *The Caine Mutiny*	Lowell *The Mills of the Kavanaughs* Moore *Collected Poems* Williams *Collected Earlier Poems*	CBS broadcasts colour television American Studies Association founded
1952	Ellison *Invisible Man* Hemingway *The Old Man and the Sea* McCarthy *The Groves of Academe* Steinbeck *East of Eden*	MacLeish *Collected Poems* O'Hare *A City Winter and Other Poems*	Eisenhower defeats Stevenson in presidential election *Mad* magazine founded 'Panty raids' at colleges

DATE	AMERICAN FICTION	OTHER WORKS	HISTORICAL/CULTURAL EVENTS
1953	Baldwin *Go Tell it on the Mountain*	Olson *The Maximus Poems*	Rosenbergs executed Korean War ends *Playboy* Magazine founded
	Bellow *The Adventures of Augie March*	Roethke *The Waiting*	
	Cheever *The Enormous Radio*	Warren *Brother to Dragons*	
	Malamud *The Natural*		
	Salinger *Nine Stories*		
	Wright *The Outsider*		
1954	Arnow *The Dollmaker*	Stevens *Collected Poems*	Supreme court rules school segregation unconstitutional
	Faulkner *The Fable*	Williams *The Desert Music*	Hemingway wins Nobel Prize
	Jarrell *Pictures from an Institution*		
	Welty *The Ponder Heart*		
1955	Gaddis *The Recognitions*	Dickinson The Complete Poems 3 vols. edition edited by Thomas H. Johnson; first properly edited text of Dickinson's poems	Birmingham, Alabama bus boycott begins Bill Haleys' *Rock Around the Clock* popularizes rock music
	McCarthy *A Charmed Life*		
	Nabokov *Lolita*		
	O'Connor *A Good Man is Hard to Find*	Lewis *The American Adam*	

DATE	AMERICAN FICTION	OTHER WORKS	HISTORICAL/CULTURAL EVENTS
1956	Barth *The Floating Opera* Bellow *Seize the Day* Morris *The Field of Vision* Thurber *Fables for Our Time*	Berryman *A Homage to Mistress Bradstreet and Other Poems* Ginsberg *Howl and Other Poems* O'Neill *Long Day's Journey into Night*	Supreme Court rules segregation on buses unconstitutional Elvis Presley emerges
1957	Agee *A Death in the Family* Cheever *The Wapshot Chronicle* Cozzens *By Love Possessed* Kerouac *On the Road* Malamud *The Assistant* Nabokov *Pnin*	Chase *The American Novel and its Traditions* Stevens *Opus Posthumous*	US troops sent to Little Rock to enforce school integration
1958	Barth *The End of the Road* Berger *Crazy in Berlin* Donleavy *The Ginger Man* (pub. in Paris, 1955) Malamud *The Magic Barrel*	Felinghetti *A Coney Island of the Mind* Roethke *Words for the Wind*	John Birch Society formed Launch of first US satellite Quiz show scandal
1959	Bellow *Henderson the Rain King*	Goffman *The Presentation of Self in Everyday Life*	Lawrence's *Lady Chatterley's Lover* published after

THE LIBRARY
GUILDFORD COLLEGE
of Further and Higher Education

DATE	AMERICAN FICTION	OTHER WORKS	HISTORICAL/CULTURAL EVENTS
	Paley *The Little Disturbances of Man* Roth *Goodbye, Columbus* Updike *The Poorhouse Fair*	Lowell, *Life Studies* Snodgrass *Heart's Needle*	thirty-year ban Alaska and Hawaii become 49th and 50th states
1960	Barth *The Sot Weed Factor* Doctorow *Welcome to Hard Times* Morris *Ceremony in Lone Tree* O'Connor *The Violent Bear it Away* Updike *Rabbit, Run*	Fiedler *Love and Death in the American Novel* Jarrell *The Woman at the Washington Zoo* Olson *The Distances* Patchen *Because It Is* Sexton *To Bedlam and Part Way Back*	Contraceptive pills introduced Kennedy–Nixon television debates Kennedy defeats Nixon for presidency African American sit-ins begin in North Carolina
1961	Hawkes *The Lime Twig* Heller *Catch-22* Malamud *A New Life* Miller *Tropic of Cancer* (first American publication) Percy *The Moviegoer* Wright *Eight Men*	H.D. *Helen in Egypt* Ginsberg *Kaddish and Other Poems*	Bay of Pigs invasion fiasco Kennedy institutes televised press conference Berlin Wall erected Attacks on 'Freedom Riders' testing transportation integration in the South

DATE	AMERICAN FICTION	OTHER WORKS	HISTORICAL/CULTURAL EVENTS
	Yates *Revolutionary Road*		

DATE	AMERICAN FICTION	OTHER WORKS	HISTORICAL/CULTURAL EVENTS
1962	Baldwin *Another Country* Berger *Reinhart in Love* Burroughs *Naked Lunch* (pub. in Paris 1959, as *The Naked Lunch*) Kesey *One Flew over the Cuckoo's Nest* Nabokov *Pale Fire* Porter *Ship of Fools* Powers *Morte D'Urban*	Albee *Who's Afraid of Virginia Woolf?* Carson *Silent Spring* Williams *Pictures from Brenghel*	Cuban missile crisis US troops go to Vietnam Tab-opening beer cans introduced Emergence of pop art
1963	McCarthy *The Group* Plath *The Bell Jar* Pynchon *V.* Salinger *Raise High the Roofbeam. Carpenters and Seymour – An Introduction* Updike *The Centaur*	Arendt *Eichmann in Jerusalem* Friedan *The Feminine Mystique* Rich *Snapshots of a Daughter-in-Law*	Murder of Kennedy in Dallas Johnson becomes President Civil Rights march on Washington Martin Luther King's 'I have a dream' speech

DATE	AMERICAN FICTION	OTHER WORKS	HISTORICAL/CULTURAL EVENTS
1964	Barthelme *Come Back, Dr Caligari* Bellow *Herzog* Berger *Little Big Man* Cheever *The Wapshot Scandal* Hawkes *Second Skin* Selby *Last Exit to Brooklyn* Southern and Hoffenberg *Candy*	Berryman *77 Dream Songs* Lowell *For the Union Dead*	Beatles and Bob Dylan emerge Johnson re-elected; signs major Civil Rights Bill Student Free Speech Movement at the University of California Gulf of Tonkin resolution authorizes Vietnam War
1965	Kosinski *The Painted Bird* Lurie *The Nowhere City* Mailer *An American Dream* O'Connor *Everything that Rises Must Converge* Porter *Collected Stories*	Malcolm X *The Autobiography of Malcolm X* Plath *Ariel* Tanner *The Reign of Wonder*	Civil Rights demonstrations in Selma, Alabama Malcolm X killed Watts riots
1966	Barth *Giles Goat Boy* Gass *Omensetter's Luck* McMurtry *The Last Picture Show*	Poirier *A World Elsewhere* Rich *Necessities of Life* Roethke *Complete Poems*	Miniskirts become fashionable Race riots in Cleveland, Chicago and Atlanta Stokely Carmichael calls for 'Black Power'

DATE	AMERICAN FICTION	OTHER WORKS	HISTORICAL/CULTURAL EVENTS
	Malamud *The Fixer* Pynchon *The Crying of Lot 49*		
1967	Barthelme *Snow White* Mailer *Why Are We in Vietnam?* Styron *The Confessions of Nat Turner* Williams *The Man Who Cried I Am*	Bly *The Light Around the Body* Creeley *Words* Moore *The Complete Poems*	Major race riots and Vietnam protests Thurgood Marshall first African American Supreme Court Justice Anti-war march on Pentagon
1968	Barth *Lost in the Funhouse* Barthelme *Unspeakable Practices, Unnatural Acts* Coover *The Universal Baseball Association* Gass *In the Heart of the Heart of the Country* Oates *Expensive People*	Berryman *His Toy, His Dream, His Rest* Exley *A Fan's Notes* Mailer *Armies of the Night*	Robert F. Kennedy and Martin Luther King murdered Chicago Democratic convention riots My Lai massacre Nixon elected President
1969	Cheever *Bullet Park* Coover *Pricksongs and Descants*	Bishop *Complete Poems* Jarrell *Complete Poems*	US moon landing Woodstock music festival

DATE	AMERICAN FICTION	OTHER WORKS	HISTORICAL/CULTURAL EVENTS
	Oates *them*		
	Reed *Yellow Back Radio Broke Down*		
	Roth *Portnoy's Complaint*		
	Taylor *Collected Stories*		
	Vonnegut *Slaughterhouse-Five*		
1970	Barthelme *City Life*	Olson *Collected Poems*	US population 203,000,000 National Guard kills
	Bellow *Mr Sammler's Planet*	Millett *Sexual Politics*	four students at Kent State anti-war protest Chicago Seven trial of
	Dickey *Deliverance*		anti-war protesters
	Didion *Play it as it Lays*		
	Morrison *The Bluest Eye*		
	Oates *The Wheel of Love*		
	Updike *Bech: A Book*		
1971	Doctorow *The Book of Daniel*	O'Hara *Complete Poems*	Eighteen-year olds get the vote *New York Times*
	Gardner *Grendel*	Sexton *Transformations*	publishes Pentagon Papers revealing government lies
	Gass *Willie Masters' Lonesome Wife*	Tate *The Swimmers and Other Poems*	

DATE	AMERICAN FICTION	OTHER WORKS	HISTORICAL/CULTURAL EVENTS
	Malamud *The Tenants*.		
	Updike *Rabbit Redux*		
1972	Barth *Chimera*	Ammons *Collected Poems*	US ground troops removed from Vietnam
	Barthelma *Sadness*	Berryman *Love and Fame*	Nixon goes to China Nixon re-elected
	Reed *Mumbo Jumbo*		
	Welty *The Optimist's Daughter*		
	Williams *Captain Blackman*		
1973	Elkin *Searches and Seizures*	Lowell *History*	Ceasefire in Vietnam Vice-President Agnew forced to resign
	Jong *Fear of Flying*	Rich *Diving into the Wreck*	Supreme Court legalizes abortion during first six months of pregnancy
	Morrison *Sula*		
	Pynchon *Gravity's Rainbow*		
1974	Heller *Something Happened*	Snyder *Turtle Island*	Watergate scandal forces Nixon's resignation; succeeded by Ford
	Lurie *The War between the Tates*	Pirsig *Zen and the Art of Motorcycle Maintenance*	Television anchorwoman commits suicide on air
	Paley *Enormous Changes at the Last Minute*		Patty Hearst kidnapping Violence in Boston against bussing for school integration
	Stone *Dog Soldiers*		

DATE	AMERICAN FICTION	OTHER WORKS	HISTORICAL/CULTURAL EVENTS
	Tyler *Celestial Navigation*		
1975	Barthelme *The Dead Father* Bellow *Humboldt's Gift* Doctorow *Ragtime* Gaddis *JR*	Ashberry *Self-Portrait in a* *Convex Mirror* Dorn *Collected Poems*	Watergate trials 'Catfish' Hunter signs five-year $3.75 million baseball contract
1976	Beattie *Chilly Scenes of Winter* Carver *Will You Please Be* *Quiet, Please* Kingston *The Woman Warrior* Walker *Meridian*	Bishop *Geography III* Haley *Roots* Rich *Of Woman Born*	Equal Rights Amendment for women becomes a political issue Bellow receives Nobel Prize Carter elected President
1977	Cheever *Falconer* Coover *The Public Burning* DeLillo *Players* Morrison *Song of Solomon* Percy *Lancelot*	Lowell *Day by Day* Warren *Selected Poems,* *1923–1975*	Carter pardons Vietnam War draft evaders Gary Gilmore executed

DATE	AMERICAN FICTION	OTHER WORKS	HISTORICAL/CULTURAL EVENTS
1978	Beattie *Secrets and Surprises*	Bercovitch *The American Jeremiad*	California constitutional amendment reduces property tax
	Cheever *The Stories of John Cheever*	Gardner *On Moral Fiction*	
	Gordon *Final Payments*	Levertov *Life in the Forest*	
	O'Brien *Going after Cacciato*	Rich *The Dream of a Common Language*	
	Updike *The Coup*	Shepard *Curse of the Starving Class*	
1979	Barth *Letters*	Lasch *The Culture of Narcissism*	Iranian hostage crisis Gasoline shortages Economic stagnation combines with inflation
	Roth *The Ghost Writer*	Mailer *The Executioner's Song*	Accident at Three Mile Island nuclear plant
	Updike *Too Far to Go*		
1980	Beattie *Falling in Place*	Dickey *Moon under Saturn*	Reagan elected President
	Percy *The Second Coming*		
	Toole *A Confederacy of Dunces*		
	Welty *The Collected Stories*		
1981	Berger *Reinhart's Women*	Ashberry *Shadow Train*	Iranian hostage crisis ends First space shuttle, Columbia launched
	Bowles *Collected Stories*	Sorrentino *Selected Poems 1958–80*	Reagan reduces taxes and increases defence spending

DATE	AMERICAN FICTION	OTHER WORKS	HISTORICAL/CULTURAL EVENTS
	Carver *What We Talk about when We Talk about Love*		
	Morrison *Tar Baby*		
	Roth *Zuckerman Unbound*		
	Updike *Rabbit is Rich*		
1982	Barth *Sabbatical*	Bukowski *Love is a Dog from Hell*	Equal Rights Amendment falls short of ratification
	Bellow *The Dean's December*	Creeley *The Collected Poems 1945–1975*	Federal budget deficit balloon
	Ozick *Levitation*		
	Tyler *Dinner at the Homesick Restaurant*		
	Walker *The Color Purple*		
	Williams *!Click Song!*		
1983	Barthelme *Overnight to Many Distant Cities*	Clampitt *The Kingfisher*	Reagan proposes 'Star Wars' and a five-year military budget for over 2 trillion dollars
	Carver *Cathedral*	Walker *In Search of Our Mother's Gardens*	Record foreign trade deficit
	Kennedy *Ironweed*		
	Roth *The Anatomy Lesson*		
	Wideman *Sent for You Yesterday*		

DATE	AMERICAN FICTION	OTHER WORKS	HISTORICAL/CULTURAL EVENTS
1984	Bellow *Him with his Foot in* *his Mouth* Chute *The Beans of Egypt,* *Maine* Erdrich *Love Medicine* Humphreys *Dreams of Sleep*	Ginsberg *Collected Poems* *1947–80* Wakosi *The Collected Greed* *Parts 1–13*	Reagan re-elected in a landslide US population over 236,000,000
1985	Beattie *Love Always* Gaddis *Carpenter's Gothic* Mason *In Country* Paley *Later the Same Day* Roth *Zuckerman Bound: A* *Trilogy and an Epilogue* Tyler *The Accidental Tourist*	Ashberry *A Wave* Merrill *Late Settings*	The threat of AIDS becomes apparent US increases support of 'Contras' in Nicaragua Corporate mergers financed with 'junk bonds'
1986	Erdrich *The Beet Queen* Ford *The Sports Writer* Pelletier *The Funeral Makers* Roth *The Counterlife* Taylor *A Summons to Memphis*	Bercovitch and Jehlen (eds) *Ideology and Classic* *American Literature*	Tax rates lowered Explosion of Challenger space shuttle National debt doubled over five years

DATE	AMERICAN FICTION	OTHER WORKS	HISTORICAL/CULTURAL EVENTS
	Updike *Roger's Version*		
1987	Humphreys *Rich in Love*	Ashberry *April Galleons*	Bicentennial celebration of the American Constitution
	McMurty *Texasville*	Dobyns *Cemetery Nights*	FBI revealed to have been spying on major American writers
	Morrison *Beloved*		Iran–contra hearings
	Percy *The Thanatos Syndrome*		
	Wolfe *The Bonfire of the Vanities*		
1988	DeLillo *Libra*	Blumenthal *Against Romance*	Bush wins presidency Farm population shrinks to lowest level since the Civil War
	Kennedy *Quinn's Book*	Roth *The Facts*	
1989	Banks *Affliction*	Hirsch *The Night Parade*	
	Kingston *Tripmaster Monkey, His Fake Book*		
	Tan *The Joy-Luck Club*		
1990	Updike *Rabbit at Rest*	Clampitt *Westward*	The deregulated savings and loans industry loses billions of dollars
		Jordan *Channel*	

General Bibliographies

Note: Each section is arranged alphabetically. Place of publication is New York, unless otherwise stated.

(i) Bibliographies and Reference Guides

Gale Research — *Contemporary Authors: A Bio-Bibliographical Guide to Current Authors and their Works* (Detroit, 1962–). (This very useful ongoing project provides biographical information, cites representative criticism and lists works by and on the authors.)

Gohdes, C. and Marovitz, S. E. — *Bibliographical Guide to the Study of the Literature of the USA* (Durham, NC, 1954; 5th revised edn 1984). (An essential starting place for research.)

Hart, J. — *The Oxford Companion to American Literature* (Oxford 1941; 5th revised edn 1983). (A standard reference work, with expectable omissions on more recent authors and more recently recuperated authors.)

Inge, M. T. (ed.) — *Handbook of American Popular Literature* (Westport, Ct, 1988). (Chapters on best sellers, detective and mystery novels, fantasy, etc. Highly useful starting place for study of popular genres.)

Leary, L. — *Articles on American Literature, 1900–1950* (Durham, NC, 1954); also *1950–1967* (1970); *1968–1975* (1979). (An excellent resource though it should be noted that it does not cover critical work in less academic or literarily identified periodicals.)

Martine, J. J. (ed.)	*Contemporary Authors: Bibliographical Series: American Novelists*, Vol. 1 (Detroit 1986). (Bibliographical essays on Baldwin, Barth, Bellow, Cheever, Heller, Mailer, Malamud, McCullers, Updike, Welty. Good starting place for these writers, with, one hopes, more authors to come.)
Reader's Guide	Reader's Guide to Periodical Literature, 1900– . (A necessary supplement to *Articles on American Literature* and *American Literary Scholarship* for contemporary authors.)
Salzman, J. (ed.)	*The Cambridge Handbook of American Literature* (Cambridge, 1986). (A fine guide with the usual problems on more recent emergences.)
Spiller, R. *et al.*	*Literary History of the United States* (1948; 4th revised edn 1974). (The individual essays on writers are uneven, some excellent, some obsolete. But this work is now most historically important as an instance of the institutionalization of American literature. Useful bibliographies.)
Weixlmann, J.	*American Short-Fiction Criticism and Scholarship 1959–1977: A Checklist* (Chicago1982). (A helpful resource in finding short story criticism.)
Woodress, J. and Robbins, J. A.	*American Literary Scholarship: An Annual* (Durham, NC, 1965–). (An annual survey of books and articles that critiques as well as lists. An excellent resource.)

(ii)   The Social, Cultural and Intellectual Contexts

Adorno, T. W. *et al.*	*The Authoritarian Personality* (1950). (Important for its influence on cultural thinking in the 1950s.)
Allen, F.L.	*The Big Change* (1952). (A good popular account of historical change up to 1950.)
Arendt, H.	*The Origins of Totalitarianism* (1951). (Powerful and influential book on the structural similarity of Nazism and Stalinism.)
Bell, D.	*The End of Ideology* (1960); *The Cultural Contradictions of Capitalism* (1976). (Interesting in both their analysis and exemplification of ideology. In *The Cultural Contradictions of Capitalism* Bell sees as dangerously subversive of capitalism forces which seem actually

intrinsic to it.)

Bellah, R. N. *et al.*   *Habits of the Heart: Individualism and Commitment in American Life* (1985). (A sociological study important for its attack on the extreme value put on individualism in American society and its call for community and spiritual values.)

Berger, P. L. and Luckmann, T.   *The Social Construction of Reality* (Garden City, 1966). (A classic anaysis of how 'reality' is a social construction. Compare Goffman and Kuhn.)

Bonn, T. L.   *Heavy Traffic and High Culture: New American Library as Literary Gatekeeper* (Carbondale, 1989). (An account of the role a paperback publishing company played in the selection and distribution of literary high culture.)

Boorstin, D.   *The Americans: The Democratic Experience* (1973); *The Image: A Guide to Pseudo-Events in America* (1962). (*The Image* traces the prevalence of manufactured image marketing in American political and social life. The later book is an excellent account of the effects of technological change, especially in the communications industries.)

Brackman, J.   *The Put-On: Modern Feeling and Modern Mistrust* (Chicago, 1971). (The put-on as used by Bob Dylan and others to undermine and evade conventional ideas. What Brackman defines we would see now as a form of postmodernist irony.)

Branch, T.   *Parting the Waters: America in the King Years 1954–63* (1988). (A superbly detailed study of King and the civil rights struggle generally, fascinating in its vignettes of the historical actors in the midst of crisis.)

Brantlinger, P.   *Bread and Circuses: Theories of Mass Culture as Social Decay* (Ithaca, 1983). (Traces the intellectuals' attack on popular culture.)

Bridgman, P.W.   'Quo Vadis' in *The New Scientist*, ed. W. Ober and A. Estrin (Garden City, 1962). (A lucid presentation of the philosophical implications of interdeterminacy theory in physics and Gödel's law in mathematics by a physicist. Both these topics influence postmodernist thinking.)

Caputo, P.   *A Rumour of War* (New Brunswick, NJ, 1977). (An intense autobiographical exploration of the Vietnam experience by the officer in charge of the dead.)

Carroll, P.N.   *It Seemed Like Nothing Happened: America in the 1970s* (1990). (An interesting study of this period.)

Cash, W.J.   *The Mind of the South* (1941). (A tortured book on Southern identity by a Southern intellectual who committed suicide on its publication; it has been frequently attacked but never superseded.)

Chase, R.   *The Democratic Vista* (Garden City, 1958). (1950s political and cultural dilemmas as seen by a participant–observer.)

Chodorow, N.   *The Reproduction of Mothering: Psychoanalysis and the Sociology of Gender* (Berkeley, 1978). (An important carefully argued theory of the structure of women's development and its relation to social forces. See also Miller, Gilligan.)

Connor, S.   *Postmodernist Culture* (Oxford, 1989). (A sympathetic but not hagiographical analysis of various forms of postmodernist art and culture.)

Conot, R.   *Rivers of Blood, Years of Darkness* (1967). (The Detroit riot of 1967 and its causes.)

Cowley, M.   *The Literary Situation* (1954). (The perspective is that of an intellectual who was as involved in the publishing as in the writing end of making books.)

Cruse, H.   *The Crisis of the Negro Intellectuals* (1967). (Important book on major developments in African American political and cultural thought.)

D'Emilio, J. and E. B. Friedman   *Intimate Matters: A History of Sexuality in America* (1988). (Useful factual background to contemporary gender ideologies.)

Dickstein, M.   *Gates of Eden: American Culture in the Sixties* (1977). (A lively cultural history which, however, overrates the cultural influence of literature and criticism as opposed to that of popular music.)

Diggins, J. P.   *The Proud Decades: America in War and Peace, 1941–1960* (1988). (A perceptive historical analysis.)

Erikson, E.   *Childhood and Society* (1950; 1963). (Highly influential psychiatric theory of identity development, now questioned for insufficient attention to gender and class differences.)

Foster, H. (ed.)   *The Anti-Aesthetic: Essays on Postmodern Culture* (Port Townsend; Washington, 1983). (Essays on contemporary culture from a postmodernist perspective.)

Friedan, B.   *The Feminine Mystique* (1963). (Pioneering feminist manifesto by the founder of the National Organization for Women. Attacked the limitation of women to the arbitrary roles of housewife and mother.)

Gans, H. J.   *Deciding What's News* (1979). (Shows how television 'news' is a cultural construction, especially in its choice of what to regard as news. The evening 'news' reflects rather than examines American cultural and political mythology.)

Geertz, C. *The Interpretation of Cultures* (1973). (Two of these essays in anthropology, 'Thick Description: Toward an Interpretive Theory of Culture' and 'Deep Play: Notes on the Balinese Cockfight', are influences on contemporary literary criticism.)

Gilbert, J.B. *Writers and Partisans: A History of Literary Radicalism in America* (1968). (A study of the *Partisan Review*, a periodical central to the cultural conflicts of the 1940s and 1950s.)

Gilligan, C. *In a Different Voice* (Cambridge, Mass., 1982). (Defines the different values developed by women and men from childhood on, arguing the validity of maligned female perceptions and values. Gilligan, Chodorow and Miller have been attacked by some feminist theorists for 'essentialism', that is, the idea that there is such a thing as a female self, but their opponents seem at least as essentialist despite various forms of disguise.)

Goffman, E. *The Presentation of Self in Everyday Life* (Garden City, 1959); *Frame Analysis* (1974). (Extreme and brilliant analyses of the social construction of the self. The self as solely role player and performer. Compare Berger and Luckmann.)

Goldman, A. *Lenny Bruce* (1974). (An extravagant, disturbing account of a comedian partly a critic of his culture, partly a reflection of its most self destructive tendencies.)

Goodheart, E. *Culture and the Radical Consciousness* (Cambridge, Mass., 1973). (An attack on formalist criticism and on the counterculture.) *The Skeptic Disposition in Contemporary Fiction* (Princeton 1984). (A vigorous polemic against postmodernist theory and practice.)

Harvey, D. *The Condition of Postmodernity* (Oxford, 1980). (An economically oriented study of postmodern society.)

Herr, M. *Dispatches* (1978). (A Vietnam War correspondent's experience. One of the sources for the Coppola Film *Apocalypse Now.*)

Hodgson, G. *America in Our Time* (1976). (A fresh look at contemporary American history that takes a cool look at the mythicized Kennedy presidency.)

Jeffords, S. *The Remasculinization of America: Gender and the Vietnam War* (Bloomington, 1989) (Argues that fiction and films about Vietnam are coded to privilege white male supremacy.)

Kaplan, E.A. (ed.)   *Women in Film Noir* (London, 1980.) (Brilliant essays on the misogynistic social construction of women in this film genre.)

Kolko, G.   *Main Currents in Modern American History* (1984). (A useful radical perspective.)

Kubler-Ross, E.   *On Death and Dying* (1969). (Known for its analysis of the five stages of response to terminal illness, this book has been drawn on by novelists and film-makers as well as being a psychiatric classic.)

Kuhn, T.S.   *The Structure of Scientific Revolutions* (Chicago, 1962; 1970). (Kuhn's analysis of paradigm revolutions in science has been a major influence on contemporary literary history, especially when Kuhn is most misunderstood.)

Laing, R.D.   *The Divided Self* (Baltimore, 1965). (A British psychiatrist's influential argument on the social construction of mental illness.)

Lasch, C.   *The Culture of Narcissism: American Life in an Age of Diminishing Expectations* (1979). (Powerful, discouraging jeremiad on the loss of communal values.)

Lifton, R.J.   *Home from the War* (1974); *History and Human Survival* (1970). (Brilliant analyses of the effects of war, the emergence of new personality types such as 'protean man' and other topics by a major culture critic.)

Lippard, L.   *Pop Art* (1966). (An incisive study by a critic with an inside knowledge of the New York art world.)

Lyotard, J.F.   *The Postmodern Condition* (Minneapolis, 1979)

MacDonald, D.   *Against the Grain* (1965). (These essays are part of the construction of the modern case against popular culture to which postmodernism is to some degree a reaction.)

Miller, J.B.   *Toward a New Psychology of Women* (Boston, 1976). (A feminist revision of developmental psychological theory. Compare Chadorow and Gilligan.)

Navasky, V.S.   *Naming Names* (Harmondsworth, 1980). (On the House Committee on Unamerican Activities 'investigation' of Hollywood; who informed and who refused to.)

Niebuhr, R.   *The Children of Light and the Children of Darkness: A Vindication of Democracy and a Critique of its Traditional Defense* (1944); *The Irony of American History* (1952).

(Niebuhr was an important influence on political and cultural thinking of the 1940s and 1950s.)

Noble, D. W. — *The End of American History: Democracy, Capitalism, and the Metaphor of Two Worlds in Anglo-American Historical Writing 1880–1980* (Minneapolis, 1985). (A study of the historical myths embedded in the most influential American historical works.)

Phillips, W. and P. Rahv (eds) — *The Partisan Review Anthology* (1962). (Essays central to the cultural controversies of the 1940s and 1950s. *The Partisan Reader* (1946). (See also the important symposium, 'Our Country and Our Culture', *Partisan Review* (1952), 282–326.)

Quinn, E. and P.J. Dolan (eds) — *The Sense of the Sixties* (1968). (Essays that do in fact give a sense of the 1960s.)

Reich, W. — *Character Analysis* (1949). (A psychiatric theory that was a source for Saul Bellow and others.)

Riesman, D., N. Glazer and R. Denney — *The Lonely Crowd* (1950). (A seminal sociological study that has become part of American intellectual history. *Riesman's Individualism Reconsidered* (1954) is a set of essays updating his reflections on the same concerns.)

Rorty, R. — *Contigency, Irony, and Solidarity* (Cambridge, 1989), (Combines pragmatism and irony into a philosophy of contingency. Witty, brilliant insights that reflect but fail to ground a postmodernist philosophical perspective.)

Rose, T. (ed) — *Violence in America* (1970). (More interesting as a typical response to 1960s political violence than in its analysis of it. John Lukacs' essay argues the real problem is the prevalence of personal rather than political violence.)

Rosenberg, B. and D.M. White (eds) — *Mass Culture* (1957). (Invaluable for its expression of the intellectual response to pop culture in the 1950s. See especially the essays by Macdonald, Greenberg, Fiedler and Van Den Haag.)

Ross, A. — *No Respect: Intellectuals and Popular Culture* (London, 1989). (Good coverage of the popular culture explosion and the intellectual response to it. Supplements Brantlinger with more emphasis on recent cultural history.)

Showalter, E. (ed) — *The New Feminist Criticism* (1985). (Probably the most influential collection of feminist literary criticism. A major critical work.)

Solotaroff, T. — *A Few Good Voices in My Head: Occasional Pieces on Writing, Editing and Reading My Contemporaries* (1987).

(Especially interesting in its insights into the state of contemporary American publishing.)

Susman, W.I. — *Culture as History: The Transformation of American Society in the Twentieth Century* (1984). (A seminal set of essays on cultural history.)

Swingewood, A. — *The Myth of Mass Culture* (Atlantic Highlands, NJ, 1977). (A critique of the theory of popular culture formulated in the 1950s. Swingewood shows the similarity of Marxist and conservative theories and the lack of historical specification in either. See also Brantlinger and Ross.)

Trilling, L. — *The Liberal Imagination* (Garden City, 1957). (Interesting now primarily as a cultural document.)

Vance, C.S. (ed) — *Pleasure and Danger: Exploring Female Sexuality* (London, 1984). (An interestingly unorthodox selection of feminist essays. Questions tendency towards 'political correctness'.)

Wahl, J. — *Existence humaine et transcendence* (Neuchatel, France, 1944). (A brilliant existentialist work from which Saul Bellow drew the notion of 'transcendence downwards' in *Herzog*.)

Wald, A.M. — *The New York Intellectuals: The Rise and Decline of the Anti-Stalinist Left from the 1930s to the 1980s* (Chapel Hill, 1987). (An account of the culture wars of the New York intellectuals.)

Whyte, W.H. — *The Organization Man* (Garden City, 1956). (An important document for 1950s cultural history.)

Wills, G. — *Nixon Agonistes: The Crisis of the Self-Made Man* (Boston, 1970). (Nixon in relation to American culture and American culture in relation to Nixon.)

Wise, G. — '"Paradigm Dramas" in American Studies: A Cultural and Institutional History of the Movement', *American Quarterly* **31** (1979). (Applies Kuhn's paradigm theory to the historical vagaries of canonical and theoretical perspectives in American studies. A major essay.)

(iii) Interview Collections

Bellamy, J. D. (ed.) — *The New Fiction: Interviews with Innovative American Writers* (Urbana, 1975). (Barth, Barthelme, Gardner, Gass, Hawkes, Kosinski, Reed, Sukenick, Vonnegut.)

Brans, J. (ed.)   *Listen to the Voices* (Dallas, 1988). (Interviews with Barthelme, Bellow, Cheever, Gass, Welty.)

Cowley, M. (ed.)   *Writers at Work*, First Series (Harmondsworth, 1958). (The first collection of the *Paris Review* interviews: Capote, Faulkner, Styron, Warren.)

Dembo, L. S. and C. S. Podrom (eds)   *The Contemporary Writer* (1972). (Barth, Bellow, Hawkes, Nabokov.)

LeClair, T. and L. McCaffery (eds)   *Anything Can Happen: Interviews with Contemporary American Writers* (Urbana, 1988). (Barth, Barthelme, Coover, DeLillo, Doctorow, Elkin, Federman, Gardner, Gass, Hawkes, McElroy, Morrison, O'Brien, Sukenick.)

McCaffery, L. and S. Gregory (eds)   *Alive and Writing: Interviews with American Authors of the 1980s* (Urbana, 1987). (Abish, Beattie, Carver, Kennedy.)

O'Brien, J. (ed.)   *Interviews with Black Writers* (1973). (Ellison, Petry, Reed, Wideman.)

Plimpton, G. (ed.)   *Writers at Work*, Second Series (Harmondsworth, 1963). (Ellison, Hemingway, McCarthy, Porter.) *Writers at Work*, Third Series (Harmondsworth, 1967). (Bellow, Burroughs, Jones, Mailer.) *Writers at Work*, Fourth Series (Harmondsworth, 1976). (Dos Passos, Kerouac, Nabokov, Steinbeck, Updike, Welty.) *Writers at Work*, Fifth Series (Harmondsworth, 1981). (Cheever, Didion, Gass, Heller, Kosinski, Oates.) *Writers at Work*, Seventh Series (Harmondsworth, 1986). (Barth, Roth, Carver.) *Writers at Work,* Eighth Series (Harmondsworth, 1988). (Ozick.)

Ruas, C. (ed.)   *Conversations with American Writers* (1984). (Burroughs, Capote, Doctorow, Heller, Mailer, Morrison, Stone, Welty.)

(iv) History and Criticism

Aldridge, J. W.   *After the Lost Generation: A Critical Study of the Writers of Two Wars* (1951). (Argues a loss of substance and value in fiction after the Second World War.)

Alter, R.   *After the Tradition: Essays on Modern Jewish Writing* (1969). (The best book on the subject.)

Alter, R.   *Partial Magic* (Berkeley, 1975). (A balanced and penetrating study of literary self-reflectiveness.)

Baker, H. A. — *Workings of the Spirit: The Poetics of Afro-American Women's Writing* (Chicago, 1991). (Theoretically informed interpretations of Hurston, Morrison and others.)

Bawer, B. — *Diminishing Fictions: Essays on the American Novel and its Critics* (St Paul, 1988). (An enjoyably unfair polemic against postmodernist fiction and criticism which is a useful counterstatement to the tendency to accept uncritically postmodernist ideas and conventions.)

Baumbach, J. — *The Landscape of Nightmare* (1965). (Sees Bellow, Ellison, Malamud and others as presenting a nightmare vision of the modern world.)

Beidler, P. D. — *Re-writing America: Vietnam Authors in their Generation* (Athens, Georgia, 1991). (An account of Vietnam War literature.)

Bell, B. W. — *The Afro-American Novel and its Tradition* (Amherst, 1987). (The best survey of African American fiction.)

Bigsby, C. W. E. — *The Second Black Renaissance* (Westport, CT, 1980). (Interesting commentary on Wright, Ellison and others.)

Blotner, J. — *The Modern American Political Novel* (Austin, 1966).

Bone, R. A. — *The Negro Novel in America* (New Haven, 1958; 1965). (Now dated but so important as a pioneering study that it should be considered part of American literary history.)

Bradbury, M. — *The Modern American Novel* (Oxford, 1983). (A useful general study.)

Braxton, J. and A. N. McLaughlin (eds) — *Wild Women in the Whirlwind: Afro-American Culture and the Continuing Literary Renaissance* (New Brunswick, NJ, 1991) (Essays on African American women writers.)

Bryant, J. — *The Open Decision: The Contemporary American Novel and its Intellectual Background* (1970). (Argues an existentialist orientation in American fiction since the Second World War.)

Caramello, C. — *Silverless Mirrors* (Tallahassee, 1983). (Less a critique than an insider's presentation of the experimentalist aesthetics of Federman, Sukenick, etc.)

Chametzky, J. — *Our Decentralized Literature: Cultural Mediations in Selected Jewish and Southern Writers* (Amherst, 1986).

(Sees a similar exploitation of the literary possibilities of marginal perception as a way of attaining centrality in Southern and Jewish American fiction.)

Conder, J. J. *Naturalism in American Fiction: The Classic Phase* (Lexington, 1984). (Contributes to the reassessment of naturalism.)

Cook, B. *The Beat Generation* (1971). (This and Tytell's book are the most helpful general studies of the beat writers.)

Core, G. (ed.) *Southern Fiction Today: Renascence and Beyond* (Athens, Georgia 1969). (Essays by leading critics of Southern fiction.)

Davis, A. P. *From the Dark Tower: Afro-American Writers, 900–1960* (Washington DC., 1974). (Judicious assessment of African American writing.)

Dewey, J. *The Apocalyptic Temper in the American Novel of the Nuclear Age* (West Lafayette, Indiana, 1989). (Apocalyptic themes in Vonnegut, Coover, Percy, Pynchon, Gaddis and DeLillo.)

Elliott, E. (ed.) *Columbia Literary History of the United States* (1988). (Incorporates new perspectives on canonization and the politics of literature but, like Spiller's *Literary History of the United States*, it may prove more useful as an example than as an analysis of literary ideology. Compare with the *Harvard Guide* (see Hoffman, D.) for how much critical orthodoxy has changed over less than ten years.)

Eisinger, C. *Fiction of the Forties* (Chicago, 1963). (An excellent study of the politics and cultural politics implicit in 1940s fiction. A model book of its kind.)

Fiedler, L. A. *Love and Death in the American Novel* (1960). (Fiedler claims too much for his thesis which is, however, brilliantly conceived and developed. He argues the fear of women and domesticity as the theme of American fiction.)

Ford, B. (ed.) *American Literature* (Harmondsworth, 1988). (An unpretentious set of essays that give a reasonable version of American literary history.)

Fetterley, J. *The Resisting Reader* (Bloomington, 1978). (An early feminist critique that is still the best exploration of how male writers misconstruct women characters.)

Galloway, D. *The Absurd Hero in American Fiction* (Austin, 1966;1970). (An optimistic existentialist humanist reading of Bellow, Mailer, Salinger, Styron and Updike. The 1970 edition is considerably updated.)

Gates, H. L. (ed.)   *Black Literature and Literary Theory* (London, 1984). (State of the art criticism of African American writers. Especially important for its argument on *how* to read African American texts.)

Geismar, M.   *American Moderns: From Rebellion to Conformity* (1958). (A refreshingly 'vulgar Marxist' perspective on the retreat from politics in the fiction of the 1940s and 1950s.)

Gibson, D. B.   *The Politics of Literary Expression: A Study of Major Black Writers* (Westport CT,1981). (Explores the political positions implicit in the writings of Wright, Ellison, Baldwin and others.)

Gilman, R.   *The Confusion of Realms* (1969). (Essays primarily on postmodern writers.)

Gossett, L. Y.   *Violence in Recent Southern Fiction* (Durham, NC, 1965). (Follows the theme of violence and its stylistic expression through Southern fiction.)

Graff, G.   *Literature Against Itself: Literary Ideas in Modern Society* (Chicago, 1979). (Polemic essays on literary and cultural politics. In 'The Politics of Anti-Realism' Graff notes certain critical mystifications used to valorize postmodernist fiction.)

Gray, R.   *The literature of Memory: Modern Writers of the American South* (Baltimore, 1977). (A perceptive study that demonstrates the value of Southern literature without being prayerful about it.)

Harap, L.   *In the Mainstream: The Jewish Presence in Twentieth Century American Literature* (1978). (Describes the movement of Jewish American literature from margin to centre.)

Harper, H. M.   *Desperate Faith: A Study of Bellow, Salinger, Mailer, Baldwin, and Updike* (Chapel Hill, 1967). (A humanist existentialist reading of these writers.)

Harris, C. B.   *Contemporary American Novelists of the Absurd* (New Haven, 1971). (On the black humour phase of postmodernism.)

Hassan, I.   *Radical Innocence* (Princeton, 1961). (A passionate endorsement of the romance theme of Adamic, anarchic individualism in American fiction.)

Hauck, R. B.   *A Cheerful Nihilism: 'Confidence' and 'The Absurd' in American Humorous Fiction* (Bloomington, 1971). (Examines some major themes of black humour.)

Hicks, J.   *In the Singer's Temple: Prose Fictions of Barthelme, Gaines, Brautigan, Percy, Kesey, and Kosinski* (Chapel Hill, 1981). (An enthusiastic account of these writers.)

Hoffman, D. (ed.)   *Harvard Guide to Contemporary American Writing*
                     (Cambridge, Mass., 1979). (Important as an instance
                     of the orthodox categories and canons of American
                     criticism in the mid 1970s.)

Hoffman, F. J.   *The Modern Novel in America 1900–1950* (Chicago,
                     1951). (Overview from a 'New Critical' perspective.)

Howard, J.   *Form and History in American Literary Naturalism*
                     (Chapel Hill, 1985). (An acute study of the generic
                     conventions of naturalistic fiction. Includes
                     contemporary writers.)

Howe, I.   *The Critical Point in Literature and Culture* (1971).
                     (Essays by a leading cultural as well as literary critic,
                     including the one on Philip Roth that inspired
                     Roth's *The Anatomy Lesson*.)

Hutcheon, L.   *A Poetics of Postmodernism* (London, 1988) (Argues
                     that true postmodernist fiction is in the form of the
                     historical fable.)

Johnson, C.   *Being and Race: Black Writing since 1970*
                     (Bloomington, 1988). (On contemporary African
                     American writing.)

Johnson, I. D. and *Les Américanistes* (Port Washington, 1978).
  C. Johnson (eds.) (Stimulating French critical perspectives on
                     contemporary American literature.)

Karl, F. R.   *American Fictions 1940/1980* (1983). (An exhaustive,
                     informative survey, offering a somewhat abstract
                     thematic analysis.)

Kazin, A.   *Bright Book of Life* (1973) and *Contemporaries* (1982).
                     (Vigorously intelligent assessments by a critic who,
                     like Howe and Trilling, is a cultural figure in his
                     own right.)

Klein, M.   *After Alienation: American Novels in Mid-Century*
                     (Cleveland, 1964). (The titular thesis was premature
                     but the book is a sound study of 1950s fiction.)

Klein, M. (ed.)   *The American Novel since World War II* (1969). (A
                     valuable set of essays that contains important anticip-
                     ations of postmodernism by Howe, Roth and Barth.)

Klinkowitz, J.   *The Life of Fiction* (Urbana, 1977); *Literary Disruptions:
                     The Making of a Post-Contemporary American Fiction*
                     (1975); *The Practice of Fiction in America* (Ames, Iowa
                     1980). (A partisan viewpoint on postmodernist
                     writers. Informative.)

Knopp, J. Z.   *The Trial of Judaism in Contemporary Jewish Writing*
                     (Urbana, 1975). (An analysis of what is Jewish and
                     what is American in Jewish American writing.)

Kuehl, J.   *Alternate Worlds: A Study of Postmodern Antirealistic
                   American Fiction* (1989). (A useful account of the
                   metafictional phase of postmodern American fiction.
                   An introductory essay by James Tuttleton notes how
                   many postmodernist themes and devices were
                   actually anticipated by the nineteenth-century
                   American realists.)

Kumar, P. S.   *Tablet Breakers in the American Wilderness* (Delhi,
                   1981). (Useful insights on Jewish American fiction.)

Lewis, R. W. B.   *Trials of the Word* (New Haven, 1965). (Includes an
                   excellent early consideration of black humour: 'Days
                   of Wrath and Laughter'.)

McCaffery, L.   *The Metafictional Muse: The Works of Robert Coover,
                   Donald Barthelme, and William Gass* (Pittsburgh,
                   1982). (An informative study of three metafictional
                   writers.)

McCarthy, M.   *The Writing on the Wall and Other Literary Essays*
                   (1970). (Acute assessments of contemporary
                   American novelists. Essays on Burroughs, Nabokov
                   and Salinger.)

MacConell, F.   *Four Postwar American Novelists: Bellow, Mailer, Barth,
                   and Pynchon* (Chicago, 1977). (Commentary on the
                   ethical response of these writers to American
                   conditions.)

Malin, I. and I. Stark   *Breakthrough: A Treasury of Contemporary
        (eds)   American–Jewish Literature* (Philadelphia, 1964). (Essays
                   on Jewish American identity and literature.)

Malin, I.   *The New Gothic Novel* (1962). (Explores Capote,
                   Hawkes, McCullers, O'Connor, Purdy and Salinger
                   as creators of the psychological gothic.)

Mellard, J. M.   *The Exploded Form: The Modernist Novel in America*
                   (Urbana, 1980). (Argues that modern American
                   fiction explodes the novel genre into modes: satire,
                   lyric, elegy, etc.)

Millgate, M.   *American Social Fiction: James to Cozzens* (1964). (On
                   American fiction involved with society rather than
                   celebrating Adamic individualism. This and Tuttleton
                   usefully complement each other.)

Muecke, D. C.   *The Compass of Irony* (London, 1969). (The best book
                   on literary irony. Essential for understanding the
                   prevalence of irony in modern fiction.)

Newman, C.   *The Post-Modern Aura: The Act of Fiction in an Age of
                   Inflation* (Evanston, 1985). (A polemic against
                   postmodernism that does not finally cohere.)

O'Connor, W. V.   *The Grotesque: An American Genre and Other Essays* (Carbondale, 1962). (Covers much the same ground as Malin on the gothic.)

O'Donnell, P.   *Passionate Doubts: Designs of Interpretation in Contemporary American Literature* (Iowa City, 1986). (A poststructuralist reading of Barth, Nabokov, Elkin, O'Connor, Hawkes and Pynchon.)

Olderman, M.   *Beyond the Wasteland: A Study of the American Novel in the 1960s* (New Haven, 1972). (Emphasis is on black humour.)

Parkinson, T. (ed.)   *A Casebook on the Beat* (1961). (Useful Information.)

Pearce, R.   *The Novel in Motion* (1983). (Focused on black humour.)

Peden, W.   *The American Short Story: Continuity and Change 1940–1975* (Boston, 1975). (One of several useful but partial studies of the short story.)

Pizer, D.   *Twentieth–Century American Literary Naturalism: An Interpretation* (Carbondale, 1982). (Useful but unaccountably leaves out Wright.)

Podhoretz, N.   *Doings and Undoings: The Fifties and After in American Writing* (1964). (Essays on Mailer, Roth and cultural politics by the Jewish intellectual who became the neo-conservative editor of the important Jewish American periodical *Commentary*.)

Poirier, R.   *The Performing Self: Compositions in the Languages of Contemporary Life* (1971). (Mailer is considered the exemplary performer.)

Pryse, M. and H.J. Spillers (eds)   *Conjuring: Black Women, Fiction, and Literary Tradition* (Bloomington, 1985). (Essays on African American women writers.)

Rainwater, C. and W. Scheick (eds)   *Contemporary American Women Writers: Narrative Strategies* (Lexington, 1985). (Original perspectives on Beattie, Tyler, Kingston and others.)

Roller, J. M.   *The Politics of the Feminist Novel* (Westport, CT, 1986). (Argues that Petry, McCarthy and Arnow wrote clearly feminist texts.)

Rubin, L. D. Jr et al. (eds)   *The History of Southern Literature* (Baton Rouge, 1985). (Uneven in quality. Does not respond to current questionings of critical tradition.)

Rubin, L. D. Jr and R. D. Jacobs (eds)   *South: Modern Southern Literature in its Cultural Setting* (Garden City, 1961). (Good set of essays on Southern writing.)

Safer, E.   *The Contemporary American Comic Epic: The Novels of Barth, Pynchon, Gaddis, and Kesey* (Detroit, 1988). (Persuasive treatment of the topic, relating it to Cotton Mather's Puritan epic biographizing in *Magnolia Christi Americana [The Wonders of Christ in America.]*

Saldivar, R.   *Chicano Narrative: The Dialectics of Difference* (Madison, 1990). (Important both for arguing the value of a body of Hispanic American narrative and for interpreting it from the perspective of contemporary high theory – Marxist, deconstructionist, feminist.)

Sale, R.   *On Not Being Good Enough* (Oxford, 1979). (A refreshingly independent assessment of various American writers. Excellent insights into the strengths and flaws of postmodernist fiction.)

Scholes, R.   *Fabulation and Metafiction* (1979). (This book influentially defined metafiction.)

Schaub, T. H.   *American Fiction in the Cold War* (Madison, 1991). (Relates literary consciousness to political and social thought.)

Schulz, M.   *Radical Sophistication* (Athens, Ohio, 1969). (On contemporary Jewish American fiction). *Black Humor Fiction of the Sixties: A Pluralistic Definition of Man and his World* (Athens, Ohio, 1973). (A rather sanguine vew of black humour.)

Scott, N. A.   *Three American Moralists: Mailer, Bellow, Trilling* (South Bend, Indiana, 1973). (Theologically informed interpretations.)

Sontag, S.   *Against Interpretation* (1966); *Styles of Radical Will* (1969). (Brilliant if rather absolutist essays on literature and culture, some of which have attained classic status.)

Stark, J.   *The Literature of Exhaustion: Borges, Nabokov, Barth* (Durham, NC, 1974). (Treats a major theme in metafictional postmodernism.)

Stevick, P.   *Alternative Pleasures: Postrealist Fiction and the Tradition* (Urbana, 1981). (Striking and precise essays. One of the most balanced considerations of postmodernist fiction.)

Sullivan, D.   *Death by Melancholy* (Baton Rouge, 1972); *A Requiem for the Renaissance* (Athens, Georgia, 1976). (Traditionalist laments for lost Southern cultural traditions leading, Sullivan argues, to fictional decline.)

Tanner, T.   *City of Words* (1971). (Far and away the best general study of contemporary American fiction. It can be supplemented by essays on more recent writers in

Tanner's *Scenes of Nature, Signs of Man* (Cambridge, 1987). Tanner, however, too uncritically accepts the romance paradigm of Adamic individualism as the centre of American fiction.)

Tuttleton, J.   *The Novel of Manners in America* (Chapel Hill, 1972). (Excellent study of this critically marginalized genre.)

Walden, D. (ed.)   *Studies in American Jewish Literature from Marginality to Mainstream: A Mosaic of Jewish Writers* (1982). (Attempts to define Jewish American literature.)

Waugh, P.   *Metafiction* (London, 1984). (Lucid distinction of types of postmodernist fiction.) *Feminine Fictions: Revisiting the Postmodern* (London, 1989). (Reads Paley and Tyler as postmodernists.)

West, R. B. Jr.   *The Short Story in America 1900–1950* (Chicago, 1952). (New Critical formalist perspective.)

Wilde, A.   *Horizons of Assent* (Philadephia, 1981); *Middle Ground* (Philadelphia, 1987). (Well–argued reassessments of irony and postmodernism as fictional modes. The second book posits 'mid-fiction' as the valid middle ground between traditional and experimental fiction.)

Wisse, R.   *The Schlemiehl as Modern Hero* (Chicago, 1971). (A central topic for Jewish American fiction.)

Young, T. D. (ed)   *Modern American Fiction: Form and Function* (Baton Rouge, 1989).

Individual Authors

Notes on biography, major works, and criticism

BALDWIN, James (1924–87), was born in New York City where his stepfather was a factory worker and a preacher. Baldwin was converted at fourteen and became a youth minister. After high school he had to work to support his family, his stepfather having become incapacitated. In the 1940s he directly experienced virulent race prejudice while working in a defence plant in New Jersey. In 1944 Richard Wright helped him get a writing fellowship but he was unable to get his writing untracked until he moved to Paris in 1948. His autobiographical novel *Go Tell it on the Mountain* appeared in 1953. *Giovanni's Room* (1956) explored homosexual experience but most of his fiction thereafter centred on the wounds of racism. His finest writing after his first novel may be in his essays: *Notes of a Native Son* (1955), *Nobody Knows My Name* (1961), *The Fire Next Time* (1963) and *The Price of the Ticket: Collected Nonfiction 1948–1985* (1985).

Weatherby, W.J. *James Baldwin: Artist on Fire* (1989).

See: Kinnamon, K. (ed.), *James Baldwin: A Collection of Critical Essays* (Englewood Cliffs, NJ, 1974).
Sylvander, C.W., *James Baldwin* (1980).
Porter, H.A., *Stealing the Fire: The Art and Protest of James Baldwin* (Middletown, Ct, 1989).
Standley, F.L. and L. Pratt (eds.), *Conversations with James Baldwin* (Jackson, Miss., 1989).

BARTH, John (1930–), was born in Cambridge on the eastern shore of Maryland, the locale for much of his writing. He went to the Julliard school of music, intending to become a jazz arranger, but his interests shifted to literature. He received an AB and an MA from Johns Hopkins to which he returned as a professor in 1973 after teaching at Pennsylvania State University and State University of New York at Buffalo. His 'nihilistic trilogy', beginning with *The Floating Opera* (1956) and *The End of the Road* (1958), merged into metafiction with *The Sot Weed Factor* (1960). *Giles Goat Boy* (1966), *Lost in the Funhouse*

(1968) and *Chimera* (1972) play out various metafictional games. *The Last Voyage of Somebody the Sailor* (1991) puts a modern American into the mythic Baghdad of the Arabian nights. Barth's essays, including 'The Literature of Exhaustion' and 'The Literature of Replenishment', are collected in *The Friday Book* (1984).

> See: Morrell, J., *Barth: An Introduction* (University Park, Pa, 1976).
> Waldmeir, J.J., *Critical Essays on John Barth* (Boston, 1980).
> Harris, C.B., *Passionate Virtuosity: The Fiction of John Barth* (Urbana, 1983).
> Schulz, M.F., *The Muses of John Barth* (Baltimore, 1990).

BARTHELME, Donald (1931–89), was born in Philadelphia, Pennsylvania but grew up in Houston, Texas where his father was a modernist architect. His brother Frederick is also a writer of talent. Graduating from the University of Houston, Donald Barthelme worked as a museum director before moving to New York City in the early 1960s and beginning to publish the innovative short stories collected in *Come Back, Dr Caligari* (1964), *Unspeakable Practices, Unnatural Acts* (1968), *City Life* (1970), *Sadness* (1972), *Amateurs* (1976), *Great Days* (1979) and *Overnight to Many Distant Cities* (1983). His novels proved as unpredictable as his short stories although *Paradise* (1986) seemed almost conventional after the brilliance of *Snow White* (1967) and *The Dead Father* (1975). Barthelme also published *Guilty Pleasures* (1974), a book of parodies, and a number of children's books.

> See: Gordon, L.G., *Donald Barthelme* (Boston, 1981).
> Couturier, M., *Donald Barthelme* (London, 1982).
> Molesworth, C., *Donald Barthelme's Fiction: The Ironist Saved From Drowning* (Columbia, Sc, 1982).
> Stengel, W.B., *The Shape of Art in the Short Stories of Donald Barthelme* (1985).
> Trachtenberg, S., *Understanding Donald Barthelme* (Columbia, Sc, 1990).

BELLOW, Saul (1915–), was born in Lachine, Quebec, to which his parents had immigrated from Latvia. The family moved to Chicago when he was nine. After military service in the Merchant Marine Corps from 1944 to 1945, Bellow attended the University of Chicago, graduated from Northwestern and did graduate work at Wisconsin University in anthropology. He has taught at the University of Chicago, where he became a member of the Commitee of Social Thought, from 1962 on. His first novel, *Dangling Man*, appeared in 1944 followed by *The Victim* in 1947. Bellow's new voice appears in *The Adventures of Augie March* (1953) and is further elaborated in *Seize the Day* (1956) and *Henderson the Rain King* (1959). *Herzog* (1964), *Mr Sammler's Planet* (1970) and *Humbolt's Gift* (1975) are more self-consciously intellectual novels. Bellow's short fiction has been somewhat overshadowed by his novels but the excellence of it is demonstrated in *Mosby's Memoirs* (1968) and *Him with his Foot in his Mouth* (1984). Bellow was awarded the Croix de Chevalier in 1968 (wittily played on in *Humboldt's Gift*) and received the Nobel Prize for literature in 1976. The nearest to a biography of him is Mark Harris, *Saul Bellow: Drumlin Woodchuck* (1980), which is about Harris's inability to find enough information on Bellow to write one.

> See: Tanner, T. *Saul Bellow* (Boston, 1965).
> Opdahl, K., *The Novels of Saul Bellow* (University Park, 1967).
> Rovit, M.G. (ed.), *Saul Bellow: A Collection of Critical Essays* (Englewood Cliffs, NJ, 1975).

Porter, M.G., *Whence the Power? The Artistry and Humanity of Saul Bellow* (Columbia, SC, 1974).
Clayton, J.J., *In Defense of Man* (Bloomington, 1979).
Trachtenberg, S. (ed.), *Critical Essays on Saul Bellow* (Boston, 1979).
Fuchs, D., *Saul Bellow: Vision and Revision* (Durham, NC, 1984).
Bloom, Harold (ed.), *Saul Bellow* (1986).
Pifer, E., *Saul Bellow: Against the Grain* (Philadelphia, 1990).

BERGER, Thomas (1924–), born in Cincinnati, served in a medical unit of the US Army from 1943 to 1946, arriving with first American occupation troops in Berlin. He graduated from the University of Cincinnati in 1948 and did a year of graduate study at Columbia. Has occasionally taught at universities. His Reinhart series began with *Crazy in Berlin* (1958), followed by *Reinhart in Love* (1962), *Vital Parts* (1970) and *Reinhart's Women* (1981). *Neighbors* (1980) is an eerily funny, critically ungraspable novel but Berger's masterpiece is *Little Big Man* (1964) which, it should be remembered, was not immediately recognized.

See: Landon, B. *Thomas Berger* (Boston, 1989).

BEATTIE, Ann (1947–), was born in Washington, DC; she graduated from the American University in Washington and went on to do an MA there. Beattie taught at the University of Connecticut for three years and now lives in that state. Her first novel was the critically well received *Chilly Scenes of Winter* (1976). Other novels are *Falling In Place* (1980), *Love Always* (1985) and *Picturing Will* (1989). Her short stories are collected in *Secrets and Surprises* (1979), *The Burning Bush* (1982) and *Where You'll Find Me* (1986).

See: Murphy, C., *Ann Beattie* (Boston, 1986).

BOWLES, Jane (1917–73), was born in New York City. Jane Auer studied at private schools in America and Switzerland. She married Paul Bowles in 1938, travelling with him to Panama and other places, settling in Morocco in 1952. *Two Serious Ladies* appeared in 1943. A collection including this and other of Bowles's best writings is *My Sister's Hand in Mine: An Expanded Edition of the Complete Works of Jane Bowles* (1978). Bowles suffered many years from a debilitating illness that prevented further writing until her death in 1973. *Out in the World: Selected Letters of Jane Bowles* was published in 1985.

Dillon, M., *A Little Original Sin: The Life and Work of Jane Bowles* (1981).

BOWLES, Paul (1910–), born in New York City, studied music with Aaron Copland and Virgil Thomson and has composed for drama, film, opera and ballet. Found a mentor in Gertrude Stein in an early trip to Paris but he started writing in emulation of his wife, Jane Bowles. In addition to *The Sheltering Sky* (1949), *The Delicate Prey and Other Stories* (1950), *Collected Stories of Paul Bowles (1939–1976)* (1979) and *Points in Time* (1982), he has written a number of translations of Arab oral tales. He is a longtime resident of Tangier.

Sawyer-Lauçanno, C., *An Invisible Spectator: A Biography of Paul Bowles* (1989).

See: Pounds, W., *The Fiction of Paul Bowles* (1985).
Patteson, R.F., *A World Outside: The Fiction of Paul Bowles* (Austin, 1987).

BURNS, John Horne (1916–53), born in Andover, Massachusetts, served in the Army in Italy during the Second World War. His best known work is *The Gallery* (1947), a book set in Milan at the time of the American occupation.

Mitzel, J., *John Horne Burns: An Appreciative Biography* (Rochester, Vt, 1974).

BURROUGHS, William (1914–), born in St Louis, Missouri where he failed to attain his ambition of becoming sewer commissioner, was the grandson of the inventor of the adding machine and founder of the Burroughs Corporation although William Burroughs's family had no share of the wealth. Burroughs graduated from Harvard and worked at a succession of dead-end jobs – advertising copywriter, exterminator and private detective among them – before meeting Jack Kerouac and Allen Ginsberg in 1946. Burroughs is William Lee in Kerouac's *On the Road*. Burroughs got hooked on morphine in about 1944 and did not recover from addiction until 1957. Because of police pressure he moved from New York City to Texas to Louisiana, finally fleeing to Mexico. The stay in Mexico ended in 1951 when Burroughs, playing William Tell with a revolver, accidentally killed his wife who had balanced a glass on her head. *The Naked Lunch*, published in Paris by Olympia Press in 1959, was assembled out of a manuscript mass accumulated while Burroughs lived in Tangier. It appeared as *Naked Lunch* in the USA in 1962. *The Soft Machine* (Paris, 1961; USA 1966) and *The Ticket that Exploded* (Paris, 1962; USA, 1967) came out of the same accumulation. *The Wild Boys* (1971) and *Cities of the Red Night* (1981) marked a new departure for Burroughs and some critics consider the latter his best work since *Naked Lunch*. After a stay in London Burroughs moved back to the USA, settling in Lawrence, Kansas. He is a mainstay of the college lecture circuit with his readings.

See: Mottram, E., *William Burroughs: The Algebra of Need* (London, 1971).
Lydenberg, R., *Word Cultures: Radical Theory and Practice in William S. Burroughs' Fiction.* (Urbana, 1987).
Skerl, J. and R. Lydenberg (eds.), *William S. Burroughs at the Front: Critical Reception 1959–1989* (Carbondale, 1991).

CAPOTE, Truman (1924–84), born in New Orleans, was initially raised by relatives in Monroeville, Alabama after his parents divorced. His closest friend was Harper Lee, herself to become author of *To Kill a Mockingbird* and the model for Idabel in *Other Voices, Other Rooms*. His mother finally sent for Capote to join her in New York City in 1932. A high-school graduate, Capote worked at an office job at *The New Yorker* before publishing his first novel, *Other Voices, Other Rooms* (1948), which startled readers almost as much with the cover photograph of Capote lounging languidly on a divan as with its taboo story line. Capote's 'Southern gothic' short stories are in *A Tree of Night and Other Stories* (1949). *Breakfast at Tiffany's* (1958) is piquant, though derivative of Isherwood's Sally Bowles. *A Christmas Memory* (1966), originally a story in *Mademoiselle* (1956), is one of his best writings. His final, abortive *roman à clef*, *Answered Prayers*, excerpts from which had cost him many of his café society friends, was published posthumously in 1986. Capote's most notable work of non-fiction was the brilliant, creepy *In Cold Blood* (1966).

Clarke, G., *Capote: A Biography* (1988).
Moates, M., *A Bridge of Childhood: Truman Capote's Southern Years* (1989).

See: Garson, H.S., *Truman Capote* (1980).

Reed, T., Truman Capote (Boston, 1981).
Capote, T., Conversations with Truman Capote (Jackson, 1985).

CARVER, Raymond (1933–88), born in Clatskanie, Oregon where his father was a labourer, graduated from Humboldt State College in California and studied at the University of Iowa. Carver married young and worked at a succession of low-level jobs, pumping gas, managing an apartment complex, etc., while his wife worked as a waitress and door-to-door salesperson, occupations appearing in many of his stories. Carver taught at Syracuse from 1980 to 1983. In his last years he was in recovery from alcoholism, in a relationship with Tess Gallagher, the poet, and beginning to work on a novel, a form previously too connected with belief in future possibility to be available for him. His stories are collected in Will You Please Be Quiet, Please (1976), What We Talk about when We Talk about Love (1981) and the book revelatory of his new belief in possibility, Cathedral (1984). Fires: Essays, Poems, Stories 1966–1982 (1983) has essays reflecting his aesthetic views.

See: Saltzman, A.M., Understanding Raymond Carver (Columbia, 1988).
Carver, R., Conversations with Raymond Carver (Jackson, 1990).

CHEEVER, John (1912–82), born in Quincy, Massachusetts, was expelled from Thayer Academy, the topic of his first story. He served in the Army from 1943 to 1945. His early stories record New York City life but he is best known as the laureate of the suburbs where, in the fashion of the 1950s, he had moved. Cheever's life was tormented by the split between his alcoholism and unadmitted homosexual inclinations, and his middle-class Christian values. In his last years he was in recovery from alcoholism, financially solvent and had come to terms with his bisexuality. Cheever largely repudiated his first book of short stories, The Way Some People Live (1943), but found his voice in The Enormous Radio (1953). His stories, most of them written for The New Yorker, were collected in The Stories of John Cheever (1978). His best known novels are The Wapshot Chronicle (1957), The Wapshot Scandal (1964), Bullet Park (1969) and Falconer (1977).

Cheever, S., Home Before Dark (Boston, 1984).
Donaldson, S., John Cheever (1988).

See: Coale, S., John Cheever (1977).
Collins, R.G. (ed.), Critical Essays on John Cheever (Boston, 1982).
Hunt, G.W., John Cheever: The Hobgoblin Company of Love (Grand Rapids, 1983).
Cheever, J., Conversations with John Cheever (Jackson, 1987).

COOVER, Robert (1932–), born in Charles City, Iowa, graduated from Indiana in 1953 and received his MA from the University of Chicago. He has taught several times at various universities. He is the author of The Origin of the Brunists (1966), The Universal Baseball Association, Inc., J. Henry Waugh, Prop. (1968), Pricksongs and Descants (1969), The Public Burning (1969) and Spanking the Maid (1982).

See: Andersen, R., Robert Coover (Boston, 1981).
Cope, J.I., Robert Coover's Fictions (Baltimore, 1986).

COZZENS, James Gould (1903–78), born in Chicago, attended Harvard, withdrawing due to ill health and debts. He served in the Army Air Force from 1942 to 1945, attaining the rank of major. His novel *The Last Adam* (1933) features a crusty individualist but his fiction after the Second World War centres on characters who are loyal to institutional rules and structures, as in his Air Force novel *Guard of Honor* (1948). *By Love Possessed* (1957) was his greatest success but caused an intense critical backlash.

Bruccoli, M., *James Gould Cozzens: A Life Apart* (San Diego, 1983).

See: Bracher, F., *The Novels of James Gould Cozzens* (1959).
   Mooney, H.J. Jr., *James Gould Cozzens: Novelist of Intellect* (Pittsburgh, 1963).
   Maxwell, D.E.S., *Cozzens* (Edinburgh, 1964).

DELILLO, Don (1936–), born in New York City, attended Cornell 1954–58. His first novel, *End Zone* (1972), is a parable relating football to nuclear apocalypse. *Great Jones Street* (1973) is about an alienated rock star and a government drug conspiracy. *Ratner's Star* (1976) is semiotic science fiction and *Players* (1977), *Running Dog* (1978) and *The Names* (1982) are postmodern thrillers. *Libra* (1988) is a fictional account of the Kennedy assassination.

See: LeClair, T., *In the Loop: Don DeLillo and the Systems Novel* (Urbana, 1987).

DIDION, Joan (1934–), was born in Sacramento and is a graduate of the University of California, Berkeley. Her finest novel is her second, *Play it as it Lays* (1970), but she is best known for her essays in *Slouching Towards Bethlehem* (1968) and *The White Album* (1979).

See: Winchell, M.R., *Joan Didion* (Boston, 1980).
   Henderson, K.U., *Joan Didion*(1981).
   Friedman, E.G. (ed.), *Joan Didion: Essays and Conversations* (1984).

DOCTOROW, E.L. (1931–), born in New York City, graduated from Kenyon and did a year of graduate study at Columbia. Doctorow's best novels play with historical fact and myth, as in his upside-down western *Welcome to Hard Times* (1960), his use of the Rosenberg executions in *The Book of Daniel* (1971), on the teens in *Ragtime* (1975) and depression gangster lore in *Billy Bathgate* (1989).

See: Cooper, B.E., *The Artist as Historian in the Novels of E.L. Doctorow* (Emporia, 1980).
   Levine, P., *E.L. Doctorow* (London, 1985)
   Harter, C.C., *E.L. Doctorow* (Boston, 1990).

DONLEAVY, J.P. (1926–), born in Brooklyn, New York, attended Trinity College, Dublin after military service in the United States Navy during the Second World War and is now an Irish citizen. Forty-five publishers rejected *The Ginger Man* before Olympia Press accepted it but published it as part of a pornographic series leading to a lengthy lawsuit eventuating in Donleavy's ownership of the long inactive Press. Later novels such as *The Saddest Summer of Samuel S* (1966) and *The Beastly Beatitudes of Balthazar B* (1968) failed to match the energy of *The Ginger Man* (1955, Olympia Press; in 1958 a revised, somewhat toned-down edition was published in the United States. The complete and unexpurgated edition was published by Delacorte in 1965 and issued by Dell in paperback in 1969).

ELKIN, Stanley (1930–), born in New York City, the son of a salesman, was
     educated at the University of Illinois, going on through a PhD there. He has
     taught at the University of Washington at St Louis since 1960. In recent years
     a serious illness has not overcome his literary versatility. His fiction includes
     Criers and Kibbitzers, Kibbitzers and Criers (1966), The Dick Gibson Show
     (1971), *Searches and Seizures* (1973), *The Franchiser* (1976), *The Living End*
     (1979) and *The Magic Kingdom* (1985), a novel about a group of children with
     various terminal illnesses. His most recent novel is *The MacGuffin* (1991).

     See: Bargen, D.G., *The Fiction of Stanley Elkin* (Frankfurt, 1980).
           Bailey, P.J., *Reading Stanley Elkin* (Urbana, 1985).
           Dougherty, D.C., *Stanley Elkin* (Boston, 1990).

ELLISON, Ralph (1914–), born in Oklahoma City, attended Tuskegee Institute but
     was sidetracked from returning to finish his degree. A music major, he
     planned to compose in both classical and jazz styles, an epitome of the literary
     style he developed. He has taught at various universities, including nine years
     at New York University, has lectured extensively in the United States and
     Europe, and has occupied a number of public service positions, such as
     Trustee of the Williamsburg Foundation and President of PEN. He has been
     honoured with the Medal of Freedom, and is a Chevalier de l'Ordre des Arts
     et Lettres, and a library has been named after him in Oklahoma City. *Invisible
     Man* (1953) won the National Book Award and is generally considered the
     most important American novel since the Second World War. Ellison has
     long been working on a novel tentatively titled 'And Hickman Arrives',
     excerpts from which have been published in *Noble Savage* (March 1960) and
     American Review **16**, (1973) and other periodicals. Ellison had to reconstruct
     the book from scratch when his only manuscript of it was lost in a house fire.
     Ellison's political and critical views as expressed in his essay collections,
     Shadow and Act (1964) and *Going to the Territory* (1986) have been
     controversial for their moderate conservatism. His exchange with Irving
     Howe after Howe's invidious contrast of him to Richard Wright is a *cause
     célèbre* and in 1979 Susan Blake's *PMLA* essay accused him of softening the
     political implications of African American folklore, an attack tacitly responded
     to by Houston Baker Jr's 1983 *PMLA* essay with its sophisticated analysis of
     Ellison's folk motifs. Ellison's other major fictional creation is the frequently
     anthologized short story 'The King of the Bingo Game'.

     See: Reilly, J.M. (ed.), *Twentieth-Century Interpretations of Invisible Man*
                (Englewood Cliffs, NJ, 1970).
           Trimmer, J.F. (ed.), *A Casebook on Ralph Ellison's Invisible Man* (1976).
                (Has Howe's attack and Ellison's response.)
           Hersey, J., *Ralph Ellison: A Collection of Critical Essays* (Englewood
                Cliffs, 1974).
           Blake, S., '*Ritual and Rationalization: Black Folklore in the Works of Ralph
                Ellison*', *PMLA* **94** (1979).
           O'Meally, R.G., *The Craft of Ralph Ellison* (Cambridge, Mass, 1980).
           Baker, H.A., 'To Move without Moving: An Analysis of Creativity
                and Commerce in Ralph Ellison's Trueblood Episode', *PMLA* **98**
                (1983) reprinted in Gates, ed., *Black Literature and Literary Theory*.
           Nadel, A., *Invisible Criticism: Ralph Ellison and the American Canon*
                (Iowa City, 1988).
           O'Meally, R.G. (ed.), *New Essays on Invisible Man* (Cambridge, Mass., 1988).

ERDRICH, Louise (1954–), born in Little Falls, Minnesota, is of
German–American and Chippewa Indian descent. Her father taught with the
Bureau of Indian Affairs. She graduated from Dartmouth and has an MA from
Johns Hopkins. She has written *Love Medicine* (1985) and *The Beet Queen*
(1986).

EXLEY, Frederick (1929–), born in Watertown, New York, graduated from the
University of Southern California. Though highly autobiographical, *A Fan's
Notes* (1968) is a fiction, with some invented characters. The book reflects the
disturbances of a life of two marriages ending in divorce, alcoholism, and
recurrent mental illness.

FAULKNER, William (1897–1962), was born in New Albany, Mississippi, and
raised in Oxford which, minus the university, became the Jefferson of his
fiction. Faulkner looked to his great-grandfather, William Clark Falkner
(William Faulkner changed the spelling of the family name), Civil War
veteran and railroad entrepreneur, as an exemplar of Southern family honour
from which both region and family had declined. Faulkner joined the Royal
Flying Corps in Canada in the First World War but the war was over before
he had completed his training. He went to the University of Mississippi for a
time but was largely self-educated by reading suggested by his friend Phil
Stone, a lawyer. His fictional breakthrough was the extraordinary *The Sound
and the Fury* (1929). In his great decade of the 1930s he wrote *As I Lay Dying*
and *Light in August* in 1932 and *Absalom, Absalom!* in 1936. His best novels of
the 1940s were *The Hamlet* (1940) and *Go Down Moses* (1942). It was not
until Malcolm Cowley's edition of *The Portable Faulkner* in 1946 that Faulkner
achieved widespread critical respect. That *Intruder in the Dust* (1948) sold
better than any previous Faulkner work was a sign of the change in his
critical standing. *Collected Stories* (1950) was published the year he won the
Nobel Prize. Faulkner extended the story of *The Hamlet* into *The Town* (1957)
and *The Mansion* (1959).

> Blotner, J., *Faulkner. A Biography*, 2 vols (1974) – the revised and updated
>   one-volume edition of 1984 adds important new material.
> Mintner, D., *William Faulkner. His Life and Work* (Baltimore, 1980).
> Karl, F., *William Faulkner, American Writer: A Biography* (1989).

> See:

> > Howe, I., *William Faulkner. A Critical Study*, 2nd edn (1952).
> > Beck, W., *Man in Motion: Faulkner's Trilogy* (Madison, 1961).
> > Brooks, C., *William Faulkner. The Yoknapatawpha Country* (New Haven,
> >   1963).
> > Vickery, O.W., *The Novels of William Faulkner. A Critical Introduction*,
> >   rev. edn (Baton Rouge, 1964).
> > Millgate, M., *The Achievement of William Faulkner* (1966).
> > Warren, R.P. (ed.), *Faulkner: A Collection of Critical Essays* (Englewood
> >   Cliffs, 1966).
> > Reed, J.W., *Faulkner's Narrative* (New Haven, 1973).
> > Irwin, J.T., *Doubling and Incest/Repetition and Revenge: A Speculative
> >   Reading of Faulkner* (Baltimore, 1975).
> > Bassett, W.J. (ed.), *William Faulkner. The Critical Heritage* (London, 1975).
> > Guerard, A.J., *The Triumph of the Novel: Dickens, Dostoevsky, Faulkner*
> >   (1976).
> > Sensibar, J., *The Origins of Faulkner's Art* (Austin, 1984).

Wadlington, W., *Reading Faulkner's Tragedy* (Ithaca, 1987).
Grimshaw, M., *Heart in Conflict: Faulkner's Struggles with Vocation* (Athens, Georgia, 1987).
Schwartz, L.H., *Creating Faulkner's Reputation* (Knoxville, 1988).
Duvall, J.D., *Faulkner's Marginal Couples: Invisible, Outlaw, and Unspeakable Communities* (Austin, 1990).

GADDIS, William (1922–), was born in New York City and raised in Massapequa, Long Island, in a Calvinist atmosphere. Attended Harvard 1941–45 and travelled in Latin America, Europe and north Africa from 1947 to 1952. Kerouac's character Howard Sands in *The Subteranneans* is based on Gaddis. His novels, *The Recognitions* (1955), *JR* (1975) and *Carpenter's Gothic* (1985), are highly regarded by critics although only the last has found many readers.

See: Moore, S., *A Reader's Guide to William Gaddis's The Recognitions* (Lincoln, 1982).
Kuehl, J. and S. Moore (eds.), *In Recognition of William Gaddis* (Syracuse, 1984).
Moore, S., *William Gaddis* (Boston, 1989).
Johnston, J., *Carnival of Repetition: Gaddis's The Recognitions and Postmodern Theory* (Philadelphia, 1990).

GARDNER, John (1933–82), born in Batavia, New York, graduated from Washington University, St Louis and received his PhD in English from the University of Iowa, specializing in medieval literature. Gardner died in a motorcycle accident in 1982. Gardner's *Grendel* was published in 1971, his *The Sunlight Dialogues* in 1972 and *Freddy's Book* in 1980. *On Moral Fiction* (1978) caused a stir with its accusations of literary immorality against many of Gardner's peers. His own scholarly work on Chaucer came under fire when questions were raised about its originality.

See: Morace, R.A. and K. Vanopankeren, *John Gardner: Critical Perspectives* (Carbondale, 1982).
Cowart, D., *Arches and Light: The Fiction of John Gardner* (Carbondale, 1983).
Morris, G.L., *A World of Order and Light: The Fiction of John Gardner* (Athens, Georgia, 1984).
McWilliams, D., *John Gardner* (Boston, 1990).
Gardner, J., *Conversations with John Gardner* (Jackson, 1990).

GASS, William (1924–), was born in Fargo, North Dakota into a desperately unhappy family situation to which Gass eventually responded with formalism and creativity. Gass graduated from Kenyon and did his PhD in philosophy at Cornell. He taught at Purdue and has been teaching philosophy at Washington University, St Louis since 1969. Gass had completely to rewrite his first novel, *Omensetter's Luck* (1966), when a colleague at Cornell stole the only copy, but the result was a more brilliant work. *In the Heart of the Heart of the Country* (1968) is a set of innovative stories that was followed by the extraordinary *tour de force Willie Masters' Lonesome Wife* (1971). His critical essays, collected in *Fiction and the Figures of Life* (1970) *The World within the Word* (1978) and *Habitations of the Word* (1985), are as much plays on as analyses of language. *On Being Blue* (1976) is a language performance that resists categorization. He has been working on a novel, *The Tunnel*, for many years, some excerpts from which have appeared.

See: Saltzman, A., *The Fiction of William Gass: The Consolations of Language*
(Carbondale, 1985).
Holloway, W.L., *William Gass* (Boston, 1990).

HAWKES, John (1925–), born in Stamford, Connecticut, was an ambulance driver
in Italy and Germany during the Second World War. He graduated from
Harvard and his teaching career was at Brown University. *The Cannibal*
(1949), set in a phantasmagoric Germany, was followed by *The Lime Twig*
(1961), set in an England purely of Hawkes's imagination (with perhaps some
assistance from Graham Greene's). *Second Skin* (1964) is an elusive, sometimes
grim comedy. *Lunar Landscapes* (1969) includes early, surrealistic tales. *The
Blood Oranges* (1971), *Travesty* (1976) and *The Passion Artist* (1979) have not
received as much critical favour as the earlier works. Hawkes's critical essays
are helpful in understanding his fiction, especially 'Notes on Violence',
Audience **7** (1960); 'Flannery O'Connor's Devil', *Southern Review* **70** (1962)
and 'John Hawkes and his Novels', *Massachusetts Review* **7** (1966).

See: Busch, F., *Hawkes: A Guide to his Works* (Syracuse, 1973).
Greiner, D.J., *Comic Terror: The Novels of John Hawkes* (Memphis, 1973)
Kuehl, J., *John Hawkes and the Craft of Conflict* (New Brunswick, 1975).
O'Donnell, P., *John Hawkes* (Boston, 1982).

HELLER, Joseph (1923–), born in Brooklyn, New York, flew sixty missions as
wing bombardier for the Air Force during the Second World War. After the
war he graduated from New York University, got his MA from Columbia
and did a year of graduate study at Oxford. He taught at City College of the
City University of New York until 1975. *Catch-22* (1961) was not
immediately noticed but became a word of mouth sensation in paperback.
Something Happened (1974) and *Good as Gold* (1979) are later novels of note.
In 1986 Heller co-authored with Speed Vogel a book about his struggle with
a near-fatal illness, *No Laughing Matter* (1986). His most recent novels are *God
Knows* (1984) and *Picture This* (1988).

See: Kiley, F. and W. McDonald (eds), *A Catch-22 Casebook* (1973).
Scotto, R.M. (ed.), *Catch-22: A Critical Edition* (1973).
Nagel, J. (ed.), *Critical Essays on Joseph Heller* (Boston, 1984).
Potts, S.W., *Catch-22: An Antiheroic Antinovel* (Boston, 1989).
Seed, D., *The Fiction of Joseph Heller: Against the Grain* (1989).

HINOJOSA, Rolando (1929–), was born in Mercedes in the valley region of South
Texas, the locale of his fiction. He served in the Army in Korea, graduated
from the University of Texas and did his PhD at the University of Illinois. He
now teaches at the University of Texas. His extended work is the *Klail City
Death Trip*, better known in Latin America than in the USA, the itinerary of
which is specified in his bilingual novels, in Spanish and English. *The Valley*
(1983) was originally published as *Estampas del valle y otras obras* (1972).
Partners in Crime (1985) is a valley thriller and *Becky and her Friends* (1990)
shows the effects of feminist realizations on a traditional society.

HUMPHREYS, Josephine (1945–), born in Charleston, South Carolina, graduated
from Duke where her mentor was the North Carolina writer Reynolds Price.
Her first novel, *Dreams of Sleep*, won the P.E.N. Hemingway award for best
first novel of 1985 and was followed by *Rich in love* (1987). Both these were
set in Charleston but Humphreys won a Guggenheim grant to travel through

the South in order to broaden her regional horizons, as will appear in subsequent works.

HURSTON, Zora Neal (1903–60), was born and raised in Eatonville, Florida, an all-Black town. She attended Howard University, graduated from Barnard College and did graduate work with Franz Boas in anthropology at Columbia. She collected folklore in Jamaica, Bermuda, Haiti and the South. In her later years she returned to the South after an injurious experience in Harlem and was discovered working as a maid in Florida. *Their Eyes Were Watching God* (1937) is her classic. The short story 'The Gilded Six Bits' now appears in most American literature anthologies.

   Hemenway, R., *Zora Neal Hurston: A Literary Biography* (Urbana, 1980).

   See: Holloway, K.F., *The Character of the Word: The Texts of Zora Neal Hurston* (1987).

JONES, James (1921–77), born in Robinson, Illinois, served in the peacetime and wartime Army from 1939 to 1944. Known for the force rather than the form of his fiction, Jones regarded himself as 'the last of the proletarian novelists'. War was his best subject, as in *From Here to Eternity* (1951) and *The Thin Red Line* (1962).

KENNEDY, William (1928–), was born in Albany, New York, which he imaginatively owns. He graduated from Siena and worked as a newspaper reporter up to 1961. He began teaching at the State University of New York at Albany in 1974, and started writing about Albany while working for a newspaper in Puerto Rico. His most celebrated work is *Ironweed* (1983). *O Albany* (1983) is a work of non-fiction.

KEROUAC, Jack (1922–69), born in Lowell, Massachusetts, to French Canadian working-class parents, attended Columbia and the New School for Social Research and worked at garages, as a sportswriter, a railroad brakeman and a fire lookout in Washington state. *On the Road* (1957) was influenced by the letter style of his friend Neal Cassady, its co-hero as well as the bus driver for Ken Kesey's Merry Pranksters as featured in Tom Wolfe's *The Electric Kool-Aid Acid Test*. Kerouac became alienated from the literary and cultural scene in his unhappy later years.

   Cassady, C., *Heart Beat: My Life with Jack and Neal* (Berkeley, 1976).
   Gifford, B. and L. Lee, *Jack's Book: An Oral Biography of Jack Kerouac* (1977).
   McNally, D., *Desolate Angel: Jack Kerouac, the Beat Generation and America* (1979).
   Clark, T., *Jack Kerouac* (San Diego, 1984).

   See: Donaldson, S., *On the Road: Text and Criticism* (1979).
      Weinreich, R., *The Spontaneous Poetics of Jack Kerouac: A Study of the Fiction* (Carbondale, 1987).

KINGSTON, Maxine Hong (1940–), was born in Stockton, California. Graduated from the University of California, Berkeley where, after teaching some years in Hawaii, she is now a professor. *The Woman Warrior* (1976) is a fictionalized memoir. The dazzlingly verbally inventive *Tripmaster Monkey: His Fake Book* appeared in 1989.

LURIE, Alison (1926–), born in Chicago, Illinois, graduated from Radcliffe and has taught at Cornell since 1969. She is divorced from a university professor. She is author of *The Nowhere City* (1965), *The War between the Tates* (1974) and *Foreign Affairs* (1984).

McCARTHY, Mary (1912–89), born in Seattle, Washington, was a Vassar graduate. Her first husband was Harold Johnsrud, an actor. She later married Edmund Wilson and, after their divorce, twice more. She had a long time association with the *Partisan Review*, doing its drama criticism from 1937 to 1962. Among her novels are *The Company She Keeps* (1942) and *The Group* (1963), both of which excited controversy by including taboo subject matter. Other novels of note are *A Charmed Life* (1955), *Groves of Academe* (1952) and *Birds of America* (1971). *Memoirs of a Catholic Girlhood* (1957) is a classic of its kind and *The Writings on the Wall and Other Literary Essays* (1970) include critical essays on Burroughs, Salinger and Nabokov.

Gelderman; C., *Mary McCarthy: A Life* (1988).

See: McKenzie, B., *Mary McCarthy* (1966).
Stock, I., *Mary McCarthy* (Minneapolis, 1968).
Hardy, W.S. *Mary McCarthy* (1981)
McCarthy, M., *Conversations with Mary McCarthy* (Jackson, 1991)

McCULLERS, Carson (1917–67), born in Columbus, Georgia, attended Columbia and New York University. Her theme of loneliness and unreciprocated love was carried through *The Heart is a Lonely Hunter* (1940), *Reflections in a Golden Eye* (1941), *The Member of the Wedding* (1946) and *The Ballad of the Sad Café* (1951). Her work fell off in her later years as she struggled with serious illness.

Carr, V.S., *The Lonely Hunter: A Biography of Carson McCullers* (Garden City, 1975).

See: Evans, D., *The Ballad of Carson McCullers* (1966).
Graver, L., *Carson McCullers* (Minneapolis, 1969).
Westling, L.H., *Sacred Groves and Ravaged Gardens: The Fiction of Eudora Welty, Carson McCullers, and Flannery O'Connor* (Athens, Georgia, 1985).
Carr, V.S., *Understanding Carson McCullers (Columbia, 1985)*.

McELROY, Joseph (1930–), born in Brooklyn, New York, graduated from Williams and did his PhD at Columbia. He has taught at Queens College, City of New York since 1964. Author of *A Smuggler's Bible* (1966), *Lookout Cartridge* (1974) and a story about a suspended mind in space, *Plus* (1977).

McMURTRY, Larry (1936–), was born in Wichita Falls, Texas, the son of a rancher. McMurtry does not sentimentalize his native Southwest. He graduated from North Texas State, received an MA from Rice and taught at the University of Houston in the 1960s. McMurtry owns a bookstore in Washington, DC where he spends half his time, the other half being in Texas. *Horseman Pass By* (1961) is less well known than the movie, *Hud*, which was adapted from it and, in McMurtry's opinion, improved on it. *The Last Picture Show* (1966) was his best known work until the cowboy epic *Lonesome Dove* (1985), but *Texasville* (1987) may be his best novel so far. The essays collected in *In a Narrow Grave* (1968) sharply criticize Texas mythology. McMurtry used to wear a sweatshirt with the slogan 'Minor Regional Novelist'.

See: Landless, T., *Larry McMurtry* (Austen, 1969).
Neinstein, R.L., *The Ghost Country: A Study of the Novels of Larry McMurtry* (Berkeley, 1976).
Peavy, C.D., *Larry McMurtry* (Boston, 1977).

MAILER, Norman (1923–) born in Long Branch, New Jersey, graduated from Harvard in 1943 and served as a rifleman in the Philippines in 1944–46. *The Naked and the Dead* (1948) won acclaim which did not carry over to *Barbary Shore* (1951) or *The Deer Park* (1955), though both these books are interesting for their political thinking. *The White Negro* (1957) scandalized many, as did Mailer's stabbing of his wife in 1960 as he was in the midst of a campaign for the Democrat nomination to run for Mayor of New York. Though there are defenders of *An American Dream* (1965), in which the hero successfully murders his wife, and of *Why Are We in Vietnam?* (1967), the general critical view is that Mailer's best writing from the 1960s on is his reportage, especially *Armies of the Night* (1968) and his account of anomie and murder in the American West, *The Executioner's Song* (1979). *Ancient Evenings* (1983), a novel set in ancient Egypt, could have used help from Cecil B. DeMille. Mailer got into some public difficulty when he helped Jack Abbott, a convict writer, get released from prison only to commit a murder almost immediately.

Mills, H., *Mailer: A Biography* (1982).
Manso, P., *Norman Mailer: His Life and Times* (1985).

See: Leeds, B., *The Structured Vision of Norman Mailer* (1969).
Lucid, R.F. (ed.), *Norman Mailer: The Man and his Work* (Boston, 1971).
Gutman, S.I., *Mankind in Barbary: The Individual and Society in the Novels of Norman Mailer* (Hanover, NH, 1975).
Bloom, H. (ed.), *Modern Critical Views: Norman Mailer* (1986).
Mailer, N., *Conversations with Norman Mailer* (Jackson, 1988).

MALAMUD, Bernard (1914–86), was born in Brooklyn, New York, his father a grocery store manager who sometimes worked sixteen hours a day. Malamud graduated from City College of New York and attained an MA from Columbia. He taught at Oregon State University – clearly the locale of *A Charmed Life* – from 1949 to 1961. *The Natural* (1952) was Malamud's first novel but his innovative voice appears more in *The Assistant* (1957) and *The Magic Barrel* (1958). He also wrote *The Fixer* (1966) and *The Tenants* (1971) and was working on a novel about an immigrant Jewish pedlar of the nineteenth century who encounters Indians in the far West.

See: Ducharne, R., *Art and Idea in the Novels of Bernard Malamud: Toward The Fixer* (The Hague, 1974).
Helterman, J., *Understanding Bernard Malamud* (Columbia, 1985).
Solotaroff, R., *Bernard Malamud: A Study of the Short Fiction* (Boston, 1989).

MARQUAND, John P. (1893–60), born in Wilmington, Delaware, graduated from Harvard. *The Late George Apley* (1937) is a minor classic as a novel of manners. Later books are *Point of No Return* (1949) and *Sincerely, Willis Wade* (1955). Marquand also wrote a series of detective novels about Mr Moto.

Bell, M.M., *Marquand: An American Life* (Boston, 1979).

MORRIS, Wright (1910–), was born and raised in Central City, Nebraska, once known as Lone Tree. From 1925 to 1930 he worked with his uncle on a dustbowl farm in Texas. He attended Crane College and Pomona College and taught at California State University in San Francisco from 1962 to 1975. He lives in Mill Valley, California, and is known as the most honoured and least read author in America. Among his novels are *My Uncle Dudley* (1942), *The Field of Vision* (1956), *Love Among the Cannibals* (1957), *Ceremony in Lone Tree* (1960) and *One Day* (1965). More recently, *Plains Song, for Female Voices* (1980) reminded critics of Morris's neglected talent. He has also written *Will's Boy: A Memoir* (1981), *The Cloak of Light: Writing My Life* (1985) and the critical book *The Territory Ahead* (1958).

See: Madden, D., *Wright Morris* (1964).
Howard, L., *Wright Morris* (Minneapolis, 1968).
Knoll, R.E. (ed.), *Conversations with Wright Morris* (Jackson, 1977).
Crump, G.B., *The Novels of Wright Morris: A Critical Interpretation* (Lincoln, 1978)

MORRISON, Toni (1931–), born in Lorain, Ohio, graduated from Howard University and did her MA at Cornell. She was a university teacher from 1955 to 1964 and then became a senior editor at Random House. She became a Professor at State University of New York at Albany in 1984 and from 1989 she has taught at Princeton. Her novels are *The Bluest Eye* (1970), *Sula* (1973), *Song of Solomon* (1977), *Tar Baby* (1981) and *Beloved* (1987).

See: Jones, E.W. and A.L. Vinson, *The World of Toni Morrison* (Dubuque, 1985).
Holloway, K.F.C. and S.A. Demetrakopoulos, *New Dimensions of Spirituality* (1987).
McKay, N.Y. (ed.), *Critical Essays on Toni Morrison* (Boston, 1988).
Otten, T., *The Crime of Innocence in Toni Morrison* (Columbia, 1989).

NABOKOV, Vladimir (1899–1977), was born in St Petersburg (Leningrad), Russia. Nabokov's father, a liberal at odds with both the tsarist autocracy and the Soviet one that succeeded it, fled with his family in 1919. Vladimir Nabokov graduated from Trinity College, Cambridge in 1922, lived in Berlin from 1922 to 1937, fled Nazism to Paris in 1937 and thence to the USA where he taught at Wellesley from 1941 to 1948 and at Cornell from 1948–1959. He became a US citizen in in 1945. In his later years he lived at the Palace Hotel in Montreux, Switzerland. Nabokov was an important Russian writer before he began to write in English. *Invitation to a Beheading* (translated 1959) is one of his brilliant Russian-language novels. *The Real Life of Sebastian Knight* (1941) and *Bend Sinister* (1947) were his first English-language novels but he did not become widely known until *Lolita* (1955). *Pnin* (1957), *Pale Fire* (1962) and *Ada or Ardor* (1969) are the most notable of his later works. *Speak Memory* (1966) is a luminous memoir.

Field, A., *Nabokov: His Life in Part* (1977). (It should be noted that Nabokov scholars and Nabokov himself disputed the factual accuracy of this book.)
Boyd, B., *Vladimir Nabokov: The Russian Years* (Princeton, 1990).
Boyd, B., *Vladimir Nabokov: The American Years* (Princeton, 1991).

See: Proffer, C., *Keys to Lolita* (Bloomington, 1968).
Appel, A. (ed.), *The Annotated Lolita* (1970).

Roth, P.A. (ed.), *Critical Essays on Vladimir Nabokov* (Boston, 1984).
Bader, J., *Crystal Land* (Berkeley, 1972).
Nabokov, V., *Strong Opinions* (1973) (interviews).
Appel, A., *Nabokov's Dark Cinema* (1974).
Fowler, D., *Reading Nabokov* (Ithaca, 1974).
Maddox, L., *Nabokov's Novels in English* (Athens, Georgia, 1983).
Johnson, D.B., *Worlds in Regression: Some Novels of Vladimir Nabokov* (Ann Arbor, 1985).

OATES, Joyce Carol (1938–), born in Lockport, New York, graduated from Syracuse, received an MA at Wisconsin and taught at the University of Detroit and University of Windsor in Canada, and has been at Princeton since 1978. The year 1963 saw her first short story collection, *By the North Gate*, and 1964 her first novel, *With Shuddering Fall* (1964). *Expensive People* (1968) and *them* (1969) are among the most powerful of her novels. Some of her finest short stories, such as 'Where Are You Going, Where Have You Been?' and 'How I Contemplated the World from the Detroit House of Correction and Began Life Over Again', are in *The Wheel of Love* (1972).

See: Grant, K., *The Tragic Vision of Joyce Carol Oates* (Durham, NC, 1978).
Wagner, L.W. (ed.), *Joyce Carol Oates: The Critical Reception* (Boston, 1979).
Waller, G.F. *Dreaming America: Obsession and Transcendence in the Fiction of Joyce Carol Oates* (Baton Rouge, 1979).
Bender, E., *Joyce Carol Oates* (Bloomington, 1987).
Johnson, G., *Understanding Joyce Carol Oates* (Columbia, 1987).
Bloom, H. (ed.), *Modern Critical Views: Joyce Carol Oates* (1987).
Oates, J.C., *Conversations with Joyce Carol Oates* (Jackson, 1989).

O'CONNOR, Flannery (1925–64), born in Savannah and brought up in Milledgeville, Georgia, graduated from the Women's College of Georgia and received a Master of Fine Arts degree at Iowa. She suffered during most of her life from a serious illness but this did not prevent her from writing some of the best American fiction of her time. She wrote two novels, *Wise Blood* (1952) and *The Violent Bear it Away* (1960), and two books of short stories, *A Good Man is Hard to Find* (1955) and *Everything that Rises Must Converge* (1965). *The Complete Stories* (1971) contains some previously uncollected work. Some of her critical writings are in *Mystery and Manners: Occasional Prose* (1969). Her letters, *The Habit of Being*, express both her caustic wit and Catholic faith.

See: Martin, C.W., *The True Country: Themes in the Fiction of Flannery O'Connor* (Nashville, 1969).
Orvell, M., *The Invisible Parade: The Fiction of Flannery O'Connor* (Philadelphia, 1972).
Eggenschwiler, D., *The Christian Humanism of Flannery O'Connor* (Detroit, 1972).
Stephens, M. *The Question of Flannery O'Connor* (Baton Rouge, 1973).
Asals, F., *Flannery O'Connor: The Imagination of Extremity* (Athens, Georgia, 1982).
Friedman, M.J. and B.L. Clark (eds), *Critical Essays on Flannery O'Connor* (Boston, 1985).
O'Connor, F., *Conversations with Flannery O'Connor* (Jackson, 1987).

Brinkmeyer, R.H., *The Art and Vision of Flannery O'Connor* (Baton Rouge, 1989).

Ragen, B.A., *A Wreck on the Road to Damascus: Innocence, Guilt and Conversion in Flannery O'Connor* (Chicago, 1989).

O'HARA, John (1905–70), born in Pottsville, Pennsylvania, attended Niagara Preparatory School. O'Hara's short stories and novels sharply observe marriage, adultery, alcoholism and moral compromise among the American middle classes. His masterwork is *Appointment in Samarra* (1934). *Butterfield 8* (1935) and *Pal Joey* (1940) look into the worlds of high-level prostitution and low-level show business. Some of his best stories are in *Sermons and Sodawater* (1960) and *The Hat on the Bed* (1963).

McShane, F., *The Life of John O'Hara* (1980).

See: Carson, E.R., *The Fiction of John O'Hara* (Pittsburgh, 1961).

Grebstein, S.N., *John O'Hara* (1966).

OZICK, Cynthia (1928–), was born in New York City, graduated from New York University and has an MA from Ohio State. Her most notable writings are *The Pagan Rabbi* (1971), *Bloodshed and Three Novellas* (1976) and *Levitation: Five Fictions* (1982). Her critical essays have been collected in *Art and Ardor* (1983) and *Metaphor and Memory* (1988).

See: Rainwater, C. and W. Scheick (eds), *Three Contemporary Women Novelists: Hazzard, Ozick, and Redmon* (Lexington, 1983).

Pinsker, S., *The Uncompromising Fictions of Cynthia Ozick* (Columbia, 1987).

Lowin, J., *Cynthia Ozick* (Boston, 1988).

PALEY, Grace (1922–), was born in New York City. She has married twice and has two children, experience drawn on in her stories. Paley attended Hunter College and New York University and taught at Columbia and Syracuse in the 1960s before a long-term engagement at Sarah Lawrence. Her books of short stories are *The Little Disturbances of Man* (1959), *Enormous Changes at the Last Minute* (1974) and *Later the Same Day* (1985).

See: Taylor, J., *Grace Paley: Illuminating the Dark Lives* (Austin, 1990).

PERCY, Walker (1916–90), was born in Birmingham, Alabama. After the suicide of his father and his mother's death in an automobile accident, Percy was brought up by his uncle, William Alexander Percy, author of the memoir *Lanterns on the Levee*, in Greenville, Mississippi. Percy graduated from the University of North Carolina and got his MD at Columbia. He quit medicine after becoming infected with tuberculosis while working as a pathologist at Bellevue Hospital. In 1947 Percy became a Roman Catholic. He moved to New Orleans, then Covington, Louisiana. His novels are *The Moviegoer* (1961), *The Last Gentleman* (1966), *Love in the Ruins* (1971), *Lancelot* (1977), *The Second Coming* (1980) and *The Thanatos Syndrome* (1987). The essays in *The Message in the Bottle* (1975) show the interest in semiology Percy developed when one of his children was born deaf.

See: Broughton, P.R. (ed.), *The Art of Walker Percy: Stratagems for Being* (Baton Rouge, 1979).

Lawson, L. and V.A. Kramer (eds), *Conversations with Walker Percy* (Jackson, 1985).

Hardy, J.E., *The Fiction of Walker Percy* (Urbana, 1987).
Sweeny, M.K., *Walker Percy and the Postmodern World* (Chicago, 1987).
Crowley, J.D., *Critical Essays on Walker Percy* (Boston, 1989).

PETRY, Ann (1908–), born in Old Saybrook, Connecticut, graduated from the
University of Connecticut and did a year of graduate study at Columbia. Her
father was a pharmicist and Petry pursued this career from 1931 to 1938
before moving to Harlem and becoming a writer for the *Amsterdam News* and
then *People's Voice* from 1938 to 1944. Author of *The Street* (1946), *Country
Place* (1947) and *The Narrows* (1953), she turned to children's literature
thereafter. She lives in her home town of Old Saybrook.

PORTER, Katherine Anne (1890–1980), was born in Indian Creek, Texas, near
Brownwood, and brought up in Kyle and San Antonio, Texas. Porter married
at sixteen, divorced, appeared in a silent film, worked as a reporter, went
through other marriages and became one of the finest of any American short
story writers. Accounts of her life before Joan Givner's biography are
unreliable because based on Porter's own fictitious version which recreated as
Catholic and aristocratic a background that was Protestant and marginally
middle class. All her short fiction collections are major: *Flowering Judas and
Other Stories* (1930), *Pale Horse, Pale Rider: Three Short Novels* (1939), *The
Leaning Tower and Other Stories* (1944). A compendium is *Collected Stories*
(1965). Her one full-length novel was *Ship of Fools* (1962).
　　Givner, J., *Katherine Anne Porter: A Life* (1982).

　See: Mooney, H.J., *The Criticism and Fiction of Katherine Anne Porter*
　　　　 (Pittsburg, 1962).
　　　 West, Ray B., *Katherine Anne Porter* (Minneapolis, 1963).
　　　 Nance, W.B., *Katherine Anne Porter and the Art of Rejection* (Chapel
　　　　 Hill, 1964).
　　　 DeMouy, J.K., *Katherine Anne Porter's Women: The Eye of her Fiction*
　　　　 (Austin, 1983).
　　　 Unrue, D.H., *Truth and Vision in Katherine Anne Porter's Fiction*
　　　　 (Athens, Georgia, 1985).
　　　 Porter, K.A., *Conversations with Katherine Anne Porter* (Jackson, 1987).

PRICE, Reynolds (1933–), was born in Macon, North Carolina, and educated with
a BA at Duke and a B. Litt. at Merton College, Oxford, as a Rhodes Scholar.
Price has taught at Duke since 1958, serving as mentor to such novelists as
Josephine Humphreys and Anne Tyler. Two of his finer novels are *A Long
and Happy Life* (1962) and *Kate Vaiden* (1986). In 1984 a spinal cord condition
resulted in paraplegia. Reynolds comments at the end of his book of essays, *A
Common Room* (1987): 'This new access of time and energy has enabled him
to complete two novels . . . a collection of poems . . . this collection of
essays . . . and a trilogy of plays.'

PYNCHON, Thomas (1937–), born in Glen Cove, Long Island, graduated from
Cornell, switching to English from engineering physics. He served in the
Navy before completing his education and worked as a technical writer for
Boeing after it. The last known photograph of Pynchon is from his college
years. He leads a life so private that where he has lived for over the last two
decades is unknown. Pynchon's novels are *V.* (1963), *The Crying of Lot 49*
(1966), *Gravity's Rainbow* (1973) and *Vineland* (1990). His early work is
collected in *Slow Learner* (1984), for which he wrote an Introduction, and a

reminiscence of his college days can be found in his Introduction to the 1983 reprint of his college friend Richard Farina's *Been Down so Long it Looks Like up to Me* (1983). Farina, Joan Baez's brother-in-law, died young in a motorcycle accident. Pynchon was a student of Nabokov's at Cornell but only Nabokov's wife, who graded for him, remembered Pynchon – for his handwriting.

See: Levine, G. and D. Leverenz (eds), *Mindful Pleasures* (Boston, 1976).
   Mendelson, E. (ed.), *Pynchon: A Collection of Critical Essays* (Englewood Cliffs, 1978).
   Stark, J.O., *Pynchon's Fictions: Thomas Pynchon and the Literature of Information* (Athens, Georgia, 1980).
   Fowler, D., *A Reader's Guide to 'Gravity's Rainbow'* (Ann Arbor, 1980).
   Cowart, D., *Thomas Pynchon: The Art of Allusion* (Carbondale, 1980).
   Schaub, T.H., *Pynchon: The Voice of Ambiguity* (Urbana, 1981).
   Tanner, T., *Thomas Pynchon* (London, 1982).
   Hite, M., *Ideas of Order in the Novels of Thomas Pynchon* (Columbus, 1983).
   Hume, K., *Mythography: An Approach to Gravity's Rainbow* (Carbondale, 1987).
   Eddins, D., *The Gnostic Pynchon* (Bloomington, 1990).

REED, Ishmael (1938–), born in Chattanooga, Tennessee, attended the State University of New York at Buffalo. He is the co-founder of Yardbird Publishing Company in Berkeley, California. He is author of *The Free-Lance Pallbearers* (1967), *Yellow Back Radio Broke Down* (1969), *Mumbo Jumbo* (1972) and *Reckless Eyeballing* (1986).

See: Martin, R., *Ishmael Reed and the New Black Aesthetic* (1987).

ROBINSON, Marilynn (1944–), received her PhD from the University of Washington. *Housekeeping* (1981) is her first novel.

See: Heller, D., *The Feminization of Quest Romance* (Austin, 1990).

ROTH, Philip (1933–), born in Newark, New Jersey, currently lives in London. His wife is the actress, Clare Bloom. Roth graduated from Bucknell and got his MA from University of Chicago. His first book, *Goodbye, Columbus* (1959), consists of a novella and several short stories. *Letting Go* (1962) and *When She Was Good* (1969) are the novels of his realist phase. *Portnoy's Complaint* (1969) was a scandal due to its subject matter but is more important for its stylistic breakthrough. The matter of (with) Zuckerman begins with *The Ghost Writer* (1979) and continues through *Zuckerman Unbound* (1981) and *The Anatomy Lesson* (1983). These were published in a single volume, *Zuckerman Bound*, with *The Prague Orgy* as an 'Epilogue' (1985). *The Counterlife* (1986) introduces a new set of Zuckerman variations and so does the memoir, *The Facts* (1988), wherein Zuckerman finally displaces his creator. *Deception* (1990) consists of enigmatic conversational exchanges between a man and a woman. *Patrimony* (1991) is nonfiction, a moving account of the death of his father.

See: Jones, J.R. and G.A., Nance, *Reading Philip Roth* (1981).
   Bloom, H. (ed.), *Modern Critical Views: Philip Roth* (1986).
   Baumgarten, N. and B., Gottfield, *Understanding Philip Roth* (Columbia, 1990)

SALINGER, J.D. (1919–), born in New York City, now lives in New Hampshire, in relative reclusiveness. He recently stymied a would-be biographer by suing to prevent quotations from his books. Salinger went to Valley Forge Military Academy and attended New York University, Ursinus College and Columbia. He was in the army from 1942-1946. His critically acclaimed novel was *The Catcher in the Rye* (1951). He is also author of *Nine Stories* (1953) and the Glass saga: *Franny and Zooey* (1961), *Raise High the Roofbeam, Carpenters, and Seymour – An Introduction* (1963). Seymour Glass's origin is 'A Good Day for Bananafish' in *Nine Stories*.

> See: Gwynn F.L. and J.L. Blotner, *The Fiction of J.D. Salinger* (Pittsburgh, 1958).
> Belcher, W.F. and J.W. Lee (eds), *J.D. Salinger and the Critics* (Belmont, California, 1962).
> French, W., *J.D. Salinger* (1963).
> Lunquist, J. *J.D. Salinger* (1979).

SELBY, Hubert (1928–), born in Brooklyn, New York, had a year of high school education. He served with the Merchant Marines from 1944 to 1946 and spent four years recovering from tuberculosis. He has worked as a freelance copywriter for the *National Enquirer* since 1965. *Last Exit to Brooklyn* (1964) was prosecuted for obscenity in England and banned in Italy.

SOUTHERN, Terry (1926–), born in Alvarado, Texas, graduated from Northwestern. With Mason Hoffenberg he co-authored *Flash and Filigree* (1958) and *Candy* (1958: Paris; published in the USA by Putnam, 1964). *The Magic Christian*, an anarchic comic novel, has a chapter in the London publication (Deutsch, 1959) suppressed in the American (Random House, 1960). Southern worked on the screenplays of the films *Doctor Strangelove, Or How I Learned to Stop Worrying and Love the Bomb* (1964) and *Easy Rider* (1969).

STAFFORD, Jean (1915–79), was born in Covina, California. She was married to and divorced from Robert Lowell and married to A.J. Liebling. She received her BA and MA from the University of Colorado and studied at Heidelberg University in 1936–37. Her most notable works are the novel *Boston Adventure* (1944), the short novel *The Mountain Lion* (1947) and *The Collected Stories of Jean Stafford* (1969). Also notable is her interview with the mother of the presidential assassin Lee Harvey Oswald, *A Mother in History* (1966).

> Goodman, C.M., *Jean Stafford: The Savage Heart* (1990).

> See: Heller, D., *The Feminization of Quest Romance* (1990).

STONE, Robert (1937–), born in New York City, attended New York University and Stanford. He has taught at Princeton, Stanford and other universities. Author of *A Hall of Mirrors* (1967), *Dog Soldiers* (1974), *A Flag for Sunrise* (1981) and *Children of Light* (1986).

STYRON, William (1925–), born in Newport News, Virginia, is a graduate of Duke University. He wrote *Lie Down in Darkness* (1951), *The Long March* (1956) *The Confessions of Nat Turner* (1967) and *Sophie's Choice* (1979). Styron has also written an account of a severe depression from which he suffered, *Darkness Visible: A Memoir of Madness* (1990).

> See: Clark, J.H. (ed.), *William Styron's Nat Turner: Ten Black Writers Respond* (Boston, 1968).
> Friedman, M.J., *William Styron* (Bowling Green, Ohio, 1974).

Morris, R.K. and I. Malin (eds), *The Achievement of William Styron* (Athens, Georgia, 1975).

Casciato, A.D. and J.L.W. West (eds), *Critical Essays on William Styron* (Boston, 1982).

Crane, J.K., *The Root of All Evil: The Thematic Unity of William Styron's Fiction* (Columbia, 1984).

Styron, W. *Conversations with William Styron* (Jackson, 1985).

Ruderman, J., *William Styron* (1987).

TAYLOR, Peter (1917–), born in Trenton, Tennessee, served in the Army from 1941 to 1945. He graduated from Kenyon College and taught at the University of North Carolina at Greensboro before moving to the University of Virginia in 1967. His novels are *A Woman of Means* (1950), *The Collected Stories of Peter Taylor* (1969) and *A Summons to Memphis* (1986).

See: Griffith, A.J., *Peter Taylor* (Boston, 1970; rev. edn. 1990).

TYLER, Anne (1941–), was born in Minneapolis, Minnesota and lived in various Quaker communes in the Midwest and South before settling in the North Carolina mountains for a time. She attended high school at Raleigh and entered Duke where Reynolds Price encouraged her writing. In 1967 she settled in Baltimore, Maryland, the site of much of her fiction. Among her novels are *Celestial Navigation* (1974), *Searching for Caleb* (1976), *Dinner at the Homesick Restaurant* (1982) and *The Accidental Tourist* (1985).

See: Voelker, J.C., *Art and the Accidental in Anne Tyler* (Columbia, 1989).

Petry, A.H., *Understanding Anne Tyler* (Columbia, 1990).

UPDIKE, John (1932–) was born in Shillington, Pennsylvania. His father was a high school teacher. Updike graduated from Harvard and studied a year at the Ruskin School of Drawing and Fine Art, Oxford. He was married in 1955 and divorced in 1977, events shadowed in *Too Far to Go* (1979), the Maples stories. *The Poorhouse Fair* (1959) was his first novel. The Rabbit cycle began with *Rabbit, Run* (1960), continued through *Rabbit Redux* (1971) and *Rabbit is Rich* (1981), ending with *Rabbit at Rest* (1990). Other important novels are *The Centaur* (1963) and *The Coup* (1978). Updike's distinguished short fiction was first collected in *The Same Door* (1959) and *Pigeon Feathers* (1962). *Museums and Women* (1972) is an important collection. He has compiled three books of criticism and assorted prose: *Assorted Prose* (1965), *Picked-up Pieces* (1975) and *Hugging the Shore* (1983). *Self-Consciousness: Memoirs* (1989) is a characteristically unusual memoir.

See: Hunt, G.W. and S.J. *John Updike and the Three Great Secret Things: Sex, Religion and Art* (Grand Rapids, 1980).

Tallent, E. *Married Men and Magic Tricks: John Updike's Erotic Heroes* (Berkeley, 1982).

Greiner, D.J., *John Updike's Novels* (Athens, Georgia, 1984).

Bloom, H. (ed.), *Modern Critical Views: John Updike* (1987).

Newman, J., *John Updike* (1988).

VONNEGUT, Kurt (1922–), born in Indianapolis, Indiana, served in the Army from 1942 to 1945 and survived the Dresden fire bombing as a prisoner of war. He was educated at Cornell and the Carnegie Institute of Technology and worked at public relations for General Electric in Schenectady. He received an MA from the University of Chicago in 1971. Among his novels are *Player Piano* (1952), the science fiction satire *The Sirens of Titan* (1959), *Cat's Cradle* (1963), *Slaughterhouse Five*, or *The Children's Crusade* (1969), about the Dresden horror, and *Breakfast of Champions* (1973).

See: Giannone, R., *Vonnegut: A Preface to his Novels* (Port Washington, 1977).
Klinkowitz, J., *Kurt Vonnegut* (London, 1982).

WALKER, Alice (1944–), born in Eatonton, Georgia, graduated from Sarah Lawrence College. Walker worked at voter registration of African Americans in Mississippi in dangerous times. She is the author of *Meridian* (1976), *The Color Purple* (1982) and a selection of essays, *In Search of Our Mother's Gardens* (1983).

WARREN, Robert Penn (1905–89), born in Guthrie, Kentucky graduated from Vanderbilt, received an MA from the University of California, Berkeley, did graduate work at Yale and received a B. Litt. from Oxford in 1931. He taught at Vanderbilt, at Louisiana State University from 1934 to 1936 where he observed the Huey Long melodrama unfold, at Minnesota and at Yale. His most important novels are *Night Rider* (1939), *At Heaven's Gate* (1943), *All the King's Men* (1946) and *World Enough and Time* (1950). *Selected Essays* (1958) contains some of his best criticism, though his major critical influence comes from the 'New Criticism' poetry anthology *Understanding Poetry* (1938) that he co-authored with Cleanth Brooks. Warren defines himself more as a poet than a novelist and was one of the Fugitive group of Southern poets centred at Vanderbilt. Among his poetic works are *Brother to Dragons* (1953), *Selected Poems 1923–1975* (1976) and *Now and Then: Poems 1976–8* (1978). He was a contributor to the Southern Agrarian manifesto *I'll Take My Stand* (1930) but evolved to become concerned with *Segregation: The Inner Conflict of the South* (1956) and *Who Speaks for the Negro?* (1965).

See: Caper, L., *Robert Penn Warren: The Dark and Bloody Ground* (Seattle, 1960).
Bohner, C.H., *Robert Penn Warren* (Boston, 1964).
Gray, R. (ed.), *Robert Penn Warren: A Collection of Critical Essays* (Englewood Cliffs, 1980).
Watkins, F.C. and J.T. Hiers (eds), *Robert Penn Warren Talking: Interviews 1950–1978* (1980).
Justus, J.H., *The Achievement of Robert Penn Warren* (Baton Rouge, 1981).

WELTY, Eudora (1909–), born in Jackson, Mississippi, graduated from Wisconsin and attended the Columbia School of Advertising. During the 1930s she worked at newspapers, radio stations and as a publicity agent for the state office of the WPA. Her early short story collections, *A Curtain of Green* (1941) and *The Wide Net* (1943), contain a number of classic stories. *The Robber Bridegroom* (1942) is a quirky historical novel about Mississippi and *The Optimist's Daughter* (1972) is her finest novel. *The Collected Stories* came out in 1980. Her critical writings were collected in *The Eye of the Story* (1978). Welty's memoir is *One Writer's Beginnings* (1984), a book attacked by feminist critics for representing her childhood as secure and relatively happy. In 1989 *Eudora Welty Photographs*, a very handsome book of Mississippi photographs she took during her work for the WPA, appeared.

See: Vandekieft, R.M., *Eudora Welty* (Boston, 1962).
Appel, A., *A Season of Dreams: The Fiction of Eudora Welty* (Baton Rouge, 1965).

Prenshaw, P.W., *Eudora Welty: Critical Essays* (Jackson, 1979).
Kreyling, M., *Eudora Welty's Achievement of Order* (Baton Rouge, 1979).
Evans, E., *Eudora Welty* (1981).
Prenshaw, P.W. (ed.), *Conversations with Eudora Welty* (Jackson, 1984).

WIDEMAN, John Edgar (1941–), born in Washington, DC, graduated from the University of Pennsylvania where he was a basketball star. He went to Oxford on a Rhodes scholarship and attained his B.Phil. He taught at the University of Pennsylvania from 1966 to 1974 and has taught at Wyoming University since 1975. Wideman's Homewood trilogy – *Damballah* (1981), *Hiding Place* (1981) and *Sent For You Yesterday* (1983) – draw on his experience growing up in the Homewood ghetto of Pittsburgh, Pennsylvania.

WRIGHT, Richard (1908–60), was born near Natchez, Mississippi. His father was a mill worker who abandoned the family and Wright was brought up by his mother and her family, as recounted in his autobiography, *Black Boy* (1945). He spent some years in Memphis, then moved to Chicago where he was active in the Communist Party. He had becomed disillusioned with communism by the time he moved to New York City but his public break did not come immediately. His experience with the Communist Party is recorded in his section of *The God that Failed*. In 1947 he moved to France, where he was influenced by Sartre's style of existentialism though it is arguable he had worked out his personal equivalent much earlier. Wright was one of the first black writers that American readers found unavoidable. His short stories of race violence appeared in *Uncle Tom's Children* (1938) and *Native Son* (1940) caused a literary shock wave. *The Outsider* (1953) is a somewhat programmatically existential novel. *Eight Man* (1961) includes the extraordinary novella '*The Man Who Lived Underground*'. Wright's political anger fuelled much of his non-fiction as in the photographically illustrated *12 Million Black Voices* (1941) which graphically depicts the sociological deprivations implicit in *Native Son*.

Fabre, M., *The Unfinished Quest of Richard Wright* (1973).

See: McCall, D., *The Example of Richard Wright* (1969).
Baker, H.A. (ed.), *Twentieth-Century Interpretations of Native Son* (Englewood Cliffs, 1972).
Reilly, J.M. (ed.), *Richard Wright: The Critical Reception* (1978).
Fabre, M., *The World of Richard Wright* (Jackson, 1985).
Felgar, R., *Richard Wright* (Boston, 1980).
Macksey, R. and F. Moorer (eds), *Richard Wright: A Collection of Critical Essays* (Englewood Cliffs, 1984).
Joyce, J.A., *Richard Wright's Art of Tragedy* (Iowa City, 1984).
Kinnamon, K. (ed.), *New Essays on Native Son* (Cambridge, 1990).
Miller, E.E., *Voice of a Native Son: The Poetics of Richard Wright* (Jackson, 1990).

YATES, Richard (1926–), was born in Yonkers, New York. He served in the Army from 1944 to 1946. His first marriage ended in divorce in 1959. He worked at commercial writing jobs, as a screenwriter and as a university teacher, but in the 1970s his publisher put him on a contract basis, cutting down on his need to work at things other than writing. He is the author of *Revolutionary Road* (1961), *Eleven Kinds of Loneliness* (1962) and *The Easter Parade* (1976), among other works.

Index